20

7531

104
NC

Travels Through North and South Carolina

William Bartram

Table of Contents

Table of Contents

Table of Contents

Travels Through North and South Carolina

William Bartram

Kessinger Publishing reprints thousands of hard–to–find books!

Visit us at http://www.kessinger.net

Travels Through North &South Carolina, Georgia, East &West Florida,
the Cherokee Country, the Extensive Territories of the Muscogulges, or

Creek Confederacy, and the Country of the Chactaws; Containing An
Account of the Soil and Natural Productions of Those Regions, Together
with Observations on the Manners of the Indians.

TO
HIS EXCELLENCY
THOMAS MIFFLIN, ESQ.
PRESIDENT OF THE STATE
OF
PENNSYLVANIA,
THIS VOLUME OF TRAVELS
IS GRATEFULLY INSCRIBED,

By his respectful friend and servant
WILLIAM BARTRAM.

INTRODUCTION.

The attention of a traveller, should be particularly turned, in the first place, to the various works of Nature, to mark the distinctions of the climates he may explore, and to offer such useful observations on the different productions as may occur. Men and manners undoubtedly hold the first rank—whatever may contribute to our existence is also of equal importance, whether it be found in the animal or vegetable kingdoms; neither are the various articles, which tend to promote the happiness and convenience of mankind, to be disregarded. How far the writer of the following sheets has succeeded in furnishing information on these subjects, the reader will be capable of determining. From the advantages the journalist enjoyed under his father JOHN BARTRAM, botanist to the king of Great–Britain, and fellow of the Royal Society, it is hoped that his labours will present new as well as useful information to the botanist and zoologist.

THIS world, as a glorious apartment of the boundless palace of the sovereign Creator, is furnished with an infinite variety of animated scenes, inexpressibly beautiful and pleasing, equally free to the inspection and enjoyment of all his creatures.

PERHAPS there is not any part of creation, within the reach of our observations, which exhibits a more glorious display of the Almighty hand, than the vegetable world. Such a variety of pleasing scenes, ever changing, throughout the seasons, arising from various causes and assigned each to the purpose and use determined.

IT is difficult to pronounce which division of the earth, within the polar circles, produces the greatest variety. The tropical division certainly affords those which principally contribute to the more luxurious scenes of splendor, as Myrtus communis, Myrt. caryophyllata, Myrt. pimenta, Caryophylus aromaticus, Laurus cinam. Laurus camphor. Laurus Persica, Nux mosch. Illicium, Camellia, Punica, Cactus melo–cactus; Cactus grandiflora, Gloriosa superba, Theobroma, Adansonia digitata, Nyctanthes, Psidium, Musa paradisica, Musa sapientum, Garcinia mangostana, Cocos nucifera, Citrus, Citrus aurantium, Cucurbita citrullus, Hyacinthus, Amaryllis, Narcissus, Poinciana pulcherima, Crinum, Cactus cochinellifer.

BUT the temperate zone (including by far the greater portion of the earth, and a climate the most favourable to the increase and support of animal life, as well as for the exercise and activity of the human faculties) exhibits scenes of infinitely greater variety, magnificence and consequence, with respect to human economy, in regard to the various uses of vegetables.

FOR instance, Triticum Cereale, which affords us bread, and is termed, by way of eminence, the staff of life, the most pleasant and nourishing food—to all terrestrial animals. Vitis vinifera, whose exhilirating juice is said to cheer the hearts of gods and men. Oryza, Zea, Pyrus, Pyrus malus, Prunus, Pr. cerasus, Ficus, Nectarin, Apricot, Cydonia. Next follows the illustrious families of forest–trees, as the Magnolia grandiflora and Quercus sempervirens, which form the venerated groves and solemn shades, on the Mississipi, Alatamaha and Florida, the magnificent Cupressus disticha of Carolina and Florida, the beautiful Water Oak

* Quercus Hemispherica.

whose vast hemispheric head, presents the likeness of a distant grove in the fields and savannas of Carolina. The gigantic Black Oak

* Quercus tinctoria.

Platanus occidentalis, Liquid–amber styraciflua, Liriodendron tulipifera, Fagus castania, Fagus sylvatica, Juglans nigra, Juglans cinerea, Jug. pecan, Ulmus, Acher sacharinum, of Virginia and Pennsylvania; Pinus phoenix, Pinus toeda, Magnolia acuminata, Nyssa aquatica, Populus heterophylla and the floriferous Gordonia lasianthus, of Carolina and Florida; the exalted Pinus strobus, Pin. balsamica, Pin. abies, Pin. Canadensis, Pin. larix, Fraxinus excelsior, Robinia pseudacacia, Guilandina dioica, Æsculus Virginica, Magnolia acuminata, of Virginia, Maryland, Pennsylvania, New–Jersey, New–York, New–England, Ohio and the regions of Erie and the Illinois; and the aromatic and floriferous shrubs, as Azalea coccinia, Azalea rosea, Rosa, Rhododendron, Kalmia, Syringa, Gardinia, Calycanthus, Daphne, Franklinia, Styrax and others equally celebrated.

IN every order of nature, we perceive a variety of qualities distributed amongst individuals, designed for different purposes and uses, yet it appears evident, that the great Author has impartially distributed his favours to his creatures, so that the attributes of each one seem to be of sufficient importance to manifest the divine and inimitable workmanship. The pompous Palms of Florida, and glorious Magnolia, strikes us with the sense of dignity and magnificence; the expansive umbrageous Live–Oak*

* Quercus Sempervirens.

with awful veneration, the Carica papaya, supercilious with all the harmony of beauty and gracefulness; the Lillium superbum represents pride and vanity; Kalmia latifolia and Azalea coccinea, exhibit a perfect show of mirth and gaiety; the Illisium Floridanum, Crinum Floridanum, Convalaria majalis of the Cherokees, and Calycanthus floridus, charm with their beauty and fragrance. Yet they are not to be compared for usefulness with the nutritious Triticum, Zea, Oryza, Solanum tuberosa, Musa, Convolvulous, Batata, Rapa, Orchis, Vitis vinifera, Pyrus, Olea; for clothing, Linum Canabis, Gossypium, Morus; for medical virtues, Hyssopus, Thymus, Anthemis nobilis, Papaver somniferum, Quinqina, Rheum rhabarbarum, Pisum, &c. though none of these most useful tribes are conspicuous for stateliness, figure or splendor, yet their valuable qualities and virtues, excite love, gratitude and adoration to the great Creator, who was such to endow them with such eminent qualities, and reveal them to us for our sustenance, amusement and delight.

Travels Through North and South Carolina

BUT there remains of the vegetable world, several tribes that are distinguished by very remarkable properties, which excite our admiration, some for the elegance, singularity and splendor of their vestment, as the Tulipa, Fritillaria, Colchicum, Primula, Lillium superbum, Kalmia, &c. Others astonish us by their figure and disposal of their vestiture, as if designed only to embellish and please the observer, as in the Nepenthes distillatoria, Ophrys insectoria, Cypripedium calceolus, Hydrangia quercifolia, Bartramia bracteata, Viburnum Canadense, Bartsea, &c.

OBSERVE these green meadows how they are decorated; they seem enamelled with the beds of flowers. The blushing Chironia and Rhexia, the spiral Ophrys with immaculate white flowers, the Limodorum, Arethusa pulcherima, Sarracenia purpurea, Sarracenia galeata, Sarracenia lacunosa, Sarracenia flava. Shall we analyze these beautiful plants, since they seem cheerfully to invite us? How greatly the flowers of the yellow Sarracenia represent a silken canopy, the yellow pendant petals are the curtains, and the hollow leaves are not unlike the cornucopia or Amaltheas horn, what a quantity of water a leaf is capable of containing, about a pint! taste of it—how cool and animating—limpid as the morning dew: nature seems to have furnished them with this cordated appendage or lid, which turns over, to prevent a too sudden, and copious supply of water from heavy showers of rain, which would bend down the leaves, never to rise again; because their streight parallel nerves, which extend and support them, are so rigid and fragile, the leaf would inevitably break when bent down to a right angle; therefore I suppose these waters which contribute to their supplies, are the rebounding drops or horizontal streams wasted by the winds, which adventitiously find their way into them, when a blast of wind shifts the lid; see these short stiff hairs, they all point downwards, which direct the condensed vapours down into the funiculum; these stiff hairs also prevent the varieties of insects, which are caught, from returning, being invited down to sip the mellifluous exuvia, from the interior surface of the tube, where they inevitably perish; what quantities there are of them! These latent waters undoubtedly contribute to the support and refreshment of the plant; perhaps designed as a reservoir in case of long continued droughts, or other casualties, since these plants naturally dwell in low savannas liable to overflows, from rain water: for although I am not of the opinion that vegetables receive their nourishment, only through the ascending part of the plant, as the stem, branches, leaves, &c. and that their descending part, as the root and fibres, only serve to hold and retain them in their places, yet I believe they imbibe rain and dews through their leaves, stems and branches, by extremely minute pores, which open on both surfaces of the leaves and on the branches, which may communicate to little auxiliary ducts or vessels; or, perhaps the cool

7

dews and showers, by constricting these pores, and thereby preventing a too free perspiration, may recover and again invigorate the languid nerves, of those which seem to suffer for want of water, in great heats and droughts; but whether the insects caught in their leaves, and which dissolve and mix with the fluid, serve for aliment or support to these kind of plants, is doubtful. All the Sarracenia are insect catchers, and so is the Drossea rotundiflolia.

BUT admirable are the properties of the extraordinary Dionea muscipula! A great extent on each side of that serpentine rivulet, is occupied by those sportive vegetables—let us advance to the spot in which nature has seated them. Astonishing production! see the incarnate lobes expanding, how gay and ludicrous they appear! ready on the spring to intrap incautious deluded insects, what artifice! there behold one of the leaves just closed upon a struggling fly, another has got a worm, its hold is sure, its prey can never escape—carnivorous vegetable! Can we after viewing this object, hesitate a moment to confess, that vegetable beings are endued with some sensible faculties or attributes, similar to those that dignify animal nature; they are organical, living and self–moving bodies, for we see here, in this plant, motion and volition.

WHAT power or faculty is it, that directs the cirri of the Cucurbita, Momordica, Vitis and other climbers, towards the twigs of shrubs, trees and other friendly support? we see them invariably leaning, extending and like the singers of the human hand, reaching to catch hold of what is nearest, just as if they had eyes to see with, and when their hold is fixed, to coil the tendril in a spiral form, by which artifice it becomes more elastic and effectual, than if it had remained in a direct line, for every revolution of the coil adds a portion of strength, and thus collected, they are enabled to dilate and contract as occasion or necessity require, and thus by yielding to, and humouring the motion of the limbs and twigs, or other support on which they depend, are not so liable to be torn off by sudden blasts of wind or other assaults; is it sense or instinct that influences their actions? it must be some impulse; or does the hand of the Almighty act and perform this work in our fight?

THE vital principle or efficient cause of motion and action, in the animal and vegetable*

* Vid. Sponsalia plantarum, Amoen. Acad 1. n, 12. Linn.

system, perhaps, may be more similar than we generally apprehend. Where is the essential difference between the seed of peas, peaches and other tribes of plants and trees, and that of oviparous animals? as the eggs of birds, snakes or butterflies, spawn of fish, &c. Let us begin at the source of terrestrial existence. Are not the seed of vegetables, and the eggs of oviparous animals fecundated, or influenced with the vivific principle of life, through the aproximation and intimacy of the sexes, and immediately after the eggs and seeds are hatched, the young larva and infant plant, by heat and moisture, rises into existence, increases, and in due time arrives to a state of perfect maturity. The physiologists agree in opinion, that the work of generation in viviparious animals, is exactly similar, only more secret and inveloped. The mode of operation that nature pursues in the production of vegetables, and oviparous animals is infinitely more uniform and manifest, than that which is or can be discovered to take place in viviparous animals.

THE most apparent difference between animals and vegetables are, that animals have the powers of sound, and are locomotive, whereas vegetables are not able to shift themselves from the places where nature has planted them: yet vegetables have the power of moving and exercising their members, and have the means of transplanting or colonising their tribes almost over the surface of the whole earth, some seeds, for instance, grapes, nuts, smilax, peas, and others, whose pulp or kernel is food for animals, such seed will remain several days without injuring in stomachs of pigeons and other birds of passage; by this means such sorts are distributed from place to place, even across seas; indeed some seeds require this preparation, by the digestive heat of the stomach of animals, to dissolve and detach the oily, viscid pulp, and to soften the hard shells of others. Small seeds are sometimes furnished with rays of hair or down, and others with thin light membranes attached to them, which serve the purpose of wings, on which they mount upward, leaving the earth, float in the air, and are carried away by the swift winds to very remote regions before they settle on the earth; some are furnished with hooks, which catch hold of the wool and hair of animals passing by them, are by that means spread abroad; other seeds ripen in pericarpes, which open with elastic force, and shoot their seed to a very great distance round about; some other seeds, as of the Mosses and Fungi, are so very minute as to be invisible, light as atoms, and these mixing with the air, arc wasted all over the world.

THE animal creation also, excites our admiration, and equally manifests the almighty power, wisdom and beneficence of the Supreme Creator and Sovereign Lord of the universe; some in their vast size and strength, as the mamoth, the elephant, the whale, the lion and alligator; others in agility; others in their beauty and elegance of colour, plumage and rapidity of flight, have the faculty of moving and living in the air; others for their immediate and indispensable use and convenience to man, in furnishing means for our clothing and sustenance, and administering to our help in the toils and labours through life; how wonderful is the mechanism of these finely formed, self–moving beings, how complicated their system, yet what unerring uniformity prevails through every tribe and particular species! the effect we see and contemplate, the cause is invisible, incomprehensible, how can it be otherwise? when we cannot see the end or origin of a nerve or vein, while the divisibility of mater or fluid, is infinite. We admire the mechanism of a watch, and the fabric of a piece of brocade, as being the production of art; these merit our admiration, and must excite our esteem for the ingenious artist or modifier, but nature is the work of God omnipotent: and an elephant, even this world is comparatively but a very minute part of his works. If then the visible, the mechanical part of the animal creation, the mere material part is so admirably beautiful, harmonious and incomprehensible, what must be the intellectual system? that inexpressibly more essential principle, which secretly operates within? that which animates the inimitable machines, which gives them motion, impowers them to act speak and perform, this must be divine and immortal?

I AM sensible that the general opinion of philosophers, has distinguished the moral system of the brute creature from that of mankind, by an epithet wich implies a mere mechanical impulse, which leads and impels them to necessary action without any premeditated design or contrivance, this we term instinct which faculty we suppose to be inferior to reason in man.

THE parental, and filial affections seem to be as ardent, their sensibility and attachment, as active and faithful, as those observed to be in human nature.

WHEN travelling on the East coast of the isthmus of Florida, ascending the South Musquitoe river, in a canoe, we observed numbers of deer and bears, near the banks, and on the islands of the river, the bear were feeding on the fruit of the dwarf creeping Chamerops, (this fruit is of the form and size of dates, and are delicious and nourishing food:) we saw eleven bears in the course of the day, they seemed no way surprized or affrighted at the sight of us; in the evening my hunter, who was an excellent marksman, said that he would shoot one of them, for the sake of the skin and oil, for we had plenty and variety of provisions in our bark. We accordingly, on sight of two of them, planned our approaches, as artfully as possible, by crossing over to the opposite shore, in order to get under cover of a small island, this we cautiously coasted round, to a point, which we apprehended would take us within shot of the bear, but here finding ourselves at too great a distance from them, and discovering that we must openly show ourselves, we had no other alternative to effect our purpose, but making oblique approaches; we gained gradually on our prey by this artifice, without their noticing us, finding ourselves near enough, the hunter fired, and laid the largest dead on the spot, where she stood, when presently the other, not seeming the least moved, at the report of our piece, approached the dead body, smelled, and pawed it, and appearing in agony, fell to weeping and looking upwards, then towards us, and cried out like a child. whilst our boat approached very near, the hunter was loading his rifle in order to shoot the survivor, which was a young cub, and the slain supposed to be the dam; the continual cries of this afflicted child, bereft of its parent, affected me very sensibly, I was moved with compassion, and charging myself as if accessary to what now appeared to be a cruel murder, and endeavoured to prevail on the hunter to save its life, but to no effect! for by habit he had become insensible to compassion towards the brute creation, being now within a few yards of the harmless devoted victim, he fired, and laid it dead, upon the body of the dam.

IF we bestow but a very little attention to the economy of the animal creation, we shall find manifest examples of premeditation, perseverance, resolution, and consumate artifice, in order to effect their purpose. The next morning, after the slaughter of the bears whilst my companions were striking our tent and preparing to re-embark, I resolved to make a little botanical excursion alone; crossing over a narrow isthmus of sand hills which separated the river from the ocean, I passed over a pretty high hill, its summit crested with a few Palm trees, surrounded with an Orange grove; this hill, whose base was washed on one side, by the floods of the Musquitoe river, and he other side by the billows of the ocean, was about one hundred yards diameter, and seemed to be an entire heap of sea hills. I continued along the beech, a quarter of a mile, and came up to a forest of the Agave vivipara (though composed of herbaceous plants, I term it a forest, because their scapes or flower-stems arose erect near 30 feet high) their tops regularly branching in the form of a pyramidal tree, and these plants growing near to each other, occupied a space of ground of several acres: when their seed is ripe they vegetate, and grow on the branches, until the scape dries when the young plants fall to the ground, take root, and fix themselves in the sand: the plant grows to a prodigious size before the scape shoots up from its centre. Having contemplated this admirable grove, I proceeded towards the

Travels Through North and South Carolina

shrubberies on the banks of the river, and though it was now late in December, the aromatic groves appeared in full bloom. The broad leaved sweet Myrtus, Erythrina corrallodendrum, Cactus cochenellifer, Cacalia suffruticosa, and particularly, Rhizophora conjugata, which stood close to, and in the salt water of the river, were in full bloom, with beautiful white sweet scented flowers, which attracted to them, two or three species of very beautiful butterflies, one of which was black, the upper pair of its wings very long and narrow, marked with transverse stripes of pale yellow, with some spots of a crimson colour near the body. Another species remarkable for splendor, was of a larger size, the wings were undulated and obtusely crenated round their ends, the nether pair terminating near the body, with a long narrow forked tail; the ground light yellow, striped oblique–transversely, with stripes of pale celestial blue, the ends of them adorned with little eyes encircled with the finest blue and crimson, which represented a very brilliant rosary. But those which were the most numerous were as white as snow, their wings large, their ends lightly crenated and ciliated, forming a fringed border, faintly marked with little black crescents, their points downward, with a cluster of little brilliant orbs of blue and crimson, on the nether wings near the body; the numbers were incredible, and there seemed to be scarcely a flower for each fly, multitudinous as they were, besides clouds of them hovering over the mellifluous groves. Besides these papiles, a variety of other insects come in for share, particularly several species of bees.

As I was gathering specimens of flowers from the shrubs, I was greatly surprised at the sudden appearance of a remarkable large spider, on a leaf of the genus Araneus saliens, at sight of me he boldly faced about, and raised himself up as if ready to spring upon me; his body was about the size of a pigeons egg, of a buff colour, which with his legs were covered with short silky hair, on the top of the abdomen was a round red spot or ocelle encircled with black; after I had recovered from the surprise, and observing the wary hunter had retired under cover, I drew near again, and presently discovered that I had surprised him on predatory attempts against the insect tribes, I was therefore determined to watch his proceedings, I soon noticed that the object of his wishes was a large fat bomble bee (apis bombylicus) that was visiting the flowers, and piercing their nectariferous tubes; this cunning intripid hunter (conducted his subtil approaches, with the circumspection and perseverance of a Siminole, when hunting a deer) advancing with slow steps obliquely, or under cover of dense foliage, and behind the limbs, and when the bee was engaged in probing a flower he would leap nearer, and then instantly retire out of sight, under a leaf or behind a branch, at the same time keeping a sharp eye upon me; when he had now got within two feet of his prey, and the bee was intent on sipping the delicious nectar from a flower, with his back next the spider, he instantly sprang upon him, and grasped him over the back and shoulder, when for some moments they both disappeared, I expected the bee had carried of his enemy, but to my surprise they both together rebounded back again, suspended at the extremity of a strong clastic thread or web, which the spider had artfully let fall, or fixed on the twig, the instant he leaped from it; the rapidity of the bee's wings, endeavouring to extricate him–self, made them both together appear as a moving vapor, until the bee became fatigued by whirling round, first one way and then back again; at length, in about a quarter of an hour, the bee quite exhausted by his struggles, and the repeated wounds of the butcher, became motionless, and quickly expired in the arms of the devouring spider, who, ascending the rope with his game, retired to feast on it under cover of leaves; and perhaps before night became himself, the delicious evening repast of a bird or lizard.

BIRDS are in general social and benevolent creatures; intelligent, ingenious, volatile, active beings; and this order of animal creation consists of various nations, bands or tribes, as may be observed from their different structure, manners and laguages or voice, as each nation, though subdivided into many different tribes, retain their general form or structure, a similarity of customs, and a sort of dialect or language, particular to that nation or genus from which they seem to have descended or separated: what I mean by a language in birds, is the common notes or speech, that they use when employed in feeding themselves and their young, calling on one another, as well as their menaces against their enemy; for their songs seem to be musical compositions, performed only by the males, about the time of incubation, in part to divert and amuse the female, entertaining her with melody, &c. this harmony, with the tender solicitude of the male, alleviates the toils, cares and distresses of the female, consoles her in solitary retirement whilst setting, and animate her with affection and attachment to himself in preference to any other. The volatility of their species, and operation of their passions and affections, are particularly conspicuous in the different tribes of the thrush, famous for song; on a sweet May morning we see the red thrush (turdus rufus) perched on an elevated sprig of the snowy Hawthorn, sweet flowering Crab, or other hedge shrubs, exerting their accomplishments in song, striving by varying and elevating their voices to excel each other, we observe a very agreeable variation, not only in tonc but in modulation; the voice of one is shrill, another lively and elevated, others sonorous and quivering. The mock–bird (turdus polyglottos) who excels, distinguishes himself in variety of action as well as air; from a turret he bounds aloft with the celerity of an arrow, as it were to recover or recal his very soul, expired in the last elevated strain. The high forests are

13

filled with the symphony of the song or wood–thrush (turdus minor.)

BOTH sexes of some tribes of birds sing equally fine, and it is remarkable, that these reciprocally assist in their domestic cares, as building their nests and setting on their eggs, feeding and defending their young brood, &c. The oriolus (icterus, Cat.) is an instance in this case, and the female of the icterus minor is a bird of more splendid and gay dress than the male bird. Some tribes of birds will relieve and rear up the young and helpless, of their own and other tribes, when abandoned. Animal substance seems to be the first food of all birds, even the granivorous tribes.

HAVING passed through some remarks, which appeared of sufficient consequence to be offered to the public, and which were most suitable to have a place in the introduction, I shall now offer such observations as must necessarily occur, from a careful attention to, and investigation of the manners of the Indian nations; being induced, while travelling among them, to associate with them, that I might judge for myself whether they were deserving of the severe censure, which prevailed against them among the white people, that they were incapable of civilization.

IN the consideration of this important subject it will be necessary to enquire, whether they were inclined to adopt the European modes of civil society? whether such a reformation could be obtained, without using coercive or violent means? and lastly, whether such a revolution would be productive of real benefit to them, and consequently beneficial to the public? I was satisfied in discovering that they were desirous of becoming united with us, in civil and religious society.

IT may, therefore, not be foreign to the subject, to point out the propriety of sending men of ability and virtue, under the authority of government, as friendly visitors, into their towns; let these men be instructed to learn perfectly their languages, and by a liberal and friendly intimacy, become acquainted with their customs and usages, religious and civil; their system of legislation and police, as well as their most ancient and present traditions and history. These men thus enlightened and instructed, would be qualified to judge equitably, and when returned to us, to make true and just reports, which might assist the legislature of the United States to form, and offer to them a judicious plan, for their civilization and union with us.

BUT I presume not to dictate in these high concerns of government, and I am fully convinced that such important matters are far above my ability; the duty and respect we owe to religion and rectitude, the most acceptable incense we can offer to the Almighty, as an attonement for our negligence, in the care of the present and future well being of our Indian brethren, induces me to mention this matter, though perhaps of greater concernment than we generally are aware of.

BARTRAM's
TRAVELS.

CHAP. I. THE AUTHOR SETS SAIL FROM PHILADELPHIA, AND ARRIVES AT CHARLESTON, FROM WHENCE HE BEGINS HIS TRAVELS.

AT the request of Dr. Fothergill, of London, to search the Floridas, and the western parts of Carolina and Georgia, for the discovery of rare and useful productions of nature, chiefly in the vegetable kingdom; in April, 1773, I embarked for Charleston, South-Carolina, on board the brigantine Charleston Packet, Captain Wright, the brig——, Captain Mason, being in company with us, and bound to the same port. We had a pleasant run down the Delaware, 150 miles to Cape Henlopen, the two vessels entering the Atlantic together. For the first twenty-four hours, we had a prosperous gale, and were cheerful and happy in the prospect of a quick and pleasant voyage; but, alas! how vain and uncertain are human expectations! how quickly is the flattering scene changed! The powerful winds, now rushing forth from their secret abodes, suddenly spread terror and devastation; and the wide ocean, which, a few moments past, was gentle and placid, is now thrown into disorder, and heaped into mountains, whose white curling crests seem to sweep the skies!

THIS furious gale continued near two days and nights, and not a little damaged our sails, cabin furniture, and state-rooms, besides retarding our passage. The storm having abated, a lively gale from N. W. continued four or five days, when shifting to N. and lastly to N. E. on the tenth of our departure from Cape Henlopen, early in the morning, we descried a sail astern, and in a short time discovered it to be Capt. Mason, who soon came up with us. We hailed each other, being joyful to meet again, after so many dangers. He suffered greatly by the gale, but providentially made a good harbour within Cape Hatteras. As he ran by us, he threw on board ten or a dozen bass, a large and delicious fish, having caught a great number of them whilst he was detained in harbour. He got into Charleston that evening, and we the next morning, about eleven o'clock.

THERE are few objects out at sea to attract the notice of the traveller, but what are sublime, awful, and majestic: the seas themselves, in a tempest, exhibit a tremendous scene, where the winds assert their power, and, in furious conflict, seem to set the ocean on fire. On the other hand, nothing can be more sublime than the view of the encircling horizon, after the turbulent winds have taken their flight, and the lately agitated bosom of the deep has again become calm and pacific; the gentle moon rising in dignity from the east, attended by millions of glittering orbs; the luminous appearance of the seas at night, when all the waters seem transmuted into liquid silver; the prodigious bands of porpoises foreboding tempest, that appear to cover the ocean; the mighty whale, sovereign of the watery realms, who cleaves the seas in his course; the sudden appearance of land from the sea, the strand stretching each way, beyond the utmost reach of sight; the alternate appearance and recess of the coast, whilst the far distant blue hills slowly retreat and disappear; or, as we approach the coast, the capes and promontories first strike our sight, emerging from the watery expanse, and like mighty giants, elevating their crests towards the skies; the water suddenly–alive with its scaly inhabitants; squadrons of sea–fowl sweeping through the air, impregnated with the breath of fragrant aromatic trees and flowers; the amplitude and magnificence of these scenes are great indeed, and may present to the imagination, an idea of the first appearance of the earth to man at the creation.

ON my arrival at Charleston, I waited on Doctor Chalmer, a gentleman of eminence in his profession and public employments, to whom I was recommended by my worthy patron, and to whom I was to apply for counsel and assistance, for carrying into effect my intended travels: the Doctor received me with perfect politeness, and, on every occasion, treated me with friendship; and by means of the countenance which he gave me, and the marks of esteem with which he honoured me, I became acquainted with many of the worthy families, not only of Carolina and Georgia, but also in the distant countries of Florida.

CHAP. II.

ARRIVING in Carolina very early in the spring vegetation was not sufficiently advanced to invite me into the western parts of this state; from which circumstance, I concluded to make an excursion into Georgia; accordingly, I embarked on board a coasting vessel, and in twenty–four hours arrived in Savanna, the capital, where, acquainting the Governor, Sir J. Wright, with my business, his Excellency received me with great politeness, shewed me every mark of esteem and regard, and furnished me with letters to the principal inhabitants of the state, which were of great service to me. Another circumstance very opportunely occurred on my arrival: the Assembly was then fitting in Savanna, and several members lodging in the same house where I took up my quarters, I became acquainted with several worthy characters, who invited me to call at their seats occasionally, as I passed through the country; particularly the Hon. B. Andrews, Esq; a distinguished, patriotic and liberal, character. This gentleman's seat, and well cultivated plantations, are situated near the south high road, which I often travelled; and I seldom passed his house without calling to see him, for it was the seat of virtue, where hospitality, piety, and philosophy, formed the happy family; where the weary traveller and stranger found a hearty welcome, and from whence it must be his own fault, if he departed without being greatly benefited.

AFTER resting, and a little recreation for a few days in Savanna, and having in the mean time purchased a good horse, and equipped myself for a journey southward, I sat off early in the morning for Sunbury, a sea–port town, beautifully situated on the main, between Medway and Newport rivers, about fifteen miles south of Great Ogeeche river. The town and harbour are defended from the fury of the seas by the north and south points of St. Helena and South Catherine's islands; between which is the bar and entrance into the sound: the harbour is capacious and safe, and has water enough for ships of great burthen. I arrived here in the evening, in company with a gentleman, one of the inhabitants, who politely introduced me to one of the principal families, where I supped and spent the evening in a circle of genteel and polite ladies and gentlemen. Next day, being desirous of visiting the islands, I forded a narrow shoal, part of the sound, and landed on one of them, which employed me the whole day to explore. The surface and vegetable mould here is generally a loose sand, not very fertile, except some spots bordering on the sound and inlets, where are found heaps or mounds of sea–shell, either formerly brought there, by the Indians, who inhabited the island, or which were perhaps thrown up in ridges, by the beating surface of the sea: possibly both these circumstances may have contributed to their formation. These sea–shells, through length of time, and the subtle penetrating effects of the air, which dissolve them to earth, render these ridges very fertile, and which, when clear of their trees, and cultivated, become profusely productive of almost every kind of vegetable. Here are also large plantations of indigo, corn, and potatoes,

* Convolvulus batata.

with many other sorts of esculent plants. I observed, amongst the shells of the conical mounds, fragments of earthen vessels, and of other utensils, the manufacture of the ancients: about the centre of one of them, the rim of an earthen pot appeared amongst the shells and earth, which I carefully removed, and drew it out, almost whole: this pot was curiously wrought all over the outside, representing basket work, and was undoubtedly esteemed a very ingenious performance, by the people, at the age of its construction. The natural produce of these testaceous ridges, besides many of less note, are, the great Laurel Tree, (Magnolia grandiflora) Pinus taeda, Laurus Borbonia, Quercus sempervirens, or Live Oak, Prunus, Laura–cerasa, Ilex aquifolium, Corypha palma, Juniperus Americana. The general surface of the island being low, and generally level, produces a very great variety of trees, shrubs and herbaceous plants; particularly the great long–leaved Pitch–Pine, or Broom–Pine, Pinus Palustris, Pinus Squamosa, Pinus lutea, Gordonia Lasianthus, Liquid Amber (Styraciflua) Acer rubrum, Fraxinus excelcior, Fraxinus aquatica, Quercus aquatica, Quercus phillos, Quercus dentata, Quercus humila varietas, Vaccinium varietas, Andromeda varietas, Prinof varietas, Ilex varietas, Viburnum prunifolium, V. dentatum, Cornus Florida, C. alba, C. sanguinea, Carpinus betula, C. ostrya, Itea Clethra alnifolia, Halesia taetraptera, H. diptera, Iva Khamnus frangula, Callicarpa, Morus rubra Sapindus, Cassine, and of such as grow near water–courses, round about ponds and savannas, Fothergilla gardini, Myrica cerifera, Olea Americana, Cyrilla racemiflora, Magnolia glauca, Magnolia pyramidata, Cercis, Kalmia angustifolia, Kalmia ciliata, Chionanthus, Cephalanthos, Aesculus parva, and the intermediate spaces, surrounding and lying between the ridges and savannas, are intersected with plains of the dwarf prickly fan–leaved Palmetto, and lawns of grass variegated with stately trees of the great Broom–Pine, and the spreading ever–green Water–Oak, either disposed in clumps, or scatteringly planted by nature. The upper surface, or vegetative soil of the island, lies on a foundation, or stratum, of tenaceous cinerious coloured clay, which perhaps is the principal support of the vast growth of timber that arises from the surface, which is little more than a mixture of fine white sand and dissolved vegetables, serving as a nursery bed to hatch, or bring into existence, the infant plant, and to supply it with aliment and food, suitable to its delicacy and tender frame, until the roots, acquiring sufficient extent and solidity to lay hold of the clay, soon attain a magnitude and stability sufficient to maintain its station. Probably if this clay were dug out, and cast upon the surface, after being meliorated by the saline or nitrous qualities of the air, it would kindly incorporate with the loose sand, and become a productive and lasting manure.

The roebuck, or deer, are numerous on this island; the tyger, wolf, and bear, hold yet some possession; as also raccoons, foxes, hares, squirrels, rats and mice, but I think no moles; there is a large ground–rat, more than twice the size of the common Norway rat. In the night time, it throws out the earth, forming little mounds, or hillocks. Opposoms are here in abundance, as also pole–cats, wild–cats, rattle–snakes, glass–snake, coach–whip snake, and a variety of other serpents.

HERE are also a great variety of birds, through out the seasons, inhabiting both sea and land. First I shall name the eagle, of which there are three species: the great grey eagle is the largest, of great strength and high flight; he chiefly preys on fawns and other young quadrupeds.

THE bald eagle is likewise a large, strong, and very active bird, but an execrable tyrant: he supports his assumed dignity and grandeur by rapine and violence, extorting unreasonable tribute and subsidy from all the feathered nations.

THE last of this race I shall mention is the falco piscatorius, or fishing–hawk: this is a large bird, of high and rapid flight; his wings are very long and pointed, and he spreads a vast sail, in proportion to the volume of his body. This princely bird subsists entirely on fish, which he takes himself, scorning to live and grow fat on the dear earned labours of another; he also contributes liberally to the support of the bald eagle.

WATER–FOWL, and the various species of land–birds, also abound, most of which are mentioned by Catesby, in his Hist. Carolina, particularly his painted finch (Emberiza Ceris Linn.) exceeded by none of the feathered tribes, either in variety and splendour of dress, or melody of song.

Travels Through North and South Carolina

CATESBY'S ground doves are also here in abundance: they are remarkably beautiful, about the size of a sparrow, and their soft and plaintive cooing perfectly enchanting.

How chaste the dove! "never known to violate the conjugal contract."

She flees the seats of envy and strife, and seeks the retired paths of peace.

THE sight of this delightful and productive island, placed in front of the rising city of Sunbury, quickly induced me to explore it; which I apprehended, from former visits to this coast, would exhibit a comprehensive epitome of the history of all the sea–coast islands of Carolina and Georgia, as likewise in general of the coast of the main; and as I considered this excursion along the coast of Georgia and northern border of Florida, a deviation from the high road of my intended travels, yet I performed it in order to employ to the most advantage the time on my hands, before the treaty of Augusta came on, where I was to attend, about May or June, by desire of the Superintendant, J. Stewart, Esq; who, when I was in Charleston, proposed, in order to facilitate my travels in the Indian territories, that, if I would be present at the Congress, he would introduce my business to the chiefs of the Cherokees, Creeks, and other nations, and recommend me to their friendship and protection; which promise he fully performed, and it proved of great service to me.

OBEDIENT to the admonitions of my attendant spirit, curiosity, as well as to gratify the expectations of my worthy patron, I again sat off on my southern excursion, and left Sunbury, in company with several of its polite inhabitants, who were going to Medway meeting, a very large and well constructed place of worship, in St. John's parish, where I associated with them in religious exercise, and heard a very excellent sermon, delivered by their pious and truly venerable pastor, the Rev.—— Osgood. This respectable congregation is independent, and consist chiefly of families, and proselytes to a flock, which this pious man led, about forty years ago, from South–Carolina, and settled in this fruitful district. It is about nine miles from Sunbury to Medway meeting–house, which stands on the high road, opposite the Sunbury road. As soon as the congregation broke up, I re–assumed my travels, proceeding down the high road, towards Fort Barrington, on the Alatamaha, passing through a level country, well watered by large streams, branches of Medway and Newport rivers, coursing from extensive swamps and marshes, their sources: these swamps are daily clearing and improving into large fruitful rice plantations, aggrandizing the well inhabited and rich district of St. John's parish. The road

20

is strait, spacious, and kept in excellent repair by the industrious inhabitants; and is generally bordered on each side with a light grove, consisting of the following trees and shrubs: Myrica Cerifera, Calycanthus, Halesia tetraptera, Itea stewartia, Andromeda nitida, Cyrella racemiflora, entwined with bands and garlands of Bignonia sempervirens, B. crucigera, Lonicera sempervirens and Glycene frutescens; these were overshadowed by tall and spreading trees, as the Magnolia grandiflora, Liquid Amber, Liriodendron, Catalpa, Quercus sempervirens, Quercus dentata, Q. Phillos; and on the verges of the canals, where the road was causwayed, stood the Cupressus disticha, Floriferus Gordonia Lacianthus, and Magnolia glauca, all planted by nature, and left standing, by the virtuous inhabitants, to shade the road and perfume the sultry air. The extensive plantations of rice and corn, now in early verdure, decorated here and there with groves of floriferous and fragrant trees and shrubs, under the cover and protection of pyramidal laurels and plumed palms, which now and then break through upon the sight from both sides of the way as we pass along; the eye at intervals stealing a view at the humble, but elegant and neat habitation, of the happy proprietor, amidst arbours and groves, all day, and moon–light nights, filled with the melody of the chearful mockbird, warbling nonpareil, and plaintive turtle dove, altogether present a view of magnificence and joy, inexpressibly charming and animating.

IN the evening, I arrived at the seat of the Hon. B. Andrews, Esq; who received and entertained me in every respect, as a worthy gentleman could a stranger, that is, with hearty welcome, plain but plentiful board, free conversation and liberality of sentiment. I spent the evening very agreeably, and the day following (for I was not permitted to depart sooner) I viewed with pleasure this gentleman's exemplary improvements in agriculture; particularly in the growth of rice, and in his machines for shelling that valuable grain, which stands in the water almost from the time it is sown, until within a few days before it is reaped, when they draw off the water by sluices, which ripens it all at once, and when the heads or panicles are dry ripe, it is reaped and left standing in the field, in small ricks, until the straw is quite dry, when it is hauled, and stacked in the barn yard. The machines for cleaning the rice are worked by the force of water. They stand on the great reservoir which contains the waters that flood the rice fields below.

TOWARDS the evening we made a little party at fishing. We chose a shaded retreat, in a beautiful grove of magnolias, myrtles, and sweet bay trees, which were left standing on the bank of a fine creek, that, from this place, took a slow serpentine course through the plantation. We presently took some fish, one kind of which is very beautiful; they call it

21

the red–belly. It is as large as a man's hand, nearly oval and thin, being compressed on each side; the tail is beautifully formed; the top of the head and back, of an olive green, besprinkled with russet specks; the sides of a sea grean, inclining to azure, insensibly blended with the olive above, and beneath lightens to a silvery white, or pearl colour, elegantly powdered with specks of the finest green, russet and gold; the belly is of a bright scarlet red, or vermilion, darting up rays or fiery streaks into the pearl on each side; the ultimate angle of the branchiostega extends backwards with a long spatula, ending with a round, or oval particoloured spot, representing the eye in the long feathers of a peacock's train, verged round with a thin flame–coloured membrane, and appears like a brilliant ruby fixed on the side of the fish; the eyes are large, encircled with fiery iris; they are a voracious fish, and are easily caught with a suitable bait.

THE next morning I took leave of this worthy family, and sat off for the settlements on the Alatahama, still pursuing the high road for Fort Barrington, till towards noon, when I turned off to the left, following the road to Darian, a settlement on the river, twenty miles lower down, and near the coast. The fore part of this day's journey was pleasant, the plantations frequent, and the roads in tolerable good repair. But the country being now less cultivated, the roads became bad, pursuing my journey almost continually, through swamps and creeks, waters of Newport and Sapello, till night, when I lost my way; but coming up to a fence, I saw a glimmering light, which conducted me to a house, where I stayed all night, and met with very civil entertainment. Early next morning, I sat off again, in company with the overseer of the farm, who piloted me through a large and difficult swamp, when we parted; he in chase of deer, and I towards Darian. I rode several miles through a high forest of pines, thinly growing on a level plain, which admitted an ample view, and a free circulation of air, to another swamp; and crossing a considerable branch of Sapello river, I then came to a small plantation by the side of another swamp: the people were remarkably civil and hospitable. The man's name was M'Intosh, a family of the first colony established in Georgia, under the conduct of General Oglethorpe. Was there ever such a scene of primitive simplicity, as was here exhibited, since the days of the good King Tammany! The venerable grey headed Caledonian smilingly meets me coming up to his house. "Welcome, stranger, come in, and rest; the air is now very sultry; it is a very hot day." I was there treated with some excellent venison, and here found friendly and secure shelter from a tremendous thunder storm, which came up from the N. W. and soon after my arrival, began to discharge its fury all around. Stepping to the door to observe the progress and direction of the tempest, the fulgour and rapidity of the streams of lightning, passing from cloud to cloud, and from the clouds to the earth, exhibited a very awful scene; when instantly the lightning, as it were, opening a fiery chasm in the black cloud, darted with inconceivable rapidity on the trunk of a large pine tree, that stood thirty or forty yards from me, and set it in a blaze. The flame instantly ascended upwards of ten or twelve feet, and continued flaming about fifteen minutes, when it was gradually extinguished, by the deluges of rain that fell upon it.

I SAW here a remarkably large turkey of the native wild breed: his head was above three feet from the ground when he stood erect; he was a stately beautiful bird, of a very dark dusky brown colour, the tips of the feathers of his neck, breast, back, and shoulders, edged with a copper colour, which in a certain exposure looked like burnished gold, and he seemed not insensible of the splendid appearance he made. He was reared from an egg, found in the forest, and hatched by a hen of the common domestic fowl.

OUR turkey of America is a very different species from the mileagris of Asia and Europe; they are nearly thrice their size and weight. I have seen several that have weighed between twenty and thirty pounds, and some have been killed that weighed near forty. They are taller, and have a much longer neck proportionally, and like wise longer legs, and stand more erect; they are also very different in colour. Ours are all, male and female, of a dark brown colour, not having a black feather on them; but the male exceedingly splendid, with changeable colours. In other particulars they differ not.

THE tempest being over, I waited till the floods of rain had run off the ground, then took leave of my friends, and departed. The air was now cool and salubrious, and riding seven or eight miles, through a pine forest, I came to Sapello bridge, to which the salt tide flows. I here stopped, at Mr. Bailey's, to deliver a letter from the Governor. This gentleman received me very civilly, inviting me to stay with him; but upon my urging the necessity of my accelerating my journey, he permitted me to proceed to Mr. L. M'Intosh's, near the river, to whose friendship I was recommended by Mr. B. Andrews.

PERHAPS, to a grateful mind, there is no intellectual enjoyment, which regards human concerns, of a more excellent nature, than the remembrance of real acts of friendship. The heart expands at the pleasing recollection. When I came up to his door, the friendly man, smiling, and with a grace and dignity peculiar to himself, took me by the hand, and accosted me thus: "Friend Bartram, come under my roof, and I desire you to make my house your home, as long as convenient to your self; remember, from this moment, that you are a part of my family, and, on my part, I shall endeavour to make it agreeable," which was verified during my continuance in, and about, the southern territories of Georgia and Florida; for I found here sincerity in union with all the virtues, under the influence of religion. I shall yet mention a remarkable instance of Mr. M'Intosh's friendship and respect for me; which was, recommending his eldest son, Mr. John M'Intosh, as a companion in my travels. He was a sensible virtuous youth, and a very agreeable companion through a long and toilsome journey of near a thousand miles.

HAVING been greatly refreshed, by continuing a few days with this kind and agreeable family, I prepared to prosecute my journey southerly.

CHAP. III.

I SAT off early in the morning for the Indian trading–house, in the river St. Mary, and took the road up the N. E. side of the Alatamaha to Fort–Barrington. I passed through a well inhabited district, mostly rice plantations, on the waters of Cathead creek, a branch of the Alatamaha. On drawing near the fort, I was greatly delighted at the appearance of two new beautiful shrubs, in all their blooming graces. One of them appeared to be a species of Gordonia,

* Franklinia Alatahama.

but the flowers are larger, and more fragrant than those of the Gordonia Lascanthus, and are sessile; the seed vessel is also very different. The other was equally distinguished for beauty and singularity; it grows twelve or fifteen feet high, the branches ascendant and opposite, and terminate with large panicles of pale blue tubular flowers, specked on the inside with crimson; but, what is singular, these panicles are ornamented with a number of ovate large brachtae, as white, and like fine paper, their tops and verges stained with a rose red, which, at a little distance, has the appearance of clusters of roses, at the extremities of the limbs; the flowers are of the Bl. Pentandria monogynia; the leaves are nearly ovate, pointed and petioled, standing opposite to one another on the branches.

AFTER fifteen miles riding, I arrived at the ferry, which is near the site of the fort. Here is a considerable height and bluff on the river, and evident vestiges of an ancient Indian town may be seen, such as old extensive fields, and conical mounds, or artificial heaps of earth. I here crossed the river, which is about five hundred yards over, in a good large boat, rowed by a Creek Indian, who was married to a white woman; he seemed an active, civil, and sensible man. I saw large, tall trees of the Nyssa coccinea, si. Ogeeche, growing on the banks of the river. They grow in the water, near the shore. There is no tree that exhibits a more desirable appearance than this, in the autumn, when their fruit is ripe, and the tree divested of its leaves; for then they look as red as scarlet, with their fruit, which is of that colour also. It is of the shape, but larger than the olive, containing an agreeable acid juice. The leaves are oblong lanciolate and entire, somewhat hoary underneath; their upper surface of a full green, and shining; the petioles short, pedunculis multifloris. The most northern settlement of this tree, yet known, is on Great Ogeeche, where they are called Ogeeche limes, from their acid fruit being about the size of limes, and their being sometimes used in their stead.

BEING safely landed on the opposite bank, I mounted my horse, and followed the high road to the ferry on St. Ille, about sixty miles south of the Alatamaha, passing through an uninhabited wilderness. The sudden transition from rich cultivated settlements, to high pine forests, dark and grassy savannas, forms in my opinion no disagreeable contrast; and the new objects of observation in the works of nature soon reconcile the surprised imagination to the change. As soon as I had lost sight of the river, ascending some sand−hills, I observed a new and most beautiful species of Annona, having clusters of large white fragrant flowers, and a diminutive but elegant Kalmia. The stems are very small, feeble, and for the most part undivided, furnished with little ovate pointed leaves, and terminate with a simple racemi, or spike of flowers, salver−formed, and of a deep rose red. The whole plant is ciliated. It grows in abundance all over the moist savannas, but more especially near ponds and bay−swamps. In similar situations, and commonly a near neighbour to this new Kalmia, is seen a very curious species of Annona. It is a very dwarf, the stems seldom extending from the earth more than a foot or eighteen inches, and are weak and almost decumbent. The leaves are long, extremely narrow, almost lineal. However, small as they are, they retain the figure common to the species, that is, lanciolate, broadest at the upper end, and attenuating down to the petiole, which is very short; their leaves stand alternately, nearly erect, forming two series, or wings, on the arcuated stems. The flowers, both in size and colour, resemble those of the Antrilobe, and are single from the axillae of the leaves on incurved pedunculi, nodding downwards. I never saw the fruit. The dens, or caverns, dug in the sand hills, by the great land−tortoise, called here Gopher,*

25

* Testudo Polyphaemus.

present a very singular appearance; these vast caves are their castles and diurnal retreats, from whence they issue forth in the night, in search of prey. The little mounds, or hillocks of fresh earth, thrown up in great numbers in the night, have also a curious appearance.

IN the evening I arrived at a cow–pen, where there was a habitation, and the people received me very civilly. I staid here all night, and had for supper plenty of milk, butter, and very good cheese of their own make, which is a novelty in the maritime parts of Carolina and Georgia; the inhabitants being chiefly supplied with it from Europe and the northern states. The next day's progress, in general, presented scenes similar to the preceding, though the land is lower, more level and humid, and the produce more varied: high open forests of stately pines, flowery plains, and extensive green savannas, checquered with the incarnate Chironia, Pillcherima, and Assclepias fragrans, perfumed the air whilst they pleased the eye. I met with some troublesome cane swamps, saw herds of horned cattle, horses and deer, and took notice of a procumbent species of Hibiscus, the leaves palmated, the flowers large and expanded, pale yellow and white, having a deep crimson eye; the whole plant, except the corolla, armed with stiff hair. I also saw a beautiful species of Lupin, having pale green villous lingulate *

* Lupinus breunis, solus integerimis oblongis villosia.

leaves; the flowers are disposed in long erect spikes; some plants produce flowers of the finest celestial blue, others incarnate, and some milk white, and though they all three seem to be varieties of one species, yet they associate in separate communities, sometimes approaching near each other's border, or in sight at a distance. Their districts are situated on dry sandy heights, in open pine forests, which are naturally thin of undergrowth, and appear to great advantage; generally, where they are found, they occupy many acres of surface. The vegetative mould is composed of fine white sand, mixed, and coloured, with dissolved and calcined vegetable substances; but this stratum is not very deep, and covers one of a tenacious cinereous coloured clay, as we may observe by the earth adhering to the roots of trees, torn up by storms, &c. and by the little chimnies, or air holes of cray–fish, which perforate the savannas. Turkeys, quails, and small birds, are here to be seen; but birds are not numerous in desert forests; they draw

26

near to the habitations of men, as I have constantly observed in all my travels.

I ARRIVED at St. Ille's in the evening, where I lodged, and next morning having crossed over in a ferry boat, sat forward for St. Mary's. The situation of the territory, it's soil and productions between these two last rivers, are nearly similar to those which I had passed over, except that the savannas are more frequent and extensive.

IT may be proper to observe, that I had now passed the utmost frontier of the white settlements on that border. It was drawing on towards the close of day, the skies serene and calm, the air temperately cool, and gentle zephyrs breathing through the fragrant pines; the prospect around enchantingly varied and beautiful; endless green savannas, checquered with coppices of fragrant shrubs, filled the air with the richest perfume. The gaily attired plants which enamelled the green had begun to imbibe the pearly dew of evening; nature seemed silent, and nothing appeared to ruffle the happy moments of evening contemplation: when, on a sudden, an Indian appeared crossing the path, at a considerable distance before me. On percieving that he was armed with a rifle, the first sight of him startled me, and I endeavoured to elude his sight, by stopping my pace, and keeping large trees between us; but he espied me, and turning short about, sat spurs to his horse, and came up on full gallop. I never before this was afraid at the sight of an Indian, but at this time, I must own that my spirits were very much agitated: I saw at once, that being unarmed, I was in his power, and having now but a few moments to prepare, I resigned myself entirely to the will of the Almighty, trusting to his mercies for my preservation; my mind then became tranquil, and I resolved to meet the dreaded foe with resolution and chearful confidence. The intrepid Siminole stopped suddenly, three or four yards before me, and silently viewed me, his countenance angry and fierce, shifting his rifle from shoulder to shoulder, and looking about instantly on all sides. I advanced towards him, and with an air of confidence offered him my hand, hailing him, brother; at this he hastily jerked back his arm, with a look of malice, rage and disdain, seeming every way disconcerted; when again looking at me more attentively, he instantly spurred up to me, and, with dignity in his look and action, gave me his hand. Possibly the silent language of his soul, during the moment of suspense (for I believe his design was to kill me when he first came up) was after this manner: "White man, thou art my enemy, and thou and thy brethren may have killed mine; yet it may not be so, and even were that the case, thou art now alone, and in my power. Live; the Great Spirit forbids me to touch thy life; go to thy brethren, tell them thou sawest an Indian in the forests, who knew how to be humane and compassionate." In fine, we shook hands, and parted in a friendly manner,

27

in the midst of a dreary wilderness; and he informed me of the course and distance to the tradinghouse, where I found he had been extremely ill treated the day before.

I now sat forward again, and after eight or ten miles riding, arrived at the banks of St. Mary's, opposite the stores, and got safe over before dark. The river is here about one hundred yards across, has ten feet water, and, following its course, about sixty miles to the sea, though but about twenty miles by land. The trading company here received and treated me with great civility. On relating my adventures on the road, particularly the last with the Indian, the chief replied, with a countenance that at once bespoke surprise and pleasure, "My friend, consider yourself a fortunate man: that fellow," said he, "is one of the greatest villains on earth, a noted murderer, and outlawed by his countrymen. Last evening he was here, we took his gun from him, broke it in pieces, and gave him a severe drubbing: he, however, made his escape, carrying off a new rifle gun, with which, he said, going off, he would kill the first white man he met."

On seriously contemplating the behaviour of this Indian towards me, so soon after his ill treatment, the following train of sentiments insensibly crouded in upon my mind.

Can it be denied, but that the moral principle, which directs the savages to virtuous and praiseworthy actions, is natural or innate? It is certain they have not the assistance of letters, or those means of education in the schools of philosophy, where the virtuous sentiments and actions of the most illustrious characters are recorded, and carefully laid before the youth of civilized nations: therefore this moral principle must be innate, or they must be under the immediate influence and guidance of a more divine and powerful preceptor, who, on these occasions, instantly inspires them, and as with a ray of divine light, points out to them at once the dignity, propriety, and beauty of virtue.

THE land on, and adjacent to, this river, notwithstanding its arenacious surface, appears naturally fertile. The Peach trees are large, healthy, and fruitful; and Indian Corn, Rice, Cotton, and Indigo, thrive exceedingly. This sandy surface, one would suppose, from it's loose texture, would possess a percolating quality, and suffer the rainwaters quickly to drain off; but it is quite the contrary, at least in these low maritime sandy countries of Carolina and Florida, beneath the mountains, for in the sands, even the heights, where the arenaceous stratum is perhaps five, eight, and ten feet above the clay, the earth, even in the longest droughts, is moist an inch or two under the surface; whereas, in the rich tenacious low lands, at such times, the ground is dry, and, as it were, baked many inches, and sometimes some feet deep, and the crops, as well as almost all vegetation, suffer in such soils and situations. The reason of this may be, that this kind of earth admits more freely of a transpiration of vapours, arising from intestine watery canals to the surface; and probably these vapours are impregnated with saline or nitrous principles, friendly and nutritive to vegetables; however, of these causes and secret operations of nature I am ignorant, and resume again my proper employment, that of discovering and collecting data for the exercise of more able physiologists.

THE savannas about St. Mary's, at this season, display a very charming appearance of flowers and verdure; their more elevated borders are varied with beds of Violets, Lupins, Amaryllis atamasco, and plats of a new and very beautiful species of Mimosa sensitiva, which I think as admirable, and more charming than the celebrated Humble plant, equally chaste and fearful of the hasty touch of the surprised admirer; the flower is larger, of a bright damask rose colour, and exceedingly fragrant: the whole plant is destitute of prickles, but hairy; it is precumbent, reclining itself upon the green turf, and from these trailing branches proceed an upright peduncle, six or eight inches high, supporting an oblong head of flowerets, which altogether, at a small distance, have the appearance of an exuberant field of clover; and, what is singular, and richly varies the scene, there are interspersed patches of the same species of plants, having flowers of the finest golden yellow, and others snow white; but the incarnate is most prevalent. Magnolia glauca, Itea Clethra, Chionanthus, Gordonia lasianthus, Ilex angustifolium, Olea Americana, Hopea tinctoria, &c. are seated in detached groves or clumps, round about the ponds or little lakes, at the lower end of the savannas. I observed, growing on the banks of this sequestered river, the following trees and shrubs: Quercus sempervirens, Q. aquatica, Q. Phillos, Q. dentata, Nyssa aquatica, N. sylvatica, N. Ogeeche, si. coccinea, Cupressus disticha, Fraxinus aquatica, Rhamnus frangula, Prunus laura cerapa, Cyrilla racemiflora, Myrica cericera, Andromeda ferruginia, Andr. nitida, and the great evergreen Andromeda of Florida, called Pipe–stem Wood, to which I gave the name of Andromeda formosissima, as it far exceeds in beauty every one of this family.

THE river St. Mary has its source from a vast lake, or marsh, called Ouaquaphenogaw, which lies between Flint and Oakmulge rivers, and occupies a space of near three hundred miles in circuit. This vast accumulation of waters, in the wet season, appears as a lake, and contains some large islands or knolls, of rich high land; one of which the present generation of the Creeks represent to be a most blissful spot of the earth: they say it is inhabited by a peculiar race of Indians, whose women are incomparably beautiful;

29

they also tell you, that this terrestrial paradise has been by some of their enterprising hunters, when in pursuit of game, who being lost in inextricable swamps and bogs, and on the point of perishing, were unexpectedly relieved by a company of beautiful women, whom they call daughters of the sun, who kindly gave them such provisions as they had with them, which were chiefly fruit, oranges, dates, &c. and some corn cakes, and then enjoined them to fly for safety to their own country; for that their husbands were fierce men, and cruel to strangers: they further say, that these hunters had a view of their settlements, situated on the elevated banks of an island, or promontory, in a beautiful lake; but that in their endeavours to approach it, they were involved in perpetual labyrinths, and, like inchanted land, still as they imagined they had just gained it, it seemed to fly before them, alternately appearing and disappearing. They resolved, at length, to leave the delusive pursuit, and to return; which, after a number of inexpressible difficulties, they effected. When they reported their adventures to their countrymen, their young warriors were enflamed with an irresistable desire to invade, and make a conquest of, so charming a country; but all their attempts have hitherto proved abortive, never having been able again to find that enchanting spot, nor even any road or pathway to it; yet they say that they frequently meet with certain signs of its being inhabited, as the building of canoes, footsteps of men, &c. They tell another story concerning the inhabitants of this sequestered country, which seems probable enough, which is, that they are the posterity of a fugitive remnant of the ancient Yamases, who escaped massacre after a bloody and decisive conflict between them and the Creek nation (who, it is certain, conquered, and nearly exterminated, that once powerful people) and here found an asylum, remote and secure from the fury of their proud conquerors. It is, however, certain that there is a vast lake, or drowned swamp, well known, and often visited both by white and Indian hunters, and on its environs the most valuable hunting grounds in Florida, well worth contending for, by those powers whose territories border upon it. From this great source of rivers,*

* Source of rivers. It is said, that St. Ille, St. Mary, and the beautiful river Little St. Juan, which discharges its waters into the bay of Apalachi, at St. Mark's, take their rise from this swamp.

St. Mary arises, and meanders through a vast plain and pine forest, near an hundred and fifty miles to the ocean, with which it communicates, between the points of Amelia and Talbert islands; the waters flow deep and gently down from its source to the sea.

HAVING made my observations on the vegetable productions of this part of the country, and obtained specimens and seeds of some curious trees and shrubs (which were the principal objects of this excursion) I returned by the same road to the Alatamaha, and arrived safe again at the seat of my good friend, L. M'Intosh, Esq; where I tarried a few days to rest and refresh myself, and to wait for my young companion and fellow pilgrim, Mr. John M`Intosh, who, being fond of the enterprize, had been so active during my absence, in the necessary preparations, that we had nothing to wait for now but Mrs. M`Intosh's final consent to give up her son to the perils and hardships of so long a journey; which difficult point being settled, we set off with the prayers and benevolent wishes of my companion's worthy parents.

CHAP. IV.

EARLY in the morning, we mounted our horses, and in two days arrived in Savanna; here we learned that the superintendant of Indian affairs had left the capital, and was on his way to Augusta. I remained but one day in Savanna, which was employed in making up and forwarding the collections for Charleston.

THE day following we sat off for Augusta, which is on Savanna river, at least an hundred and fifty miles by land from the capital, and about three hundred by water. We followed the course of the river, and arrived there after having had a prosperous journey, though a little incommoded by the heats of the season.

As nothing very material occurred on the road, I shall proceed to give a summary account of the observations I made concerning the soil, situation, and natural productions of the country.

IN our progress from the sea coast, we rise gradually, by several steps or ascents, in the following manner: first, from the sea–coast, fifty miles back, is a level plain, generally of a loose sandy soil, producing spacious high forests, of Pinus taeda, P. lutea, P. squarpsa, P. echinata, 1. Quercus sempervirens, 2. Quercus aquatica, 3. Q. phillos, 4. Q. tinctoria, 5. Q. dentata, 6. Q. prinos, 7. Q. alba, 8. Q. finuata, 9. Q. rubra,

* 1. Live Oak. 2. Della leaved Water Oak. 3. Willow–leaved Oak. 4. Great Black Oak. 5. Narrow–leaved Wintergreen Oak. 6. Swamp White Oak. 7. White Oak. 8. Spanish Oak.

9. Red Oak.

Liriodendron tulipifera, Liquid amber styraciflua, Morus rubra, Cercis tilia, Populus heterophylla, Platanus occidentalis, Laurus sasafras, Laurus Borbonia, Hopea tinctoria, Fraxinus excelsior, Nyssa, Ulmus, Juglans exaltata, Halesa, Stewartia. Nearly one third of this vast plain is what the inhabitants call swamps, which are the sources of numerous small rivers and their branches: these they call salt rivers, because the tides flow near to their sources, and generally carry a good depth and breadth of water for small craft, twenty or thirty miles upwards from the sea, when they branch and spread abroad like an open hand, interlocking with each other, and forming a chain of swamps across the Carolinas and Georgia, several hundred miles parallel with the sea coast. These swamps are fed and replenished constantly by an infinite number of rivulets and rills, which spring out of the first bank or ascent; their native trees and shrubs are, besides most of those already enumerated above, as follow: Acer rubrum, Nyssa aquatica, Chionanthus, Celtis, Fagus sylvatica, Sambricus; and the higher knolls afford beautiful clumps of Azalea nuda and Azalea viscosa, Corypha palma, Corypha pumila, and Magnolia grandiflora; besides, the whole surface of the ground between the trees and shrubs appears to be occupied with canes (Arundo gigantea) intangled with festoons of the floriferous Glycine frutescens, Bignonia sempervirens, Glycine apios, Smilax, various species, Bignonia crucigera, Bign. radicans, Lonicera sempervirens, and a multitude of other trees, shrubs, and plants less conspicuous; and, in very wet places, Cupressus disticha. The upper soil of these swamps is a perfectly black, soapy, rich earth, or stiff mud, two or three feet deep, on a foundation or stratum of calcarious fossil, which the inhabitants call white marle; and this is the heart or strength of these swamps; they never wear out or become poor, but, on the contrary, are more fertile by tillage; for when they turn up this white marle, the air and winter frosts causing it to fall like quicklime, it manures the surface: but it has one disadvantage, that is, in great droughts, when they cannot have water sufficient in their reservoirs to lay the surface of the ground under water, it binds, and becomes so tough as to burn and kill the crops, especially the old cleared lands; as, while it was fresh and new, the great quantity of rotten wood, roots, leaves, &c. kept the surface loose and open. Severe droughts seldom happen near the sea coast.

WE now rise a bank of considerable height, which runs nearly parallel to the coast, through Carolina and Georgia; the ascent is gradual by several flights or steps, for eight or ten miles, the perpendicular height whereof, above the level of the ocean, may be two or three hundred feet (and these are called the sand–hills) when we find ourselves on the entrance of a vast plain, generally level, which extends west sixty or seventy miles, rising gently as the former, but more perceptibly. This plain is mostly a forest of the great long–leaved pine (P. palustris Linn.) the earth covered with grass, interspersed with an infinite variety of herbacious plants, and embellished with extensive savannas, always green, sparkling with ponds of water, and ornamented with clumps of evergreen, and other trees and shrubs, as Magnolia grandiflora, Magnolia glauca, Gordonia, Ilex aquifolium, Quercus, various species, Laurus Borbonia, Chionanthus, Hopea tinctoria, Cyrilla, Kalmia angustifolia, Andromeda, varieties, Viburnum, Azalea, Rhus vernix, Prinos, varieties, Fothergilla, and a new shrub of great beauty and singularity; it grows erect, seven or eight feet high; a multitude of erect stems arise from its root; these divide themselves into ascendant branches, which are garnished with abundance of narrow lanciolate obtuse pointed leaves, of a light green, smooth and shining. These branches, with their many subdivision, terminate in simple racemes of pale incarnate flowers, which make a fine appearance among the leaves; the flowers are succeeded by desiccated triquetrous pericarpi, each containing a single kernel.

THE lowest sides of these savannas are generally joined by a great cane swamp, varied with coppices and hommocks of the various trees and shrubs already mentioned. In these swamps several rivulets take their rise, which drain them and the adjoining savannas, and thence meandering to the rivers through the forests, with their banks decorated with shrubs and trees. The earth under this level plain may be described after the following manner: the upper surface, or vegetative mould, is a light sandy loam, generally nine inches or a foot deep, on a stratum of cinerious coloured clay, except the sand–hills, where the loose sandy surface is much deeper upon the clay; stone of any sort, or gravel, is seldom seen.

THE next ascent, or flight, is of much greater and more abrupt elevation, and continues rising by broken ridges and narrow levels, or vales, for ten or fifteen miles, when we rest again on another extensive nearly level plain of pine forests, mixed with various other forest trees, which continues west forty or fifty miles farther, and exhibits much the same appearance with the great forest last mentioned; its vegetable productions nearly the same, excepting that the broken ridges by which we ascend to the plain are of a better soil; the vegetative mould is mixed with particles of clay and small gravel, and the soil of a dusky brown colour, lying on a stratum of redish brown tough clay. The trees and

33

shrubs are, Pinus taeda, great black Oak, Quercus tinctoria, Q. rubra, Laurus, Sasafras, Magnolia grandiflora, Cornus Florida, Cercis, Halesia, Juglans acuminata, Juglans–exaltata, Andromeda arborea; and, by the sides of rivulets (which wind about and between these hills and swamps, in the vales) Styrax latifolia, Ptelea trifoliata, Stewartia, Calycanthus, Chionanthus, Magnolia tripetala, Azalea, and others.

THUS have I endeavoured to give the reader a short and natural description of the vast plain lying between the region of Augusta and the sea coast; for from Augusta the mountainous country begins (when compared to the level sandy plain already passed) although it is at least an hundred and fifty miles west, thence to the Cherokee or Apalachean mountains; and this space may with propriety be called the hilly country, every where fertile and delightful, continually replenished by innumerable rivulets, either coursing about the fragrant hills, or springing from the rocky precipices, and forming many cascades; the coolness and purity of which waters invigorate the air of this otherwise hot and sultry climate.

THE village of Augusta is situated on a rich and fertile plain, on the Savanna river; the buildings are near its banks, and extend nearly two miles up to the cataracts, or falls, which are formed by the first chain of rocky hills, through which this famous river forces itself, as if impatient to repose on the extensive plain before it invades the ocean. When the river is low, which is during the summer months, the cataracts are four or five feet in height across the river, and the waters continue rapid and broken, rushing over rocks five miles higher up: this river is near five hundred yards broad at Augusta.

A FEW days after our arrival at Augusta, the chiefs and warriors of the Creeks and Cherokees being arrived, the Congress and the business of the treaty came on, and the negociations continued undetermined many days; the merchants of Georgia demanding at least two millions of acres of land from the Indians, as a discharge of their debts, due, and of long standing; the Creeks, on the other hand, being a powerful and proud spirited People, their young warriors were unwilling to submit to so large a demand, and their conduct evidently betrayed a disposition to dispute the ground by force of arms, and they could not at first be brought to listen to reason and amicable terms; however, at length, the cool and deliberate counsels of the ancient venerable chiefs, enforced by liberal presents of suitable goods, were too powerful inducements for them any longer to resist, and finally prevailed. The treaty concluded in unanimity, pace, and good order; and the honorable Superintendant, not forgetting his promise to me, at the conclusion, mentioned my business, and recommended me to the protection of the Indian chiefs and warriors. The presents being distributed amongst the Indians, they departed, returning home to their towns. A company of surveyors were appointed, by the Governor and Council, to ascertain the boundaries of the new purchase; they were to be attended by chiefs of the Indians, selected and delegated by their countrymen, to assist, and be witnesses that the articles of the treaty were fulfilled, as agreed to by both parties in Congress.

COL. BARNET, who was chosen to conduct this business on the part of the Georgians, a gentleman every way qualified for that important trust, in a very friendly and obliging manner, gave me an invitation to accompany him on this tour.

IT was now about the middle of the month of May; vegetation, in perfection, appeared with all her attractive charms, breathing fragrance every where; the atmosphere was now animated with the efficient principle of vegetative life; the arbustive hills, gay lawns, and green meadows, which on every side invest the villa of Augusta, had already received my frequent visits; and although here much delighted with the new beauties in the vegetable kingdom, and many eminent ones have their sequestered residence near this place, yet, as I was never long satisfied with present possession, however endowed with every possible charm to attract the sight, or intrinsic value to engage and fix the esteem, I was restless to be searching for more, my curiosity being insatiable.

THUS it is with regard to our affections and attachments, in the more important and interesting concerns of human life.

UPON the rich rocky hills at the cataracts of Augusta, I first observed the perfumed Rhododendron ferruginium, white robed Philadelphus inodorus, and cerulean Malva; but nothing in vegetable nature was more pleasing than the odoriferous Pancratium fluitans, which almost alone possesses the little rocky islets which just appear above the water.

THE preparatory business of the surveyors being now accomplished, Mr. J. M'Intosh, yet anxious for travelling, and desirous to accompany me on this tour, we joined the caravan, consisting of surveyors, astronomers, artisans, chain-carriers, markers, guides and hunters, besides a very respectable number of gentlemen, who joined us, in order to speculate in the lands, together with ten or twelve Indians, altogether to the number of eighty or ninety men, all or most of us well mounted on horseback, besides twenty or thirty pack-horses, loaded with provisions, tents, and camp equipage.

Travels Through North and South Carolina

THE summer season now rapidly advancing, the air at mid–day, about this region, is insufferably hot and sultry. We sat off from Augusta, early in the morning, for the Great Buffalo Lick, on the Great Ridge, which separates the waters of the Savanna and Alatamaha, about eighty miles distant from Augusta. At this Lick the surveyors were to separate themselves, and form three companies, to proceed on different routes. On the evening of the second day's journey, we arrived at a small village on Little river, a branch of Savanna: this village, called Wrightsborough, was founded by Jos. Mattock, Esq; of the sect called Quakers; this public spirited man having obtained, for himself and his followers, a district, comprehending upwards of forty thousand acres of land, gave the new town this name, in honour of Sir James Wright, then Governor of Georgia, who greatly promoted the establishment of the settlement. Mr. Mattock, who is now about seventy years of age, healthy and active, and presides as chief magistrate of the settlement, received us with great hospitality. The distance from Augusta to this place is about thirty miles; the face of the country is chiefly a plain of high forests savannas, and cane swamps, until we approach Little River, when the landscape varies, presenting to view high hills and rich vales. The soil is a deep, rich, dark mould, on a deep stratum of redish brown tenacious clay, and that on a foundation of rocks, which often break through both strata, lifting their backs above the surface. The forest trees are chiefly of the deciduous order, as, Quercus tinctoria, Q. lasciniata, Q. alba, Q. rubra, Q. prinus, with many other species; Celtis, Fagus sylvatica, and, on the rocky hills, Fagus castania, Fag. pumila, Quercus castania; in the rich vales, Juglans nigra, Jug. cinerea, Gleditsia triacanthos, Magnolia acuminata, Liriodendron, Platanus, Fraxinus excelsior, Cercea, Juglans exaltata, Carpinus, Morus rubra, Calycanthus, Halesia, Aesculus pavia, Aesc. arborea.

LEAVING the pleasant town of Wrightsborough, we continued eight or nine miles through a fertile plain and high forest, to the north branch of Little River, being the largest of the two, crossing which, we entered an extensive fertile plain, bordering on the river, and shaded by trees of vast growth, which at once spoke its fertility. Continuing some time through these shade groves, the scene opens, and discloses to view the most magnificent forest I had ever seen. We rise gradually a sloping bank of twenty or thirty feet elevation, and immediately entered this sublime forest; the ground is perfectly a level green plain, thinly planted by nature with the most stately forest trees, such as the gigantic Black*

* Gigantic Black Oak. Querc. tinctoria; the bark of this species of oak is found to afford a valuable yellow dye. This tree is known by the name of Black Oak in Pennsylvania, New–Jersey, New–York, and New England.

Oak (Q. tinctoria) Liriodendron, Juglans nigra, Platanus, Juglans exaltata, Fagus sylvatica, Ulmus sylvatica, Liquid–amber styraciflua, whose mighty trunks, seemingly of an equal height, appeared like superb columns. To keep within the bounds of truth and reality, in describing the magnitude and grandeur of these trees, would, I fear, fail of credibility; yet, I think I can assert, that many of the black oaks measured eight, nine, ten, and eleven feet diameter five feet above the ground, as we measured several that were above thirty feet girt, and from hence they ascend perfectly strait, with a gradual taper, forty or fifty feet to the limbs; but, below five or six feet, these trunks would measure a third more in circumference, on account of the projecting jambs, or supports, which are more or less, according to the number of horizontal roots that they arise from: the Tulip tree, Liquid–amber, and Beech, were equally stately.

NOT far distant from the terrace, or eminence, overlooking the low grounds of the river, many very magnificent monuments of the power and industry of the ancient inhabitants of these lands are visible. I observed a stupendous conical pyramid, or artificial mount of earth, vast tetragon terraces, and a large sunken area, of a cubical form, encompassed with banks of earth; and certain traces of a large Indian town, the work of a powerful nation, whose period of grandeur perhaps long preceded the discovery of this continent.

AFTER about seven miles progress through this forest of gigantic Black Oaks, we enter on territories which exhibit more varied scenes: the land rises almost insensibly by gentle ascents, exhibiting desart plains, high forests, gravelly and stony ridges, ever in fight of rapid rivulets; the soil, as already described. We then passed over large rich savannas, or natural meadows, wide–spreading cane swamps, and frequently old Indian settlements, now deserted and overgrown with forest. These are always on or near the banks of rivers, or great swamps, the artificial mounts and terraces elevating them above the surrounding groves. I observed, in the antient cultivated fields, 1. Diospyros, 2. Gleditsia triacanthos, 3. Prunus Chicasaw,*

* The Chicasaw plumb I think must be excepted, for though certainly a native of America, yet I never saw it wild in the forests, but always in old deserted Indian

plantations: I suppose it to have been brought from the S. W. beyond the Missisippi, by the Chicasaws.

4. Callicarpa, 5. Morus rubra, 6. Juglans exaltata, 7. Juglans nigra, which inform us, that these trees were cultivated by the ancients, on account of their fruit, as being wholesome and nourishing food. Tho' these are natives of the forest, yet they thrive better, and are more fruitful, in cultivated plantations, and the fruit is in great estimation with the present generation of Indians, particularly Juglans exaltata* commonly called shell–barked hiccory; the Creeks store up the latter in their towns. I have seen above an hundred bushels of these nuts belonging to one family. They pound them to pieces, and then cast them into boiling water, which, after passing through fine strainers, preserves the most oily part of the liquid: this they call by a name which signifies Hiccory milk; it is as sweet and rich as fresh cream, and is an ingredient in most of their cookery, especially homony and corn cakes.

AFTER four days moderate and pleasant travelling, we arrived in the evening at the Buffalo Lick. This extraordinary place occupies several acres of ground, at the foot of the S. E. promontory of the Great Ridge, which, as before observed, divides the rivers Savanna and Alatamaha. A large cane swamp and meadows, forming an immense plain, lies S. E. from it; in this swamp I believe the head branches of the great Ogeeche river take their rise. The place called the Lick contains three or four acres, is nearly level, and lies between the head of the cane swamp and the ascent of the Ridge. The earth, from the superficies to an unknown depth, is an almost white or cinerious coloured tenacious fattish clay, which all kinds of cattle lick into great caves, pursuing the delicious vein. It is the common opinion of the inhabitants, that this clay is impregnated with saline vapours, arising from fossile salts deep in the earth; but I could discover nothing saline in its taste, but I imagined an insipid sweetness. Horned cattle, horses, and deer, are immoderately fond of it, insomuch, that their excrement, which almost totally covers the earth to some distance round this place, appears to be perfect clay; which, when dried by the sun and air, is almost as hard as brick.

WE were detained at this place one day, in adjusting and planning the several branches of the survey. A circumstance occurred during this time, which was a remarkable instance of Indian sagacity, and had nearly disconcerted all our plans, and put an end to the business. The surveyor having fixed his compass on the staff, and about to ascertain the course from our place of departure, which was to strike Savanna river at the confluence of a certain river, about seventy miles distance from us; just as he had determined upon the point, the Indian Chief came up, and observing the course he had fixed upon, spoke, and said it was not right; but that the course to the place was so and so, holding up his hand, and pointing. The surveyor replied, that he himself was certainly right, adding, that that little instrument (pointing to the compass) told him so, which, he said, could not err. The Indian answered, he knew better, and that the little wicked instrument was a liar; and he would not acquiesce in its decisions, since it would wrong the Indians out of their land. This mistake (the surveyor proving to be in the wrong) displeased the Indians; the dispute arose to that height, that the Chief and his party had determined to break up the business, and return the shortest way home, and forbad the surveyors to proceed any farther: however, after some delay, the complaisance and prudent conduct of the Colonel made them change their resolution; the Chief became reconciled, upon condition that the compass should be discarded, and rendered incapable of serving on this business; that the Chief himself should lead the survey; and, moreover, receive an order for a very considerable quantity of goods.

MATTERS being now amicably settled, under this new regulation, the Colonel having detached two companies on separate routes, Mr. M'Intosh and myself attaching ourselves to the Colonel's party, whose excursion was likely to be the most extensive and varied, we sat off from the Buffalo Lick, and the Indian Chief, heading the party, conducted us on a straight line, as appeared by collateral observation, to the desired place. We pursued nearly a north course up the Great Ridge, until we came near the branches of Broad River, when we turned off to the right hand, and encamped on a considerable branch of it. At this place we continued almost a whole day, constituting surveyors and astronomers, who were to take the course, distance, and observations on Broad River, and from thence down to its confluence with the Savanna.

THE Great Ridge consists of a continued high forest; the soil fertile, and broken into moderately elevated hills, by the many rivulets which have their sources in it. The heights and precipices abound in rock and stone. The forest trees and other vegetable productions are the same as already mentioned about Little River: I observed Halesia, Styrax, Aesculus pavia, Aesc. sylvatica, Robinia hispida, Magnolia acuminata, Mag. tripetala, and some very curious new shrubs and plants, particularly the Physic−nut, or Indian Olive. The stems arise many from a root, two or three feet high; the leaves sit opposite, on very short petioles; they are broad, lanciolate, entire, and undulated, having smooth surfaces of a deep green colour. From the bosom of each leaf is produced a single oval drupe, standing erect, on long slender stems; it has a large kernel, and thin pulp. The fruit is yellow when ripe; and about the size of an olive. The Indians, when they go in pursuit of deer, carry this fruit with them, supposing that it has the power of charming or drawing that creature to them; from whence, with the traders, it has obtained the name of the Physic—nut, which means, with them, charming, conjuring, or fascinating. Malva scandens, Felix scandens, perhaps species of Trichomanes; the leaves are palmated, or radiated; it climbs and roves about, on shrubs, in moist ground. A very singular and elegant plant, of an unknown family, called Indian Lettuce, made its first appearance in these rich vales; it is a biennial; the primary or radical leaves are somewhat spatuled, or broad, lanciolate, and obtuse pointed, of a pale yellowish green, smooth surface, and of a delicate frame, or texture; these leaves, spread equally on every side, almost reclining on the ground; from their centre arises a strait upright stem, five, six or seven feet high, smooth and polished; the ground of a dark purple colour, which is elegantly powdered with greenish yellow specks; this stem, three fourths of its length, is embellished with narrow leaves, nearly of the same form of the radical ones, placed at regular distances, in verticilate order. The superior one fourth division of this stem is formed into a pyramidal spike of flowers, rather diffuse; these flowers are of the hexandria, large, and expanded; of a dark purple colour, delicately powdered with green, yellow, and red, and divided into six parts, or petals; these are succeeded by triquetrous dry pericarpi, when ripe.

THIS great ridge is a vast extended projection of the Cherokee or Alegany mountains, gradually encreasing in height and extent, from its extremity at the Lick, to its union with the high ridge of mountains anciently called the Apalachian mountains; it every where approaches much nearer the waters of the Alatamaha than those of the Savanna: at one particular place, where we encamped, on the Great Ridge, during our repose there, part of a day. Our hunters going out, and, understanding that their route was to the low lands on the Ocone, I accompanied them: we had not rode above three miles before we came to the banks of that beautiful river. The cane swamps, of immense extent, and the oak forests, on the level lands, are incredibly fertile; which appears from the tall reeds of the one, and the heavy timber of the other.

BEFORE we left the waters of Broad River, having encamped in the evening, on one of its considerable branches, and left my companions, to retire, as usual, on botanical researches, on ascending a steep rocky hill, I accidentally discovered a new species of Caryophyllata (Geum odoratissimum) on reaching to a shrub, my foot slipped, and, in recovering myself, I tore up some of the plants, whose roots filled the air with animating scents of cloves and spicy perfumes.

ON my return towards camp, I met my philosophic companion, Mr. M'Intosh, who was seated on the bank of a rivulet, and whom I found highly entertained by a very novel and curious natural exhibition, in which I participated with high relish. The waters at this place were still and shoal, and flowed over a bed of gravel just beneath a rocky rapid: in this eddy shoal were a number of little gravelly pyramidal hills, whose summits rose almost to the surface of the water, very artfully constructed by a species of small cray–fish (Cancer macrourus) which inhabited them: here seemed to be their citadel, or place of retreat for their young, against the attacks and ravages of their enemy, the gold–fish: these, in numerous bands, continually infested them, except at short intervals, when small detachments of veteran cray–fish sallied out upon them, from their cells within the gravelly pyramids, at which time a brilliant fight presented: the little gold–fish instantly fled from every side, darting through the transparent waters like streams of lightning; some even sprang above the surface, into the air, but all quickly returned to the charge, surrounding the pyramids as before, on the retreat of the cray–fish; in this manner the war seemed to be continual.

THE gold–fish is about the size of the anchovy, nearly four inches long, of a neat slender form; the head is covered with a salade of an ultramarine blue, the back of a redish brown, the sides and belly of a flame, or of the colour of a fine red lead; a narrow dusky line runs along each side, from the gills to the tail; the eyes are large, with the iris like burnished gold. This branch of Broad River is about twelve yards wide, and has two, three, and four feet depth of water, and winds through a fertile vale, almost overshadowed on one side by a ridge of high hills, well timbered with Oak, Hiccory, Liriodendron, Magnolia acuminata, Pavia sylvatica, and on their rocky summits, Fagus castania, Rhododendron ferruginium, Kalmia latifolia, Cornus Florida, &c.

ONE of our Indian young men, this evening, caught a very large salmon trout, weighing about fifteen pounds, which he presented to the Col. who ordered it to be served up for supper. The Indian struck this fish, with a reed harpoon, pointed very sharp, barbed, and hardened by the fire. The fish lay close under the steep bank, which the Indian discovered and struck with his reed; instantly the fish darted off with it, whilst the Indian pursued, without extracting the harpoon, and with repeated thrusts drowned it, and then dragged it to shore.

41

Travels Through North and South Carolina

AFTER leaving Broad River, the land rises very sensibly, and the country being mountainous, our progress became daily more difficult and slow; yet the varied scenes of pyramidal hills, high forests, rich vales, serpentine rivers, and cataracts, fully compensated for our difficulties and delays. I observed the great Aconitum napellus, Delphinium perigrinum, the carminative Angelica lucida,*

* Called Nondo in Virginia: by the Creek and Cherokee traders, White Root.

and cerulean Malva.

WE at length happily accomplished our line, arriving at the little river, where our hunters bringing in plenty of venison and turkeys, we had a plentiful feast at supper. Next morning we marked the corner tree, at the confluence of Little river and the Savanna; and, soon after, the Indians amicably took leave of us, returning home to their towns.

THE rocks and fossils, which constitute the hills of this middle region, are of various species, as, Quartsum, Ferrum, Cos, Silex, Glarea, Arena, Ochra, Stalectites, Saxum, Mica, &c. I saw no signs of Marble, Plaster, or Lime–stone; yet there is, near Augusta, in the forests, great piles of a porous friable white rock, in large and nearly horizontal masses, which seems to be an heterogeneous concrete, consisting of pulverized sea shells, with a small proportion of sand; it is soft, and easily wrought into any form, yet of sufficient consistence for constructing any building.

As for the animal productions, they are the same which originally inhabited this part of North America, except such as have been affrighted away since the invasion of the Europeans. The buffalo (Urus) once so very numerous, is not at this day to be seen in this part of the country; a few elk, and those only in the Apalachian mountains. The dreaded and formidable rattle–snake is yet too common, and a variety of other serpents abound, particularly that admirable creature the glass–snake: I saw a very large and beautiful one, a little distance from our camp. The allegator, a species of crocodile, abounds in the rivers and swamps, near the sea coast, but is not to be seen above Augusta. Bears, tygers,*

* This creature is called, in Pennsylvania and the northern States, Panther; but in Carolina and the southern States, is called Tyger; they are very strong, much larger than any dog,

of a yellowish brown, or clay colour, having a very long tail; they are a mischievous animal, and prey on calves, young colts, &c.

wolves, and wild cats (Felis cauda truncata) are numerous enough; and there is a very great variety of Papilio and Phalina, many of which are admirably beautiful, as well as other insects of infinite variety.

THE surveyors having completed their observations, we sat off next day on our return to Augufta, taking our route generally through the low lands on the banks of the Savanna. We crossed Broad River, at a newly settled plantation, near its confluence with the Savanna. On my arrival at Augusta, finding myself a little fatigued, I staid there a day or two, and then sat off again for Savanna, the capital, where we arrived in good health.

HAVING, in this journey, met with extraordinary success, not only in the enjoyment of an uninterrupted state of good health, and escaping ill accidents, incident to such excursions, through uninhabited wildernesses, and an Indian frontier, but also in making a very extensive collection of new discoveries of natural production. On the recollection of so many and great favours and blessings, I now, with a high sense of gratitude, presume to offer up my sincere thanks to the Almighty, the Creator and Preserver.

CHAP. V.

HAVING completed my Hortus Siccus, and made up my collections of seeds and growing roots, the fruits of my late western tour, and sent them to Charleston, to be forwarded to Europe, I spent the remaining part of this season in botanical excursions to the low countries, between Carolina and East Florida, and collected seeds, roots, and specimens, making drawings of such curious subjects as could not be preserved in their native state of excellence.

DURING this recess from the high road of my travels, having obtained the use of a neat light cypress canoe, at Broughton Island, a plantation, the property of the Hon. Henry Laurens, Esq. where I stored myself with necessaries, for the voyage, and resolved upon a trip up the Alatamaha.

Travels Through North and South Carolina

I ASCENDED this beautiful river, on whose fruitful banks the generous and true sons of liberty securely dwell, fifty miles above the white settlements.

HOW gently flow thy peaceful floods, O Alatamaha! How sublimely rise to view, on thy elevated shores, yon Magnolian groves, from whose tops the surrounding expanse is perfumed, by clouds of incense, blended with the exhaling balm of the Liquid–amber, and odours continually arising from circumambient aromatic groves of Illicium, Myrica, Laurus, and Bignonia.

WHEN wearied, with working my canoe against the impetuous current (which becomes stronger by reason of the mighty floods of the river, with collected force, pressing through the first hilly ascents, where the shores on each side the river present to view rocky cliffs rising above the surface of the water, in nearly flat horizontal masses, washed smooth by the descending floods, and which appear to be a composition, or concrete, of sandy lime–stone) I resigned my bark to the friendly current, reserving to myself the controul of the helm. My progress was rendered delightful by the sylvan elegance of the groves, chearful meadows, and high distant forests, which in grand order presented themselves to view. The winding banks of the river, and the high projecting promontories, unfolded fresh scenes of grandeur and sublimity. The deep forests and distant hills re–echoed the chearing social lowings of domestic herds. The air was filled with the loud and shrill whooping of the wary sharp crane. Behold, on yon decayed, defoliated Cypress tree, the solitary wood–pelican, dejectedly perched upon its utmost elevated spire; he there, like an ancient venerable sage, sets himself up as a mark of derision, for the safety of his kindred tribes. The crying–bird, another faithful guardian, screaming in the gloomy thickets, warns the feathered tribes of approaching peril; and the plumage of the swift sailing squadrons of Spanish curlews (white as the immaculate robe of innocence) gleam in the cerulean skies.

THUS secure and tranquil, and meditating on the marvellous scenes of primitive nature, as yet unmodified by the hand of man, I gently descended the peaceful stream, on whose polished surface were depicted the mutable shadows from its pensile banks; whilst myriads of finny inhabitants sported in its pellucid floods.

THE glorious sovereign of day, cloathed in light refulgent, rolling on his gilded chariot, speeds to revisit the western realms. Grey pensive eve now admonishes us of gloomy night's hasty approach: I am roused by care to seek a place of secure repose, ere darkness comes on.

DRAWING near the high shores, I ascended the steep banks, where stood a venerable oak. An ancient Indian field, verdured o'er with succulent grass, and checquered with coppices of fragrant shrubs, offers to my view the Myrica cerifera, Magnolia glauca, Laurus benzoin, Laur. Borbonia, Rhamnus frangula, Prunus Chicasaw, Prun. Lauro cerasa, and others. It was nearly encircled with an open forest of stately pines (Pinus palustris) through which appears the extensive savanna, the secure range of the swift roebuck. In front of my landing, and due east, I had a fine prospect of the river and low lands on each side, which gradually widened to the sea coast, and gave me an unconfined prospect, whilst the far distant sea coast islands, like a coronet, limited the hoary horizon.

MY barque being securely moored, and having reconnoitered the surrounding groves, and collected fire–wood, I spread my skins and blanket by my chearful fire, under the protecting shade of the hospitable Live–oak, and reclined my head on my hard but healthy couch. I listened, undisturbed, to the divine hymns of the feathered songsters of the groves, whilst the softly whispering breezes faintly died away.

THE sun now below the western horizon, the moon majestically rising in the east; again the tuneful birds become inspired; how melodious is the social mock–bird! the groves resound the unceasing cries of the whip–poor–will; the moon about an hour above the horizon; lo! a dark eclipse*

* The air at this time being serene, and not a cloud to be seen, I saw this annual almost total autumnal eclipse, in its highest degree of perfection.

of her glorious brightness comes slowly on; at length, a silver thread alone encircles her temples: at this boding change, an universal silence prevails.

NATURE now weary, I resigned myself to rest; the night passed over; the cool dews of the morning awake me; my fire burnt low; the blue smoke scarce rises above the moistened embers; all is gloomy: the late starry skies, now overcast by thick clouds, I am warned to rise and be going. The livid purple clouds thicken on the frowning brows of the morning; the tumultuous winds from the east now exert their power. O peaceful Alatamaha! gentle by nature! how thou art ruffled! thy wavy surface disfigures every

45

object, presenting them obscurely to the sight, and they at length totally disappear, whilst the furious winds and sweeping rains bend the lofty groves, and prostrate the quaking grass, driving the affrighted creatures to their dens and caverns.

THE tempest now relaxes, its impetus is spent, and a calm serenity gradually takes place; by noon they break away, the blue sky appears, the fulgid sun–beams spread abroad their animating light, and the steady western wind resumes his peaceful reign. The waters are purified, the waves subside, and the beautiful river regains its native calmness: so it is with the varied and mutable scenes of human events on the stream of life. The higher powers and affections of the soul are so blended and connected with the inferior passions, that the most painful feelings are excited in the mind when the latter are crossed: thus in the moral system, which we have planned for our conduct, as a ladder whereby to mount to the summit of terrestrial glory and happiness, and from whence we perhaps meditated our flight to heaven itself, at the very moment when we vainly imagine ourselves to have attained its point, some unforeseen accident intervenes, and surprises us; the chain is violently shaken, we quit our hold and fall: the well contrived system at once becomes a chaos; every idea of happiness recedes; the splendour of glory darkens, and at length totally disappears; every pleasing object is defaced, all is deranged, and the flattering scene passes quite away, a gloomy cloud pervades the understanding, and when we see our progress retarded, and our best intentions frustrated, we are apt to deviate from the admonitions and convictions of virtue, to shut our eyes upon our guide and protector, doubt of his power, and despair of his assistance. But let us wait and rely on our God, who in due time will shine forth in brightness, dissipate the envious cloud, and reveal to us how finite and circumscribed is human power, when assuming to itself independent wisdom.

BUT, before I leave the river Alatamaha, we will proceed to give a further and more particular account of it. It has its source in the Cherokee mountains, near the head of Tugilo, the great west branch of Savanna, and, before it leaves the mountains, is joined and augmented by innumerable rivulets; thence it descends through the hilly country, with all its collateral branches, and winds rapidly amongst the hills two hundred and fifty miles, and then enters the flat plain country, by the name of the Oakmulge; thence meandering an hundred and fifty miles, it is joined on the east side by the Ocone, which likewise heads in the lower ridges of the mountains. After this confluence, having now gained a vast acquisition of waters, it assumes the name of Alatamaha, when it becomes a large majestic river, flowing with gentle windings through a vast plain forest, near an hundred miles, and enters the Atlantic by several mouths. The north channel, or entrance, glides by the heights of Darien, on the east bank, about ten miles above the bar, and, running from thence with several turnings, enters the ocean between Sapello and Wolf islands. The south channel, which is esteemed the largest and deepest, after its separation from the north, descends gently, winding by M`Intosh's and Broughton islands; and lastly, by the west coast of St. Simon's island, enters the ocean, through St. Simon's Sound, between the south end of the island of that name and the north end of Jekyl island. On the west banks of the south channel, ten or twelve miles above its mouth, and nearly apposite Darien, are to be seen, the remains of an ancient fort, or fortification; it is now a regular tetragon terrace, about four feet high, with bastions at each angle; the area may contain about an acre of ground, but the fosse which surrounded it is nearly filled up. There are large Live Oaks, Pines, and other trees, growing upon it, and in the old fields adjoining. It is supposed to have been the work of the French or Spaniards. A large swamp lies betwixt it and the river, and a considerable creek runs close by the works, and enters the river through the swamp, a small distance above Broughton Island. About seventy or eighty miles above the confluence of the Oakmulge and Ocone, the trading path, from Augusta to the Creek nation, crosses these fine rivers, which are there forty miles apart. On the east banks of the Oakmulge, this trading road runs nearly two miles through ancient Indian fields, which are called the Oakmulge fields: they are the rich low lands of the river. On the heights of these low grounds are yet visible monuments, or traces, of an ancient town, such as artificial mounts or terraces, squares and banks, encircling considerable areas. Their old fields and planting land extend up and down the river, fifteen or twenty miles from this site.

AND, if we are to give credit to the account the Creeks give of themselves, this place is remarkable for being the first town or settlement, when they sat down (as they term it) or established themselves, after their emigration from the west, beyond the Missisippi, their original native country. On this long journey they suffered great and innumerable difficulties, encountering and vanquishing numerous and valiant tribes of Indians, who opposed and retarded their march. Having crossed the river, still pushing eastward, they were obliged to make a stand, and fortify themselves in this place, as their only remaining hope, being to the last degree persecuted and weakened by their surrounding foes. Having formed for themselves this retreat, and driven off the inhabitants by degrees, they recovered their spirits, and again faced their enemies, when they came off victorious in a memorable and decisive battle. They afterwards gradually subdued their surrounding enemies, strengthening themselves by taking into confederacy the vanquished tribes.

AND they say, also, that about this period the English were establishing the colony of Carolina, and the Creeks, understanding that they were a powerful, warlike people, sent deputies to Charleston, their capital, offering them their friendship and alliance, which was accepted, and, in consequence thereof, a treaty took place between them, which has remained inviolable to this day: they never ceased war against the numerous and potent bands of Indians, who then surrounded and cramped the English plantations, as the Savannas, Ogeeches, Wapoos, Santees, Yamasees, Utinas, Icosans, Paticas, and others, until they had extirpated them. The Yamasees and their adherents sheltering themselves under the power and protection of the Spaniards of East Florida, they pursued them to the very gates of St. Augustine, and the Spaniards refusing to deliver them up, these faithful intrepid allies had the courage to declare war against them, and incessantly persecuted them, until they entirely broke up and ruined their settlements, driving them before them, till at length they were obliged to retire within the walls of St. Augustine and a few inferior fortified posts on the sea coast.

AFTER a few days, I returned to Broughton Island. The Cherokees and their confederates being yet discontented, and on bad terms with the white people, it was unsafe to pursue my travels into the north western regions of Carolina; and recollecting many subjects of natural history, which I had observed in the south of the isthmus of Florida, when on a journey some years ago with my father, John Bartram, that were interesting, and not taken notice of by any traveller; and as it was then in the autumn and winter, I had reason to think that very many curious subjects had escaped our researches: I now formed the resolution of travelling into East Florida; accordingly, I immediately wrote to Doctor Fothergill, in order that he might know where to direct to me.

PART II.

CHAP. I.

WE are, all of us, subject to crosses and disappointments, but more especially the traveller; and when they surprise us, we frequently become restless and impatient under them: but let us rely on Providence, and by studying and contemplating the works and power of the Creator, learn wisdom and understanding in the economy of nature, and be seriously attentive to the divine monitor within. Let us be obedient to the ruling powers in such things as regard human affairs, our duties to each other, and all creatures and concerns that are submitted to our care and controul.

IN the month of March, 1774, I sat off from Savanna, for Florida, proceeding by land to the Alatamaha, where I diverted my time agreeably in short excursions, picking up curiosities, until the arrival of a small vessel at Frederica, from Savanna, which was destined to an Indian trading house high up St. John's, in East Florida. Upon information of this vessel's arrival, I immediately took boat and descended the Alatamaha, calling by the way of Broughton Island, where I was kindly received by Mr. James Bailey, Mr. Laurens's agent. Leaving Broughton Island in the evening, I continued descending the south channel nine or ten miles, when, after crossing the sound, I arrived at Frederica, on the island of St. Simon, where I was well received and entertained by James Spalding, Esq; This gentleman carrying on a very considerable trade, and having extensive connections with the Indian tribes of East Florida, furnished me with letters to his agents residing at his trading houses, ordering them to furnish me with horses, guides, and every other convenient assistance.

BEFORE the vessel was ready to sail again for St. John's, I had time to explore the island. In the cool of the morning early, I rode out of the town, directing my course to the south end of the island. After penetrating a thick grove of oaks, which almost surrounded the town on the land side, suddenly a very extensive and beautiful green savanna opened to view, in length nearly two miles, and in breadth near a mile, well stocked with horned cattle, horses, sheep, and deer. Following an old highway, now out of repair, across the Savanna, I ascended the sloping green bank, and entered a noble forest of lofty pines, and then a venerable grove of Live Oaks, under whose shady spreading boughs opened a spacious avenue, leading to the former seat of General Oglethorp, but now the property of Capt. Raimond Demere. After leaving this town, I was led into a high pine forest; the trees were tall, and generally of the species called Broom-pine (P. palustris Linn.) the surface of the ground covered with grass, herbage, and some shrubbery: I continued through this forest nearly in a direct line towards the sea coast, five or six miles, when the land became uneven, with ridges of sand-hills, mixed with sea shells, and covered by almost impenetrable thickets, consisting of Live Oaks, Sweet-bay (L. Borbonia) Myrica, Ilex aquifolium, Rhamnus frangula, Cassine, Sideroxylon, Ptelea, Halesia, Callicarpa, Carpinus, entangled with Smilax, pseudo China, and other species, Bignonia sempervirens, B. crucigera, Rhamnus volubllis, &c. This dark labyrinth is succeeded by a great extent of salt plains, beyond which the boundless ocean is seen. Betwixt the dark forest and the salt plains, I crossed a rivulet of fresh water, where I sat down a while to

49

rest myself, under the shadow of sweet Bays and Oaks; the lively breezes were perfumed by the fragrant breath of the superb Crinum, called, by the inhabitants, White Lilly. This admirable beauty of the sea–coast dwells in the humid shady groves, where the soil is made fertile and mellow by the admixture of sea shells. The delicate structure of its spadix, its green broad leaves, and the texture and whiteness of its flowers, at once charmed me. The Euphorbia picta, Salvia coccinea, and Ipomea erecta, were also seated in front of my resting place, as well as the Lycium salsum (perhaps L. Afrum Linn.) a very beautiful ever green shrub, its cerulean flowers, and coral red berries, always on its branches, forming not the least of its beauties.

Time now admonishing me to rise and be going, I, with reluctance, broke away from this assembly of maritime beauties.

CONTINUING on, southward, the salt plains on my left hand insensibly became narrower, and I at length reached the strand, which was level, firm, and paved with shells, and afforded me a grand view of the boundless ocean.

O thou Creator supreme, almighty! how infinite and incomprehensible thy works! most perfect, and every way astonishing!

I CONTINUED nearly a mile along this firm sandy beach, the waves of the sea sometimes washing my horse's feet. I observed a great variety of shell–fish, as Echinitis, Corallinus, Patella, Medusa, Buccina, Concha venerea, Auris marina, Cancer, Squilla, &c. some alive, and others dead, having been cast upon the beach by the seas, in times of tempest, where they became a prey to sea fowl, and other maritime animals, or perished by the heat of the sun and burning sands. At length I doubled the utmost south point of St. Simon's, which forms the north cape of the south channel of the great river Alatamaha. The sound, just within this cape, forms an excellent bay, or cove, on the south end of the island, on the opposite side of which I beheld a house and farm, where I soon arrived. This delightful habitation was situated in the midst of a spacious grove of Live Oaks and Palms, near the strand of the bay, commanding a view of the inlet. A cool area surrounded the low but convenient buildings, from whence, through the groves, was a spacious avenue into the island, terminated by a large savanna; each side of the avenue was lined with bee–hives, to the number of fifty or sixty; they seemed to be well peopled, and exhibited a lively image of a colony that has attained to a state of power and affluence, by the practice of virtue and industry.

Travels Through North and South Carolina

WHEN I approached the house, the good man, who was reclining on a bear–skin, spread under the shade of a Live Oak, smoking his pipe, rose and saluted me: "Welcome, stranger, I am indulging the rational dictates of nature, taking a little rest, having just come in from the chace and fishing." After some conversation and rest, his servant brought a bowl of honey and water, a very refreshing and agreeable liquor, of which I drank. On rising to take my departure, he objected, and requested me to stay and dine with him; and on my pleading, for excuse, the necessity of my being at Frederica, "Yet, I pray you, stay a little, I will soon have some refreshment for you." Presently was laid before us a plentiful repast of venison, &c. our drink being honey and water, strengthened by the addition of brandy. Our rural table was spread under the shadow of Oaks, Palms, and Sweet Bays, fanned by the lively salubrious breezes wafted from the spicy groves. Our music was the responsive love–lays of the painted nonpareil, and the alert and gay mockbird; whilst the brilliant humming–bird darted through the flowery groves, suspended in air, and drank nectar from the flowers of the yellow Jasmine, Lonicera, Andromeda, and sweet Azalea.

BUT yet, how awfully great and sublime is the majestic scene east–ward! the solemn sound of the beating surf strikes our ears; the dashing of yon liquid mountains, like mighty giants, in vain assail the skies; they are beaten back, and fall prostrate upon the shores of the trembling island.

TAKING leave of my sylvan friend, I sat off on my return to the town, where I arrived before night, having observed, on the way, many curious vegetable productions, particularly Corypha Palma (or great Cabbage Palm) Corypha pumila, Corypha repens, frondibus expansis, flabelliformibus, plicatis, stipit. spinosis (Dwarf Saw Palmetro) Corypha) obliqua, caudex arboreus ascendens, frondibus expansis, flabelliformibus, plicatis, stipit. serratis, Cyrilla, Tillandsia monostachya, Till. lingulata, or Wild Pine; both these curious vegetables are parasites, living on the substance of others, particularly on the limbs of the Live Oak; the latter species is a very large flourishing plant, greatly resembling, at some distance, a well grown plant of the Bromelia Ananas: the large deep green leaves are placed in a imbricated order, and ascendant; but their extremities are reflex, their bases gibbous and hollowed, like a ladle, and capable of containing near a pint of water: heavy tempests of wind and rain tear these plants from the trees; yet they live and flourish on the earth, under the shadow of these great Live Oaks. A very large part of this island had formerly been cleared and planted by the English, as appeared evidently to me, by vestiges of plantations, ruins of costly buildings, highways, &c. but it is now overgrown with forests. Frederica was the first town built by the English in Georgia, and was founded by General Oglethorp, who began and established the colony. The fortress was regular and beautiful, constructed chiefly with brick, and was the largest, most regular, and perhaps most costly, of any in North America, of British construction: it is now in ruins, yet occupied by a small garrison; the ruins also of the town only remain; peach trees, figs, pomegranates, and other shrubs, grow out of the ruinous walls of former spacious and expensive buildings, not only in the town, but at a distance in various parts of the island; yet there are a few neat houses in good repair, and inhabited: it seems now recovering again, owing to the public and liberal spirit and exertions of J. Spalding, Esq; who is president of the island, and engaged in very extensive mercantile concerns.

CHAP. II.

THE vessel, in which I was to embark for East Florida, being now ready to pursue her voyage, we sat sail with a fair wind and tide. Our course was south, through the sound, betwixt a chain of sea–coast–islands, and the main. In the evening we came to, at the south end of St. Simons, having been hindred by the flood tide making against us. The Captain and myself, with one of our crew, went on shore, with a view of getting some venison and sea fowl. We had not the good fortune to see any deer, yet we were not altogether unsuccessful, having taken three young racoons (Ursus cauda elongata) which are excellent meat: we had them for supper, served up in a pillo. Next morning early, we again got under way, running by Jekyl and Cumberland Islands, large, beautiful and fertile, yet thinly inhabited, and consequently excellent haunts for deer, bears and other game.

As we ran by Cumberland Isle, keeping the channel through the sound, we saw a sail a head coming up towards us. Our Captain knew it to be the trading schooner from the stores on St. John's, and immediately predicted bad news, as she was not to sail, until our arrival there. As she approached us, his apprehensions were more and more confirmed, from the appearance of a number of passengers on deck. We laid to, until she came up, when we hailed her, "What news?" "Bad; the Indians have plundered the upper store, and the traders have escaped, only with their lives." Upon this both vessels came to anchor very near each other, when, learning the particulars, it appeared, that a large party of Indians, had surprised and plundered two trading houses, in the istmus, beyond the river

Travels Through North and South Carolina

St. Johns, and a third being timely apprised of their hostile intentions, by a faithful runner, had time to carry off part of the effects, which they secreted in a swamp at some distance from it, covering them with skins. The upper store had saved their goods in like manner, and the lower store, to which we were bound, had removed the chief of theirs, and deposited them on a small island, in the river, about five miles below the store. With these effects was my chest, which I had forwarded in this vessel, from Savanna, not being at that time determined, whether to make this journey by land, or water. The Captain of our vessel, resolved to put about and return to Frederica, for fresh instructions how to proceed; but for my part, I was determined to proceed for the island up St. John's, where my chest was lodged, there being some valuable books and papers in it, which I could not do well without. I accordingly desired our Captain to put me on shore, on Little St. Simon's, which was not far distant, intending to walk a few miles to a fort, at the south end of that island, where some fishermen resided, who, as I expected, would set me over on Amelia Island, where was a large plantation, the property of Lord Egmont, a British nobleman, whose agent, while I was at Frederica, gave me an invitation to call on him, as I passed toward East Florida; and here I had expectations of getting a boat to carry me to St. John's. Agreeably to my desire, the Captain put me on shore, with a young man, a passenger, for East Florida, who promised to continue with me, and share my adventures. We landed safely, the Captain wishing us a prosperous journey, returned on board his vessel, and we proceeded for the fort, encountering some harsh treatment from thorny thickets, and prickly vines. However we reached the fort in the evening. The commander was out in the forest, hunting. My companion being tired, or indolent, betook himself to rest, while I made a tour round the south point of the island, walking the shelly paved sea beach, and picking up novelties. I had not gone above a mile, before I came up to a roebuck, lying slain on the sands, and hearing the report of a gun, not far off, and supposing it to be from the Captain of the fort, whom I expected soon to return to take up his game, I retired to a little distance, mounted the sand hills, and sat down, enjoying a fine prospect of the rolling billows and foaming breakers, beating on the bar, and north promontory of Amelia Isle, opposite to me. The Captain of the fort soon came up, with a slain buck on his shoulders. We hailed each other, and returned together to the fort, where we were well treated, and next morning, at my request, the Captain obligingly sat us over, landing us safely on Amelia. After walking through a spacious forest of Live Oaks and Palms, and crossing a creek, that ran through a narrow salt marsh, I and my fellow traveller arrived safe at the plantation, where the agent, Mr. Egan, received us very politely and hospitably. This gentleman is a very intelligent and able planter, having already greatly improved the estate, particularly in the cultivation of indigo. Great part of this island consists of excellent hommocky land, which is the soil this plant delights in, as well as cotton, corn, batatas, and almost every other esculent vegetable. Mr. Egan politely rode with me, over great part of the island. On Egmont estate, are several very large Indian tumuli, which are called Ogeeche mounts, so named from that nation of Indians, who took shelter here, after being driven from their native settlements on the main near Ogeeche river. Here they were constantly harrassed by the Carolinians and Creeks, and at length slain by their conquerors, and their bones intombed in these heaps of earth and shells. I observed here the ravages of the common grey catterpillar, so destructive to forest and fruit trees, in Pennsylvania, and through the northern states, by stripping them of their leaves, in the spring, while young and tender (Phalena periodica.)

MR. Egan having business of importance to transact in St. Augustine, pressed me to continue with him, a few days, when he would accompany me to that place, and if I chose, I should have a passage, as far as the Cow–ford, on St. Johns, where he would procure me a boat to prosecute my voyage.

IT may be a subject worthy of some inquiry, why those fine islands, on the coast of Georgia, are so thinly inhabited; though perhaps Amelia may in some degree plead an exemption, as it is a very fertile island, on the north border of East Florida, and at the Capes of St. Mary, the finest harbour in this new colony. If I should give my opinion, the following seem to be the most probable reasons: the greatest part of these are as yet the property of a few wealthy planters, who having their residence on the continent, where lands on the large rivers, as Savanna, Ogeeche, Altamaha, St. Ille and others, are of a nature and quality adapted to the growth of rice, which the planters chiefly rely upon, for obtaining ready cash, and purchasing family articles; they settle a few poor families on their insular estates, who rear stocks of horned cattle, horses, swine and poultry, and protect the game for their proprietors. The inhabitants of these islands also lay open to the invasion and ravages of pirates, and in case of a war, to incursions from their enemies armed vessels, in which case they must either remove with their families and effects to the main, or be stripped of all their movables, and their houses laid in ruins.

THE soil of these islands appears to be particularly favourable to the culture of indigo and cotton, and there are on them some few large plantations for the cultivation and manufacture of those valuable articles. The cotton is planted only by the poorer class of people, just enough for their family consumption: they plant two species of it, the annual and West–Indian; the former is low, and planted every year; the balls of this are very large, and the phlox long, strong, and perfectly white; the West–Indian is a tall perennial plant, the stalk somewhat shrubby, several of which rise up from the root for several years successively, the stems of the former year being killed by the winter frosts. The balls of this latter species are not quite so large as those of the herbacious cotton; but the phlox, or wool, is long, extremely fine, silky, and white. A plantation of this kind will last several years, with moderate labour and care, whereas the annual sort is planted every year.

THE coasts, sounds, and inlets, environing these islands, abound with a variety of excellent fish, particularly Rock, Bass, Drum, Mullet, Sheeps–head Whiting, Grooper, Flounder, Sea–Trout, [this last seems to be a species of Cod] Skate, Skip–jack, Stingray, the Shark, and great Black Stingray, are insatiable cannibals, and very troublesome to the fishermen. The bays and lagoons are stored with oysters and varieties of other shell–fish, crabs, shrimp, &c. The clams, in particular, are large, their meat white, tender, and delicate.

THERE is a large space betwixt this chain of seacoast–islands and the main land, perhaps generally near three leagues in breadth; but all this space is not covered with water: I estimate nearly two thirds of it to consist of low salt plains, which produce Barilla, Sedge, Rushes, &c. and which border on the main land, and the western coasts of the islands. The east side of these islands are, for the most part, clean, hard, sandy beaches, exposed to the wash of the ocean. Between these islands are the mouths or entrances of some rivers, which run down from the continent, winding about through these low salt marshes, and delivering their waters into the sounds, which are very extensive capacious harbours, from three to five and six to eight miles over, and communicate with each other by parallel salt rivers, or passes, that flow into the sound: they afford an extensive and secure inland navigation for most craft, such as large schooners, sloops, pettiaugers, boats, and canoes; and this inland communication of waters extends along the sea coast with but few and short interruptions, from the bay of Chesapeak, in Virginia, to the Missisippi, and how much farther I know not, perhaps as far as Vera Cruz. Whether this chain of sea–coast–islands is a step, or advance, which this part of our continent is now making on the Atlantic ocean, we must leave to future ages to determine. But it seems evident, even to demonstration, that those salt marshes adjoining the coast of the main, and the reedy and grassy islands and marshes in the rivers, which are now overflowed at every side, were formerly high swamps of firm land, affording forests of Cypress, Tupilo, Magnolia grandiflora, Oak, Ash, Sweet Bay, and other timber trees, the same as are now growing on the river swamps, whose surface is two feet or more above the spring tides that flow at this day; and it is plainly to be seen, by every planter along the coast of Carolina, Georgia, and Florida, to the Missisippi, when they bank in these grassy tide marshes for cultivation, that they cannot sink their drains above three or four feet below the surface, before they come to strata of Cypress stumps and other trees, as close together as they now grow in the swamps.

CHAP. III.

BEING now in readiness to prosecute our voyage to St. John's, we sat sail in a handsome pleasure, manned with four stout negro slaves, to row in case of necessity. After passing Amelia Narrows, we had a pleasant run, across Fort George's sound, where, observing the pelicans fishing, Mr. Egan shot one of them, which we took into the boat. I was greatly surprised on observing the pouch or sack, which hangs under the bill: it is capable of being expanded to a prodigious size. One of the people on board, said, that he had seen more than half a bushel of bran, crammed into one of their pouches. The body is larger than that of a tame goose, the legs extremely short, the feet webbed, the bill of a great length, bent inwards like a scythe, the wings extend near seven feet from tip to tip, the tail is very short, the head, neck and breast, nearly white, the body of a light bluish grey, except the quill feathers of the wings, which are black. They seem to be of the gull kind, both in form and structure, as well as manner of fishing. The evening following, we landed on the main. It was a promontory of high land, covered with orange–trees, and projecting into the sound, forming a convenient port. We pitched our tent under the shelter of a forest of Live Oaks, Palms and Sweet Bays; and having in the course of the day, procured plenty of sea fowl, such as curlews, willets, snipes, sand birds and others; we had them dressed for supper, and seasoned with excellent oysters, which lay in heaps in the water, close to our landing place. The shrub Capsicum growing here in abundance, afforded us a very good pepper: we drank of a well of fresh water just at hand, amidst a grove of Myrtles (Myrica carefera.) Our repose however was incompleat, from the stings of musquetoes, the roaring of crocadiles, and the continual noise and restlessness of the sea fowl, thousands of them having their roosting–places very near us, particularly loons of various species, herons, pelicans, Spanish curlews, &c. all promiscuously lodging together, and in such incredible numbers, that the trees were entirely covered. They roost in inaccessible islets in the salt marshes, surrounded by lagoons, and shallow water. Just without the trees, betwixt them, the water and marshes, is a barricade of Palmetto royal

56

(Yucca gloriosa) or Adam's needle, which grows so thick together, that a rat, or bird, can scarcely pass thro' them; and the stiff leaves of this Sword plant, standing nearly horizontally, are as impenetrable to man, or any other animal, as if they were a regiment of grenadiers with their bayonets pointed at you. The Palmetto royal is, however, a very singular and beautiful production. It may be termed a tree, from its durability and magnitude, as likewise from the ligneous quality of its stem, or trunk, when old; yet from its form and texture, I should be inclined to rank it amongst the herbaceous plants, for even the glorious Palm, although it rises to the altitude of a tree, and even transcends most of them, yet it bears the characters of the herbaceous ones: and this, like the Palm tree, rises with a strait, erect stem, about ten or twelve feet high, crowned with a beautiful chaplet of sword or dagger–like leaves, of a perfect green colour, each terminated with a stiff, sharp spur, and their edges finely crenated. This thorny crown is crested with a pyramid of silver white flowers, each resembling a tulip or lilly. These flowers are succeeded by a large fruit, nearly of the form and size of a slender cucumber, and when ripe, is of a deep purple colour, the skin smooth and shining, its pulp soft, very juicy, and of an agreeable aromatic flavour but rather bitter to the taste; it is, however, frequently eaten, but if eaten to excess, proves violently purgative. The seeds are numerous, flat and lunated.

THE plant, or tree, when grown old, sometimes divides into two or three stems, which seem of equal height and thickness, and indeed nearly of the same thickness with the main stem; but generally, when they arrive to this age and magnitude, their own weight brings them to the ground, where they soon decay, the heart or pith first, leaving a hollow fibrous reticulated trunk or sleeve, which likewise soon after decays, and in fine, all is again reduced to its original earth, and replaces the vegetative mould. But the deceased are soon replaced by others, as there are younger ones of all ages and stature, ready to succeed their predecessors, and flourish for a time, with the same regal pomp and splendor. These plants are so multitudinous, whereever they get a footing, that the earth is completely occupied with them, and scarcely any other vegetable is to be seen, where they are; yet they are sometimes scattered amongst other trees and vegetables.

IN three days after leaving Amelia, we arrived at the Cow–ford, a public ferry, over St. Johns, about thirty miles above the bar or capes, the river here being above a mile wide.

MR. Egan, after procuring a neat little sail–boat for me, at a large Indigo plantation near the ferry, and for which I paid three guineas, departed for St. Augustine, which is on the sea–coast about forty–five miles over land.

IT was now about the middle of April, vegetation appearing every where in high progress, I was anxious to be advancing southerly; and having at this plantation, stored myself with necessaries for my voyage, I sailed in the morning, with a fair wind. I was now again alone, for the young man my fellow traveller, though stouter and heartier than myself, having repented of his promise to accompany me, to the Indian trading houses, I suppose not relishing the hardship and dangers, which might perhaps befall us, chose rather to stay behind, amongst the settlements. His leaving me, however, I did not greatly regret, as I could not consider it a disappointment much to my disadvantage at the moment. Our views were probably totally opposite; he, a young mechanic on his adventures, seemed to be actuated by no other motives, than either to establish himself, in some well inhabited part of the country, where, by following his occupation, he might be enabled to procure without much toil and danger, the necessaries and conveniencies of life; or by industry and frugality, perhaps establish his fortune. Whilst I, continually impelled by a restless spirit of curiosity, in pursuit of new productions of nature, my chief happiness consisted in tracing and admiring the infinite power, majesty and perfection of the great Almighty Creator, and in the contemplation, that through divine aid and permission, I might be instrumental in discovering, and introducing into my native country, some original productions of nature, which might become useful to society. Each of our pursuits, were perhaps equally laudable; and upon this supposition, I was quite willing to part with him upon amicable terms.

My little vessel being furnished with a good sail, and having fishing tackle, a neat light fusee, powder and ball, I found myself well equipped, for my voyage, about one hundred miles to the trading house.

I crossed the river to a high promontory of wood–land, on the west shore, and being struck with the magnificence of a venerable grove of Live Oak, Palms and Laurel (Magnolia grandiflora) I stepped on shore to take a view of the place. Orange trees were in full bloom, and filled the air with fragrance.

It was now past noon, and this place being about eight miles above the Cow–ford, and the river near three miles in breadth, I wanted to reach a plantation in sight, on the opposite shore, in order to get some repairs, my vessel having sustained some damage from the violence of the wind, in crossing over. I arrived late in the evening, and finding a convenient landing place and harbour, I concluded to remain here till morning, and then coast it, close along shore to the plantation.

IT beginning to thunder, I was sufficiently warned to prepare against a wet night, and observing a very large Oak tree, which had been thrown down, by a hurricane and offered me a convenient shelter, as its enormous limbs bore up the trunk, a sufficient height from the earth, to admit me to sit or lie down under it, I spread my sail, slanting from the trunk of the tree, to the ground, on the windward side; and having collected a quantity of wood, sufficient to keep up a fire, during the night, I struck one up in front, and spreading skins on the ground, and upon these placing a blanket, one half I laid down upon, turning the other over me for a covering.

THE storm came up, with a furious wind and tremendous thunder and lightning, from the opposite N. W. coast, but luckily for me, little rain fell, and I rested very well. But as the wind next morning blew very fresh, right in upon the shore, there was no possibility of moving, with safety, from my present situation. I however arose to reconnoitre the ground, round about my habitation, being roused by the report of a musquet not far off. I had not left fight of my encampment, following a winding path through a grove of Live Oak, Laurel (Magn. grandiflora) and Sapindus, before an Indian stepped out of a thicket and crossed the path just before me, having a large turkey cock, slung across his shoulders, he saw me and stepping up and smiling, spoke to me in English, bidding me good–morning. I saluted him with "Its well brother," led him to my camp, and treated him with a dram. This friendly Indian informed me that he lived at the next plantation, employed as a hunter, I asked him how far it was to the house; he answered about half a mile by land, and invited me to go there, telling me that his master was a very good, kind man, and would be glad to see me. I replied, that I would, if my boat and effects in the mean time could be safe, he said that he would immediately return to the house, and acquaint his master of it, who would send trusty Negroes to bring my vessel round the point, to the landing, I thanked him for his civility, and not willing to be troublesome, I told him I would leave my boat, and follow after him; so taking my fusee on my shoulder, and after dragging my bark as high up on shore as I could, I followed the Indian, and soon reached the house.

THE gentleman received me, in the most polite manner, and after hearing my situation, he requested me to make my abode with him, a few days, to rest and refresh myself. I thanked him and told him I would stay a day. He immediately sent slaves who brought my boat round, and having carpenters at work, on a new building, he sat them about repairing my vessel, which by night was completely refitted.

I SPENT the day in the most agreeable manner, in the society of this man of singular worth, he led me over his extensive improvements, and we returned in company with several of his neighbours. In the afternoon the most sultry time of the day, we retired to the fragrant shades of an Orange grove. The house was situated on an eminence, about one hundred and fifty yards, from the river. On the right hand was the Orangery, consisting of many hundred trees, natives of the place, and left standing, when the ground about it was cleared. These trees where large, flourishing and in perfect bloom, and loaded with their ripe golden fruit. On the other side was a spacious garden, occupying a regular slope of ground, down to the water; and a pleasent lawn lay between. Here were large plantations of the Indigo plant, which appeared in a very thriving condition: it was then about five or six inches high, growing in streight parallel rows, about eighteen inches apart. The Corn (Zea) and Potatoes (Convolv. Batata) were greatly advanced in growth, and promised a plentiful crop. The Indigo made in East Florida is esteemed almost equal to the best Spanish, especially that sort, which they call Flora. Mr. Marshall presented me, with a specimen of his own manufacture, at this plantation: it was very little, if any inferior; to the best Prussian blue.

IN the morning following, intimating my intentions of proceeding on my voyage, Mr. Marshall, again importuned me to stay, but I obtained his consent to depart, on my promising to visit him, at my return to Georgia. After breakfast I therefore took my leave, attended to the shore, by several slaves, loaded with ammunition and provisions, which my friend had provided for me. On my expressing some difficulty in receiving so large a share of his bounty, he civilly replied, that it was too little to mention, and that, if I had continued with him a day or two longer, he should have had time to have served me in a much better manner.

TAKING my leave of Mr. Marshall, I again embarked alone on board my little vessel, and blessed with a favourable steady gale, I set sail. The day was extremely pleasant, the late thunder storm had purified the air, by disuniting and dissipating the noxious vapours. The falling of heavy showers, with thunder and brisk winds, from the cool regions of the N. W. contributes greatly towards restoring the salubrity of the air, and purity of the waters, by precipitating the putrescent scum, that rises from the bottom, and floats upon the surface, near the shores of the rivers, in these southern climates, during the hot seasons. The shores of this great river St. Juan, are very level and shoal, extending in some places, a mile or two, into the river, betwixt the high land, and the clear waters of the river, which is so level, as to be covered not above a foot or two deep, with water, and at a little distance appears as a green meadow having water–grass and other amphibious vegetables, growing in the oozy bottom, and floating upon the water.

HAVING a lively leading breeze, I kept as near the East shore, as possible, often surprised by the plunging of alligators, and greatly delighted with the pleasing prospect of cultivation, and the encrease of human industry, which frequently struck my view from the elevated, distant shores.

AT night I ran in shore, at a convenient harbour, where I was received and welcomed by the gentleman, who was agent for the plantation, and at whose pleasant habitation, near the harbour, I took up my quarters for the night.

THIS very civil man, happened to be a person with whom I had formerly been acquainted in St. Augustine; and as he lived about twenty miles distant from it, I had good reason to expect that he would be a proper person, to obtain intelligence from, concerning the disturbances, which were thought still to subsist, between the Lower Creeks and the white inhabitants of East Florida. Upon enquiry, and conversation with him, I found my conjectures on that head, to have been well founded. My friend informed me, that there had, but a few days since, been a counsel held at St. Augustine, between the governor of East Florida, and the chiefs of the Lower Creeks. They had been delegated by their towns, to make enquiry, concerning the late alarm and depredations, committed by the Indians upon the traders, which the nation being apprised of, recommended these deputies to be chosen and sent, as soon as possible, in order to make reasonable concessions, before the flame, already kindled, should spread into a general war. The parties accordingly met in St. Augustine, and the affair was amicacably adjusted, to the satisfaction of both parties. The chiefs of the delinquent bands, whose young warriors had commited the mischief, promised to indemnify the traders for the loss of their goods, and requested that they might return to their store–house, with goods as usual, and that they should be safe in their persons and property, The traders at this time, were actually preparing to return. It appeared upon a strict investigation of facts, that the affair had taken its rise from the licentious conduct of a few vagrant young hunters of the Siminole nation, who, imagining themselves to have been ill treated, in their dealings, with the traders (which by the bye was likely enough to be true) took this violent method of doing themselves justified. The culprits however endeavoured to exculpate themselves, by asserting, that they had no design or intention of robbing the traders of their effects, but meant it only as a threat, and that the traders, from a conciousness of their dishonesty, had been terrified and fled, leaving their sores, which they took possession of, to prevent their being totally lost. This troublesome affair being adjusted, was very agreeable news to me, as I could now, without apprehensions, ascend this grand river, and visit its delightful shores, where, and when I pleased.

BIDDING adieu to my obliging friend, I spread my sail to the favourable breeze, and by noon, came to a–breast of fort Picolata, where, being desirous of gaining yet farther intelligence, I landed, but to my disappointment, found the fort dismantled and deserted. This fortress is very ancient, and was built by the Spaniards. It is a square tower, thirty feet high, invested with a high wall, without bastions, about breast high, pierced with loop holes and surrounded with a deep ditch. The upper story is open on each side, with battlements, supporting a cupola or roof: these battlements were formerly mounted with eight four pounders, two on each side.

THE works are constructed with hewn stone, cemented with lime. The stone was cut out of quarries, on St. Anastatius Island, opposite St. Augustine: it is of a pale redish brick colour, and a testacious composition, consisting of small fragments of sea–shells and fine sand. It is well adapted to the constructing of fortifications. It lies in horizontal masses in the quarry, and constitutes the foundation of that island. The castle at St. Augustine, and most of the buildings of the town, are of this stone.

LEAVING Picolata, I continued to ascend the river. I observed this day, during my progress up the river, incredible numbers of small flying insects, of the genus, termed by naturalists, Ephemera, continually emerging from the shallow water, near shore, some of them immediately taking their flight to the land, whilst myriads, crept up the grass and herbage, where remaining, for a short time, as they acquired sufficient strength, they took their flight also, following their kindred, to the main land. This resurrection from the deep, if I may so express it, commences early in the morning, and ceases after the sun is up. At evening they are seen in clouds of innumerable millions, swarming and wantoning in the still air, gradually drawing near the river, descend upon its surface, and there quickly end their day, after committing their eggs to the deep; which being for a little while tossed about, enveloped in a viscid scum, are hatched, and the little Larva descend into their secure and dark habitation, in the oozy bed beneath, where they remain, gradually increasing in size, until the returning spring; they then change to a Nymph, when the genial heat brings them, as it were, into existence, and they again arise into the world. This fly seems to be delicious food for birds, frogs and fish. In the morning, when they arise, and in the evening, when they return, the tumult is great indeed, and the surface of the water along shore broken into bubbles, or spirted into the air, by the contending aquatic tribes, and such is the avidity of the fish and frogs, that they spring into the air, after this delicious prey.

EARLY in the evening, after a pleasant days voyage, I made a convenient and safe harbour, in a little lagoon, under an elevated bank, on the West shore of the river, where I shall intreat the reader's patience, whilst we behold the closing scene of the short–lived Ephemera, and communicate to each other the reflections which so singular an exhibition might rationally suggest to an inquisitive mind. Our place of observation is happily situated, under the protecting shade of majestic Live Oaks, glorious Magnolias and the fragrant Orange, open to the view of the great river, and still waters of the lagoon just before us.

AT the cool eves approach, the sweet enchanting melody of the feathered songsters gradually ceases, and they betake themselves to their leafy coverts for security and repose.

SOLEMNLY and slowly move onward, to the river's shore, the rustling clouds of the Ephemera. How awful the procession! innumerable millions of winged beings, voluntarily verging on to destruction, to the brink of the grave, where they behold bands of their enemies with wide open jaws, ready to receive them. But as if insensible of their danger, gay and tranquil each meets his beloved mate, in the still air, inimitably bedecked in their new nuptial robes. What eye can trace them, in their varied wanton amorous chaces, bounding and fluttering on the odoriferous air? with what peace, love and joy, do they end the last moments of their existence?

I THINK we may assert, without any fear of exaggeration, that there are annually of these beautiful winged beings, which rise into existence, and for a few moments take a transient view of the glory of the Creator's works, a number greater than the whole race of mankind that have ever existed since the creation; and that only, from the shore of this river. How many then must have been produced since the creation, when we consider the number of large rivers in America, in comparison with which, this river is but a brook or rivulet.

THE importance of the existence of these beautiful and delicately formed little creatures, in the creation, whose frame and organization is equally wonderful, more delicate, and perhaps as complicated as that of the most perfect human being, is well worth a few moments contemplation; I mean particularly when they appear in the fly state. And it we consider the very short period, of that stage of existence, which we may reasonably suppose, to be the only space of their life that admits of pleasure and enjoyment, what a lesson doth it not afford us of the vanity of our own pursuits.

THEIR whole existence in this world, is but one compleat year, and at least three hundred and sixty days of that time, they are in the form of an ugly grub, buried in mud, eighteen inches under water, and in this condition scarcely locomotive, as each Larva or grub, has but its own narrow solitary cell, from which it never travels, or moves, but in a perpendicular progression, of a few inches, up and down, from the bottom to the surface of the mud, in order to intercept the passing atoms for its food, and get a momentary respiration of fresh air; and even here it must be perpetually on its guard, in order to escape the troops of fish and shrimps Watching to catch it, and from whom it has no escape, but by instantly retreating back into its cell. One would be apt almost to imagine them created merely for the food of fish and other animals.

HAVING rested very well during the night, I was awakened in the morning early, by the cheering converse of the wild turkey–cock (Meleagris occidentalis) saluting each other, from the sun–brightened tops of the lofty Cupressus disticha and Magnolia grandiflora. They begin at early dawn, and continue till sun rise, from March to the last of April. The high forests ring with the noise, like the crowing of the domestic cock, of these social centinels, the watch–word being caught and repeated, from one to another, for hundreds of miles around; insomuch that the whole country, is for an hour or more, in an universal shout. A little after sun–rise, their crowing gradually ceases, they quit their high lodging places, and alight on the earth, where, expanding their silver bordered train, they strut and dance round about the coy female, while the deep forests seem to tremble with their shrill noise.

THIS morning the winds on the great river, were high and against me, I was therefore obliged to keep in port, a great part of the day, which I employed in little excursions round about my encampment. The Live Oaks are of an astonishing magnitude, and one

64

tree contains a prodigious quantity of timber, yet comparatively, they are not tall, even in these forests, where growing on strong land, in company with others of great altitude (such as Fagus sylvatica, Liquid–amber, Magnolia grandiflora, and the high Palm tree) they strive while young to be upon an equality with their neighbours, and to enjoy the influence of the sun–beams, and of the pure animating air; but the others at last prevail, and their proud heads are seen at a great distance, towering far above the rest of the forest, which consists chiefly of this species of oak, Fraxinus, Ulmus, Acer rubrum, Laurus Borbonia, Quercus dentata, Ilex aquifolium, Olea Americana, Morus, Gleditsia triacanthus, and I believe a species of Sapindus. But the latter spreads abroad his brawny arms, to a great distance. The trunk of the Live Oak is generally from twelve to eighteen feet in girt, and rises ten or twelve feet erect from the earth; some I have seen eighteen or twenty; then divides itself into three, four, or five great limbs, which continue to grow in nearly an horizontal direction, each limb forming a gentle curve, or arch, from its base to its extremity. I have stepped above fifty paces, on a strait line, from the trunk of one of these trees, to the extremity of the limbs. They are ever green, and the wood almost incorruptible, even in the open air. It bears a prodigious quantity of fruit; the acorn is small, but sweet and agreeable to the taste when roasted, and is food for almost all animals. The Indians obtain from it a sweet oil, which they use in the cooking of hommony, rice, &c. and they also roast them in hot embers, eating them as we do chesnuts.

THE wind being fair in the evening, I sat sail again, and crossing the river, made a good harbour on the East shore, where I pitched my tent for the night. The bank of the river was about twelve or fifteen feet perpendicular, from its surface, but the ascent gentle. Although I arrived here early in the evening, I found sufficient attractions to choose it for my lodging–place, and an ample field for botanical employment. It was a high, airy situation, and commanded an extensive and varied prospect of the river and its shores, up and down.

BEHOLD yon promontory, projecting far into the great river, beyond the still lagoon, half a mile distance from me, what a magnificent grove arises on its banks! how glorious the Palm! how majestically stands the Laurel, its head forming a perfect cone! its dark green foliage, seems silvered over with milk–white flowers. They are so large, as to be distinctly visible at the distance of a mile or more. The Laurel Magnolia, which grows on this river are the most beautiful and tall, that I have any where seen, unless we except those, which stand on the banks of the Missisippi; yet even these must yield, to those of

St. Juan, in neatness of form, beauty of foliage, and I think, in largeness and fragrance of flower. Their usual height is about one hundred feet, and some greatly exceed that. The trunk is perfectly erect, rising in the form of a beautiful column, and supporting a head like a an obtuse cone. The flowers are on the extremities of the subdivisions of the branches, in the center of a coronet of dark green, shining, ovate pointed entire leaves: they are large, perfectly white, and expanded like a full blown Rose. They are polypetalous, consisting of fifteen, twenty, or twenty–five petals: these are of a thick coriaceous texture, and deeply concave, their edges being somewhat reflex, when mature. In the center stands the young cone, which is large, of a flesh colour, and elegantly studded with a gold coloured stigma; that by the end of summer, is greatly enlarged, and in the autumn ripens to a large crimson cone or strobile, disclosing multitudes of large coral red berries, which for a time hang down from them, suspended by a fine, white silky thread, four, six to nine inches in length. The flowers of this tree are the largest, and most compleat of any yet known: when fully expanded, they are of six, eight and nine inches diameter. The pericarpium and berries, possess an agreeable spicy scent, and an aromatic bitter taste. The wood when seasoned is of a straw colour, compact, and harder and firmer than that of the Poplar.

IT is really astonishing to behold the Grape–Vines in this place. From their bulk and strength, one would imagine, they were combined to pull down these mighty trees, to the earth, when in fact, amongst other good purposes, they serve to uphold them: they are frequently nine, ten, and twelve inches in diameter, and twine round the trunks of the trees, climb to their very tops, and then spread along their limbs, from tree to tree, throughout the forest; the fruit is but small and ill tasted. The Grape vines with the Rhamnus volubilis, Bignonia radicans, Bignonia crucigera, and another rambling shrubby vine, which seems allied to the Rhamnus, perhaps Zizyphus scandens, seem to tie the trees together, with garlands and festoons, and form enchanting shades. The long moss, so called, (Tillandsea usneascites) is a singular and surprising vegetable production: it grows from the limbs and twigs of all trees in these southern regions, from N. lat. 35 down as far as 28, and I believe every where within the tropics. Wherever it fixes itself, on a limb, or branch, it spreads into short and intricate divarications; these in time collect dust, wasted by the wind, and which, probably by the moisture it absorbs, softens the bark and sappy part of the tree, about the roots of the plant, and renders it more fit for it to establish itself; and from this small beginning, it encreases, by sending downwards and obliquely, on all sides, long pendant branches, which divide and subdivide themselves ad infinitum. It is common to find the spaces, betwixt the limbs of large trees, almost occupied by this plant; it also hangs waving in the wind, like streamers, from the lower limbs, to the length of fifteen or twenty feet, and of bulk and weight, more than several men together could carry; and in some places, cart loads of it are lying on the ground, torn off, by the violence of the wind. Any part of the living plant, torn off and caught, in the limbs of a tree, will presently take root, grow and encrease, in the same degree of perfection, as if it had sprung up from the seed. When fresh, cattle and deer will eat it in the winter season. It seems particularly adapted to the purpose of stuffing mattrasses, chairs, saddles, collars, &c. and for these purposes, nothing yet known equals it. The Spaniards in South America, and the West–Indies, work it into cables that are said to be very strong and durable; but, in order to render it useful, it ought to be thrown into shallow ponds of water, and exposed to the sun, where it soon rots, and the outside furry substance is dissolved. It is then taken out of the water, and spread to dry; when, after a little beating and shaking, it is sufficiently clean, nothing remaining but the interior, hard, black, elastic filament, entangled together, and greatly resembling horse–hair.

THE Zanthoxilum clava Herculis also grows here. It is a beautiful spreading tree, and much like a well grown apple tree. Its aromatic berry is delicious food for the little turtle dove; and epicures say that it gives their flesh a fine flavor.

HAVING finished my observation, I betook myself to rest; and when the plunging and roaring of the crocodiles, and the croaking of the frogs, had ceased, I slept very well during the remainder of the night, as a breeze from the river had scattered the clouds of musquitoes that at first infested me.

IT being a fine cool morning, and fair wind, I sat sail early, and saw, this day, vast quantities of the Pistia stratiotes, a very singular aquatic plant. It associates in large communities, or floating islands, some of them a quarter of a mile in extent, and are impelled to and fro, as the wind and current may direct. They are first produced on, or close to the shore, in eddy water, where they gradually spread themselves into the river, forming most delightful green plains, several miles in length, and in some places a quarter of a mile in breadth. These plants are nourished and kept in their proper horizontal situation, by means of long fibrous roots, which descend from the nether center, downwards, towards the muddy bottom. Each plant, when full grown, bears a general resemblance to a well grown plant of garden lettice, though the leaves are more nervous, of a firmer contexture, and of a full green colour, inclining to yellow. It vegetates on the surface of the still stagnant water, and in its natural situation, is

67

propagated from seed only. In great storm of wind and rain, when the river is suddenly raised, large masses of these floating plains are broken loose, and driven from the shores, into the wide water, where they have the appearance of islets, and float about, until broken to pieces by the winds and waves; or driven again to shore, on some distant coast of the river, where they again find footing, and there, forming new colonies, spread and extend themselves again, until again broken up and dispread as before. These floating islands present a very entertaining prospect; for although we behold an assemblage of the primary productions of nature only, yet the imagination seems to remain in suspence and doubt; as in order to enliven the delusion and form a most picturesque appearance, we see not only flowery plants, clumps of shrubs, old weather–beaten trees, hoary and barbed, with the long moss waving from their snags, but we also see them compleatly inhabited, and alive, with crocodiles, serpents, frogs, otters, crows, herons, curlews, jackdaws, &c. there seems, in short, nothing wanted but the appearance of a wigwam and a canoe to complete the scene.

KEEPING along the West or Indian shore, I saw basking on the sedgy banks, numbers of alligators*

* I have made use of the terms alligator and crocodile indiscriminately for this animal, alligator being the country name.

some of them of an enormous size.

THE high forests on this coast, now wore a grand and sublime appearance, the earth rising gradually, from the river Westward, by easy swelling ridges, behind one another, and lifted the distant groves up into the skies. The trees are of the lofty kind, as the grand Laurel Magnolia, Palm elata, Liquid–amber styraciflua, Fagus sylvatica, Querci, Juglans hiccory, Fraxinus, and others.

ON my doubling a long point of land, the river appeared surprisingly widened, forming a large bay, of an oval form, and several miles in extent. On the West side it was bordered round with low marshes, and invested with a swamp of Cypress, the trees so lofty, as to preclude the sight of the high–land forests, beyond them; and these trees, having flat tops, and all of equal height, seemed to be a green plain, lifted up and supported upon columns in the air, round the West side of the bay.

Travels Through North and South Carolina

THE Cupressus disticha stands in the first order of North American trees. Its majestic stature is surprising, and on approaching them, we are struck with a kind of awe, at beholding the stateliness of the trunk, lifting its cumbrous top towards the skies, and casting a wide shade upon the ground, as a dark intervening cloud, which, for a time, precludes the rays of the sun. The delicacy of its colour, and texture of its leaves, exceed every thing in vegetation. It generally grows in the water, or in low flat lands, near the banks of great rivers and lakes, that are covered, great part of the year, with two or three feet depth of water, and that part of the trunk, which is subject to be under water, and four or five feet higher up, is greatly enlarged, by prodigious buttresses, or pilasters, which, in full grown trees, project out on every side, to such a distance, that several men might easily hide themselves in the hollows between. Each pilaster terminates under ground, in a very large, strong, serpentine root, which strikes off, and branches every way, just under the surface of the earth; and from these roots grow woody cones, called cypress knees, four, five, and fix feet high, and from fix to eighteen inches and two feet in diameter at their bases. The large ones are hollow, and serve very well for beehives; a small space of the tree itself is hollow, nearly as high as the buttresses already mentioned. From this place the tree, as it were, takes another beginning, forming a grand strait column eighty or ninety feet high, when it divides every way around into an extensive flat horizontal top, like an umbrella, where eagles have their secure nests, and cranes and storks their temporary resting places; and what adds to the magnificence of their appearance, is the streamers of long moss that hang from the lofty limbs and float in the winds. This is their majestic appearance, when standing alone, in large rice plantations, or thinly planted on the banks of great rivers.

PAROQUETS are commonly seen hovering and fluttering on their tops: they delight to shell the balls, its feed being their favourite food. The trunks of these trees when hollowed out, make large and durable pettiaugers and canoes, and afford excellent shingles, boards, and other timber, adapted to every purpose in frame buildings. When the planters fell these mighty trees, they raise a stage round them, as high as to reach above the buttresses; on this stage, eight or ten negroes ascend with their axes, and fall to work round its trunk. I have seen trunks of these trees that would measure eight, ten, and twelve feet in diameter, for forty and fifty feet strait shaft.

As I continued coasting the Indian shore of this bay, on doubling a promontory, I suddenly saw before me an Indian settlement, or village. It was a fine situation, the bank rising gradually from the water. There were eight or ten habitations, in a row, or street,

69

fronting the water, and about fifty yards distance from it. Some of the youth were naked, up to their hips in the water, fishing with rods and lines, whilst others, younger, were diverting themselves in shooting frogs with bows and arrows. On my near approach, the little children took to their heels, and ran to some women, who were hoeing corn; but the stouter youth stood their ground, and, smiling, called to me. As I passed along, I observed some elderly people reclined on skins spread on the ground, under the cool shade of spreading Oaks and Palms, that were ranged in front of their houses; they arose, and eyed me as I passed, but perceiving that I kept on, without stopping, they resumed their former position. They were civil, and appeared happy in their situation.

THERE was a large Orange grove at the upper end of their village; the trees were large, carefully pruned, and the ground under them clean, open, and airy. There seemed to be several hundred acres of cleared land, about the village; a considerable portion of which was planted, chiefly with corn (Zea) Batatas, Beans, Pompions, Squash, (Cucurbita verrucosa) Melons (Cucurbita citrullus) Tobacco (Nicotiana) &c. abundantly sufficient for the inhabitants of the village.

AFTER leaving this village, and coasting a considerable cove of the lake, I percieved the river before me much contracted within its late bounds, but still retaining the appearance of a wide and deep river, both coasts bordered, for several miles, with rich deep swamps, well timbered with Cypress, Ash, Elm, Oak, Hiccory, Scarlet Maple, Nyssa aquatica, Nyssa tupilo, Gordonia lasianthus, Corypha palma, Corypha pumila, Laurus Borbonia, &c. The river gradually narrowing, I came in sight of Charlotia, where it is not above half a mile wide, but deep; and as there was a considerable current against me, I came here to an anchor. This town was founded by Den. Rolle, Esq; and is situated on a high bluff, on the east coast, fifteen or twenty feet perpendicular from the river, and is in length half a mile, or more, upon its banks. The upper stratum of the earth consists entirely of several species of fresh water Cochlae, as Cochelix, Coch. labyrinthus, and Coch. voluta; the second, of marine shells, as Concha mytulus, Concostrea, Conc. peeton, Haliotis auris marina, Hal. patella, &c. mixed with sea sand; and the third, or lower stratum, which was a little above the comman level of the river, was horizontal masses of a pretty hard rock, composed almost entirely of the above shell, generally whole, and lying in every direction, petrefied or cemented together, with fine white sand; and these rocks were bedded in a stratum of clay. I saw many fragments of the earthen ware of the ancient inhabitants, and bones of animals, amongst the shells, and mixed with the earth, to a great depth. This high shelly bank continues, by gentle parallel ridges, near a quarter of a mile back from the river, gradually diminishing to the level of the sandy plains, which widen before and on each side eastward, to a seemingly unlimited distance, and appear green and delightful, being covered with grass and the Corypha repens, and thinly planted with trees of the long leaved, or Broom Pine, and decorated with clumps, or coppices of floriferous, evergreen, and aromatic shrubs, and enamelled with patches of the beautiful little Kalmea ciliata. These shelly ridges have a vegetable surface of loose black mould, very fertile, and naturally produces Orange groves, Live Oak, Laurus Borbonia, Palma elata, Carica papaya, Sapindus, Liquid–amber, Fraxinus exelsior, Morus rubra, Ulmns, Tilia, Sambucus, Ptelea, Tallow–nut, or Wild Lime, and many others.

MR. Rolle obtained from the crown, a grant of forty thousand acres of land, in any part of East Florida, where the land was unlocated. It seems his views were to take up his grant near St. Marks, in the bay of Aplatchi; and sat sail from England, with about one hundred families, for that place; but by contrary winds, and stress of weather, he missed his aim, and being obliged to put into St. Juan's, he, with some of the principal of his adherents, ascended the river in a boat, and being struck with its majesty, the grand situation of its banks, and fertility of its lands, and at the same time, considering the extensive navigation of the river, and its near vicinity to St. Augustine, the capital and seat of government, he altered his views on St. Marks, and suddenly determined on this place, where he landed his first little colony. But it seems from an ill concerted plan, in its infant establishment, negligence, or extreme parsimony, in sending proper recruits, and other necessaries, together with a bad choice of citizens, the settlement by degrees grew weeker, and at length totally fell to the ground. Those of them who escaped the constant contagious fevers, fled the dreaded place, betaking themselves for subsistence, to the more fruitful and populous regions of Georgia and Carolina.

THE remaining old habitations, are mouldering to earth, except the mansion house, which is a large frame building, of Cypress wood, yet in tolerable repair, and inhabited by an overseer and his family. There is also a black–smith with his shop and family, at a small distance from it. The most valuable district belonging to Mr. Rolle's grant, lies on Dunn's lake, and on a little river, which runs from it into St. Juan. This district consists of a vast body of rich swamp land, fit for the growth of Rice, and some very excellent high land surrounding it. Large swamps of excellent rice land are also situated on the West shore of the river, opposite to Charlotia.

71

THE aborigines of America, had a very great town in this place, as appears from the great tumuli, and conical mounts of earth and shells, and other traces of a settlement which yet remain. There grew in the old fields on these heights great quantities of Callicarpa and of the beautiful shrub Annona: the flowers of the latter are large, white and sweet scented.

HAVING obtained from the people here, directions for discovering the little remote island, where the traders and their goods were secreted, which was about seven miles higher up, I sat sail again, with a fair wind, and in about one hour and an half, arrived at the desired place, having fortunately taken the right channel of the river, amongst a multitude of others, occasioned by a number of low swampy islands. But I should have ran by the landing, if the centinels had not, by chance seen me drawing near them; and who perceiving that I was a whiteman, ventured to hail me; upon which I immediately struck sail, and came too. Upon my landing they conducted me to their encampment, forty or fifty yards from the river, in an almost impenetrable thicket. Upon my inquiry, they confirmed the accounts of the amicable treaty at St. Augustine, and in consequence thereof, they had already removed great part of the goods, to the trading–house, which was a few miles higher up, on the Indian shore. They shewed me my chest, which had been carefully preserved, and upon inspection I found every thing in good order. Having learned from them, that all the effects would, in a few days time, be removed to the store–house, I bid adieu to them, and in a little time, arrived at the trading–house, where I was received with great politeness, and treated during a residence of several months, with the utmost civility and friendship, by Mr. C. M'Latche, Messrs. Spalding and Kelsall's agent.

THE river almost form Charlotia, and for near twelve mile higher up is divided into many channels by a great number of islands.

CHAP. IV.

HAVING rested myself a few days, and by ranging about the neighbouring plains and groves, surrounding this pleasant place, pretty well recovered my strength and spirits, I began to think of planning my future excursions, at a distance round about this center. I found from frequent conferrences with Mr. M'Latche, that I might with safety, extend my journeys every way, and with prudence, even into the towns and settlement of the Indians, as they were perfectly reconciled to us, and sincerely wished for the renewal of our trade.

THERE were three trading–houses to be established this summer, each of which had its supplier from the store on St. Juan, where I now had my residence, and in which the produce or returns were to center annually, in order to be shipped for Savanna or Sunbury, and from thence to Europe.

ONE of these trading–houses was to be fixed about sixty miles higher up the river, from this place, by the name of Spalding's upper store; a second at Alachua, about fifty miles West from the river St. Juan; and a third at Talahasochte, a considerable town of the Siminoles, on the river Little St. Juan, near the bay of Apalachi, about one hundred and twenty miles distance. Each of these places I designed to visit, before the return of the vessel to Frederica, in the autumn, that I might avail myself of an opportunity so favourable, for transporting my collections so far on their way towards Charleston.

THE company for Alachua, were to set off in about a month. That to Little St. Juan, in July, which suited me exceedingly well, as I might make my tour to the upper store directly, that part of the country being at this season, enrobed in her richest and gayest apparel.

ABOUT the middle of May, every thing being in readiness, to proceed up the river, we sat sail. The traders with their goods in a large boat, went ahead, and myself in my little vessel followed them; and as their boat was large, and deeply laden, I found that I could easily keep up with them, and if I chose, out–sail them; but I preferred keeping them company, as well for the sake of collecting what I could from conversation, as on account of my safety in crossing the great lake, expecting to return alone, and descend the river at my own leisure.

WE had a pleasant day, the wind fair and moderate, and ran by Mount Hope, so named by my father John Bartram, when he ascended this river, about fifteen years ago. It is a very high shelly bluff, upon the little lake. It was at that time a fine Orange grove, but now cleared and converted into a large Indigo plantation, the property of an English gentleman, under the care of an agent. In the evening we arrived at Mount Royal, where we came to, and stayed all night: we were treated with great civility, by a gentleman whose name was——— Kean, and had been an Indian trader.

Travels Through North and South Carolina

FROM this place we enjoyed a most enchanting prospect of the great Lake George, through a grand avenue, if I may so term this narrow reach of the river, which widens gradually for about two miles, towards its entrance into the lake, so as to elude the exact rules of perspective and appears of an equal width.

AT about fifty yards distance from the landing place, stands a magnificent Indian mount. About fifteen years ago I visited this place, at which time there were no settlements of white people, but all appeared wild and savage; yet in that uncultivated state, it possessed an almost inexpressible air of grandeur, which was now entirely changed. At that time there was a very considerable extent of old fields, round about the mount; there was also a large Orange grove, together with Palms and Live Oaks, extending from near the mount, along the banks, downwards, all of which has since been cleared away to make room for planting ground. But what greatly contributed towards compleating the magnificence of the scene, was a noble Indian highway, which led from the great mount, on a strait line, three quarters of a mile, first through a point or wing of the Orange grove, and continuing thence through an awful forest, of Live Oaks, it was terminated by Palms and Laurel Magnolias, on the verge of an oblong artificial lake, which was on the edge of an extensive green level savanna. This grand highway was about fifty yards wide, sunk a little below the common level, and the earth thrown up on each side, making a bank of about two feet high. Neither nature nor art, could any where present a more striking contrast, as you approach this savanna. The glittering water pond, plays on the sight, through the dark grove, like a brilliant diamond, on the bosom of the illumined savanna, bordered with various flowery shrubs and plants; and as we advance into the plain, the sight is agreeably relieved by a distant view of the forest, which partly environ the green expanse, on the left hand, whilst the imagination is still flattered and entertained by the far distant misty points of the surrounding forests, which project into the plain, alternately appearing and disappearing, making a grand sweep round on the right, to the distant banks of the great lake. But that venerable grove is now no more. All has been cleared away and planted with Indigo, Corn and Cotton, but since deserted: there was now scarcely five acres of ground under fence. It appeared like a desart, to a great extent, and terminated, on the land side, by frightful thickets, and open Pine forests.

IT appears however, that the late proprietor had some taste, as he has preserved the mount, and this little adjoining grove inviolate. The prospect from this station is so happily situtated by nature, as to comprise at one view, the whole of the sublime and pleasing.

Travels Through North and South Carolina

AT the reanimating appearance of the rising sun, nature again revives; and I obey the chearful summons of the gentle monitors of the meads and groves.

YE vigilant and faithful servants of the Most High! ye who worship the Creator, morning, noon and eve, in simplicity of heart; I haste to join the universal anthem. My heart and voice unite with yours, in sincere homage to the great Creator, the universal sovereign.

O MAY I be permitted to approach the throne of mercy! may these my humble and penitent supplications, amidst the universal shouts of homage, from thy creatures, meet with thy acceptance.

AND although, I am sensible, that my service, cannot encrease, or diminish thy glory, yet it is pleasing to thy servant, to be permitted to sound thy praise; for O sovereign Lord! we know that thou alone art perfect, and worthy to be worshiped. O universal Father! look down upon us we beseech thee, with an eye of pity and composition, and grant that universal peace and love, may prevail in the earth, even that divine harmony, which fills the heavens, thy glorious habitation.

AND O sovereign Lord! since it has pleased thee to endue man with power, and pre—eminence, here on earth, and establish his dominion over all creatures, may we look up to thee, that our understanding may be so illuminated with wisdom and our hearts warmed and animated, with a due sense of charity, that we may be enabled to do thy will, and perform our duty towards those submitted to our service, and protection, and be merciful to them even as we hope for mercy.

THUS may we be worthy of the dignity, and superiority of the high, and distinguished station, in which thou hast placed us here on earth.

THE morning being fair, and having a gentle favourable gale, we left our pleasant harbour, in pursuit of our desired port.

NOW as we approach the capes, behold the little ocean of Lake George, the distant circular coast gradually rising to view, from his misty fringed horizon. I cannot entirely suppress my apprehension of danger. My vessel at once diminished to a nut–shell, on the swelling seas, and at the distance of a few miles, must appear to the surprised observer, as some aquatic animal, at intervals emerging from its surface. This lake is a large and beautiful piece of water ; it is a dilatation of the river St. Juan, and is about fifteen miles wide, and generally about fifteen or twenty feet deep, excepting at the entrance of the river, where lies a bar, which carries eight or nine feet water. The lake is beautified with two or three fertile islands. The first lies in the bay, as we ascend into the lake, near the West coast, about S. W. from Mount Royal, from whence it appears to form part of the West shore of the bay. The second island seems to ride on the lake before us as we enter, about a mile within it. This island is about two miles in breadth, and three quarters of a mile where broadest, mostly high land, well timbered, and fertile. The third and last, lies at the South end of the lake, and near the entrance of the river; it is nearly circular, and contains but a few acres of land, the earth high and fertile, and almost an entire Orange grove, with grand Magnolias and Palms.

SOON after entering the lake, the wind blew so briskly from the West, and thunder–clouds gathering upon the horizon, we were obliged to seek a shelter, from the approaching tempest, on the large beautiful island, before mentioned. Where, having gained the South promontory, we met with an excellent harbour, in which we continued the remaining part of the day and the night. This circumstance gave me an opportunity to explore the greatest part of it.

THIS island appears, from obvious vestiges, to have been once the chosen residence of an Indian prince, there being to this day, evident remains of a large town of the Aborigines. It was situated on an eminence, near the banks of the lake, and commanded a comprehensive and charming prospect of the waters, island, East and West shore of the lake, the capes, the bay and Mount Royal, and to the South the view is in a manner infinite, where the skies and waters seem to unite. On the site of this ancient town, stands a very pompous Indian mount, or conical pyramid of earth, from which runs in a strait line, a grand avenue or Indian highway, through a magnificent grove of Magnolias, Live Oaks, Palms and Orange trees, terminating at the verge of a large green level savanna. This island appears to have been well inhabited, as is very evident, from the quantities of fragments of Indian earthen–ware, bones of animals and other remains, particularly in the shelly heights and ridges, all over the island. There are no habitations at present on the island, but a great number of deer, turkeys, bears, wolves, wild cats, squirrels, racoons, and opossoms. The bears are invited here to partake of the fruit of the Orange tree, which they are immoderately fond of, and both they and turkeys are made extremely fat and delicious, from their feeding on the sweet acorns of the Live Oak.

THERE grows on this island, many curious shrubs, particularly a beautiful species of Lantana (perhaps Lant. camerara. Lin. Syst. Veget. p. 473.) It grows in coppices in old fields, about five or six feet high, the branches adorned with rough serrated leaves, which sit opposite, and the twigs terminate with umbeliferous tufts of orange coloured blossoms, which are succeeded by a cluster of small blue berries: the flowers are of various colours, on the same plant, and even in the same cluster. As crimson, scarlet, orange and golden yellow: the whole plant is of a most agreeable scent. The orange flowered shrub Hibiscus is also conspicuously beautiful (perhaps Hibisc. spinifex of Linn.) it grows five or fix feet high, and subramous. The branches are divergent, and furnished with cordated leaves, which are crenated. The flowers are of a moderate size, and of a deep splendid yellow. The pericarpii are spiny. I also saw a new and beautiful palmated leaved convolvulus.*

* Convol. dissectus.

This Vine rambles over the shrubs, and strolls about on the ground, its leaves are elegantly sinuated, of a deep grass green, and sit on long petioles. The flowers are very large, infundibuliform, of a pale incarnate colour, having a deep crimson eye.

THERE are some rich swamps on the shores of the island, and these are verged on the outside with large marshes, covered entirely with tall grass, rushes, and herbacious plants: amongst these are several species of Hibiscus, particularly the Hibiscus coccineus. This most stately of all herbacious plants, grows ten or twelve feet high, branching regularly, so as to form a sharp cone. These branches also divide again, and are embellished with large expanded crimson flowers: I have seen this plant of the size and figure of a beautiful little tree, having at once several hundred of these splendid flowers, and which may be then seen at a great distance. They continue to flower in succession all summer and autumn, when the stems wither and decay; but the perennial root sends forth new stems the next spring, and so on for many years. Its leaves are large, deeply and elegantly sinuated, having fix or seven very narrow dentated segments; the surface of the leaves, and of the whole plant, are smooth and polished. Another species of Hibiscus, worthy of particular notice, is likewise a tall flourishing plant; several strong stems arise from a root, five, six, and seven feet high, embellished with ovate lanciolate leaves, covered with a fine down on their nether surfaces: the flowers are very large, and of a deep incarnate colour.

Travels Through North and South Carolina

THE last we shall now mention seems nearly allied to the Alcea; the flowers are a size less than the Hibiscus, and of a fine damask rose colour, and are produced in great profusion on the tall pyramidal stems.

THE Lobelia cardinalis grows in great plenty here, and has a most splendid appearance amidst extensive meadows of the golden Corymbous Jacobea (Senecio Jacobea) and odorous Pancratium.

HAVING finished my tour, on this princely island, I prepared for repose. A calm evening had succeeded the stormy day. The late tumultuous winds had now ceased, the face of the lake had become placid, and the skies serene; the balmy winds breathed the animating odours of the groves around me; and as I reclined on the elevated banks of the lake, at the foot of a Live Oak, I enjoyed the prospect of its wide waters, its fringed coasts, and of the distant horizon.

THE squadrons of aquatic fowls, emerging out of the water, and hastening to their leafy coverts on shore, closed the varied scenes of the past day. I was lulled asleep by the mixed sounds of the wearied surf, lapsing on the hard beaten shore, and the tender warblings of the painted nonpareil and other winged inhabitants of the groves.

AT the approach of day, the dreaded voice of the alligators shook the isle, and resounded along the neighbouring coasts, proclaiming the appearance of the glorious sun. I arose, and prepared to accomplish my daily task. A gentle favourable gale led us out of the harbour: we sailed across the lake, and, towards evening, entered the river, on the opposite South coast, where we made a pleasant and safe harbour, at a shelly promontory, the East cape of the river on that side of the lake. It is a most desirable situation, commanding a full view of the lake. The cape opposite to us was a vast cypress swamp, environed by a border of grassy marshes, which were projected farther into the lake, by floating fields of the bright green Pistia stratoites, which rose and fell alternately with the waters. Just to leeward of this point, and about half a mile in the lake, is the little round island already mentioned. But let us take notice of our harbour and its environs: it is a beautiful little cove, just within the sandy point, which defends it from the beating surf of the lake. From a shelly bank, ten or twelve feet perpendicular from the water, we entered a grove of Live Oaks, Palm, Magnolia, and Orange trees, which grow amongst shelly hills, and low ridges, occupying about three acres of ground, comprehending the isthmus, and a part of the peninsula, which joins it to the grassy plains. This enchanting little forest is partly encircled by a deep creek, a branch of the river, that has its source in the high forests of the main, South East from us, and winds through the extensive grassy plains which surround this peninsula, to an almost infinite distance, and then unites its waters with those of the river, in this little bay which formed our harbour. This bay, about the mouth of the creek, is almost covered with the leaves of the Nymphaea nilumbo: its large sweet–scented yellow flowers are listed up two or three feet above the surface of the water, each upon a green starol, representing the cap of Liberty.

THE evening drawing on, and there being no convenient landing place, for several miles higher up the river, we concluded to remain here all night. Whilst my fellow travellers were employing themselves in collecting fire–wood, and fixing our camp, I improved the opportunity, in reconnoitering our ground; and taking my fusee with me, I penetrated the grove, and afterwards entered some almost unlimited savannas and plains, which were absolutely enchanting; they had been lately burnt by the Indian hunters, and had just now recovered their vernal verdure and gaiety.

HOW happily situated is this retired spot of earth! What an elisium it is! where the wandering Siminole, the naked red warrior, roams at large, and after the vigorous chase retires from the scorching heat of the meridian sun. Here he reclines, and reposes under the odoriferous shades of Zanthoxilon, his verdant couch guarded by the Deity; Liberty, and the Muses, inspiring him with wisdom and valour, whilst the balmy zephyrs fan him to sleep.

SEDUCED by these sublime enchanting scenes of primitive nature, and these visions of terrestrial happiness, I had roved far away from Cedar Point, but awakening to my cares, I turned about, and in the evening regained our camp.

ON my return, I found some of my companions fishing for trout, round about the edges of the floating nymphaea, and not unsuccessfully, having then caught more than sufficient for us all. As the method of taking these fish is curious and singular, I shall just mention it.

THEY are taken with a hook and line, but without any bait. Two people are in a little canoe, one sitting in the stern to steer, and the other near the bow, having a rod ten or twelve feet in length, to one end of which is tied a strong line, about twenty inches in length, to which is fastened three large hooks, back to back. These are fixed very securely, and covered with the white hair of a deer's tail, shreds of a red garter, and some particoloured feathers, all which form a tuft, or tassel, nearly as large as one's fist, and entirely cover and conceal the hooks: this is called a bob. The steersman paddles softly, and proceeds slowly along shore, keeping the boat parallel to it, at a distance just sufficient to admit the fisherman to reach the edge of the floating weeds along shore: he now ingeniously swings the bob backwards and forwards, just above the surface, and sometimes tips the water with it; when the unfortunate cheated trout instantly springs from under the weeds, and seizes the supposed prey. Thus he is caught without a possibility of escape, unless he break the hooks, line, or rod, which he, however, sometime does by dint of strength; but, to prevent this, the fisherman used to the sport is careful not to raise the reed suddenly up, but jerks it instantly backwards, then steadily drags the sturdy reluctant fish to the side of the canoe, and with a sudden upright jerk brings him into it.

THE head of this fish makes about one third of his length, and consequently the mouth is very large: birds, fish, frogs, and even serpents, are frequently found in its stomach.

THE trout is of lead colour, inclining to a deep blue, and marked with transverse waved lists, of a deep slate colour, and when fully grown, has a cast of red, or brick colour. The fins, with the tail, which is large, and beautifully formed, are of a light reddish purple, or flesh colour, the whole body is covered with large scales. But what is most singular, this fish is remarkably ravenous; nothing living, that he can seize upon, escapes his jaws, and the opening and extending of the branchiostega, at the moment he rises to the surface to seize his prey, discovering his bright red gills, through the transparent waters, give him a very terible appearance. Indeed it may be observed, that all fish of prey have this opening and covering of the gills very large, in order to discharge the great quantity of water, which they take in at their mouth, when they strike at their prey. This fish is nearly cuniform, the body tapering gradually from the breast to the tail, and lightly compressed on each side. They frequently weigh fifteen, twenty and thirty pounds, and are delicious food.

MY companion, the trader, being desirous of crossing the river to the opposite shore, in hopes of getting a turkey, I chose to accompany him, as it offered a good opportunity to observe the natural productions of those rich swamps and islands of the river. Having crossed the river, which is here five or six hundred yards wide, we entered a narrow channel, which after a serpentine course, for some miles, rejoins the main river again, above; forming a large fertile island, of rich low land. We landed on this island, and soon saw a fine roebuck*

* Cervus sylvaticus. The American deer.

a some distance from us, who appeared leader of a company of deer, that were feeding near him, on the verge of a green meadow. My companion parting from me, in pursuit of the deer, one way, and I, observing a flock of turkeys at some distance, on the other, directed my steps towards them, and with great caution, got near them; when singling out a large cock, and being just on the point of firing, I observed that several young cocks were affrighted, and in their language, warned the rest to be on their guard, against an enemy, whom I plainly perceived was industriously making his subtile approaches towards them, behind the fallen trunk of a tree, about twenty yards from me. This cunning fellow hunter, was a large fat wild cat (lynx) he saw me, and at times seemed to watch my motions, as if determined to seize the delicious prey before me. Upon which I changed my object, and levelled my piece at him. At that instant, my companion, at a distance, also discharged his piece at the deer, the report of which alarmed the flock of turkeys, and my fellow hunter, the cat, sprang over the log and trotted off. The trader also missed his deer: thus we foiled each other. By this time it being near night, we returned to camp, where having a delicious meal, ready prepared for our hungry stomachs, we sat down in a circle round our wholesome repast.

How supremely blessed were our hours at this time! plenty of delicious and healthful food, our stomachs keen, with contented minds; under no controul, but what reason and ordinate passions dictated, far removed from the seats of strife.

OUR situation was like that of the primitive state of man, peaceable, contented, and sociable. The simple and necessary calls of nature, being satisfied. We were altogether as brethren of one family, strangers to envy, malice and rapine.

THE night being over we arose, and pursued our course up the river, and in the evening reached the trading–house, Spalding's upper store, where I took up my quarters for several weeks.

Travels Through North and South Carolina

ON our arrival at the upper store, we found it occupied by a white trader, who had for a companion, a very handsome Siminole young woman. Her father, who was a prince, by the name of the White Captain, was an old chief of the Siminoles, and with part of his family, to the number of ten or twelve, were encamped in an Orange grove near the stores, having lately come in from a hunt.

THIS white trader, soon after our arrival, delivered up the goods and store–houses to my companion, and joined his father–in–law's camp, and soon after went a way into the forests on hunting and trading amongst the flying camps of Siminoles.

HE is at this time, unhappy in his connections with his beautiful savage. It is but a few years since he came here, I think from North Carolina, a stout genteel well–bred man, active, and of a heroic and amiable disposition and by his industry, honesty, and engaging manners, had gained the affections of the Indians, and soon made a little fortune by traffic with the Siminoles: when, unfortunately, meeting with this little charmer, they were married in the Indian manner. He loves her sincerely, as she possesses every perfection in her person to render a man happy. Her features are beautiful, and manners engaging. Innocence, modesty, and love, appear to a stranger in every action and movement; and these powerful graces she has so artfully played upon her beguiled and vanquished lover, and unhappy slave, as to have already drained him of all his possessions, which she dishonestly distributes amongst her savage relations. He is now poor, emaciated, and half distracted, often threatening to shoot her, and afterwards put an end to his own life; yet he has not resolution even to leave her; but now endeavours to drown and forget his sorrows, in deep draughts of brandy. Her father condemns her dishonest and cruel conduct.

THESE particulars were related to me by my old friend the trader, directly after a long conference which he had with the White Captain on the subject, his son in law being present. The scene was affecting; they both shed tears plentifully. My reasons for mentioning this affair, so foreign to my business, was to exhibit an instance of the power of beauty in a savage, and their art and finesse in improving it to their private ends. It is, however, but doing justice to the virtue and moral conduct of the Siminoles, and American Aborigines in general, to observe, that the character of this woman is condemned and detested by her own people, of both sexes; and if her husband should turn her away; according to the customs and usages of these people, she would not get a husband again, as a divorce seldom takes place but in consequence of a deliberate impartial trial, and public condemnation, and then she would be looked upon as a harlot.

SUCH is the virtue of these ututored savages: but I am afraid this is a common phrase epithet, having no meaning, or at least improperly applied; for these people are both well tutored and civil; and it is apparent to an impartial observer, who resides but a little time amongst them, that it is from the most delicate sense of the honour and reputation of their tribes and families, that their laws and customs receive their force and energy. This is the divine principle which influences their moral conduct, and solely preserves their constitution and civil government in that purity in which they are found to prevail amongst them.

CHAP. V.

BEING desirous of continuing my travels and observations, higher up the river, and having an invitation from a gentleman who was agent for, and resident at a large plantation, the property of an English gentleman, about sixty miles higher up, I resolved to persue my researches to that place; and having engaged in my service a young Indian, nephew to the White Captain, he agreed to assist me in working my vessel up as high as a certain bluff, where I was, by agreement, to land him, on the west or Indian shore, whence he designed to go in quest of the camp of the White Trader, his relation.

PROVISIONS and all necessaries being procured, and the morning pleasant, we went on board and stood up the river. We passed for several miles on the left, by islands of high swamp land, exceedingly fertile, their banks for a good distance from the water, much higher than the interior part, and sufficiently so to build upon, and be out of the reach of inundations. They consist of a loose black mould, with a mixture of sand, shells and dissolved vegetables. The opposite Indian coast is a perpendicular bluff; ten or twelve feet high, consisting of a black sandy earth, mixed with a large proportion of shells, chiefly various species of fresh water Cochlea and Mytuli. Near the river, on this high shore, grew Corypha palma, Magnolia grandiflora, Live Oak, Callicarpa, Myrica cerifera, spinifex, and the beautiful evergreen shrub called Wild lime or Tallow nut. This last shrub grows six or eight feet high, many erect rising from a root; the leaves are lanciolate and intire, two or three inches in length and one in breadth, of a deep green colour, and polished; at the foot of each leaf grows a stiff, sharp thorn; the flowers are small and in clusters, of a greenish yellow colour, and sweet scented; they are succeeded by a large oval fruit, of the consistence and taste of an ordinary plumb, of a fine yellow colour when ripe, a soft sweet pulp covers a nut which has a thin shell, enclosing a white kernel somewhat of the consistence and taste of the sweet Almond, but more oily and very much like hard tallow, which induced my father when he first observed it, to call it the Tallow nut.

AT the upper end of this bluff is a fine Orange grove. Here my Indian companion requested me set him on shore, being already tired of rowing under a fervid sun, and having for some time intimated a dislike to his situation, I readily complied with his desire, knowing the impossibility of compelling an Indian against his own inclinations, or even prevailing upon him by reasonable arguments, when labour is in the question; before my vessel reached the shore, he sprang out of her and landed, when uttering a thrill and terrible whoop, he bounded off like a roebuck, and I lost sight of him. I at first apprehended that as he took his gun with him, he intended to hunt for some game and return to me in the evening. The day being excessively hot and sultry, I concluded to take up my quarters here until next morning.

THE Indian not returning this morning, I sat sail alone. The coasts on each side had much the same appearance as already described. The Palm trees here seem to be of a different species from the Cabbage tree; their strait trunks are sixty, eighty or ninety feet high, with a beautiful taper of a bright ash colour, until within six or seven feet of the top, where it is a fine green colour, crowned with an orb of rich green plumed leaves: I have measured the stem of these plumes fifteen feet in length, besides the plume, which is nearly of the same length.

THE little lake, which is an expansion of the river, now appeared in view; on the East side are extensive marshes, and on the other high forests and Orange groves, and then a bay, lined with vast Cypress swamps, both coasts gradually approaching each other, to the opening of the river again, which is in this place about three hundred yards wide; evening now drawing on, I was anxious to reach some high bank of the river, where I intended to lodge, and agreeably to my wishes, I soon after discovered on the West shore, a little promontory, at the turning of the river, contracting it here to about one hundred and fifty yards in width. This promontory is a peninsula, containing about three acres of high ground, and is one entire Orange grove, with a few Live Oaks, Magnolias and Palms. Upon doubling the point, I arrived at the landing, which is a circular harbour, at the foot of the bluff, the top of which is about twelve feet high; and back of it is a large

Travels Through North and South Carolina

Cypress swamp, that spreads each way, the right wing forming the West coast of the little lake, and the left stretching up the river many miles, and encompassing a vast space of low grassy marshes. From this promontory, looking Eastward across the river, we behold a landscape of low country, uparalleled as I think; on the left is the East coast of the little lake, which I had just passed, and from the Orange bluff at the lower end, the high forests begin, and increase in breadth from the shore of the lake, making a circular sweep to the right, and contain many hundred thousand acres of meadow, and this grand sweep of high forests encircles, as I apprehend, at least twenty miles of these green fields, interspersed with hommocks or islets of evergreen trees, where the sovereign Magnolia and lordly Palm stand conspicuous. The islets are high shelly knolls, on the sides of creeks or branches of the river, which wind about and drain off the super–abundant waters that cover these meadows, during the winter season.

THE evening was temperately cool and calm. The crocodiles began to roar and appear in uncommon numbers along the shores and in the river. I fixed my camp in an open plain, near the utmost projection of the promontory, under the shelter of a large Live Oak, which stood on the highest part of the ground and but a few yards from my boat. From this open, high situation, I had a free prospect of the river, which was a matter of no trivial consideration to me, having good reason to dread the subtle attacks of the allegators, who were crouding about my harbour. Having collected a good quantity of wood for the purpose of keeping up a light and smoke during the night, I began to think of preparing my supper, when, upon examining my stores, I found but a scanty provision, I there upon determined, as the most expeditious way of supplying my necessities, to take my bob and try for some trout. About one hundred yards above my harbour, began a cove or bay of the river, out of which opened a large lagoon. The mouth or entrance from the river to it was narrow, but the waters soon after spread and formed a little lake, extending into the marshes, its entrance and shores within I observed to be verged with floating lawns of the Pistia and Nymphea and other aquatic plants; these I knew were excellent haunts for trout.

THE verges and islets of the lagoon were elegantly embellished with flowering plants and shrubs; the laughing coots with wings half spread were tripping over the little coves and hiding themselves in the tufts of grass; young broods of the painted summer teal, skimming the still surface of the waters, and following the watchful parent unconscious of danger, were frequently surprised by the voracious trout, and he in turn, as often by the subtle, greedy alligator. Behold him rushing forth from the flags and reeds. His enormous body swells. His plaited tail brandished high, floats upon the lake. The waters like a cataract descend from his opening jaws. Clouds of smoke issue from his dilated nostrils. The earth trembles with his thunder. When immediately from the opposite coast of the lagoon, emerges from the deep his rival champion. They suddenly dart upon each other. The boiling surface of the lake marks their rapid course, and a terrific conflict commences. They now sink to the bottom folded together in horrid wreaths. The water becomes thick and discoloured. Again they rise, their jaws clap together, re–echoing through the deep surrounding forests. Again they sink, when the contest ends at the muddy bottom of the lake, and the vanquished makes a hazardous escape, hiding himself in the muddy turbulent waters and sedge on a distant shore. The proud victor exulting returns to the place of action. The shores and forests resound his dreadful roar, together with the triumphing shouts of the plaited tribes around, witnesses of the horrid combat.

MY apprehensions were highly alarmed after being a spectator of so dreadful a battle; it was obvious that every delay would but tend to encrease my dangers and difficulties, as the sun was near setting, and the alligators gathered around my harbour from all quarters; from these considerations I concluded to be expeditious in my trip to the lagoon, in order to take some fish. Not thinking it prudent to take my fusee with me, lest I might lose it overboard in case of a battle, which I had every reason to dread before my return, I therefore furnished myself with a club for my defence, went on board, and penetrating the first line of those which surrounded my harbour, they gave way; but being pursued by several very large ones, I kept strictly on the watch, and paddled with all my might towards the entrance of the lagoon, hoping to be sheltered there from the multitude of my assailants; but ere I had half–way reached the place, I was attacked on all sides, several endeavouring to overset the canoe. My situation now became precarious to the last degree: two very large ones attacked me closely, at the same instant, rushing up with their heads and part of their bodies above the water, roaring terribly and belching floods of water over me. They struck their jaws together so close to my ears, as almost to stun me, and I expected every moment to be dragged out of the boat and instantly devoured, but I applied my weapons so effectually about me, though at random, that I was so successful as to beat them off a little; when, finding that they designed to renew the battle, I made for the shore, as the only means left me for my preservation, for, by keeping close to it, I should have my enemies on one side of me only, whereas I was before surrounded by them, and there was a probability, if pushed to the last extremity, of saving myself, by jumping out of the canoe on shore, as it is easy to outwalk them on land, although comparatively as swift as lightning in the water. I found this last expedient alone could fully answer my expectations, for as soon as I gained the shore they drew off and kept aloof. This was a happy relief, as my confidence was, in some degree, recovered by it. On recollecting myself, I discovered that I had almost reached the entrance of the lagoon, and determined to venture in, if possible to take a few fish and then return to my harbour, while day–light continued; for I could now, with caution and resolution, make my way with safety along shore, and indeed there was no other way to regain my camp, without leaving my boat and making my retreat through the marshes and reeds, which, if I could even effect, would have been in a manner throwing myself away, for then there would have been no hopes of ever recovering my bark, and returning in safety to any settlements of men. I accordingly proceeded and made good my entrance into the lagoon, though not without opposition from the alligators, who formed a line across the entrance, but did not pursue me into it, nor was I molested by any there, though there were some very large ones in a cove at the upper end. I soon caught more trout than I had present occasion for, and the air was too hot and sultry to admit of their being kept for many hours, even though salted or barbecued. I now prepared for my return to camp, which I succeeded in with but little trouble, by keeping close to the shore, yet I was opposed upon re–entering the river out of the lagoon, and pursued near to my landing (though not closely attacked) particularly by an old daring one, about twelve feet in length, who kept close after me, and when I stepped on shore and turned about, in order to draw up my canoe, he rushed up near my feet and lay there for some time, looking me in the face, his head and shoulders out of water; I resolved he should pay for his temerity, and having a heavy load in my fusee, I ran to my camp, and returning with my piece, found him with his foot on the gunwale of the boat, in search of fish, on my coming up he withdrew sullenly and slowly into the water, but soon returned and placed himself in his former position, looking at me and seeming neither fearful or any way disturbed. I soon dispatched him by lodging the contents of my gun in his head, and then proceeded to cleanse and prepare my fish for supper, and accordingly took them out of the boat, laid them down on the sand close to the water, and began to scale them, when, raising my head, I saw before me, through the clear water, the head and shoulders of a very large alligator, moving slowly towards me; I instantly stepped back, when, with a sweep of his tail, he brushed off several of my fish. It was certainly most providential that I looked up at that instant, as the monster would probably, in less than a minute, have seized and dragged me into the river. This incredible boldness of the animal disturbed me greatly, supposing there could now be no reasonable safety for me during the night, but by keeping continually on the watch; I therefore, as soon as I had prepared the fish, proceeded to secure myself and effects in the best manner I could: in the first place, I hauled my bark upon the shore, almost clear out of the water, to prevent their oversetting or sinking her, after this every moveable was taken out and carried to my camp, which was but a few yards off; then ranging some dry wood in such order as was the most convenient, cleared the ground round about it, that there might be no impediment in my way, in case of an attack in the night, either from the water or the land; for I discovered by this time, that this small isthmus, from its remote situation and fruitfulness, was resorted to by bears and wolves. Having prepared myself in the best manner I could, I charged my gun and proceeded to reconnoitre my camp and the adjacent grounds; when I discovered that the peninsula and grove, at the distance of about two hundred yards from my encampment, on the land side, were invested by a Cypress swamp, covered with water, which below was jointed to the shore of the little lake, and above to the marshes surrounding the lagoon, so that I was confined to an islet exceedingly circumscribed, and I found there was no other retreat for me, in case of an attack, but by either ascending one of the large Oaks, or pushing off with my boat.

IT was by this time dusk; and the alligators had nearly ceased their roar, when I was again alarmed by a tumultuous noise that seemed to be in my harbour, and therefore engaged my immediate attention. Returning to my camp I found it undisturbed, and then continued on to the extreme point of the promontory, where I saw a scene, new and surprising, which at first threw my senses into such a tumult, that it was some time before I could comprehend what was the matter; however, I soon accounted for the prodigious assemblage of crocodiles at this place, which exceeded every thing of the kind I had ever heard of.

How shall I express myself so as to convey an adequate idea of it to the reader, and at the same time avoid raising suspicions of my want of veracity. Should I say, that the river (in this place) from shore to shore, and perhaps near half a mile above and below me, appeared to be one solid bank of fish, of various kinds, pushing through this narrow pass of St. Juans into the little lake, on their return down the river, and that the alligators were in such incredible numbers, and so close together from shore to shore, that it would have been easy to have walked across on their heads, had the animals been harmless. What expressions can sufficiently declare the shocking scene that for some minutes continued, whilst this mighty army of fish were forcing the pass? During this attempt, thousands, I may say hundreds of thousands of them were caught and swallowed by the devouring alligators. I have seen an alligator take up out of the water several great fish at a time, and just squeeze them betwixt his jaws, while the tails of the great trout flapped about his eyes and lips, ere he had swallowed them. The horrid noise of their closing jaws, their plunging amidst the broken banks of fish, and rising with their prey some feet upright above the water, the floods of water and blood rushing out of their mouths, and the clouds of vapour issuing from their wide nostrils, were truly frightful. This scene continued at intervals during the night, as the fish came to the pass. After this sight, shocking and tremendous as it was, I found myself somewhat easier and more reconciled to my situation, being convinced that their extraordinary assemblage here, was owing to this annual feast of fish, and that they were so well employed in their own element, that I had little occasion to fear their paying me a visit.

IT being now almost night, I returned to my camp, where I had left my fish broiling, and my kettle of rice stewing, and having with me, oil, pepper and salt, and excellent oranges hanging in abundance over my head (a valuable substitute for vinegar) I sat down and regaled myself chearfully; having finished my repast, I re–kindled my fire for light, and whilst I was revising the notes of my past day's journey, I was suddenly roused with a noise behind me toward the main land; I sprang up on my feet, and listning, I distinctly heard some creature wading in the water of the isthmus; I seized my gun and went cautiously from my camp, directing my steps towards the noise; when I had advanced about thirty yards, I halted behind a coppice of Orange trees, and soon perceived two very large bears, which had made their way through the water, and had landed in the grove, about one hundred yards distance from me, and were advancing towards me. I waited until they were within thirty yards of me, they there began to snuff and look towards my camp, I snapped my piece, but it flashed, on which they both turned about and galloped off, plunging through the water and swamp, never halting as I suppose, until they reached fast land, as I could hear them leaping and plunging a long time; they did not presume to return again, nor was I molested by any other creature, except being occasionally awakened by the whooping of owls, screaming of bitterns, or the wood–rats running amongst the leaves.

THE wood–rat is a very curious animal, they are not half the size of the domestic rat; of a dark brown or black colour; their tail slender and shorter in proportion, and covered thinly with short hair; they are singular with respect to their ingenuity and great labour in the construction of their habitations, which are conical pyramids about three or four feet high, constructed with dry branches, which they collect with great labour and perseverance, and pile up without any apparent order, yet they are so interwoven with one another, that it it would take a bear or wild–cat some time to pull one of these castles to pieces, and allow the animals sufficient time to secure a retreat with their young.

THE noise of the crocodiles kept me awake the greater part of the night, but when I arose in the morning, contrary to my expectations, there was perfect peace; very few of them to be seen, and those were asleep on the shore, yet I was not able to suppress my fears and apprehensions of being attacked by them in future; and indeed yesterday's combat with them, notwithstanding I came off in a manner victorious, or at least made a safe retreat, had left sufficient impression on my mind to damp my courage, and it seemed too much for one of my strength, being alone in a very small boat to encounter such collected danger. To pursue my voyage up the river, and be obliged every evening to pass such dangerous defiles, appeared to me as perilous as running the gauntlet betwixt two rows of Indians armed with knives and fire brands; I however resolved to continue my voyage one day longer, if I possibly could with safety, and then return down the river, should I find the like difficulties to oppose. Accordingly I got every thing on board, charged my gun, and set sail cautiously along shore; as I passed by Battle lagoon, I began to tremble and keep a good look out, when suddenly a huge alligator rushed out of the reeds, and with a tremendous roar, came up, and darted as swift as an arrow under my boat, emerging upright on my lea quarter, with open jaws, and belching water and smoke that fell upon me like rain in a hurricane; I laid soundly about his head with my club and beat him off, and after plunging and darting about my boat, he went off on a strait line through the water, seemingly with the rapidity of lightning, and entered the cape of the lagoon; I now employed my time to the very best advantage in padling close along shore, but could not forbear looking now and then behind me, and presently perceived one of them coming up again; the water of the river hereabouts, was shoal and very clear, the monster came up with the usual roar and menaces, and passed close by the side of my boat, when I could distinctly see a young brood of alligators to the number of one hundred or more, following after her in a long train, they kept close together in a column without straggling off to the one side or the other, the young appeared to be of an equal size, about fifteen inches in length, almost black, with pale yellow transverse waved clouds or blotches, much like rattle snakes in colour. I now lost sight of my enemy again.

STILL keeping close along shore; on turning a point or projection of the river bank, at once I beheld a great number of hillocks or small pyramids, resembling hay cocks, ranged like an encampment along the banks, they stood fifteen or twenty yards distant from the water, on a high marsh, about four feet perpendicular above the water; I knew them to be the nests of the crocodile, having had a description of them before, and now expected a furious and general attack, as I saw several large crocodiles swimming abreast of these buildings. these nests being so great a curiosity to me, I was determined at all events immediately to land and examine them. Accordingly I ran my bark on shore at one of their landing places, which was a sort of nick or little dock, from which ascended a sloping path or road up to the edge of the meadow, where their nests where, most of them were deserted, and the great thick whitish egg–shells lay broken and scattered upon the ground round about them.

THE nests or hillocks are of the form of an obtuse cone, four feet high and four or five feet in diameter at their bases; they are constructed with mud, grass and herbage: at first they lay a floor of this kind of tempered mortar on the ground, upon which they deposit a layer of eggs, and upon this a stratum of mortar seven or eight inches in thickness, and then another layer of eggs, and in this manner one stratum upon another, nearly to the top: I believe they commonly lay from one to two hundred eggs in a nest: these are hatched I suppose by the heat of the sun, and perhaps the vegetable substances mixed with the earth, being acted upon by the sun, may cause a small degree of fermentation, and so increase the heat in those hillocks. The ground for several acres about these nests shewed evident marks of a continual resort of alligators; the grass was every where beaten down, hardly a blade or straw was left standing; whereas, all about, at a distance, it was five or six feet high, and as thick as it could grow together. The female, as I imagine, carefully watches her own nest of eggs until they are all hatched, or perhaps while she is attending her own brood, she takes under her care and protection, as many as the can get at one time, either from her own particular nest or others: but certain it is, that the young are not left to shift for themselves, having had frequent opportunities of seeing the female alligator, leading about the shores her train of young ones, just like a hen does her brood of chickens, and she is equally assiduous and courageous in defending the young, which are under their care, and providing for their subsistence; and when the is basking upon the warm banks, with her brood around her, you may hear the young ones continually whining and barking, like young puppies. I believe but few of a brood live to the years of full growth and magnitude, as the old feed on the young as long as they can make prey of them.

THE alligator when full grown is a very large and terrible creature, and of prodigous strength, activity and swiftness in the water. I have seen them twenty feet in length, and some are supposed to be twenty–two or twenty–three feet; their body is as large as that of a horse; their shape exactly resembles that of a lizard, except their tail, which is flat or cuniform, being compressed on each side, and gradually diminishing from the abdomen to the extremity, which, with the whole body is covered with horny plates or squammae, impenetrable when on the body of the live animal, even to a rifle ball, except about their head and just behind their fore–legs or arms, where it is said they are only vulnerable. The head of a full grown one is about three feet, and the mouth opens nearly the fame length, the eyes are small in proportion and seem funk deep in the head, by means of the prominency of the brows; the nostrils are large, inflated and prominent on the top, so that the head in the water, resembles, at a distance, a great chunk of wood floating about. Only the upper jaw moves, which they raise almost perpendicular, so as to form a right angle with the lower one. In the fore part of the upper jaw, on each side, just under the nostrils, are two very large, thick, strong teeth or tusks, not very sharp, but rather the shape of a cone, these are as white as the finest polished ivory, and are not covered by any skin or lips, and always in sight, which gives the creature a frightful appearance; in the lower jaw are holes opposite to these teeth, to receive them; when they clap their jaws together it causes a surprising noise, like that which is made by forcing a heavy plank with violence upon the ground, and may be heard at a great distance.

BUT what is yet more surprising to a stranger, is the incredible loud and terrifying roar, which they are capable of making, especially in the spring season, their breeding time; it most resembles very heavy distant thunder, not only shaking the air and waters, but causing the earth to tremble; and when hundreds and thousands are roaring at the same time, you can scarcely be persuaded, but that the whole globe is violently and dangerously agitated.

AN old champion, who is perhaps absolute sovereign of a little lake or lagoon (when fifty less than himself are obliged to content themselves with swelling and roaring in little coves round about) darts forth from the reedy coverts all at once, on the surface of the waters, in a right line; at first seemingly as rapid as lightning, but gradually more slowly until he arrives at the center of the lake, when he stops; he now swells himself by drawing in wind and water through his mouth, which causes a loud sonorous rattling in the throat for near a minute, but it is immediately forced out again through his mouth and nostrils, with a loud noise, brandishing his tail in the air, and the vapour ascending from his nostrils like smoke. At other times, when swolen to an extent ready to burst, his head and tail lifted up, he spins or twirls round on the surface of the water. He acts his part like an Indian chief when rehearsing his feats of war, and then retiring, the exhibition is continued by others who dare to step forth, and strive to excel each other, to gain the attention of the favourite female.

HAVING gratified my curiosity at this general breeding place and nursery of crocodiles, I continued my voyage up the river without being greatly disturbed by them: in my way I observed islets or floating fields of the bright green Pistia, decorated with other amphibious plants, as Senecio Jacobea, Persicaria amphibia, Coreopsis bidens, Hydrocotile fluitans, and many others of less note.

THE swamps on the banks and island of the river, are generally three or four feet above the surface of the water, and very level; the timber large and growing thinly, more so than what is observed to be in the swamps below Lake George; the black, rich earth is covered with moderately tall, and very succulent tender grass, which when chewed is sweet and agreeable to the taste, some what like young sugarcane: it is a jointed decumbent grass, sending out radiculae at the joints into the earth, and so spreads itself, by creeping over its surface.

THE large timber trees, which possess the low lands, are Acer rubrum, Ac. nigundo, Ac. glaucum, Ulmus sylvatica, Fraxinus excelsior, Frax. aquatica, Ulmus suberifer, Gleditsia monosperma, Gledit. triacanthus, Diospyros Virginica, Nyssa aquatica, Nyssa sylvatica, Juglans cinerea, Quercus dentata, Quercus phillos, Hopea tinctoria, Corypha palma, Morus rubra, and many more. The Palm grows on the edges of the banks, where they are raised higher than the adjacent level ground, by the accumulation of sand, river–shells, &c. I passed along several miles by those rich swamps, the channels of the river which encircle the several fertile islands, I had passed, now uniting, formed one deep channel near three hundred yards over. The banks of the river on each sided, began to rise and present shelly bluffs, adorned by beautiful Orange groves, Laurels and Live Oaks. And now appeared in sight, a tree that claimed my whole attention: it was the Carica papaya, both male and female, which were in flower; and the latter both in flower and fruit, some of which were ripe, as large, and of the form of a pear, and of a most charming appearance.

THIS admirable tree, is certainly the most beautiful of any vegetable production I know of; the towering Laurel Magnolia, and exalted Palm, indeed exceed it in grandeur and magnificence, but not in elegance, delicacy and gracefulness; it rises erect, with a perfectly strait tapering them, to the height of fifteen or twenty feet, which is smooth and polished, of a bright ash colour, resembling leaf silver, curiously inscribed with the footsteps of the fallen leaves, and these vestiges, are placed in a very regular uniform imbricated order, which has a fine effect, as if the little column were elegantly carved all over. Its perfectly spherical top, is formed of very large lobe–sinuate leaves, supported on very long footstalks; the lower leaves are the largest as well as their petioles the longest, and make a graceful sweep or flourish, like the long *S* on the branches of a sconce candlestick. The ripe and green fruit are placed round about the stem or trunk, from the lowermost leaves, where the ripe fruit are, and upwards almost to the top; the heart or inmost pithy part of the trunks is in a manner hollow, or at best consists of very thin porous medullae or membranes; the tree very seldom branches or divides into limbs, I believe never unless the top is by accident broken off when very young: I saw one which had two tops or heads, the stem of which divided near the earth. It is always green, ornamented at the same time with flowers and fruit, which like figs come out singly from the trunk or stem.

AFTER resting and refreshing myself in these delightful shades, I left them with reluctance, embarking again after the fervid heats of the meridian sun were abated, for some time I passed by broken ridges of shelly high land, covered with groves of Live Oak, Palm, Olea Americana, and Orange trees; frequently observing floating islets and green fields of the Pistia near the shores of the river and lagoons.

HERE is in this river and in the waters all over Florida, a very curious and handsome bird, the people call them Snake Birds, I think I have seen paintings of them on the Chinese screens and other India pictures: they seeem to be a species of cormorant or loon (Colymbus cauda elongata) but far more beautiful and delicately formed than any other species that I have ever seen. The head and neck of this bird are extremely small and slender, the latter very long indeed, almost out of all proportion, the bill long, strait and slender, tapering from its ball to a sharp point, all the upper side, the abdomen and thighs, are as black and glossy as a raven's, covered with feathers so firm and elastic, that they in some degree resemble fish–scales, the breast and upper part of the belly are covered with feathers of a cream colour, the tail is very long, of a deep black, and tipped with a silvery white, and when spread, represent an unfurled fan. They delight to sit in little peaceable communities, on the dry limbs of trees, hanging over the still waters, with their wings and tails expanded, I suppose to cool and air themselves, when at the same time they behold their images in the watery mirror: at such times, when we approach them, they drop off the limbs into the water as if dead, and for a minute or two are not to be seen; when on a sudden at a vast distance, their long slender head and neck only appear, and have very

94

much the appearance of a snake, and no other part of them are to be seen when swimming in the water, except some the tip end of their tail. In the heat of the day they are seen in great numbers, sailing very high in the air, over lakes and rivers.

I DOUBT not but if this bird had been an inhabitant of the Tiber in Ovid's days, it would have furnished him with a subject, for some beautiful and entertaining metamorphoses. I believe they feed intirely on fish, for their flesh smells and tastes intolerably strong of it, it is scarcely to be eaten unless constrained by insufferable hunger.

I HAD now swamps and marshes on both sides of me, and evening coming on apace, I began to look out for high land to encamp on, but the extensive marshes seemed to have no bounds; and it was almost dark when I found a tolerable suitable place, and at last was constrained to take up on a narrow strip of high shelly bank, on the West side. Great numbers of crocodiles were in sight on both shores: I ran my bark on shore at a perpendicular bank four or five feet above the water, just by the roots and under the spreading limbs of a great Live Oak: this appeared to have been an ancient camping place by Indians and strolling adventurers, from ash heaps and old rotten fire brands, and chunks, scattered about on the surface of the ground; but was now evidently the harbour and landing place of some sovereign alligator: there led up from it a deep beaten path or road, and was a convenient ascent.

I DID not approve of my intended habitation from these circumstances; and no sooner had I landed and moored my canoe to the roots of the tree, than I saw a huge crocodile rising up from the bottom close by me, who, when he perceived that I saw him, plunged down again under my vessel; this determined me to be on my guard, and in time to provide against a troublesome night: I took out of my boat every moveable, which I carried upon the bank, then chose my lodging close to my canoe, under the spreading Oak; as hereabouts only, the ground was open and clear of high grass and bushes, and consequently I had some room to stir and look round about. I then proceeded to collect firewood which I found difficult to procure. Here were standing a few Orange trees. As for provisions, I had saved one or two barbecued trout; the remains of my last evenings collection in tolerable good order, though the sultry heats of the day had injured them; yet by stewing them up afresh with the lively juice of Oranges, they served well enough for my supper: having by this time but little relish or appetite for my victuals; for constant watching at night against the attacks of alligators, stinging of musquitoes and sultry heats of the day; together, with the fatigues of working my bark, had almost deprived me of every desire but that of ending my troubles as speedy as possible. I had the good fortune to collect together a sufficiency of dry sticks, to keep up a light and smoke, which I laid by me, and then spread my skins and blankets upon the ground, kindled up a little fire and supped before it was quite dark. The evening was however, extremely pleasant, a brisk cool breeze sprang up, and the skies were perfectly serene, the stars twinkling with uncommon briliancy. I stretched myself along before my fire; having the river, my little harbour and the stern of my vessel in view, and now through fatigue and weariness I fell asleep, but this happy temporary release from cares and troubles I enjoyed but a few moments, when I was awakened and greatly surprised, by the terrifying screams of Owls in the deep swamps around me, and what encreased my extreme misery was the difficulty of geting quite awake, and yet hearing at the same time such screaming and shouting, which increased and spread every way for miles around, in dreadful peals vibrating through the dark extensive forests, meadows and lakes, I could not after this surprise recover the former peaceable state and tranquility of mind and repose, during the long night, and I believe it was happy for me that I was awakened, for at that moment the crocodile was dashing my canoe against roots roots of the tree, endeavouring to get into her for the fish, which I however prevented. Another time in the night I believe I narrowly escaped being dragged into the river by him, for when again through excessive fatigue I had fallen asleep, but was again awakened by the screaming owl, I found the monster on the top of the bank, his head towards me not above two yards distant, when starting up and seizing my fuzee well loaded, which I always kept under my head in the night time, he drew back and plunged into the water. After this I roused up my fire, and kept a light during the remaining part of the night, being determined not to be caught napping so again, indeed the musquitoes alone would have been abundantly sufficient to keep any creature awake that possessed their perfect senses, but I was overcome, and stupified with incessant watching and labour: as soon as I discovered the first signs of day—light, I arose, got all my effects and implements on board and set sail, proceeding upwards, hoping to give the musquitoes the slip, who were now, by the cool morning dews and breezes, driven to their shelter and hiding places; I was mistaken however in these conjectures, for great numbers of them, which had concealed themselves in my boat, as soon as the sun arose, began to revive, and sting me on my legs, which obliged me to land in order to get bushes to beat them out of their quarters.

IT is very pleasing to observe the banks of the river ornamented with hanging garlands, composed of varieties of climbing vegetables, both shrubs and plants, forming perpendicular green walls, with projecting jambs, pilasters and deep apartments, twenty or thirty feet high and compleatly covered, with Glycine frutescens, Glyc. apios, Vitis labrusca, Vitis vulpina, Rajana, Hedera quinquifolia, Hedera arborea, Eupatorium scandens, Bignonia crucigera, and various species of Convolvulus, particularly an amazing tall climber of this genus, or perhaps an Ipomea. This has a very large white flower, as big as a small funnel, its tube is five or fix inches in length and not thicker than a pipe stem; the leaves are also very large, oblong and cordated, sometimes dentated or angled, near the insertion of the foot–stalk; they are of a thin texture, and of a deep green colour: it is exceedingly curious to behold the Wild Squash *

* Cucurbita peregrina.

climbing over the lofty limbs of the trees; their yellow fruit somewhat of the size and figure of a large orange, pendant from the extremities of the limbs over the water.

TOWARDS noon, the sultry heats being intolerable, I put into shore, at a midling high bank, five or fix feet above the surface of the river; this low sandy testaceous ridge along the river side was but narrow, the surface is light, black and exceedingly fertile, producing very large venerable Live Oaks, Palms and grand Magnolias, scatteringly planted by nature: there being no underwood to prevent the play of the breezes from the river, afforded a desirable retreat from the sun's heat: immediately back of this narrow ridge, was deep wet swamps, where stood some astonishingly tall and spreading Cypress trees; and now being weary and drowsy, I was induced to indulge and listen to the dictates of reason and invitations to repose, which consenting to, after securing my boat and reconnoitring the ground, I spread my blanket under the Oaks near my boat, on which I extended myself, where, falling to sleep, I instantaneously passed away the sultry hours of noon, what a blissful tranquil repose! undisturbed I awoke, refreshed and strengthened; I chearfully stepped on board again and continued to ascend the river. The afternoon being cool and pleasant, and the trees very lofty on the higher Western banks of the river, by keeping near that shore I passed under agreeable shades the remaining part of the day. During almost all this day's voyage, the banks of the river on both shores were midling high, perpendicular, and washed by the brisk current; the shores were not lined with the green lawns of floating aquatics, and consequently not very commodious resorts or harbours for crocodiles, I therefore was not disturbed by them, and saw but few, but those were very large. I however did not like to lodge on those narrow ridges, invested by such dreary swamps, and evening approaching, I began to be anxious for high land for a

97

camping place; it was quite dark before I came up to a bluff, which I had in view a long time, over a very extensive point of meadows. I landed however at last, in the best manner I could, at a magnificent forest of Orange groves, Oaks and Palms. I here, with little labour or difficulty, soon collected a sufficient quantity of dry wood: there was a pleasant vista of grass betwixt the grove and the edge of the river bank, which afforded a very convenient, open, airy camping place, under the protection of some spreading Oaks.

THIS was a high perpendicular bluff, fronting more than one hundred yards on the river, the earth black, loose and fertile, it is a composition of river–shells, sand, &c. back of it from the river, were open Pine forests and savannas. I met with a circumstance here, that, with some, may be reckoned worthy of mentioning, since it regards the monuments of the ancients; as I have already observed, when I landed it was quite dark, and in collecting wood for my fire, stroling in the dark about the groves, I found the surface of the ground very uneven, by means of little mounts and ridges; in the morning I found I had taken up my lodging on the border of an ancient burying ground; sepulchres or tumuli of the Yamasees, who were here slain by the Creeks in the last decisive battle, the Creeks having driven them into this point, between the doubling of the river, where few of them escaped the fury of the conquerors. These graves occupied the whole grove, consisting of two or three acres of ground; there were near thirty of these cemeteries of the dead, nearly of an equal size and form, they were oblong, twenty feet in length, ten or twelve feet in width and three or four feet high, now overgrown with Orange trees, Live Oaks, Laurel Magnolias, Red bays and other trees and shrubs, composing dark and solemn shades.

I HERE, for the first time since I left the trading house, enjoyed a night of peaceful repose; I arose, greatly refreshed and in good spirits, stepped on board my bark and continued my voyage. After doubling the point I passed by swamps and meadows on each side of me, The river here is something more contracted within perpendicular banks, the land of an excellent quality, fertile, and producing prodigiously large timber and luxuriant herbage.

THE air continued sultry and scarcely enough wind to flutter the leaves on the trees. The Eastern coast of the river now opens, and presents to view ample plains, consisting of grassy marshes and green meadows, and affords a prospect almost unlimited and extremely pleasing. The opposite shore presents to view a sublime contrast; a high bluff bearing magnificent forests of grand Magnolia, glorious Palms, fruitful Orange groves,

Travels Through North and South Carolina

Live Oaks, Bays and others. This grand elevation continues four or five hundred yards, discribing a gentle curve on the river, ornamented by a sublime grove of Palms, consisting of many hundreds of trees together; they intirely shade the ground under them. Above and below the bluff the grounds gradually descend to the common level swamps on the river: back of this eminence opens to view, expansive green meadows or savannas, in which are to be seen glittering ponds of water, surrounded at a great distance, by high open Pine forests and hommocks, and islets of Oaks and Bays projecting into the savannas. After ranging about these solitary groves and peaceful shades, I re–embarked and continued some miles up the river, between elevated banks of the swamps or low lands, when on the East shore in a capacious cove or winding of the river, were pleasing fields of Pistia, and in the bottom of this cove opened to view a large creek or branch of the river, which I knew to be the entrance to a beautiful lake, on the banks of which was the farm I was going to visit, and which I designed should be the last extent of my voyage up the river.

ABOUT noon the weather became extremely sultry, not a breath of wind stirring, hazy or cloudy, and very heavy distant thunder, which is answered by the crocodiles, sure presage of a storm!

SOON after ascending this branch of the river, on the right hand presents to view, a delightful little bluff, consisting chiefly of shells, and covered with a dark grove of Red Cedar, Zanthoxilon and Myrtle, I could not resist the temptation to stop here, although the tremendous thunder all around the hemisphere alarmed me greatly, having a large lake to cross. From this grove presents to view, an expansive and pleasing prospect. The beauteous long lake in front, about North East from me, its most distant East shores adorned with dark, high forests of stately trees; North and South almost endless green plains and meadows, embellished with islets and projecting promontories of high, dark forests, where the pyramidal Magnolia grandiflora, Palma elata and shady Oak conspicuously tower.

BEING heretofore so closely invested, by high forests and deep swamps of the great river, I was prevented from feeing the progress and increase of the approaching tempest, the terrific appearance of which now at once confounded me; how purple and fiery appeared the tumultious clouds! swiftly ascending or darting from the horizon upwards; they seemed to oppose and dash against each other, the skies appeared streaked with blood or purple flame overhead, the flaming lightning streaming and darting about in every direction around, seems to fill the world with fire; whilst the heavy thunder keeps the earth in a constant tremor. I had yet some hopes of crossing the lake to the plantation in sight. On the opposite shore of the creek before me, and on the cape as we enter the lake, stood a large islet or grove of Oaks and Palms, here I intended to seek shelter and abide till the fury of the hurricane was overpast, if I found it too violent to permit me to cross the lake; in consequence of this precipitate determination I stepped into my boat and pushed off, what a dreadful rushing and roaring there is every where around me; and to my utter confusion and astonishment I could not find from what particular quarter its strongest current or direction came, where by I might have a proper chance of taking measures of securing a harbour or running from it. The high forests behind me bend to the blast, and the sturdy limbs of the trees crack; I had by this time got up a breast of the grove or hommock, the hurricane close by, pursuing me, I found it dangerous and imprudent in the highest degree to put in here, as the groves were already torn up, and the spreading limbs of the ancient Live Oaks were flying over my head, and carried about in the air as leaves and stubble; I ran by and boldly entered the lake, (being hurried in by a strong current, which seemed a prodigy, the violent wind driving the stream of the creek back again into the lake) and as soon as possible took shelter under the high reedy bank of the lake, made fast my bark to the boughs of a low shrubby Hickory, that leaned over the water: such was the violence of the wind, that it raised the waters on the opposite shores of the lake several feet perpendicular, and there was a rapid flow of water from the creek into it, which was contrary to its natural course; such floods of rain fell during the space of half or three quarters of an hour that my boat was filled, and I expected every moment, when I should see her sink to the bottom of the lake; and the violence of the wind kept the cable so constantly extended, that it was beyond my ability to get to her; my box which contained my books of specimens and other collections, was floating about in her; and for a great part of the time the rain came down with such rapidity and fell in such quantities, that every object was totally obscured, excepting the continual streams or rivers of lightning, pouring from the clouds; all seemed a frightful chaos. When the wind and rain abated, I was overjoyed to see the face of nature again appear.

IT took me an hour or more to clear the water out of my bark. I then crossed the lake before a brisk and favourable breeze (it was about a mile over) and landed safely at the plantation.

WHEN I arrived my friend was affrighted to see me, and immediately enquired of me in what manner I came there, supposing it impossible (until I had shewed him my boat) that

I could have arrived by water, through so tremendous a hurricane.

INDEED I saw plainly that they were greatly terrified, having suffered almost irreparable damages from the violence of the storm; all the buildings on the plantation except his own dwelling–house, were laid almost flat to the ground, or the logs and roof rent asunder and twisted about; the mansion–house shook and reeled over their heads. He had nearly one hundred acres of the Indigo plant almost ripe for the first cutting, which was nearly ruined, and several acres of very promising Sugar–cane, totally spoiled for the season. The great Live Oaks which had been left standing about the fields, were torn to pieces, their limbs lying scattered over the ground: and one very large one which stood near his house torn down, which could not have been done by the united strength of a thousand men. But what is incredible, in the midst of this devastation and ruin, providentially no lives were lost, although there were about sixty Negro slaves on the plantation, and most of them in their huts when the storm came on, yet they escaped with their lives, though several were badly wounded.

I CONTINUED here three days, indeed it took most of the time of my abode with him, to dry my books and specimens of plants. But with attention and care I saved the greatest number of them; though some were naturally so delicate and fragile, that it was impossible to recover them. Here is a vast body of land belonging to this estate; of high ridges fit for the culture of Corn, Indigo, Cotton, Batatas, &c. and of low swamps and marshes, which when properly drained and tilled, would be suitable for Rice, these rich low grounds when drained and ridged, are as productive as the natural high land, and vastly more durable, especially for Sugar–cane, Corn and even Indigo; but this branch of agriculture being more expensive, these rich lands are neglected, and the upland only is under culture. The farm is situated on the East shore of the beautiful Long Lake, which is above two miles long, and near a mile broad, which communicates with the St. Juan, by the little river which I ascended; it is about one and an half mile in length, and thirty or forty yards wide; this river, as well as the lake, abounds with fish, and wild fowl of various kinds, and incredible numbers especially during the winter season, when the geese and ducks arrive here from the North.

NEW–SMYRNA,

* New–Smyrna is built on a high shelly bluff, on the West bank of the South branch of Mosquito river, about ten miles above the capes of that river, which is about thirty miles

Travels Through North and South Carolina

North of Cape Canaveral, Lat 28. I was there about ten years ago, when the surveyour run the lines or precincts of the colony, where there was neither habitation nor cleared field. It was then a famous Orange grove, the upper or South promontory of a ridge, nearly half a mile wide and stretching North about forty miles, to the head of the North branch of the Musquito, to where the Tomoko river unites with it, nearly parallel to the sea coast, and not above two miles across to the sea beach, All this ridge was then one entire Orange grove, with Live Oaks, Mangolias, Palms, Red Bays and others: I observed then, near where New–Smyrna now stands, a spacious Indian mount and avenue, which stood near the banks of the river; the avenue ran on a strait line back, through the groves, across the ridge, and terminated at the verge of natural savannas and ponds.

a pretty thriving town, is a colony of Greeks and Minorquies, established by Mr. Turnbull, on the Mosquito river and very near its mouth, is about thirty miles over land from this farm.

MY friend rode with me, about four miles distance from the house, to shew me a vast fountain of warm or rather hot mineral water, which issued from a high ridge or bank on the river in a great cove or bay, a few miles above the mouth of the creek which I ascended to the lake; it boils up with great force, forming immediately a vast circular bason, capacious enough for several shallops to ride in, and runs with rapidity into the river three or four hundred yards distance. This creek, which is formed instantly by this admirable fountain, is wide and deep enough for a sloop to sail up into the bason. The water is perfectly diaphanous, and here are continually a prodigious number and variety of fish; they appear as plain as though lying on a table before your eyes, although many feet deep in the water. This tepid water has a most disagreeable taste, brassy and vitriolic, and very offensive to the smell, much like bilge water or the washings of a gun–barrel, and is smelt at a great distance. A pale bluish or pearl coloured coagulum covers every inanimate substance that lies in the water, as logs, limbs of trees, &c. Alligators and gar were numerous in the bason, even at the apertures where the ebulition emerges through the rocks, as also many other tribes of fish. In the winter season several kinds of fish and aquatic animals migrate to these warm fountains. The forbiding taste and smell of these waters seem to be owing to vitriolic and sulphurious fumes or vapours, and these being condensed, form this coagulum, which represents flakes of pearly clouds in the clear cerulean waters in the bason. A charming Orange grove, with Magnolias, Oaks and Palms; half surrounded this vast fountain. A delightful stream of cool salubrious water issues from the ridge, meandering along and enters the creek just below the bason. I returned in the evening, and next day sat off again down the river.

MY hospitable friend, after supplying me with necessaries, prevailed on me to accept of the company and assistance of his purveyor, one day's voyage down the river, whom I was to set on shore at a certain bluff, upwards of twenty miles below, but not above one third that distance by land; he was to be out in the forests one day, on a hunt for turkeys.

THE current of the river being here confined within its perpendicular banks, ran briskly down; we chearfully descended the grand river St. Juan, enjoying enchanting prospects.

BEFORE night we reached the destined port, at a spacious range grove. Next morning we separated, and I proceeded down the river. The prospects on either hand are now pleasing and I view them at leisure, and without toil or dread.

INDUCED by the beautiful appearance of the green meadows, which open to the Eastward, I determined not to pass this Elisium without a visit. Behold the loud, sonorous, watchful savanna crane (grus pratensis) with musical clangor, in detached squadrons. They spread their light elastic sail; at first they move from the earth heavy and slow, they labour and beat the dense air; they form the line with wide extended wings, tip to tip, they all rise and fall together as one bird; now they mount aloft, gradually wheeling about, each squadron performs its evolution, incircling the expansive plains, observing each one their own orbit; then lowering sail, descend on the verge of some glittering lake; whilst other squadrons, ascending aloft in spiral circles, bound on interesting discoveries, wheel round and double the promontory, in the silvery regions of the clouded skies, where, far from the scope of eye, they carefully observe the verdant meadows on the borders of the East Lake; then contract their plumes and descend to the earth, where, resting awhile on some verdant eminence, near the flowery border of the lake, with dignified, yet flow, respectful steps, approach the kindred band; they confer and treat for habitation; the bounds an precincts being settled, they confederate and take possession.

THERE is inhabiting the low shores and swamps of this river and the lakes of Florida, as well as Georgia, a very curious bird, called by an Indian name (Ephouskyca)

* Tantalus pictus.

103

which signifies in our language the crying bird. I cannot determine what genus of European birds to join it with. It is about the size of a large domestic hen; all the body, above and beneath, is of a dark lead colour, every feather edged or tipped with white, which makes the bird appear speckled on a near view; the eye is large and placed high on the head, which is very prominent; the bill or beak is five or fix inches in length, arched or bent gradually downwards, in that respect to be compared to one half of a bent bow, it is large or thick near the base, compressed on each side, and flatted at top and beneath, which makes it appear four square for more than inch, where the nostrils are placed, from whence to their tips, both mandibles are round, gradually lessening or tapering to their extremities, which are thicker for about half an inch than immediately above, by which the mandibles never fit quite close their whole length; the upper mandible is small matter longer than the under; the bill is of a dusky green colour, more bright and yellowish about the base and angles of the mouth; the tail is very short and the middle feather the longest, the others on each side shorten gradually, and are of the colour of the rest of the bird, only somewhat darker; the two shortest or outermost feathers are perfectly white, which the bird has a faculty of flirting out on either side, as quick as a flash of lightning, especially when he hears or sees any thing that disturbs him, uttering at the same instant an extreme harsh and loud shriek; his neck is long and slender, and his legs are also long and bare of feathers above the knee, like those of the bittern, and are black or of a dark lead colour.

THERE are two other species of this genus, which agree in almost every particular, with the above description, except in size and colour: the first*

* Tantalus albus. Numinus albus Cat.

of these I shall mention is a perfect white, except the prime quill feathers, which are as black as those of a crow; the bill and legs of a beautiful clear red, as also a space clear of feathers about the eyes. The other species

** Tantalus versicolor. Numinus fuscus. Cat.

is black on the upper side, the breast and belly white, and the legs and beak as white as

104

snow; both these species are about half the size of the crying bird. They fly in large flocks or squadrons, evening and morning to and from their feeding places or roosts; both species are called Spanish curlews: these and the crying bird feed chiefly on cray fish, whose cells they probe, and with their strong pinching bills drag them out: all the three species are esteemed excellent food.

IT is a pleasing sight at times of high winds and heavy thunder storms, to observe the numerous squadrons of these Spanish curlews driving to and fro, turning and tacking about, high up in the air, when by their various evolutions in the different and opposite currents of the wind high in the clouds, their silvery white plumage gleams and sparkles like the brightest chrystal, reflecting the sun–beams that dart upon them between the dark clouds.

SINCE I have turned my observation upon the birds of this country, I shall notice another very singular one, which though already most curiously and exactly figured by Catesby, yet it seems to be nearly allied to those before mentioned, I mean the bird which he calls the wood pelican.*

* Tantalus loculator. Linn.

This is a large bird, perhaps near three feet high when standing erect. The bill is very long and strong, bending with a moderate curve, from the base to the tip, the upper mandible is the largst, and receives the edges of the nether one into it its whole length; the edges are very sharp and firm, the whole of a dark ash or horn colour; the forehead round the base of the beak, and side of the head is bare of feathers, and of a dark greenish colour, in which space is placed the eyes, which are very large; the remainder of the head and neck is of a nut brown colour; the back of a light bluish grey; upper part of the wings, breast and belly almost white, with some slight dashes of grey; the quill–feathers and tail, which are very short, are of a dark slate colour, almost black; the legs which are very long, and bare of feathers a great length above the knees, are of a dark dull greenish colour: they have a small bag or pouch under their throat: they feed on serpents, young alligators, frogs and other reptiles.

THIS solitary bird does not associate in flocks, but is generally seen alone; commonly near the banks of great rivers, in vast marshes or meadows; especially such as are caused by inundations, and also in the vast deserted Rice plantations; he stands alone on the topmost limb of tall dead Cypress trees, his neck contracted or drawn in upon his shoulders, and beak resting like a long scythe upon his breast: in this pensive posture and solitary situation, they look extremely grave, sorrowful and melancholy, as if in the deepest thought. They are never seen on the salt sea coast, and yet are never found at a great distance from it. I take this bird to be of a different genus from the tantalus, and perhaps approaches the nearest to the Egyptian ibis of any other bird yet known.

THERE are two species of vultures

* Vultur sacra.

in these regions I think not mentioned in history: the first we shall describe is a beautiful bird, near the size of a turkey buzzard

** Vultu aura.

but his wings are much shorter, and consequently, he falls greatly below that admirable bird in sail. I shall call this bird the painted vulture. The bill is long and strait almost to the point, when it is hooked or bent suddenly down and sharp; the head and neck bare of feathers nearly down to the stomach, when the feathers begin to cover the skin, and soon become long and of a soft texture, forming a ruff or tippet, in which the bird by contracting his neck can hide that as well as his head; the bare skin on the neck appears loose and wrinkled, which is of a deep bright yellow colour, intermixed with coral red; the hinder part of the neck is nearly covered with short, stiff hair; and the skin of this part of the neck is of a dun–purple colour, gradually becoming red as it approaches the yellow of the sides and forepart. The crown of the head is red; there are lobed lappets of a redish orange colour, which lay on the base of the upper mandible. But what is singular, a large portion of the stomach hangs down on the breast of the bird, in the likeness of a sack or half wallet, and seems to be a duplicature of the craw, which is naked and of a redish flesh colour, this is partly concealed by the feathers of the breast, unless when it is loaded with food, (which is commonly, I believe, roasted reptiles) and then it appears prominent. The plumage of the bird is generally white or cream colour, except the quill–feathers of the wings and two or three rows of the coverts, which are of a beautiful dark brown; the tail which is large and white is tipped with this dark brown or black; the legs and feet of a clear white; the eye is encircled with a gold coloured iris; the pupil black.

THE Creeks or Muscogulges construct their royal standard of the tail feather of this bird, which is called by a name signifying the eagle's tail; this they carry with them when they go to battle, but then it is painted with a zone of red within the brown tips; and in peaceable negociations it is displayed new, clean and white, this standard is held most sacred by them on all occasions; and is constructed and ornamented with great ingenuity. These birds seldom appear but when the deserts are set on fire (which happens almost every day throughout the year, in some part or other, by the Indians, for the purpose of rousing the game, as also by the lightning:) when they are seen at a distance soaring on the wing, gathering from every quarter, and gradually approaching the burnt plains, where they alight upon the ground yet smoking with hot embers; they gather up the roasted serpents, frogs and lizards; filling their sacks with them; at this time a person may shoot them at pleasure, they not being willing to quit the feast, and indeed seem to brave all danger.

THE other species may very properly be called the coped vulture, and is by the inhabitants called the carrion crow; as to bulk or weight, he is nearly equal to either of the others before mentioned. His wings are not long and sharp pointed, but broad and round at their extremities, having a clumsy appearance; the tail is remarkably short, which he spreads like a little fan, when on the wing; they have a heavy laborious flight, flapping their wings, then sail a little and then flap their wings again, and so on as if recovering themselves when falling; the beak is very long and strait, until it makes a sudden hook at the point, in the manner of the other vultures; the whole bird is of a sable or mourning colour; the head and neck down to the breast is bare of feathers, and the skin wrinkled, this unfeathered skin is of a deep livid purple, appearing black and thinly set with short black hair; he has a ruff or tippet of long soft feathers, like a collar bearing on his breast, in which he can conceal his neck and head at pleasure.

HAVING agreeably diverted away the intolerable heats of sultry noon in fruitful fragrant groves, with renewed vigour I again resume my sylvan pilgrimage. The afternoon and evening moderately warm, and exceeding pleasant views from the river and its varied shores. I passed by Battle lagoon and the bluff, without much opposition; but the crocodiles were already assembling in the pass. Before night I came to, at a charming Orange grove bluff, on the East side of the little lake, and after fixing my camp on a high open situation, and collecting a plenty of dry wood for fuel, I had time to get some fine trout for supper and joyfully return to my camp.

WHAT a most beautiful creature is this fish before me! gliding to and fro, and figuring in the still clear waters, with his orient attendants and associates: the yellow bream*

* Cyprinus coronarius.

or sun fish. It is about eight inches in length, nearly of the shape of the trout, but rather larger in proportion over the shoulders and breast; the mouth large, and the branchiostega opens wide; the whole fish is of a pale gold (or burnished brass) colour, darker on the back and upper sides; the scales are of a proportionable size, regularly placed, and every where variably powdered with red, russet, silver, blue and green specks, so laid on the scales as to appear like real dust or opaque bodies, each apparent particle being so projected by light and shade, and the various attitudes of the fish, as to deceive the sight; for in reality nothing can be of a more plain and polished surface than the scales and whole body of the fish; the fins are of an Orange colour; and like all the species of the bream, the ultimate angle of the branchiostega terminate by a little stula, the extreme end of which represents a crescent of the finest ultramarine blue, encircled with silver, and velvet black, like the eye in the feathers of a peacock's train; he is a fish of prodigious strength and activity in the water; a warrior in a gilded coat of mail, and gives no rest or quarters to small fish, which he preys upon; they are delicious food and in great abundance.

THE Orange grove, is but narrow, betwixt the the river banks and ancient Indian fields, where there are evident traces of the habitations of the ancients, surrounded whith groves of Live Oak, Laurel Magnolia, Zanthoxilon, Liquid–amber, and others.

How harmonious and soothing is this native sylvan music now at still evening! inexpressibly tender are the responsive cooings of the innocent dove, in the fragrant Zanthoxilon groves, and the variable and tuneful warblings of the nonparel; with the more sprightly and elevated strains of the blue linnet and golden icterus; this is indeed harmony even amidst the incessant croaking of the frogs; the shades of silent night are made more chearful, with the shrill voice of the whip–poor–will*

* Caprimulgus rufus called chuck–will's–widow, from a fancied resemblance of his notes to these words: they inhabit the maritime parts of Carolina and Florida, and are more than twice the size of the night hawk or whip–poor–will.

and active mock–bird.

My situation high and airy, a brisk and cool breeze steadily and incessantly passing over the clear waters of the lake, and fluttering over me through the srrounding groves, wings its way to the moon–light savannas, while I repose on my sweet and healthy couch of the soft Tillandsi ulnea–adscites, and the latter gloomy and still hours of night passed rapidly away as it were in a moment; I arose, strengthened and chearful, in the morning. Having some repairs to make in the tackle of my vessel, I paid my first attention to them; which being accomplished, my curiosity prompted me to penetrate the grove and view the illumined plains.

WHAT a beautiful display of vegetation is here before me! seemingly unlimited in extent and variety; how the dew–drops twinkle and play upon the fight, trembling on the tips of the lucid, green savanna, sparkling as the gem that flames on the turban of the Eastern prince; fee the pearly tears rolling off the buds of the expanding Granadilla

* Passiflora incarnata, called May–Apple.

behold the azure fields of cerulean Ixea! what can equal the rich golden flowers of the Canalutea, which ornament the banks of yon serpentine rivulet, meandering over the meadows; the almost endless varieties of the gay Phlox, that enamel the swelling green banks, associated with the purple Verbena corymbosa, Viola, pearly Gnaphalium, and silvery Perdicium; how fantastical looks the libertine Clitoria, mantling the shrubs, on the vistas skirting the groves. My morning excursion finished, I returned to the camp, breakfasted, then went on board my boat, and gently descended the noble river and passed by several openings of extensive plains and meadows, environing the East Lake, charming beyond compare; at evening I came to at a good harbour, under the high banks of the river, and rested during the night, amidst the fragrant groves, exposed to the constant breezes from the river: here I made ample collections of specimens and growing roots of curious vegetables, which kept me fully employed the greatest part of the day, and in the evening arrived at a charming spot on the East bank, which I had marked on my ascent up the river, where I made some addition to my collections, and the next day I employed myself in the same manner, putting into shore frequently, at convenient places, which I had noticed; and in the evening arrived again at the upper store, where I had the pleasure of finding my old friend, the trader, in good health and chearful, and his affairs in prosperous way. There were also a small party of Indians here, who had lately arrived with their hunts to purchase goods. I continued a few days at this post, searching its environs for curious vegetable productions, collecting seeds and planting growing roots in boxes, to be transported to the lower trading house.

Now, having procured necessaries to accommodate me on my voyage down to the lower store, I bid adieu to my old friend and benefactor, Mr. Job Wiggens, embarked alone on board my little fortunate vessel, and sat sail; I chose to follow the Eastermost channel of the river to the Great Lake, because it ran by high banks and bluffs of the Eastern main the greatest part of the distance, which afforded me an opportunity of observing a far greater variety of natural subject, than if I had taken the Western or middle channel, which flowed thro' swamps and marshes.

AT evening I arrived at Cedar Point, my former safe and pleasant harbour, at the East cape of the Great Lake, where I had noticed some curious shrubs and plants; here I rested, and on the smooth and gentle current launch again into the little ocean of Lake George, meaning now, on my return, to coast his Western shores in search of new beauties in the bounteous kingdom of Flora.

I WAS however induced to deviate a little from my intended course, and touch at the inchanting little Isle of Palms. This delightful spot, planted by nature, is almost an entire grove of Palms, with a few pyramidal Magnolias, Live Oaks, golden Orange, and the animating Zanthoxilon; what a beautiful retreat is here! blessed unviolated spot of earth! rising from the limpid waters of the lake; its fragrant groves and blooming lawns invested and protected by encircling ranks of the Yucca gloriosa; a fascinating atmosphere surrounds this blissful garden; the balmy Lantana, ambrosial Citra, perfumed Crinum, perspiring their mingled odours, wafted through Zanthoxilon groves. I at last broke away from the enchanting spot, and stepped on board my boat, hoisted sail and soon approached the coast of the main, at the cool eve of day; then traversing a capacious semicircular cove of the lake, verged by low, extensive grassy meadows, I at length by dusk made a safe harbour, in a little lagoon, on the sea shore or strands of a bold sandy point, which descended from the surf of the lake; this was a clean sandy beach, hard and firm by the beating surf when the wind sets from the East coast; I drew up my light vessel on the sloping shore, that she might be safe from the beating waves in case of a sudden storm of wind in the night. A few yards back the land was a little elevated, and overgrown with thickets of shrubs and low trees, consisting chiefly of Zanthoxilon, Olea Americana, Rhamus frangula, Sideroxilon, Morus, Ptelea, Halesia, Querci, Myrica cerifera and others; these groves were but low, yet sufficiently high to shelter me from the chilling dews; and being but a few yards distance from my vessel, here I fixed my encampment. A brisk wind arising from the lake, drove away the clouds of mosquitoes into the thickets. I now, with difficulty and industries, collected a sufficiency of dry wood to keep up a light during the night, and to roast some trout which I had caught when descending the river; their heads I stewed in the juice of Oranges, which, with boiled rice, afforded me a wholesome and delicious supper: I hung the remainder of my broiled fish on the snags of some shrubs over my head. I at last, after reconnoitring my habitation, returned, spread abroad my skin and blanket upon the clean sands by my fire side, and betook myself to repose.

How glorious the powerful sun, minister of the Most High, in the rule and government of this earth, leaves our hemisphere, retiring from our sight beyond the western forests! I behold with gratitude his departing smiles, tinging the fleecy roseate clouds, now riding far away on the Eastern horizon; behold they vanish from sight in the azure skies!

ALL now silent and peaceable, I suddenly fell asleep. At midnight I awake; when raising my head effect, I find myself alone in the wilderness of Florida, on the shores of Lake George. Alone indeed, but under the care of the Almighty, and protected by the invisible hand of my guardian angel.

WHEN quite awake, I started at the heavy tread of some animal, the dry limbs of trees upon the ground crack under his feet, the close shrubby thickets part and bend under him as he rushes off.

I REKINDLED up my sleepy fire, lay in contact the exfoliated smoking brands damp with the dew of heaven.

THE bright flame ascends and illuminates the ground and groves around me.

Travels Through North and South Carolina

WHEN looking up, I found my fish carried off, though I had thought them safe on the shrubs, just over my head, but their scent, carried to a great distance by the damp noctournal breezes, I suppose were too powerful attractions to resist.

PERHAPS it may not be time lost, to rest awhile here, and reflect on the unexpected and unaccountable incident, which however pointed out to me an extraordinary deliverance, or protection of my life, from the rapacious wolf that stole my fish from over my head.

HOW much easier and more eligible might it have been for him to have leaped upon my breast in the dead of sleep, and torn my throat, which would have instantly deprived me of life, and then glutted his stomach for the present with my warm blood, and dragged off my body, which would have made a feast afterwards for him and his howling associates; I say would not this have been a wiser step, than to have made protracted and circular approaches, and then after, by chance, espying the fish over my head, with the greatest caution and silence rear up, and take them off the snags one by one, then make off with them, and that so cunningly as not to awaken me until he had fairly accomplished his purpose.

THE morning being clear, I sat sail with a favourable breeze, coasting along the shores; when on a sudden the waters became transparent, and discovered the sandy bottom, and the several nations of fish, passing and repassing each other. Following this course I was led to the cape of the little river, descending from Six mile Springs, and meanders six miles from its source, through green meadows. I entered this pellucid stream, sailing over the heads of innumerable squadrons of fish, which, although many feet deep in the water, were distinctly to be seen; I passed by charming islets of flourishing trees, as Palm, Red Bay, Ash, Maple, Nussa and others. As I approached the distant high forest on the main, the river widens, floating fields of the green Pistia surrounded me, the rapid stream winding through them. What an alluring scene was now before me! A vast bason or little lake of chrystal waters, half encircled by swelling hills, clad with Orange and odoriferous Illisium groves. The towring Magnolia itself a grove, and the exalted Palm, as if conscious of their transcendent glories, tossed about their lofty heads, painting, with mutable shades, the green floating fields beneath. The social pratling coot enrobed in blue, and the squeeling water–hen, with wings half expanded, tripped after each other, over the watery mirror.

Travels Through North and South Carolina

I PUT in at an ancient landing place, which is a sloping ascent to a level grassy plain, an old Indian field. As I intended to make my most considerable collections at this place, I proceeded immediately to fix my encampment but a few yards from my safe harbour, where I securely fastened my boat to a Live Oak which overshadowed my port.

AFTER collecting a good quantity of fire–wood, as it was about the middle of the afternoon, I resolved to reconoiter the ground about my encampment: having penetrated the groves next to me, I came to the open forests, consisting of exceedingly tall strait Pines (Pinus Palustris) that stood at a considerable distance from each other, through which appeared at N. W. an almost unlimited plain of grassy savannas, embellished with a chain of shallow ponds, as far as the sight could reach. Here is a species of Magnolia that associates with the Gordonia lasianthus; it is a tall tree, sixty or eighty feet in heighth; the trunk strait; its head terminating in the form of a sharp cone; the leaves are oblong, lanciolate, of a fine deep green, and glaucous beneath; the flowers are large, perfectly white and extremely fragrant; with respect to its flowers and leaves, it differs very little from the Magnolia glauca. The silvery whiteness of the leaves of this tree, had a striking and pleasing effect on the sight, as it stood amidst the dark green of the Quercus dentata, Nyssa sylvatica, Nys. aquatica, Gordonia lasianthus and many others of the same hue. The tall aspiring Gordonia lasianthus, which now stood in my view in all its splendour, is every way deserving of our admiration. Its thick foliage, of a dark green colour, is flowered over with large milk–white fragrant blossoms, on long slender elastic peduncles, at the extremities of its numerous branches, from the bosom of the leaves, and renewed every morning; and that in such incredible profusion, that the tree appears silvered over with them, and the ground beneath covered with the fallen flowers. It at the same time continually pushes forth new twigs, with young buds on them; and in the winter and spring the third year's leaves, now partly concealed by the new and perfect ones, are gradually changing colour, from green to golden yellow, from that to a scarlet, from scarlet to crimson; and lastly to a brownish purple, and then fall to the ground. So that the Gordonia lasianthus may be said to change and renew its garments every morning throughout the year; and every day appears with unfading lustre. And moreover, after the general flowering is past, there is a thin succession of scattering blossoms to be seen, on some parts of the tree, almost every day throughout the remaining months, until the floral season returns again. Its natural situation, when growing, is on the edges of shallow ponds, or low wet grounds on rivers, in a sandy soil, the nearest to the water of any other tree, so that in drouthy seasons its long serpentine roots which run near or upon the surface of the earth, may reach into the water. When the tree has arrived to the period of

113

perfect magnitude, it is sixty, eighty or an hundred feet high, forming a pyramidal head. The wood of old trees when sawn into plank, is deservedly admired in cabinet–work or furniture; it has a cinnamon coloured ground, marbled and veined with many colours: the inner bark is used for dying a redish or sorrel colour; it imparts this colour to wool, cotton, linnen and dressed deer skins, and is highly esteemed by tanners.

THE Zamia pumila, the Erythryna corallodendrum and the Cactus opuntia grow here in great abundance and perfection. The first grows in the open pine forests, in tufts or clumps, a large conical strobile disclosing its large coral red fruit, which appears singularly beautiful amidst the deep green fern–like pinnated leaves.

THE Erythryna corallodendrum is six or eight feet high; its prickly limbs stride and wreathe about with singular freedom, and its spikes of crimson flowers have a fine effect amidst the delicate foliage.

THE Cactus opuntia is very tall, erect and large, and strong enough to bear the weight of a man: some are seven or eight feet high: the whole plant or tree seems to be formed of great oval compressed leaves or articulations; those near the earth continually encrease, magnify and indurate as the tree advances in years, and at length lose the bright green colour and glossy surface of their youth, acquiring a ligenous quality, with a whitish scabrous cortex: every part of the plant is nearly destitute of aculea, or those fascicles of barbed bristles which are in such plenty on the common dwarf Indian Fig. The cochineal insect were feeding on the leaves: the female of this insect is very large and fleshy, covered with a fine white silk or cottony web, which feels always moist or dewy, and seems designed by nature to protect them from the violent heat of the sun. The male is very small in comparison to the female, and but very few in number, they each have two oblong pelucid wings. The large polypetalus flowers are produced on the edges of the last years leaves, are of a fine splendid yellow, and are succeeded by very large pear shaped fruit, of a dark livid purple when ripe: its pulp is charged with a juice of a fine transparent crimson colour, and has a cool pleasant taste, somewhat like that of a pomegranate; soon after eating this fruit the urine becomes of the same crimson colour, which very much surprises and affrights a stranger, but is attended with no other ill consequence, on the contrary, it is esteemed wholesome, though powerfully diuretic.

ON the left hand of those open forests and savannas, as we turn our eyes Southward, South–west and West, we behold an endless wild desert, the upper stratum of the earth of which is a fine white sand, with small pebbles, and at some distance appears entirely covered with low trees and shrubs of various kinds, and of equal heighth, as dwarf Sweet Bay (Laurus Borbonia) Olea Americana, Morus rubra, Myrica cerifera, Ptelea, Æsculus pavia, Quercus Ilex, Q. glandifer, Q. maritima, foliis obcunciformibus obsolete tribobis minoribus, Q. pumila, Rhamnus frangula, Halesia diptera, & Tetraptera, Cassine, Ilex aquifolium, Callicarpa Johnsonia, Erythryna corallodendrum, Hibiscus spinifex, Zanthoxilon, Hopea tinctoria, Sideroxilum, with a multitude of other shrubs, many of which are new to me, and some of them admirably beautiful and singular. One of them particularly engaged my notice, which, from its fructification I take to be a species of Cacalia. It is an evergreen shrub, about six or eight feet high, the leaves are generally somewhat cuniform, fleshly and of a pale whitish green, both surfaces being covered with a hoary pubescence and vesiculae, that when pressed feels clammy, and emits an agreeable scent; the ascendent branches terminate with large tufts or corymbes of rose coloured flowers, of the same agreeable scent; these cluster of flowers, at a distance, look like a large Carnation or fringed Poppy flower (Syngenesia Polyg. Oqul. Linn.) Cacalia heterophylla, foliis cuniformibus, carnosis, papil. viscidis.

HERE is also another species of the same genus, but it does not grow quite so large; the leaves are smaller, of a yet duller green colour, and the flowers are of a pale rose; they are both valuable evergreens.

THE trees and shrubs which cover these extensive wilds, are about five or six feet high, and seem to be kept down by the annual firing of the desarts, rather than the barrenness of the soil, as I saw a few large Live Oaks, Mulberry trees and Hickories, which evidently have withstood the devouring flames. These adjoining wild plains, forests and savannas, are situated lower than the hilly groves on the banks of the lake and river, but what should be the natural cause of it I cannot even pretend to conjecture, unless one may suppose that those high hills, which we call bluffs, on the banks of this great river and its lakes, and which support those magnificent groves and high forests, and are generally composed of shell and sand, were thrown up to their present heighth by the winds and waves, when the bed of the river was nearer the level of the present surface of the earth; but then, to rest upon such a supposition, would be admitting that the waters were heretofore in greater quantities than at this time, or that their present channels and receptacles are worn deeper into the earth.

Travels Through North and South Carolina

I NOW directed my steps towards my encampment, in a different direction. I seated myself upon a swelling green knoll, at the head of the chrystal bason. Near me, on the left, was a point or projection of an entire grove of the aromatic Illisium Floridanum; on my right and all around behind me, was a fruitful Orange grove, with Palms and Magnolias interspersed in front, just under my feet was the inchanting and amazing chrystal fountain, which incessantly threw up, from dark, rocky caverns below, tons of water every minute, forming a bason, capacious enough for large shallops to ride in, and a creek of four or five feet depth of water, and near twenty yards over, which meanders six miles through green meadows, pouring its limpid waters into the great Lake George, where they seem to remain pure and unmixed. About twenty yards from the upper edge of the bason, and directly opposite to the mouth or outlet to the creek, is a continual and amazing ebullition, where the waters are thrown up in such abundance and amazing force, as to jet and swell up two or three feet above the common surface: white sand and small particles of shells are thrown up with the waters, near to the top, when they diverge from the center, subside with the expanding flood, and gently sink again, forming a large rim or funnel round about the aperture or mouth of the fountain, which is a vast perforation through a bed of rocks, the ragged points of which are projected out on every side. Thus far I know to be matter of real fact, and I have related it as near as I could conceive or express myself. But there are yet remaining scenes inexpressibly admirable and pleasing.

BEHOLD, for instance, a vast circular expanse before you, the waters of which are so extremely clear as to be absolutely diaphanous or transparent as the ether; the margin of the bason ornamented with a great variety of fruitful and floriferous trees, shrub and plants, the pendant golden Orange dancing on the surface of the pellucid waters, the balmy air vibrates the melody of the merry birds, tenants of the encircling aromatic grove.

AT the same instant innumerable bands of fish are seen, some cloathed in the most brilliant colours; the voracious crocodile stretched along at full length, as the great trunk of a tree in size, the devouring garfish, inimical trout, and all the varieties of gilded painted bream, the barbed catfish, dreaded sting-ray, skate and flounder, spotted bass, sheeps head and ominous drum; all in their seperate bands and communities, with free and unsuspicious intercourse performing their evolutions: there are no signs of enmity, no attempt to devour each other; the different bands seem peaceably and complaisantly to move a little aside, as it were to make room for others to pass by.

116

Travels Through North and South Carolina

BUT behold yet something far more admirable, see whole armies descending into an abyss, into the mouth of the bubbling fountain, they disappear! are they gone forever? is it real? I raise my eyes with terror and astonishment,—I look down again to the fountain with anxiety, when behold them as it were emerging from the blue ether of another world, apparently at a vast distance, at their first appearance, no bigger than flies or minnows, now gradually enlarging, their brilliant colours begin to paint the fluid.

Now they come forward rapidly, and instantly emerge, with the elastic expanding column of chrystaline waters, into the circular bason or funnel, see now how gently they rise, some upright, others obliquely, or seem to lay as it were on their sides, suffering themselves to be gently lifted or born up, by the expanding fluid towards the surface, sailing or floating like butterflies in the cerulean ether: then again they as gently descend, diverge and move off; when they rally, form again and rejoin their kindred tribes.

THIS amazing and delightful scene, though real, appears at first but as a piece of excellent painting; there seems no medium, you imagine the picture to be within a few inches of your eyes, and that you may without the least difficulty touch any one of the fish, or put your singer upon the crocodile's eye, when it really is twenty or thirty feet under water.

AND although this paradise of fish, may seem to exhibit a just representation of the peaceable and happy state of nature which existed before the fall, yet in reality it is a mere representation; for the nature of the fish is the same as if they were in lake George or the river; but here the water or element in which they live and move, is so perfectly clear and transparent, it places them all on an equality with regard to their ability to injure or escape from one another; (as all river fish of prey, or such as feed upon each other, as well as the unwieldy crocodile, take their prey by surprise; secreting themselves under covert or in ambush, until an opportunity offers, when they rush suddenly upon them:) but here is no covert, no ambush, here the trout freely passes by the very nose of the alligator and laughs in his face, and the bream by the trout.

BUT what is really surprising, that the consciousness of each others safety or some other latent cause, should so absolutely alter their conduct, for here is not the least attempt made to injure or disturb one another.

117

THE sun passing below the horizon, and night approaching, I arose from my seat, and proceeding on arrived at my camp, kindled my fire, supped and reposed peaceably. And rising early, employed the fore part of the day in collecting specimens of growing roots and seeds. In the afternoon, left these Ellisian springs and the aromatic graves, and briskly descend the pellucid little river, re–entering the great lake; the wind being gentle and fair for Mount Royal, I hoisted sail and successfully crossing the N. West bay, about nine miles, came to at Rocky Point, the West cape or promontory, as we enter the river descending towards Mount Royal: these are horizontal slabs or flat masses of rocks, rising out of the lake two or three feet above its surface, and seem an aggregate composition or concrete of sand, shells and calcarious cement; of a dark grey or dusky colour; this stone is hard and firm enough for buildings, and serve very well for light hand mill–stones; and when calcined affords a coarse lime; they lay in vast horizontal masses upon one another, from one to two or three feet in thickness, and are easily seperated and broke to any size or form, for the purpose of building. Rocky Point is an airy cool and delightful situation, commanding a most ample and pleasing prospect of the lake and its environs; but here being no wood, I re–embarked and sailed down a little farther to the island in the bay, where I went on shore at a magnificent grove of Magnolias and Oranges, desirous of augmenting my collections. Arose early next morning, and after ranging the groves and savannas, returned, embarked again, and descending, called at Mount Royal, where I enlarged my collections; and bidding adieu to the gentleman and lady, who resided here, and who treated me with great hospitality on my ascent up the river; arrived in the evening at the lower trading house.

CHAP. VI.

ON my return from my voyage to the upper store, I understood the trading company designed for Cuscowilla, that they had been very active in their preparations, and would be ready to set off in a few days; I therefore availed myself of the little time allowed me to secure and preserve my collections, against the arrival of the trading schooner, which was hourly expected, that every thing might be in readiness to be shipped on board her, in case she should load again and return for Savanna during my absence.

EVERY necessary being now in readiness, early on a fine morning we proceeded, attended by four men under the conduct of an old trader, whom Mr. M'Latche had delegated to treat with the Cowkeeper and other chiefs of Cuscowilla, on the subject of re–establishing the trade, &c. agreeable to the late treaty of St. Augustine.

FOR the first four or five miles we travelled West–ward, over a perfectly level plain, which appeared before and on each side of us, as a charming green meadow, thinly planted with low spreading Pine trees (P. palustri.) The upper stratum of the earth is a fine white chrystaline sand, the very upper surface of which being mixed or incorporated with the ashes of burnt vegetables, renders it of sufficient strength or fertility to clothe itself perfectly, with a very great variety of grasses, herbage and remarkably low shrubs, together with a very dwarf species of Palmetto (Corypha pumila stipit. serratis.) Of the low shrubs many were new to me and of a very pleasing appearance, particularly a species of Annona (Annona incarna, floribus grandioribus paniculatis;) this grows three, four or five feet high, the leaves somewhat cuniform or broad lanciolate, attenuating down to the petiole, of a pale or light green colour, covered with a pubescence or short fine down; the flowers very large, perfectly white and sweet scented, many connected together on large loose panicles or spikes; the fruit of the size and form of a small cucumber, the skin or exterior surface somewhat rimose or scabrous, containing a yellow pulp of the consistence of a hard custard, and very delicious, wholsome food. This seems a variety, if not the same that I first remarked, growing on the Alatamaha near Fort Barrington, Charlotia and many other places in Georgia and East–Florida; and I observed here in plenty, the very dwarf decumbent Annona, with narrow leaves, and various flowers already noticed at Alatamaha (Annona pigmea.) Here is also abundance of the beautiful little dwarf Kalmea ciliata, already described. The white berried Empetrum, a very pretty evergreen, grows here on somewhat higher and drier knolls, in large patches or clumps, associated with Olea Americana, several species of dwarf Querci (Oaks) Vaccinium, Gordonia lasianthus, Andromeda ferruginia and a very curious and beautiful shrub which seems allied to the Rhododendron, Cassine, Rhamnus frangula, Andromeda nitida, &c. which being of dark green foliage, diversifies and enlivens the landscape; but what appears very extraordinary, is to behold here, depressed and degraded, the glorious pyramidal Magnolia grandiflora, associated amongst these vile dwarfs, and even some of them rising above it though not five feet high; yet still shewing large, beautiful and expansive white fragrant blossoms, and great heavy cones on slender procumbent branches, some even lying on the earth; the ravages of fire keep them down, as is evident from the vast excrescent tuberous roots, covering several feet of ground, from which these slender shoots spring.

119

Travels Through North and South Carolina

In such clumps and coverts are to be seen several kinds of birds, particularly a species of jay; they are generally of an azure blue colour, have no crest or tuft of feathers on the head, nor are they so large as the great crested blue jay of Virginia, but are equally clamorous (pica glandaria cerulea non crestata.) The towee bird (fringilla erythrophthalma) are very numerous, as are a species of bluish grey butcher bird (lanius.) Here were also lizards and snakes. The lizards were of that species called in Carolina, scorpions: they are from five to six inches in length, of a slender form; the tail in particular is very long and small; they are of a yellowish clay colour, varied with longitudinal lines or stripes of a dusky brown colour, from head to tail; they are wholly covered with very small squamae, vibrate their tail, and dart forth and brandish their forked tongue after the manner of serpents, when they are surprised or in pursuit of their prey, which are scarabei, locustae, musci, and other insects, but I do not learn that their bite is poisonous, yet I have observed cats to be sick soon after eating them. After passing over this extensive level, hard, wet savanna, we crossed a fine brook or rivulet; the water cool and pleasant; its banks adorned with varieties of trees and shrubs, particularly the delicate Cyrilla racemifiora, Chionanthus, Clethra, Nyssa sylvatica, Andromeda nitida, Andromeda formosissima: and here were great quantities of a very large and beautiful Filex osmunda, growing in great tufts or clumps. After leaving the rivulet we passed over a wet, hard, level glade or down, covered with a fine short grass, with abundance of low saw Palmetto, and a few shrubby Pine trees, Quercus nigra, Quercus sinuata or scarlet Oak: then the path descends to a wet bay–gale; the ground a hard, fine white sand, covered with black slush, which continued above two miles, when it gently rises the higher sand hills, and directly after passes through a fine grove of young long leaved Pines. The soil seemed here, loose, brown, coarse, sandy loam, though fertile. The ascent of the hill, ornamented with a variety and profusion of herbacious plants and grasses, particularly Amaryllis atamasco, Clitoria, Phlox, Ipomea, Convolvulus, Verbena corymbosa, Rucllia, Viola, &c. A magnificent grove of stately Pines, succeeding to the expansive wild plains we had a long time traversed, had a pleasing effect, rousing the faculties of the mind, awakening the imagination by its sublimity, and arresting every active inquisitive idea, by the variety of the scenery and the solemn symphony of the steady Western breezes, playing incessantly, rising and falling through the thick and wavy foliage.

THE Pine groves passed, we immediately find ourselves on the entrance of the expansive airy Pine forests, on parallel chains of low swelling mounds, called the Sand Hills, their ascent so easy, as to be almost imperceptible to the progressive traveller, yet at a distant view, before us in some degree exhibit the appearance of the mountainous swell of the ocean immediately after a tempest; but yet, as we approach them, they insensibly disappear, and seem to be lost, and we should be ready to conclude all to be a visionary scene, were it not for the sparkling ponds and lakes, which at the same time gleam through the open forests, before us and on every side, retaining them on the eye, until we come up with them; and at last the imagination remains flattered and dubious, by their uniformity, being mostly circular or eliptical, and almost surrounded with expansive green meadows; and always a picturesque dark grove of Live Oak, Magnolia, Gordonia and the fragrant Orange, encircling a rocky shaded grotto, of transparent water, on some border of the pond or lake; which, without the aid of any poetic fable, one might naturally suppose to be the sacred abode or temporary residence of the guardian spirit but is actually the possession and retreat of a thundering absolute crocodile.

ARRIVED early in the evening at the Halfway pond, where we encamped and stayed all night. This lake spreads itself in a spacious meadow, beneath a chain of elevated sand hills, the sheet of water at this time was about three miles in circumference; the upper end, and just under the hills, are surrounded by a crescent of dark groves, which shaded a rocky grotto. Near this place, was a sloping green bank, terminating by a point of flat rocks, which shaded into the lake, and formed one point of the crescent that partly surrounded the vast grotto or bason of transparent waters, which is called by the traders a sink-hole, a singular kind of vortex or conduit, to the subteranean receptacles of the waters; but though the waters of these ponds in the summer and dry seasons, evidently tend towards these sinks, yet it is so slow and gradual, as to be almost imperceptible. There is always a meandering channel winding through the savannas or meadows, which receives the waters spread over them, by several lateral smaller branches, slowly conveying them along into the lake, and finally into the bason, and with them nations of the finny tribes.

JUST by the little cape of flat rocks, we fixed our encampment, where I enjoyed a comprehensive and varied scene, the verdant meadows spread abroad, charmingly decorated by green points of grassy lawns and dark promontories of wood-land, projecting into the green plains.

BEHOLD now at still evening, the sun yet streaking the embroidered savannas, armies of fish pursuing their pilgrimage to the grand pellucid fountain, and when here arrived, all quiet and peaceable, encircle the little cerulean hemisphere, descend into the dark caverns of the earth; where probably they are separated from each other, by innumerable paths, or secret rocky avenues; and after encountering various obstacles, and beholding new and unthought of scenes of pleasure and disgust, after many days absence from the surface of the world, emerge again from the dreary vaults, and appear exulting in gladness, and sporting in the transparent waters of some far distant lake.

THE various kinds of fish and amphibious animals, that inhabit these inland lakes and waters, may be mentioned here, as many of them here assembled, pass and repass in the lucid grotto: first the crocodile alligator; great brown spotted garr, accoutred in an impenetrable coat of mail; this admirable animal may be termed a cannibal amongst fish, as fish are his prey; when fully grown he is from five to six feet in length, and of proportionable thickness, of a dusky brown colour, spotted with black. The Indians make use of their sharp teeth to scratch or bleed themselves with, and their pointed scales to arm their arrows. This fish is sometimes eaten, and to prepare them for food, they cover them whole in hot embers, where they bake them, the skin with the scales easily peel off, leaving the meat white and tender.

THE mud fish is large, thick or round, but two feet in length; his meat white and tender, but soft and tastes of the mud, and is not much esteemed. The great devouring trout and catfish are in abundance; the golden bream or sunfish, the red bellied bream, the silver or white bream, the great yellow and great black or blue bream, also abound here. The last of these mentioned, is a large, beautiful and delicious fish; when full grown they are nine inches in length, and five to six inches in breadth; the whole body is of a dull blue or Indigo colour, marked with transverse lists or zones of a darker colour, scatteringly powdered with sky blue, gold and red specks; fins and tail of a dark purple or livid flesh colour; the ultimate angel of the branchiostega forming a spatula, the extreme end of which is broad and circular, terminating like the feather of the peacock's train, and having a brilliant spot or eye like it, being delicately painted with a fringed border of a fire colour.

The great yellow or particoloured bream is in form and proportion much like the forementioned, but larger, from a foot to fifteen inches in length; the upper part of his body (i.e.) his back from head to tail, is of a dark clay and dusky colour, with transverse dashes or blotches, of redish dull purple, or bluish, according to different exposures to light; the sides and belly of a bright pale yellow, the belly faintly stained with vermillion red, insensibly blended with the yellow on the sides, and all garnished with fiery, blue, green, gold and silver specks on the scales; the branchiostega is of a yellowish clay or straw colour, the lower edge or border next the opening of the gills, is near a quarter of an inch in breadth, of a sea green or marine blue, the ulterior angle protends backwards to a considerable length, in the form of a spatula or feather, the extreme end dilated and circular, of a deep black or crow colour, reflecting green and blue, and bordered round with fiery red, somewhat like red sealing wax, representing a brilliant ruby on the side of the fish; the fins redish, edged with a dove colour: they are deservedly esteemed a most excellent fish.

HERE are, as well as in all the rivers, lakes and ponds of East Florida, the great soft shelled tortoise

* Testudo naso cylindracea elongato, truncato.

they are very large when full grown, from twenty to thirty and forty pounds weight, extremely fat and delicious, but if eaten to excess, are apt to purge people not accustomed to eat their meat.

THEY are flat and very thin; two feet and a half in length, and eighteen inches in breadth across the back; in form, appearance and texture, very much resembling the sea turtle: the whole back shell, except the vertebrae or ridge, which is not at all prominent, and ribs on each side, is soft or cartilaginous, and easily reduced to a jelly when boiled; the anterior and posterior extremities of the back shell, appear to be embossed with round, horny warts or tubercles, the belly or nether shell is but small and semicartilagenous, except a narrow cross bar connecting it at each end with the back shell, which is hard and osseous; the head is large and clubbed, of nearly an oval form, the upper mandible, however, is protended forward, and truncated, somewhat resembling a swine's snout, at the extreme end of which the nostrils are placed; on each side of the root or base of this proboscis are the eyes, which are large; the upper beak is hooked and sharp, like a hawk's bill; the lips and corners of the mouth large, tumid, wrinkled and barbed with long, pointed warts, which he can project and contract at pleasure, which gives the creature a frightful and disagreeable countenance. They bury themselves in the slushy bottoms of rivers and ponds, under the roots of flags and other aquatic herbage, leaving a hole or aperture just sufficient for their head to play through; in such places they withdraw themselves when hungry, and there seize their prey by surprise, darting out their heads as quick as lightning, upon the unwary animal that unfortunately strolls within their reach: they can extend their neck to a surprising length, which enables them to seize young fowl swimming on the surface of the water above them, which they instantly drag down. They are seen to raise their heads above the surface of the water, in the depths of the lakes and rivers, and blow, causing a faint puffing noise, somewhat like a porpoise; probably this is for pastime, or to charge themselves with a proper supply of fresh air. They are carnivorous, feeding on any animal they can seize, particularly young ducks, frogs and fish.

WE had a large and fat one served up for our supper, which I at first apprehended we had made a very extravagant waste of, not being able to consume one half of its flesh, though excellently well cooked; my companions however seemed regardless, being in the midst of plenty and variety, at any time within our reach, and to be obtained with little or no trouble or fatigue on our part; when herds of deer were feeding in the green meadows before us; flocks of turkeys, walking in the groves around us, and myriads of fish, of the greatest variety and delicacy, sporting in the chrystaline floods before our eyes.

The vultures and ravens, crouched on the crooked limbs of the lofty Pines, at a little distance from us, sharpening their beaks, in low debate, waiting to regale themselves on the offals, after our departure from camp.

AT the return of the morning, by the powerful influence of light; the pulse of nature becomes more active, and the universal vibration of life insensibly and irresistibly moves the wondrous machine: how chearful and gay all nature appears. Hark! the musical savanna cranes, ere the chirping sparrow flirts from his grassy couch, or the glorious sun gilds the tops of the Pines, spread their expansive wings, leave their lofty roosts, and repair to the ample plains.

FROM Half-way pond, we proceed Westward, through the high forests of Cuscowilla.

THE appearance of the earth for five or six miles, presented nearly the same scenes as heretofore.

Now the sand ridges become higher, and their bases proportionably more extensive; the savannas and ponds more expansive; the summit of the ridges more gravelly; here and there, heaps or piles of rocks, emerging out of the sand and gravel: these rocks are the same sort of concrete of sand and shells as noticed on St. Juans and the great lake. The vegetable productions nearly the same as already mentioned.

WE gently descend again over sand ridges, cross a rapid brook, ripling over the gravelly bed, hurrying the transparent waters into a vast and beautiful lake, through a fine fruitful Orange grove; which magnificently adorns the banks of the lake to a great distance on each side of the capes of the creek. This is a fine situation for a capital town. These waters are tributary to St. Juan's.

We alighted to refresh ourselves, and adjust our packs. Here are evident signs and traces of a powerful settlement of the ancients.

Sat off again, and continued travelling over a magnificent Pine forest, the ridges low, but their bases extensive, with proportionable plains. The steady breezes gently and continually rising and falling, fill the high lonesome forests with an awful reverential harmony, inexpressibly sublime, and not to be enjoyed any where, but in these native wild Indian regions.

crossing another large deep creek of St. Juan's, the country is a vast level plain, and the soil good for the distance of four or five miles, though light and sandy, producing a forest of stately Pines and laurels, with some others; and a vast profusion of herbage, such as Rudbeckia, Helianthus, Silphium, Polymnia, Ruellia, Verbena, Rhexea, Convolvus, Sophora, Glycine, Vitia, Clitorea, Ipomea, Urtica, Salvia graviolens, Viola and many more. How chearful and social is the rural converse of the various tribes of tree frogs, whilst they look to heaven for prolific showers!

How harmonious the shrill tuneful songs of the wood thrush, and the soothing love lays of the amorous cuckoo! * Cuculus Caroliniensis.

seated in the cool leafy branches of the stately Magnolias and shadowy Elms, Maples and Liquid–amber, together with gigantic Fagus sylvatica, which shade and perfume these sequestered groves. How unexpected and enchanting the enjoyment, after traversing a burning sandy desert!

Travels Through North and South Carolina

Now again we behold the open Pine forests, and rise the sandy hills, which continue for some miles, then gently descend again, when a level expansive savanna plain presents to view, which, after entering, and proceeding on, became wet, and covered by a fine short grass, with extensive parterres of the dwarf creeping Palmetto, their stipes sharply toothed or serrated together with clumps of low shrubs, as Kalmia, Andromeda, Annona pygmea, Myrica cerifera, Empetrum, Vaccinium and others.

WE now rise a little again, and pass through a narrow Pine forest, when suddenly opens to view, a vastly extensive and sedgy marsh, expanding Southerly like an open fan, seemingly as boundless as the great ocean: our road crossed the head of it, about three hundred yards over; the bottom here, was hard sand, a foot or more under a soft muddy surface: the traders informed me that these vast marshes lay on the borders of a great lake, many miles in length, in magnitude exceeding Lake George, and communicates with St. Juan's by a river*

* Ockli–Waha Great.

its confluence above the lower store at the Little Lake.

OBSERVED as we passed over the sand hills, the dens of the great land tortoise, called gopher: this strange creature remains yet undescribed by historians and travellers. The first signs of this animal's existence, as we travel Southerly, are immediately after we cross the Savanna River. They are to be seen only on the high dry sand hills. When arrived to their greatest magnitude, the upper shell is near eighteen inches in length, and ten or twelve inches in breadth; the back is very high, and the shell of a very hard bony substance, consisting of many regular compartments, united by sutures, in the manner of the other species of tortoise, and covered with thin horny plates. The nether or belly shell is large, and regularly divided transversely, into five parts: these compartments are not knit together like the futures of the skull, or the back shell of the tortoise, but adhere, or are connected together by a very ridgy horny cartilage, which serves as hinges for him to shut up his body within his shell at pleasure. The fore part of the belly shell towards its extremity, is formed somewhat like a spade, extends forward near three inches, and is about an inch and an half in breadth; its extremity is a little bifid, the posterior division of the belly shell, is likewise protended backwards considerably, and is deeply bifurcated.

126

Travels Through North and South Carolina

THE legs and feet are covered with flat horny squamea; he seems to have no clefts in them or toes, but long flattish nails or talons, somewhat in resemblance to the nails of the human fingers, five on the fore feet; the hind legs or feet appear as if truncated, or as stumps of feet, armed all round with sharp, flattish strong nails, the number undetermined or irregular; the head is of a moderate size, the upper mandible a little hooked, the edges hard and sharp; the eyes are large; the nose picked; the nostrils near together and very minute; the general colour of the animal is a light ash or clay, and at a distance, unless he is in motion, any one would disregard or overlook it as a stone or an old stump. It is astonishing what a weight one of these creatures will bear; it will easily carry any man standing on its back, on level ground. They form great and deep dens in the sand hills, casting out incredible quantities of earth. They are esteemed excellent food; the eggs are larger than a musket ball, perfectly round and the shell hard.

AFTER crossing over this point or branch of the marshes, we entered a noble forest, the land level, and the soil fertile, being a loose, dark brown, coarse sandy loam, on a clay or marley foundation; the forests were Orange groves, overtoped by grand Magnolias, Palms, Live Oaks, Juglans cinerea, Morus rubra, Fagus sylvatica, Telia and Liquid–amber, with various kinds of shrubs and herbacious plants, particularly Callicarpa, Halesia, Sambucus, Zanthoxilon, Ptelea, Rhamnus frangula, Rudbeckia, Silphium, Polymnia, Indigo fera, Sophora, Salvia graviolens, &c. We were chearfully received in this hospitable shade, by various tribes of birds, their sprightly songs seemed a prelude to the vicinity of human habitations. This magnificent grove was a wing of the vast forests lying upon the coast of the great and beautiful lake of Cuscowilla, at no great distance from us. Continuing eight or nine miles through this sublime forest, we entered on an open forest of lofty Pines and Oaks, on gently swelling sand hills, and presently saw the lake, its waters sparkling through the open groves. Near the path was a large artificial mound of earth, on a most charming, high situation, supposed to be the work of the ancient Floridans or Yamasees, with other traces of an Indian town; here were three or four Indian habitations, the women and children saluted us with chearfulness and complaisance. After riding near a mile farther we arrived at Cuscowilla, near the banks: a pretty brook of water ran through the town, and entered the lake just by.

WE were welcomed to the town, and conducted by the young men and maidens to the chief's house, which stood on an eminence, and was distinguished from the rest by its superior magnitude, a large flag being hoisted on a high staff at one corner. We immediately alighted; the chief, who is called the Cowkeeper, attended by several ancient

127

men, came to us, and in a very free and sociable manner, shook our hands (or rather arms) a form of salutation peculiar to the American Indians, saying at the same time, "You are come." We followed him to an apartment prepared for the reception of their guests.

THE pipe being filled, it is handed around, after which a large bowl, with what they call "Thin drink," is brought in and set down on a small low table; in this bowl is a great wooden ladle; each person takes up in it as much as he pleases, and after drinking until satisfied, returns it again into the bowl, pushing the handle towards the person in the circle, and so it goes round.

AFTER the usual compliments and enquiries relative to our adventures, &c. the chief trader informed the Cowkeeper; in the presence of his council or attendants, the purport of our business, with which he expressed his satisfaction. He was then informed what the nature of my errand was, and he received me with complaisance; giving me unlimited permission to travel over the country for the purpose of collecting flowers, medicinal plants, &c. saluting me by the name of PUC PUGGY or the Flower hunter, recommending me to the friendship and protection of his people.

THE next day being agreed on to hold a council and transact the business of our embassy, we acquainted the chief with our intention of making our encampment on the borders of the great ALACHUA SAVANNA, and to return at the time appointed to town, to attend the council according to agreement.

SOON after we had fixed on the time and manner of proceeding on the further settlement of the treaty, a considerable number of Indians assembled around their chief, when the conversation turned to common and familiar topics.

THE chief is a tall well made man, very affable and cheerful, about sixty years of age, his eyes lively and full of fire, his countenance manly and placid, yet ferocious, or what we call savage; his nose aquiline, his dress extremely simple, but his head trimmed and ornamented in the true Creek mode. He has been a great warrior, having then attending him as slaves, many Yamasee captives, taken by himself when young. They were dressed better then he, served and waited upon him with signs of the most abject fear. The manners and customs of the Alachuas, and most of the lower Creeks or Siminoles, appear evidently tinctured with Spanish civilization. Their religious and civil usages manifest a predilection for the Spanish customs. There are several Christians among them, many of whom wear little silver crucifixes, affixed to a wampum collar round their necks, or suspended by a small chain upon their breast. These are said to be baptized, and notwithstanding most of them speak and understand Spanish, yet they have been the most bitter and formidable Indian enemies the Spaniards ever had. The slaves, both male and female, are permitted to marry amongst them: their children are free, and considered in every respect equal to themselves, but the parents continue in a state of slavery as long as they live.

IN observing these slaves, we behold at once, in their countenance and manners, the striking contrast betwixt a state of freedom and slavery. They are the tamest, the most abject creatures that we can possibly imagine: mild, peaceable and tractable, they seem to have no will or power to act but as directed by their masters; whilst the free Indians, on the contrary, are bold, active and clamorous. They differ as widely from each other as the bull from the ox.

THE repast is now brought in, consisting of venison, stewed with bear's oil, fresh corn cakes, milk and homony, and our drink honey and water, very cool and agreeable. After partaking of this banquet, we took leave and departed for the great savanna.

WE soon entered a level, grassy plain, interspersed with low, spreading, three leaved Pine trees, large patches of low shrubs, consisting of Prinos glaber, low Myrica, Kalmia glauca, Andromedas of several species, and many other shrubs, with patches of Palmetto. We continued travelling through this savanna or bay–gale, near two miles, when the land ascends a little; we then entered a hommock or dark grove, consisting of various kinds of trees, as the Magnolia grandiflora, Corypha palma, Citrus Aurantium, Quercus sempervirens, Morus rubra, Ulmus sylvatica, Tilia, Juglans cinerea, Æsculus pavia, Liquid–amber, Laurus Borbonia, Hopea tinctoria, Cercis, Cornus Florida, Halesia diptera, Halesia tetraptera, Olea Americana, Callicarpa, Andromeda arborea, Sideroxilon sericium, Sid. tenax, Vitis labrusca, Hedera arborea, Hedera quinquifolia, Rhamnus volubilis, Prunus Caroliniana (pr. flor. racemosis, foliis sempervirentibus, lato–lanceolatis, accumunatis, serratis) Fagus sylvatica, Zanthoxilon clava Herculis, Acer rubrum, Acer negundo, Fraxinus excelsior, with many others already mentioned. The land still gently rising, the soil fertile, loose, loamy and of a dark brown colour. This continues near a mile, when at once opens to view, the most sudden transition from darkness to light, that can poffibly be exhibited in a natural landscape.

129

Travels Through North and South Carolina

THE extensive Alachua savanna is a level, green plain, above fifteen miles over, fifty miles in circumference, and scarcely a tree or bush of any kind to be seen on it. It is encircled with high, sloping hills, covered with waving forests and fragrant Orange groves, rising from an exuberantly fertile soil. The towering Magnolia grandiflora and transcendent Palm, stand conspicuous amongst them. At the same time are seen innumerable droves of cattle; the lordly bull, lowing cow and sleek capricious heifer. The hills and groves re–echo their cheerful, social voices. Herds of sprightly deer, squadrons of the beautiful, fleet Siminole horse, flocks of turkeys, civilized communities of the sonorous, watchful crane, mix together, appearing happy and contented in the enjoyment of peace, 'till disturbed and affrighted by the warrior man. Behold yonder, coming upon them through the darkened groves, sneakingly and unawares, the naked red warrior, invading the Elysian fields and green plains of Alachua. At the terrible appearance of the painted, fearless, uncontrouled and free Siminole, the peaceful, innocent nations are at once thrown into disorder and dismay. See the different tribes and bands, how they draw towards each other! as it were deliberating upon the general good. Suddenly they speed off with their young in the centre; but the roebuck fears him not: here he lays himself down, bathes and flounces in the cool flood. The red warrior, whose plumed head flashes lightning; whoops in vain; his proud, ambitious horse strains and pants; the earth glides from under his feet, his flowing main whistles in the wind, as he comes up full of vain hopes. The bounding roe views his rapid approaches, rises up, lifts aloft his antled head, erects the white flag*

* Alluding to his tail.

and fetching a shrill whistle, says to his fleet and free associates, "follow;" he bounds off, and in a few minutes distances his foe a mile; suddenly he stops, turns about, and laughing says, "how vain, go chase meteors in the azure plains above, or hunt butterflies in the fields about your towns."

WE approached the savanna at the South end, by a narrow isthmus of level ground, open to the light of day, and clear of trees or bushes, and not greatly elevated above the common level, having on our right a spacious meadow, embellished with a little lake, one verge of which was not very distant from us; its shore is a moderately high, circular bank, partly encircling a cove of the pond, in the form of a half moon; the water is clear and deep, and at the distance of some hundred yards, was a large floating field (if I may so express myself) of the Nymphea nilumbo, with their golden blossoms waving to and fro on their lofty stems. Beyond these fields of Nymphea were spacious plains, encompassed by dark groves, opening to extensive Pine forests, other plains still appearing beyond them.

THIS little lake and surrounding meadows, would have been alone sufficient to surprise and delight the traveller, but being placed so near the great savanna, the attention is quickly drawn off, and wholly engaged in the contemplation of the unlimited, varied, and truly astonishing native wild scenes of landscape and perspective, there exhibited: how is the mind agitated and bewildered, at being thus, as it were, placed on the borders of a new world! On the first view of such an amazing display of the wisdom and power of the supreme author of nature, the mind for a moment seems suspended, and impressed with awe.

THIS isthmus being the common avenue or road of Indian travellers, we pitched our camp at a small distance from it, on a rising knoll near the verge of the savanna, under some spreading Live Oaks: this situation was open and airy, and gave us an unbounded prospect over the adjacent plains. Dewy evening now comes on, the animating breezes, which cooled and tempered the meridian hours of this sultry season, now gently cease; the glorious sovereign of day, calling in his bright beaming emanations, leaves us in his absence to the milder government and protection of the silver queen of night, attended by millions of brilliant luminaries. The thundering alligator has ended his horrifying roar; the silver plumed ganet and stork, the sage and solitary pelican of the wilderness, have already retired to their silent nocturnal habitations, in the neighbouring forests; the sonorous savanna crane, in well disciplined squadrons, now rising from the earth, mount aloft in spiral circles, far above the dense atmosphere of the humid plain; they again view the glorious sun, and the light of day still gleaming on their polished feathers, they sing their evening hymn, then in a strait line majestically descend, and alight on the towering Palms or lofty Pines, their secure and peaceful lodging places. All around being still and silent, we repair to rest.

SOON after sun−rise, a party of Indians on horseback, appeared upon the savanna, to collect together several herds of cattle which they drove along near our camp, towards the town. One of the party came up and informed us the cattle belonged to the chief of Cuscowilla, that he had ordered some of the best steers of his droves to be slaughtered for a general feast for the whole town, in compliment of our arrival, and pacific negotiations.

Travels Through North and South Carolina

THE cattle were as large and fat as those of the rich grazing pastures of Moyomensing in Pennsylvania. The Indians drove off the lowing herds, and we soon followed them to town, in order to be at council at the appointed hours, leaving two young men of our party to protect our camp.

UPON our arrival we repaired to the public square or council–house, where the chiefs and senators were already convened, the warriors and young men assembled soon after, the business being transacted in public. As it was no more than a ratification of the late treaty of St. Augustine, with some particular commercial stipulations, with respect to the citizens of Alachua, the negociations soon terminated to the satisfaction of both parties.

THE banquet succeeds; the ribs and choisest fat pieces of the bullocks, excellently well barbecued, are brought into the apartment of the public square, constructed and appointed for feasting; bowls and kettles of stewed flesh and broth are brought in for the next course, and with it a very singular dish, the traders call it tripe soup; it is made of the belly or paunch of the beef, not overcleansed of its contents, cut and minced pretty fine, and then made into a thin soup, seasoned well with salt and aromatic herbs; but the seasoning not quite strong enough to extinguish its original savour and scent. This dish is greatly esteemed by the Indians, but is, in my judgment, the least agreeable they have amongst them.

THE town of Cuscowilla, which is the capital of the Alachua tribe contains about thirty habitations, each of which consists of two houses nearly the same size, about thirty feet in length, twelve feet wide, and about the same in height; the door is placed midway on one side or in the front; this house is divided equally, across, into two apartments, one of which is the cook room and common hall, and the other their lodging room. The other house is nearly of the same dimensions, standing about twenty yards from the dwelling house, its end fronting the door; this building is two stories high, and constructed in a different manner, it is divided transversely, as the other, but the end next the dwelling house is open on three sides, supported by posts or pillars, it has an open loft or platform, the ascent to which, is by a portable stairs or ladder; this is a pleasant, cool, airy situation, and here the master or chief of the family, retires to repose in the hot seasons, and receives his guests or visitors: the other half of this building is closed on all sides by notched logs; the lowest or ground part is a potatoe house, and the upper story over it a granary for corn and other provisions. Their houses are constructed of a kind of frame; in the first place, strong corner pillars are fixed in the ground, with others somewhat less, ranging on a line between; these are strengthened by cross pieces of timber, and the whole with the roof is covered close with the bark of the Cypress tree. This dwelling stands near the middle of a square yard, encompassed by a low bank, formed with the earth taken out of the yard, which is always carefully swept. Their towns are clean, the inhabitants being particular in laying their filth at a proper distance from their dwellings, which undoubtedly contributes to the healthiness of their habitations.

THE town stands on the most pleasant situation, that could be well imagined or desired, in an inland country; upon a high swelling ridge of sand hills, within three or four hundred yards of a large and beautiful lake, the circular shore of which continually washes a sandy beach, under a moderately high sloping bank, terminated on one side by extensive forests, consisting of Orange groves, overtopped with grand Magnolias, Palms, Poplar, Tilia, Live Oaks and others already noticed; and the opposite point of the crescent, gradually retires with hommocky projecting points, indenting the grassy marshes, and lastly terminates in infinite green plains and meadows, united with the skies and waters of the lake; such a natural landscape, such a rural scene, is not to be imitated by the united ingenuity and labour of man. At present the ground betwixt the town and the lake is adorned by an open grove of very tall Pine trees, which standing at a considerable distance from each other, admit a delightful prospect of the sparkling waters. The lake abounds with various excellent fish and wild fowl; there are incredible numbers of the latter, especially in the winter season, when they arrive here from the North to winter.

THE Indians abdicated the ancient Alachua town on the borders of the savanna, and built here, calling the new town Cuscowilla; their reasons for removing their habitation were on account of its unhealthiness, occasioned, as they say, by the stench of the putrid fish and reptiles in the summer and autumn, driven on shore by the alligators, and the exhalations from marshes of the savanna, together with the persecution of the musquitoes.

THEY plant but little here about the town, only a small garden spot at each habitation, consisting of a little Corn, Beans, Tobacco Citruls, &c. their plantations which supply them with the chief of their vegetable provisions, such as Zea, Convolvulus batata, Cucurbita citrulus, Cuc. laginaria, Cuc. pepo, Cuc. melopepo, Cuc. verrucosa, Dolichos varieties, &c. lies on the rich prolific lands bordering on the great Alachua savanna, about two miles distance, which plantation is one common inclosure, and is worked and tended

133

by the whole community; yet every family has its particular part, according to its own appointment, marked off when planted, and this portion receives the common labour and assistance until ripe, when each family gathers and deposits in its granary its own proper share, setting apart a small gift or contribution for the public granary, which stands in the centre of the plantation.

THE youth, under the supervisal of some of their ancient people, are daily stationed in their fields, who are continually whooping and hallooing, to chase away crows, jackdaws, black–birds and such predatory animals, and the lads are armed with bows and arrows, who, being trained up to it from their early youth, are sure at a mark, and in the course of the day load themselves with squirrels, birds, &c. The men in turn patrole the Corn fields at night, to protect their provisions from the depredations of night rovers, as bears, raccoons and deer; the two former being immoderately fond of young Corn, when the grain is filled with a rich milk, as sweet and nourishing as cream, and the deer are as fond of the Potatoe vines.

AFTER the feast was over, we returned to our encampment on the great savanna, towards the evening. Our companions, whom we left at the camp, were impatient for our return, having been out horse hunting in the plains and groves during our absence. They soon left us, on a visit to the town, having there some female friends, with whom they were anxious to renew their acquaintance. The Siminole girls are by no means destitute of charms to please the rougher sex: the white traders, are fully sensible how greatly it is for their advantage to gain their affections and friendship in matters of trade and commerce; and if their love and esteem for each other is sincere, and upon principles of reciprocity, there are but few instances of their neglecting or betraying the interests and views of their temporary husbands; they labour and watch constantly to promote their private interests, and detect and prevent any plots or evil designs which may threaten their persons, or operate against their trade or business.

IN the cool of the evening I embraced the opportunity of making a solitary excursion round the adjacent lawns: taking my fuzee with me, I soon came up to a little clump of shrubs, upon a swelling green knoll, where I observed several large snakes entwined together; I stepped up near them, they appeared to be innocent and peaceable, having no inclination to strike at any thing, though I endeavoured to irritate them, in order to discover their disposition, nor were they anxious to escape from me. This snake is about four feet in length and as thick as a man's wrist; the upper side of a dirty, ash colour; the

134

squamae large, ridged and pointed; the belly or under side of a reddish, dull flesh colour; the tail part not long but slender like most other innocent snakes. They prey on rats, land frogs, young rabbits, birds, &c. I left them, continuing my progress and researches, delighted with the ample prospects around and over the savanna.

STOPPING again at a natural shrubbery, when turning my eyes to some flowering shrubs, I observed near my feet, the surprising glass snake (anguis fragilis;) they seem as innocent and harmless as worms. They are, when full grown, two feet and an half in length, and three fourths of an inch in thickness; the abdomen or body part is remarkably short, and they seem to be all tail, which, though long, gradually attenuates to its extremity, yet not small and slender as in switch snakes; the colour and texture of the whole animal is so exactly like bluish green glass, which, together with its fragility, almost persuades a stranger that they are in reality of that brittle substance: but it is only the tail part that breaks off, which it does like glass, by a very gentle stroke from a slender switch. Tho' they are quick and nimble in twisting about, yet they cannot run fast from one, but quickly secrete themselves at the bottom of the grass or under leaves. It is a vulgar fable, that they are able to repair themselves after being broke into several pieces; which pieces, common report says, by a power or faculty in the animal, voluntarily approach each other, join and heal again. The sun now low, shoots the pointed shadows of the projecting promontories far on the skirts of the lucid green plain, flocks of turkeys calling upon their strolling associates, circumspectly march onward to the groves and high forests, their nocturnal retreats. Dewy eve now arrived; I turned about and regained our encampment in good time.

THE morning cool and pleasant, and the skies serene, we decamped, pursuing our progress round the Alachua savanna. Three of our companions separating from us, went a–head and we soon lost sight of them: they again parting on different excursions, in quest of game and in search of their horses; some enter the surrounding groves and forests, others strike off into the green plains. My companion, the old trader and myself kept together, he being the most intelligent and willing to oblige me; we coasted the green verge of the plain, under the surrounding hills, occasionally penetrating and crossing the projecting promontories, as the pathway or conveniency dictated, to avoid the waters and mud which still continued deep and boggy near the steep hills, in springy places; so that when we came to such places, we found it convenient to ascend and coast round the sides of the hills, or strike out a little into the savanna, to a moderately swelling ridge, where the ground being dry, and a delightful green turf, was pleasant travelling;

but then we were under the necessity to ford creeks or rivulets, which are the conduits or drains of the shallow, boggy ponds or morasses just under the hills; this range or chain of morasses continues round the South and South–West border of the savanna, and appeared to me to be fed or occasioned by the great wet bay gale or savanna Pine lands, which lay immediately back of the high, hilly forests on the great savanna, part of which we crossed in coming from Cuscowilla, which bottom is a flat, level, hard sand, lying between the sand ridge of Cuscowilla and these eminences of the great savanna, and is a vast receptacle or reservoir of the rain waters, which being defended from the active and powerful exhalations of the meridian sun, by the shadow of the Pine trees, low shrubs and grass, gradually filtering through the sand, drain through these hills and present themselves in innumerable little meandering rills, at the bases of the shady heights fronting the savanna.

OUR progress this day was extremely pleasant, over the green turf, having in view numerous herds of cattle and deer, and squadrons of horse, peaceably browsing on the tender, sweet grass, or strolling through the cool fragrant groves on the surrounding heights.

BESIDES the continued Orange groves, these heights abound with Palms, Magnolias, Red Bays, Liquid–amber, and Fagus sylvatica of incredible magnitude, their trunks imitating the shafts of vast columns: we observed Cassine, Prunus, Vitis labrusca, Rhamnus volubilis, and delightful groves of Æsculus pavia, Prunus Caroliniana, a most beautiful evergreen, decorated with its racemes of sweet, white blossoms.

PASSING through a great extent of ancient Indian fields, now grown over with forests of stately trees, Orange groves and luxuriant herbage. The old trader, my associate, informed me it was the ancient Alachua, the capital of that famous and powerful tribe, who peopled the hills surrounding the savanna, when, in days of old, they could assemble by thousands at ball play and other juvenile diversions and athletic exercises, over those, then, happy fields and green plains; and there is no reason to doubt of his account being true, as almost every step we take over those fertile heights, discovers remains and traces of ancient human habitations and cultivation. It is the most elevated eminence upon the savanna, and here the hills descend gradually to the savanna, by a range of gentle, grassy banks. Arriving at a swelling green knoll, at some distance in the plains, near the banks of a pond, opposite the old Alachua town, the place appointed for our meeting again together; it being near night our associates soon after joined us, where we lodged. Early next morning we continued our tour; one division of our company directing their course across the plains to the North coast: my old companion, with myself in company, continued our former rout, coasting the savanna W. and N. W. and by agreement we were all to meet again at night, at the E. end of the savanna.

WE continued some miles crossing over, from promontory to promontory, the most enchanting green coves and vistas, scolloping and indenting the high coasts of the vast plain. Observing a company of wolves (lupus niger) under a few trees, about a quarter of a mile from shore, we rode up towards them, they observing our approach, sitting on their hinder parts until we came nearly within shot of them, when they trotted off towards the forests, but stopped again and looked at us, at about two hundred yards distance; we then whooped, and made a feint to pursue them, when they seperated from each other, some stretching off into the plains and others seeking covert in the groves on shore; when we got to the trees we observed they had been feeding on the carcase of a horse. The wolves of Florida are larger than a dog, and are perfectly black, except the females, which have a white spot on the breast, but they are not so large as the wolves of Canada and Pennsylvania, which are of a yellowish brown colour. There were a number of vultures on the trees over the carcase, who, as soon as the wolves ran off, immediately settled down upon it; they were however held in restraint and subordination by the bald eagle (falco leucocephalus.)

ON our rout near a long projected point of the coast, we observed a large flock of turkeys; at our approach they hastened to the groves; we soon gained the promontory; on the ascending hills were vestiges of an ancient Indian town, now overshadowed with groves of the Orange, loaded with both green and ripe fruit, and embellished with their fragrant bloom, gratifying the taste, the sight and the smell at the same instant. Leaving this delightful retreat, we soon came to the verge of the groves, when presented to view, a vast verdant bay of the savanna; we discovered a herd of deer feeding at a small distance, upon the sight of us they ran off, taking shelter in the groves on the opposite point or cape of this spacious meadow. My companions being old expert hunters, quickly concerted a plan for their destruction; one of our company immediately struck off, obliquely crossing the meadow for the opposite groves, in order to intercept them, is they should continue their course up the forest, to the main; and we crossed strait over to the point, if possible to keep them in sight, and watch their motions, knowing that they would make a stand thereabouts, before they would attempt their last escape: on drawing near the point, we slackened our gate, and cautiously entered the groves, when we beheld them thoughtless and secure, flouncing in a sparkling pond, in a green meadow or cove beyond the point; some were lying down on their sides in the cool waters, whilst others were prancing like young kids; the young bucks in playsome sport, with their sharp horns hooking and spurring the others, urging them to splash the water.

I ENDEAVOURED to plead for their lives, but my old friend though he was a sensible, rational and good sort of man, would not yield to my philosophy; he requested me to mind our horses, while he made his approaches, cautiously gaining ground on them, from tree to tree, when they all suddenly sprang up and herded together; a princely buck who headed the party, whistled and bounded off, his retinue followed, but unfortunately for their chief, he led them with prodigious speed out towards the savanna very near us, and when passing by, the lucky old hunter fired and laid him prostrate upon the green turf, but a few yards from us; his affrighted followers at the instant, sprang off in every direction, streaming away like meteors or phantoms, and we quickly lost sight of them: he opened his body, took out the entrails and placed the carcase in the fork of a tree, casting his frock or hunting shirt over to protect it from the vultures and crows, who follow the hunter as regularly as his own shade.

OUR companions soon arrived, we set forward again, enjoying the like scenes we had already past; observed parties of Siminole horses coursing over the plains, and frequently saw deer, turkeys and wolves, but they knew their safety here, keeping far enough out of our reach. The wary, sharp sighted crane, circumspectly observing our progress. We saw a female of them sitting on her nest, and the male, her mate, watchfully traversing backwards and forwards, at a small distance; they suffered us to approach near them before they arose, when they spread their wings, running and tipping the ground with their feet some time, and then mounted aloft, soaring round and round over the nest; they set upon only two eggs at a time, which are very large, long and pointed at one end, of a pale ash colour, powdered or speckled with brown. The manner of forming their nests and setting is very singular; choosing a tussock and there forming a rude heap of dry grass, or such like materials, near as high as their body is from the ground, when standing upon their feet; on the summit of this they form the nest of fine soft dry grass, when she covers her eggs to hatch them, she stands over them, bearing her body and wings over the eggs.

WE again came up to a long projecting point of the high forests, beyond which opened to view an extensive grassy cove of the savanna, several miles in circuit; we crossed strait over from this promontory to the opposite coast, and on the way were constrained to wade a mile or more through the water, though at a little distance from us it appeared as a delightful meadow, the grass growing through the water, the middle of which, however, when we came up, proved to be a large space of clear water almost deep enough to swim our horses; it being a large branch of the main creek which drains the savanna; after getting through this morass, we arrived on a delightful, level, green meadow as usual, which continued about a mile, when we reached the firm land; and then gradually ascending, we alighted on a hard sandy beach, which exhibited evident signs of being washed by the waves of the savanna, when in the winter season it is all under water, and then presents the appearance of a large lake. The coast here is much lower than the opposite side, which we had left behind us, and rises from the meadows with a gradual sloping ascent, covered scatteringly with low spreading Live Oaks, short Palms, Zanthoxilon, Laurus Borbonia, Cassine, Sideroxilon, Quercus nigra, Q. sinuata and others; all leaning from the bleak winds that oppress them. About one hundred yards back of this beach, the sand hills gradually rise, and the open Pine forests appear; we coasted a mile or two along the beach, then doubled a promontory of high forests, and soon after came to a swift running brook of clear water, rolling over gravel and white sand, which being brought along with it, in its descent down the steeper sandy beach, formed an easy swelling bank or bar; the waters spread greatly at this place, exhibiting a shallow glittering sheet of clear water, but just sufficient continually to cover the clear gravelly bed, and seemed to be sunk a little below the common surface of the beach; this stream however is soon separated into a number of rivulets, by small sandy and gravelly ridges, and the waters are finally stole away from the sight, by a charming green meadow, which, again secretly uniting under the tall grass, forms a little creek, meandering through the turfy plain, marking its course by reeds and rushes, which spring up from its banks, joining the main creek that runs through the savanna, and at length delivers the water into the Great Sink. Proceeding about a mile farther we came up to, and crossed another brook larger than the former, which exhibited the like delightful appearance. We next passed over a level green lawn, a cove of the savanna, and arrived at a hilly grove. We alighted in a pleasant vista, turning our horses to graze while we amused ourselves with exploring the borders of the Great Sink. In this place a group of rocky hills almost surround a large bason, which is the general receptacle of the water, draining from every part of the vast savanna, by lateral conduits, winding about, and one after another joining the main creek or general conductor, which at length delivers them into this sink; where they descend by slow degrees, through rocky caverns, into the bowels of the earth, whence they are carried by secret subterraneous channels into other receptacles and basons.

Travels Through North and South Carolina

WE ascended a collection of eminences, covered with dark groves, which is one point of the crescent that partly encircles the sink or bason, open only on the side next the savanna, where it is joined to the great channel or general conductor of the waters; from this point over to the opposite point of the crescent (which is a similar high rocky promontory) is about one hundred yards, forming a vast semicircular cove or bason, the hills encircling it rising very steep fifty or sixty feet, high, rocky, perpendicular and bare of earth next the waters of the bason. These hills, from the top of the perpendicular, fluted, excavated, walls of rocks, slant off moderately up to their summits, and are covered with a very fertile, loose, black earth, which nourishes and supports a dark grove of very large trees, varieties of shrubs and herbacious plants. These high forest trees surrounding the bason, by their great height and spread, so effectually shade the waters, that coming suddenly from the open plains, we seem at once shut up in darkness, and the waters appear black, yet are clear; when we ascend the top of the hills, we perceive the ground to be uneven, by round swelling points and corresponding hollows, overspread with gloomy shade, occasioned by the tall and spreading trees, such as Live Oak, Morus rubra, Zanthoxilon, Sapindus, Liquid–amber, Tilia, Laurus Borbonia, Quercus dentata, Juglans cinerea, and others, together with Orange trees of remarkable magnitude and very fruitful. But that which is most singular and to me unaccountable, is the infundibuliform cavities, even on the top of these high hills, some twenty, thirty and forty yards across, at their superficial rims exactly circular, as if struck with a compass, sloping gradually inwards to a point at bottom, forming an inverted cone, or like the upper wide part of a funnel; the perpendicular depth of them from the common surface is various, some descending twenty feet deep, others almost to the bed of rocks, which forms the foundation or nucleus of the hills, and indeed of the whole country of East Florida; some of them seem to be nearly filled up with earth, swept in from the common surface, but retain the same uniformity; though sometimes so close together as to be broken one into another. But as I shall have occasion to speak further of these sinks in the earth hereafter, I turn my observation to other objects in view round about me. In and about the Great Sink, are to be seen incredible numbers of crocodiles, some of which are of an enormous size, and view the passenger with incredible impudence and avidity; and at this time they are so abundant, that, if permitted by them, I could walk over any part of the bason and the river upon their heads, which slowly float and turn about like knotty chuncks or logs of wood, except when they plunge or shoot forward to beat off their associates, pressing too close to each other, or taking up fish, which continually croud in upon them from the river and creeks, draining from the savanna, especially the great trout, mudfish, catfish and the various species of bream; the gar are rather too hard for their jaws and rough for their throats, especially here where they have a superfluous plenty and variety of those that are every way preferable; besides the gar being like themselves, a warlike voracious creature, they seem to be in league or confederacy together, to enslave and devour the numerous defenceless tribes.

IT is astonishing and incredible, perhaps, I may say, to relate what unspeakable numbers of fish repair to this fatal fountain or receptacle, during the latter summer season and autumn, when the powerful sunbeams have evaporated the waters off the savanna, where those who are so fortunate as to effect a retreat into the conductor, and escape the devouring jaws of the fearful alligator and armed gar, descend into the earth, through the wells and cavities or vast perforations of the rocks, and from thence are conducted and carried away, by secret subterranean conduits and gloomy vaults, to other distant lakes and rivers; and it does not appear improbable, but that in some future day this vast savanna or lake of waters, in the winter season will be discovered to be in a great measure filled with its finny inhabitants, who are strangers or adventurers, from other lakes, ponds and rivers, by subterraneous rivulets and communications to this rocky, dark door or outlet, whence they ascend to its surface, spread over and people the winter lake, where they breed, increase and continue as long as it is under water, or during pleasure, for they are at all seasons to be seen ascending and descending through the rocks; but towards the autumn, when the waters have almost left the plains, they then croud to the sink in such multitudes, as at times to be seen pressing on in great banks into the bason, being urged by pursuing bands of alligators and gar, and when entering the great bason or sink, are suddenly fallen upon by another army of the same devouring enemy, lying in wait for them; thousands are driven on shore, where they perish and rot in banks, which was evident at the time I was there, the stench being intollerable, although then early in the summer. There are three great doors or vent holes through the rocks in the sink, two near the centre and the other one near the rim, much higher up than the other two, which was conspicuous through the clear water. The beds of rocks lay in horizontal thick strata or laminae, one over the other, where the sink–holes or outlets are. These rocks are perforated by perpendicular wells or tubes, four, five and six feet in diameter, exactly circular as the tube of a cannon or walled well; many of these are broken into one another, forming a great ragged orifice, appearing fluted by alternate jambs and semicircular perpendicular niches or excavations.

HAVING satisfied my curiosity in viewing this extraordinary place and very wonderful work of nature, we repaired to our resting place, where we found our horses and mounted again. One of the company parting from us for the buck that we had shot and left in the fork of the tree. My friend, the old trader, led the shortest way across the plain, after repassing the wet morass which had almost swam our horses in the morning. At evening we arrived at the place of our destination, where our associates soon after rejoined us with some Indians, who were merry, agreeable guests as long as they staid; they were in full dress and painted, but before dark they mounted their horses, which were of the true Siminole breed, set spurs to them, uttering all at once a shrill whoop, and went off for Cuscowilla.

THOUGH the horned cattle and horses bred in these meadows are large, sleek, sprightly and as fat as can be in general, yet they are subject to mortal diseases. I observed several of them dreadfully mortified, their thighs and haunches ulcerated, raw and bleeding, which, like a mortification or slow cancer, at length puts an end to their miserable existence. The traders and Indians call this disease the water–rot or scald, and say it is occasioned by the warm waters of the savanna, during the heats of summer and autumn, when these creatures wade deep to feed on the water–grass, which they are immoderately fond of; whereas the cattle which only feed and range in the high forests and Pine savannas are clear of this disorder. A sacrifice to intemperance and luxury.

WE had heavy rains during the night, and though very warm yet no thunder and very little wind. It cleared away in the morning and the day very pleasant. Sat off for the East end of the savanna, collecting by the way and driving before us, parties of horse, the property of the traders; and next morning sat off on our return to the lower store on St. John's, coasting the savanna yet a few miles, in expectation of finding the remainder of their horses, though disappointed.

WE at last bid adieu to the magnificent plains of Alachua, entered the Pine forests, and soon fell into the old Spanish highway, from St. Augustine across the isthmus of Florida, to St. Mark's in the bay of Apalache. Its course and distance from E. to W. is, from St. Augustine to Fort Picolata on the river St. Juan, twenty–seven miles; thence across the river to the Poopoa Fort, three miles; thence to the Alachua Savanna, forty–five miles; thence to Talahasochte on the river Little St. Juan, seventy–five miles; thence down this river to St. Mark's, thirty miles; the whole distance from St. Augustine to St. Mark's, one hundred and eighty miles. But that road having been unfrequented for many years past, since the Creeks subdued the remnant tribes of the ancient Floridans, and drove the Spaniards from their settlements in East Florida into St. Augustine, which effectually cut off their communication between that garrison and St. Mark's; this ancient highway is grown up in many places with trees and shrubs, but yet has left so deep a track on the surface of the earth, that it may be traced for ages yet to come.

LEAVING the highway on our left hand, we ascend a sandy ridge, thinly planted by nature with stately Pines and Oaks, of the latter genera, particularly Q. sinuata, S. flamule, Q. nigra, Q. rubra. Passed by an Indian village situated on this high, airy sand ridge, consisting of four or five habitations; none of the people were at home, they were out at their hunting camps; we observed plenty of corn in their cribs. Following a hunting path eight or nine miles, through a vast Pine forest and grassy savanna, well timbered, the ground covered with a charming carpet of various flowering plants, came to a large creek of excellent water, and here we found the encampment of the Indians, the inhabitants of the little town we had passed; we saw their women and children, the men being out hunting. The women presented themselves to our view as we came up, at the door of their tents, veiled in their mantle, modestly shewing their faces when we saluted them. Towards the evening we fell into the old trading path, and before night came to camp at the Halfway Pond. Next morning, after collecting together the horses, some of which had strolled away at a great distance, we pursued our journey and in the evening arrived at the trading house on St. Juan's, from a successful and pleasant tour.

ON my return to the store on St. Juan's the trading schooner was there, but as she was not to return to Georgia until the autumn, I found I had time to pursue my travels in Florida, and might at leisure plan my excursions to collect seeds and roots in boxes, &c.

AT this time the talks (or messages between the Indians and white people) were perfectly peaceable and friendly, both with the Lower Creeks and the Nation or Upper Creeks; parties of Indians were coming in every day with their hunts: indeed the Muscogulges or Upper Creeks very seldom disturb us. Bad talks from the Nation is always a very serious affair, and to the utmost degree alarming to the white inhabitants.

THE Muscogulges are under a more strict government or regular civilization than the Indians in general. They lie near their potent and declared enemy, the Chactaws; their country having a vast frontier, naturally accessible and open to the incursions of their enemies on all sides, they find themselves under the necessity of associating in large, populous towns, and these towns as near together as convenient that they may be enabled to succour and defend one another in case of sudden invasion; this consequently

143

occasions dear and bear to be scarce and difficult to procure, which obliges them to be vigilent and industrious; this naturally begets care and serious attention, which we may suppose in some degree forms their natural disposition and manners, and gives them that air of dignified gravity, so strikingly characteristic in their aged people, and that steadiness, just and chearful reverence in the middle aged and youth, which sits so easy upon them, and appears so natural: for however strange it may appear to us, the same moral duties which with us form the amiable, virtuous character, and is so difficult to maintain, there, without compulsion or visible restraint, operates like instinct, with a surprising harmony and natural ease, insomuch that it seems impossible for them to act out of the common high–road to virtue.

WE will now take a view of the Lower Creeks or Siminoles, and the natural disposition which characterises this people, when, from the striking contrast, the philosopher may approve or disapprove, as he may think proper, from the judgment and opinion given by different men.

THE Siminoles, but a weak people, with respect to numbers, all of them I suppose would not be sufficient to people one of the towns in the Muscogulge (for instance, the Uches on the main branch of the Apalachucla river, which alone contains near two thousand inhabitants.) Yet this handful of people possesses a vast territory, all East Florida and the greastest part of West Florida, which being naturally cut and divided into thousands of islets, knolls and eminences, by the innumerable rivers, lakes, swamps, vast savannas and ponds, form so many secure retreats and temporary dwelling places, that effectually guard them from any sudden invasions or attacks from their enemies; and being such a swampy, hommocky country, furnishes such a plenty and variety of supplies for the nourishment of varieties of animals, that I can venture to assert, that no part of the globe so abounds with wild game or creatures fit for the food of man.

THUS they enjoy a superabundance of the necessaries and conveniencies of life, with the security of person and property, the two great concerns of mankind. The hides of deer, bears, tigers and wolves, together with honey, wax and other productions of the country, purchase their cloathing, equipage and domestic utensils from the whites. They seem to be free from want or desires. No cruel enemy to dread; nothing to give them disquietude, but the gradual encroachments of the white people. Thus contented and undisturbed, they appear as blithe and free as the birds of the air, and like them as volatile and active, tuneful and vociferous. The visage, action and deportment of a Siminole, being the most

144

striking picture of happiness in this life; joy, contentment, love and friendship, without guile or affection, seem inherent in them, or predominant in their vital principle, for it leaves them but with the last breath of life. It even seems imposing a constraint upon their ancient chiefs and senators, to maintain a necessary decorum and solemnity, in their public councils; not even the debility and decrepitude of extreme old age, is sufficient to erase from their visages, this youthful, joyous simplicity; but like the grey eve of a serene and calm day, a gladdening, cheering blush remains on the Western horizon after the sun is set.

I DOUBT not but some of my countrymen who may read these accounts of the Indians, which I have endeavoured to relate according to truth, at least as they appeared to me, will charge me with partiality or prejudice in their favour.

I WILL, however, now endeavour to exhibit their vices, immoralities and imperfections, from my own observations and knowledge, as well as accounts from the white traders, who reside amongst them.

THE Indians make war against, kill and destroy their own species, and their motives spring from the same erroneous source as it does in all other nations of mankind; that is, the ambition of exhibiting to their fellows, a superior character of personal and national valour, and thereby immortalize themselves, by transmitting their names with honour and lustre to posterity; or in revenge of their enemy, for public or perional insults; or lastly, to extend the borders and boundaries of their territories: but I cannot find upon the strictest enquiry, that their bloody contests, at this day are marked with deeper stains of inhumanity or savage cruelty, than what may be observed amongst the most civilized nations: they do indeed scalp their slain enemy, but they do not kill the females or children of either sex: the most ancient traders, both in the Lower and Upper Creeks, affured me they never saw an instance of either burning or tormenting their male captives; though it is said they used to do it formerly. I saw in every town in the Nation and Siminoles that I visited, more or less male captives, some extremely aged, who were free and in as good circumstances as their masters; and all slaves have their freedom when they may, which is permitted and encouraged; when they and their offspring, are every way upon an equality with their conquerors; they are given to adultery and fornication, but I suppose in no greater excess than other nations of men. They punish the delinquents, male and female, equally alike, by taking off their ears. This is the punishment for adultery. Infamy and disgrace is supposed to be a sufficient punishment

145

for fornication, in either sex.

THEY are fond of games and gambling, and amuse themselves like children, in relating extravagant stories, to cause surprise and mirth.

THEY wage eternal war against deer and bear, to procure food and clothing, and other necessaries and conveniences: which is indeed carried to an unreasonable and perhaps criminal excess, since the white people have dazzled their senses with foreign superfluities.

CHAP. VII.

A JOURNEY FROM SPALDING'S LOWER TRADING HOUSE TO TALAHASOCHTE OR WHITE KING'S TOWN, ON THE RIVER LITTLE ST. JUAN, THIRTY MILES ABOVE FORT ST. MARKS IN THE BAY OF APALATCHE.

ON my return to the trading house, from my journey to the great savanna, I found the trading company for Little St. Juan's, were preparing for that post.

MY mind yet elate with the various scenes of rural nature, which as a lively animated picture, had been presented to my view; the deeply engraven impression, a pleasing flattering contemplation, gave strength and agility to my steps, anxiously to press forward to the delightful fields and groves of Apalatche.

THE trading company for Talahasochte being now in readiness to proceed for that quarter, under the direction of our chief trader, in the cool of the morning we sat off, each of us having a good horse to ride, besides having in our caravan several pack horses laden with provisions, camp equipage and other necessaries; a young man from St. Augustine, in the service of the governor of East Florida accompanied us, commissioned to purchase of the Indians and traders, some Siminole horses. They are the most beautiful and sprightly species of that noble creature, perhaps any where to be seen; but are of a small breed, and as delicately formed as the American roe buck. A horse in the Creek or Muscogulge tongue is echoclucco, that is the great deer, (echo is a deer and clucco is big:) the Siminole horses are said to descend originally from the Andalusian breed, brought here by the Spaniards when they first established the colony of East Florida. From the forehead to their nose is a little arched or aquiline, and so are the fine Chactaw

146

horses among the Upper Creeks, which are said to have been brought thither from New–Mexico across Mississippi, by those nations of Indians who emigrated from the West, beyond the river. These horses are every way like the Siminole breed, only being larger, and perhaps not so lively and capricious. It is a matter of conjecture and enquiry, whether or not the different soil and situation of the country, may have contributed in some measure, in forming and establishing the difference in size and other qualities betwixt them. I have observed the horses and other animals in the high hilly country of Carolina, Georgia, Virginia and all along our shores, are of a much larger and stronger make, than those which are bred in the flat country next the sea coast; a back–skin of the Upper Creeks and Cherokees will weigh twice as heavy as those of the Siminoles or Lower Creeks, and those bred in the low flat country of Carolina.

OUR first days journey was along the Alachua roads, twenty–five miles to the Half–way Pond, where we encamped, the musquitoes were excessively troublesome the whole night.

DECAMPED early next morning, still pursuing the road to Alachua, until within a few miles of Cuscowilla, when the road dividing, one for the town and the other for the great savanna; here our company seperated, one party chose to pass through the town, having some concerns there; I kept with the party that went through the savanna, it being the best road, leading over a part of the savanna, when entering the groves on its borders, we travelled several miles over these fertile emminences and delightful, shady, fragrant forests, then again entered upon the savanna, and crossed a charming extensive green cove or bay of it, covered with a vivid green grassy turf, when we again ascended the woodland hills, through fruitful Orange groves and under shadowy Palms and Magnolias. Now the Pine forests opened to view, we left the magnificent savanna and its delightful groves, passing through a level, open, airy Pine forest, the stately trees scatteringly planted by nature, arising strait and erect from the green carpet, embellished with various grasses and flowering plants, and gradually ascending the sand hills soon came into the trading path to Talahasochte; which is generally, excepting a few deviations, the old Spanish highway to St. Mark's. At about five miles distance beyond the great savanna, we came to camp late in the evening, under a little grove of Live Oaks Just by a group of shelly rocks, on the banks of a beautiful little lake, partly environed by meadows. The rocks as usual in these regions partly encircled a spacious sink or grotto, which communicates with the waters of the lake; the waters of the grotto are perfectly transparent, cool and pleasant, and well replenished with fish. Soon after our arrival here,

147

our companions who passed through Cuscowilla joined us. A brisk cool wind during the night kept the persecuting musquitoes at a distance.

THE morning pleasant, we decamped early, proceeding on, rising gently for several miles, over sandy, gravelly ridges, we find ourselves in an elevated, high, open, airy region, somewhat rocky, on the backs of the ridges, and presents to view on every side, the most dreary, solitary, desart waste I had ever beheld; groups of bare rocks emerging out of the naked gravel and drifts of white sand; the grass thinly scattered and but few trees; the Pines, Oaks, Olives and Sideroxilons, poor, mishapen and tattered; scarce an animal to be seen or noise heard, save the symphony of the Western breeze, through the bristly Pine leaves, or solitary sand crickets schreech, or at best the more social converse of the frogs, in solemn chorus with the swift breezes, brought from distant fenns and forests. Next we joyfully enter the borders of the level Pine forest and savannas, which continued for many miles, never out of sight of little lakes or ponds, environed with illumined meadows, the clear waters sparking through the tall Pines.

HAVING a good spirited horse under me, I generally kept a–head of my companions, which I often chose to do, as circumstances offered or invited, for the sake of retirement and observation.

THE high road being here open and spacious, at a good distance before me, I observed a large hawk on the ground, in the middle of the road; he seemed to be in distress, endeavouring to rise, when, coming up near him, I found him closely bound up by a very long coach–whip snake, that had wreathed himself several times round the hawk's body, who had but one of his wings at liberty; beholding their struggles a while, I alighted off my horse with an intention of parting them; when, on coming up, they mutually agreed to seperate themselves, each one seaking his own safety, probably considering me as their common enemy. The bird rose aloft and fled away as soon as he recovered his liberty, and the snake as eagerly made off, I soon overtook him but could not perceive that he was wounded.

I SUPPOSE the hawk had been the aggressor, and fell upon the snake with an intention of making a prey of him, and that the snake dexterously and luckily threw himself in coils round his body, and girded him so close as to save himself from destruction.

148

Travels Through North and South Carolina

THE coach–whip snake is a beautiful creature; when full grown they are six and seven feet in length, and the largest part of their body not so thick as a cane or common walking stick; their head not larger than the end of a man's singer; their neck is very slender, and from the abdomen tapers away in the manner of a small switch or coach–whip; the top of the head and neck, for three or four inches, is as black and shining as a raven; the throat and belly as white as snow; and the upper side of their body of a chocolate colour, excepting the tail part, almost from the abdomen to the extremity, which is black: it may be proper to observe, however, that they vary in respect to the colour of the body; some I have seen almost white or cream colour, others of a pale chocolate or clay colour, but in all the head and neck is black, and the tail dark brown or black. They are extremely swift, seeming almost to fly over the surface of the ground, and that which is very singular, they can run swiftly on only their tail part, carrying their head and body upright: one very fine one accompanied me along the road side, at a little distance, raising himself erect, now and then looking me in the face, although I proceeded on a good round trot on purpose to observe how fast they could proceed in that position. His object seemed mere curiosity or observation; with respect to venom they are as innocent as a worm, and seem to be familiar with man. They seem a particular inhabitant of East Florida, though I have seen some of them in the maritime parts of Carolina and Georgia, but in these regions they are neither so large or beautiful.

WE rise again, passing over sand ridges of gentle elevation, savannas and open Pine forests. Masses or groups of rocks present to view on every side, as before mentioned, and with difficulty we escaped the circular infundibuliform cavities or sinks in the surface of the earth; generally a group of rocks, shaded by Palms, Live Oaks and Magnolias, is situated on their limb: some are partly filled up with earth, whilst others and the greater number of them are partly filled with transparent cool water, which discover the well or perforation through the rocks in the center. This day being remarkably sultry, we came to camp early, having chosen our situation under some stately Pines, near the verge of a spacious savanna.

AFTER some refeshment, our hunters went out into the forest, and returned towards evening; amongst other game, they brought with them a savanna crane*

* Grus p.

149

which they shot in the adjoining meadows. This stately bird is above six feet in length from the toes to the extremity of the beak when extended, and the wings expand eight or nine feet; they are above five feet high when standing erect; the tail is remarkably short, but the flag or pendant feathers which fall down off the rump on each side, are very long and sharp pointed, of a delicate texture, and silky softness; the beak is very long, strait and sharp pointed; the crown of the head bare of feathers, of a reddish rose colour, thinly barbed with short, stiff, black hair; the legs and thighs are very long, and bare of feathers a great space above the knees; the plumage of this bird is generally of a pale ash colour, with shades or clouds of pale brown and sky blue, the brown prevails on the shoulders and back; the barrels of the prime quill–feathers are long and of a large diameter, leaving a large cavity when extracted from the wing: all the bones of this bird have a thin shell, and consequently a large cavity or medullary receptacle. When these birds move their wings in flight, their strokes are slow, moderate and regular, and even when at a considerable distance or high above us, we plainly hear the quill–feathers, their shafts and webbs upon one another, creek as the joints or working of a vessel in a tempestuous sea.

WE had this fowl dressed for supper and it made excellent soup; nevertheless as long as I can get any other necessary food I shall prefer his seraphic music in the etherial skies, and my eyes and understanding gratified in observing their economy and social communities, in the expansive green savannas of Florida.

NEXT morning we arose early, and proceeding, gradually descended again, and continued many miles along a flat, level country, over delightful green savannas, decorated with hommocks or islets of dark groves, consisting of Magnolia grandiflora, Morus tilia, Zanthoxilon, Laurus Borbonia, Sideroxilon, Quercus sempervirens, Halesia diptera, Callicarpa, Corypha palma, &c. there are always groups of whitish testaceous rocks and sinks where these hommocks are. We next crossed a wet savanna, which is the beginning of a region still lower than we had traversed; here we crossed a rapid rivulet of exceeding cool, pleasant water, where we halted to refresh ourselves. But it must be remarked here, that this rivulet, though lively and rapid at this time, is not a permanent stream, but was formed by a heavy rain that fell the day before, as was apparent from its bed, besides it is at best but a jet or mere phantom of a brook, as the land around is rocky and hollow, abounding with wells and cavities. Soon after leaving the brook we passed off to the left hand, along the verge of an extensive savanna, and meadows many miles in circumference, edged on one border with detached groves and pompous Palms, and embellished with a beautiful sparkling lake; its verges decorated with tall, waving grass and floriferous plants; the pellucid waters gently rolling on to a dark shaded grotto, just under a semicircular, swelling, turfy ascent or bank, skirted by groves of Magnolias, Oaks, Laurels and Palms. In these expansive and delightful meadows, were feeding and roving troops of the sleet Siminole horse. We halted a while at this grotto, and after refreshing ourselves we mounted horse and proceeded across a charming lawn, part of the savanna, entering on it through a dark grove. In this extensive lawn were several troops of horse, and our company had the satisfaction of observing several belonging to themselves. One occurrance, remarkable here, was a troop of horse under the controul and care of a single black dog, which seemed to differ in no respect from the wolf of Florida, except his being able to bark as the common dog. He was very careful and industrious in keeping them together, and if any one strolled from the rest at too great a distance, the dog would spring up, head the horse and bring him back to the company. The proprietor of these horses is an Indian in Talahasochte, about ten miles distance from this place, who, out of humour and experiment, trained his dog up from a puppy to this business; he follows his master's horses only, keeping them in a separate company where they range, and when he is hungry or wants to see his master, in the evening he returns to town, but never stays at home a night.

THE region we had journied through, since we decamped this morning, is of a far better soil and quality than we had yet seen since we left Alachua; generally a dark greyish, and sometimes brown and black loam, on a foundation of whitish marl, chalk and testaceous limestone rocks, and ridges of a loose, coarse, reddish sand, producing stately Pines in the plains, and Live Oak, Mulberry, Magnolia, Palm, Zanthoxilon, &c. in the hommocks, and also in great plenty the pirennial Indigo; it grows here five, six and seven feet high, and as thick together as if it had been planted and cultivated. The higher ridges of hills afford great quantities of a species of iron ore, of that kind found in New−Jersey and Pennsylvania, and there called bog ore; it appears on the surface of the ground in large detached masses and smaller fragments; it is ponderous and seemed rich of that most useful metal; but one property remarkable in these terrigenous stones is, they appeared to be blistered, somewhat resembling cinders, or as if they had suffered a violent action of fire.

LEAVING the charming savanna and fields of Capola, we passed several miles through delightful plains and meadows, little differing from the environs of Capola, diversified with rocky islets or hommocks of dark woodland.

WE next entered a vast forest of the most stately Pine trees that can be imagined, planted by nature at a moderate distance, on a level, grassy plain, enamelled with a variety of flowering shrubs, viz. Viola, Ruellia infundibuliformea, Amaryllis atamasco, Mimosa sensitiva, Mimosa intsia and many others new to me. This sublime forest continued five or six miles, when we came to dark groves of Oaks, Magnolias, Red bays, Mulberrys, &c. through which proceeding near a mile, we entered open fields and arrived at the town of Talahasochte, on the banks of Little St. Juan.

THE river Little St. Juan may, with singular propriety, be termed the pellucid river. The waters are the clearest and purest of any river I ever saw, transmitting distinctly the natural form and appearance of the objects moving in the transparent floods, or reposing on the silvery bed, with the finny inhabitants sporting in its gently flowing stream.

THE river at the town is about two hundred yards over, and fifteen or twenty feet in depth. The great swamp and lake Oaquaphenogaw is said to be its source, which is about one hundred miles by land North of this place, which would give the river a course of near two hundred miles from its source to the sea, to follow its meanders; as in general our rivers, that run any considerable distance through the country to the sea, by their windings and roaving about to find a passage through the ridges and heights, at least double their distance.

THE Indians and traders say that this river has no branches or collateral brooks or rivers tributary to it, but that it is fed or augmented by great springs which break out through the banks. From the accounts given by them, and my own observations on the country round about, it seems a probable assertion, for there was not a creek or rivulet, to be seen, running on the surface of the ground, from the great Alachua Savanna to this river, a distance of above seventy miles; yet, perhaps, no part of the earth affords a greater plenty of pure, salubrious waters. The uparalleled transparency of these waters furnishes an argument for such a conjecture, that amounts at least to a probability, were it not confirmed by occular demonstration; for in all the flat countries of Carolina and Florida, except this isthmus, the waters of the river are, in some degree, turgid, and have a dark hue, owing to the annual firing of the forests and plains, and afterwards the heavy rains washing the light surface of the burnt earth into rivulets, and these rivulets running rapidly over the surface of the earth, flow into the rivers, and tinge the waters the colour of lye or beer, almost down to the tide near the sea coast. But here behold how different the appearance, and how manifest the cause; for although the surface of the ground produces the same vegetable substances, the soil the same, and suffers in like manner a general conflagration, and the rains, in impetuous showers, as liberally descend upon the parched surface of the ground; but the earth being so hollow and porous, these superabundant waters cannot constitute a rivulet or brook, to continue any distance on its surface, before they are arrested in their course and swallowed up, thence descending, are filtered through the sands and other strata of earth, to the horizontal beds of porous rocks, which being composed of thin seperable laminae, lying generally in obliquely horizontal directions over each other, admit these waters to pass on by gradual but constant percolation; which collecting and associating, augment and form little rills, brooks and even subterraneous rivers, which wander in darkness beneath the surface of the earth, by innumerable doublings, windings and secret labyrinths; no doubt in some places forming vast reservoirs and subterranean lakes, inhabited by multitudes of fish and aquatic animals: and possibly, when collected into large rapid brooks, meeting irresistible obstructions in their course, they suddenly break through these perforated fluted rocks, in high, perpendicular jets, nearly to their former level, flooding large districts of land: thus by means of those subterranean courses, the waters are purified and finally carried to the banks of great rivers, where they emerge and present themselves to open day–light, with their troops of finny inhabitants, in those surprising vast fountains near the banks of this river; and likewise on and near the shores of Great St. Juan, on the East coast of the isthmus, some of which I have already given an account of.

ON our arrival at Talahasochte, in the evening we repaired to the trading house formerly belonging to our chief, where were a family of Indians, who immediately and complaisantly moved out to accommodate us. The White King with most of the male inhabitants were out hunting or tending their Corn plantations.

THE town is delightfully situated on the elevated East banks of the river, the ground level to near the river, when it descends suddenly to the water; I suppose the perpendicular elevation of the ground may be twenty or thirty feet. There are near thirty habitations constructed after the mode of Cuscowilla; but here is a more spacious and neat council–house.

THESE Indians have large handsome canoes, which they form out of the trunks of Cypress trees (Cupressus disticha) some or them commodious enough to accomodate twenty or thirty warriors. In these large canoes they descend the river on trading and hunting expeditions on the sea coast, neighbouring islands and keys, quite to the point of Florida, and sometimes cross the gulph, extending their navigations to the Bahama islands and even to Cuba: a crew of these adventurers had just arrived, having returned from Cuba just a few days before our arrival, with a cargo of spiritous liquors, Coffee, Sugar, and Tobacco. One of them politely presented me with a choice piece of Tobacco, which he told me he had received from the governor of Cuba.

They deal in the way of barter, carrying with them deer skins, furs, dry fish, bees–wax, honey, bear's oil and some other articles. They say the Spaniards receive them very friendly, and treat them with the best spiritous liquors.

The Spaniards of Cuba likewise trade here or at St. Marks, and other sea ports on the West coast of the isthmus in small sloops; particularly at the bay of Calos, where are excellent fishing banks and grounds; not far from which is a considerable town of the Siminoles, where they take great quantities of fish, which they salt and cure on shore, and barter with the Indians and traders for skins, furs, &c. and return with their cargoes to Cuba.

THE trader of the town of Talahasochte informed me, that he had, when trading in that town, large supplies of goods, from these Spanish trading vessels suitable for that trade; and some very essential articles, on more advantageous terms than he could purchase at Indian stores either in Georgia or St. Augustine.

TOWARDS the evening after the sultry heats were past, a young man of our company, having previously procured the loan of a canoe from an Indian, proposed to me a fishing excursion for trout with the bob. We sat off down the river, and before we had passed two miles caught enough for our houshold: he was an excellent hand at this kind of diversion; some of the fish were so large and strong in their element, as to shake his arms stoutly and dragged us with the canoe over the floods before we got them in. It is in the eddy coves, under the points and turning of the river, where the surface of the waters for some acres is covered with the leaves of the Nymphea, pistia and other amphibious herbs and grass, where the haunts and retreats of this famous fish are, as well as others of various tribes.

Travels Through North and South Carolina

OBSERVING a fishing canoe of Indians turning a point below and coming towards us, who hailing us, we waited their coming up; they were cheerful merry fellows, and insisted on our accepting of part of their fish, they having a greater quantity and variety, especially of the bream my favourite fish; we exchanged some of our trout with them.

OUR chief being engaged with the chiefs of the town in commercial concerns, and others of our company, out in the forests with the Indians, hunting up horses belonging to the trading company; the young interpreter, my companion, who was obliging to me and whom our chief previously recommended to me as an associate; proposed to me another little voyage down the river; this was agreeable to me, being desirous of increasing my observations during our continuance at Talahasochte; as when the White King should return to town (which was expected every hour) we intended after audience and treaty to leave them and encamp in the forests, about fifteen miles distance and nearer the range of their horses.

HAVING supplied ourselves with amunition and provision, we set off in the cool of the morning, and descended pleasantly, riding on the chrystal flood, which flows down with an east, gentle, yet active current, rolling over its silvery bed; how abundantly are the waters replenished with inhabitants! the stream almost as transparent as the air we breathe; there is nothing done in secret except on its green flowery verges, where nature at the command of the Supreme Creator, hath spread a mantle, as a covering and retreat at suitable and convenient times, but by no means a secure refuge from the voracious enemy and pursuer.

BEHOLD the watery nations, in numerous bands roving to fro, amidst each other, here they seem all at peace; through incredible to relate, but a few yards off, near the verge of the green mantled shore there is eternal war, or rather slaughter! Near the banks the waters become turgid, from substance gradually diverging from each side of the swift channel, and collections of opaque particles whirled to those by the eddies, which afford a kind of nursery for young fry, and its slimy bed a prolific nidus for generating and rearing of infinite tribes and swarms of amphibious insects, which are the food of young fish, who in their turn become a prey to the older. Yet when those different tribes of fish are in the transparent channel, their very nature seems absolutely changed, for here is neither desire to destroy or persecute, but all seems peace and friendship; do they agree on a truce, a suspension of hostilities? or by some secret divine influence, is desire taken away? or they are otherwise rendered incapable of pursuing each other to destruction?

Travels Through North and South Carolina

ABOUT noon we approached the admirable Manate Spring, three or four miles down the river. This charming nympheum is the product of primitive nature, not to be imitated much less equalled by the united effort of human power and ingenuity! as we approach it by water, the mind of the enquiring traveller is previously entertained and gradually led on to greater discovery; first by a view of the sublime dark grove, lifted up on shore, by a range or curved chain of hills, at a small distance from the lively green verge of the river, on the East banks; as we gently descend floating fields of the Nymphea nilumbo, intersected with vistas of the yellow green Pista stratiotes, which cover a bay or cove of the river opposite the circular woodland hills.

IT is amazing and almost incredible, what troops and bands of fish, and other watery inhabitants are now in sight, all peaceable, and in what variety of gay colours and forms, continually ascending and descending, roving and figuring amongst one another, yet every tribe associating seperately; we now ascended the chrystal stream, the current swift, we entered the grand fountain, the expansive circular bason, the source of which arises from under the bases of the high woodland hills, near half encircling it; the ebullition is astonishing, and continual, though its greatest force or fury intermits, regularly, for the space of thirty seconds of time; the waters appear of a lucid sea green colour, in some measure owing to the reflection of the leaves above; the ebullition is perpendicular upwards, from a vast ragged orifice through a bed of rocks, a great depth below the common surface of the bason, throwing up small particles or pieces of white shells, which subside with the waters, at the moment of intermission, gently settling down round about the orifice, form a vast funnel; at those moments, when the waters rush upwards, the surface of the bason immediately over the orifice is greatly swolen or raised a considerable height; and then it is impossible to keep the boat or any other floating vessel over the fountain; but the ebullition quickly subsides, yet, before the surface becomes quite even, the fountain vomits up the waters again, and so on perpetually; the bason is generally circular, about fifty yards over, and the perpetual stream from it into the river is twelve or fifteen yards wide, and ten or twelve feet in depth; the bason and stream continually peopled with prodigious numbers and variety of fish and other animals; as the alligator and the manate*

* Trichechus manatus. Sea cow.

or sea cow, in the winter season; part of a skeleton of one, which the Indians had killed last winter, lay upon the banks of the spring; the grinding teeth were about an inch in diameter; the ribs eighteen inches in length, and two inches and an half in thickness, bending with a gentle curve, this bone is esteemed equal to ivory; the flesh of this creature is counted wholesome and pleasant food; the Indians call them by a name which signifies the big beaver. My companion, who was a trader in Talahasochte last winter, saw three of them at one time in this spring: they feed chiefly on aquatic grass and weeds. The ground round about the head of the bason is generally level, for the distance of a few yards, then gradually ascends, forming moderately high hills; the soil at top is a light, greyish, sandy mould, which continues some feet in depth, lying on a stratum of yellowish clay, then clay and gravel, then sand, and so on, stratum upon stratum, down to the general foundation of testaceous rocks. In other places a deep stratum of whitish, chalky limestone. The vegetable productions which cover and ornament those emminences, are generally Live Oaks, Magnolia grandiflora, in the Creek tongue, Tolo–chlucco, which signifies the Big Bay, Laurus Borbonia or Red Bay, in the Creek tongue, Etomico, that is King's tree, Olea Americana and Liquid–amber, with other trees, shrubs and herbacious plants common in East Florida.

THE hills and groves environing this admirable fountain, affording amusing subjects of enquiry, occasioned my stay here a great part of the day, and towards evening we returned to the town.

NEXT day, early in the morning, we crossed the river, landing on the other shore opposite the town, swimming our horses by the side of the canoe, each of us holding his horse by the bridle whilst an Indian paddled us over. After crossing, we struck off from the river into the forests, sometimes falling into, and keeping for a time, the ancient Spanish high road to Pensacola, now almost obliterated: passed four or five miles through old Spanish fields.

THERE are to be seen plain marks or vestiges of the old Spanish plantations and dwellings; as fence posts and wooden pillars of their houses, ditches and even Corn ridges and Batata hills. From the Indian accounts, the Spaniards had here a rich, well cultivated and populous settlement, and a strong fortified post, as they likewise had at the savanna and fields of Capola; but either of them far inferior to one they had some miles farther South–West towards the Apalachuchla River, now called the Apalachean Old Fields, where yet remain vast works and buildings, as fortifications, temples, some brass cannon, mortars, heavy church bells, &c.

Travels Through North and South Carolina

THE same groups of whitish, testaceous rocks and circular sinks, with natural wells, make their appearance in these groves and fields, as observed on the side of the river opposite to Capola, and the same trees, shrubs and herbage without variation. Having passed five or six miles through these ancient fields and groves, the scene suddenly changes, after riding through a high forest of Oak, Magnolia, Fraxinus, Liquid–amber, Fagus sylvatica, &c,

Now at once opens to view, perhaps, the most extensive Cane–break*

* Cane meadows, so called by the inhabitants of Carolina, &c.

that is to be seen on the face of the whole earth; right forward, about South–West, there appears no bound but the skies, the level plain, like the ocean, uniting with the firmament; and on the right and left hand, dark shaded groves, old fields and high forests, such as we had lately passed through.

THE alternate, bold promontories and misty points advancing and retiring, at length, as it were, insensibly vanishing from sight, like the two points of a crescent, softly touching the horizon, represent the most magnificent amphitheatre or circus perhaps in the whole world. The ground descends gently from the groves to the edge of the Cane–break, forming a delightful, green, grassy lawn. The Canes are ten or twelve feet in height, and as thick as an ordinary walking staff; they grow so close together, there is no penetrating them without previously cutting a road. We came up to this vast plain where the ancient Spanish high way crosses it to Pensacola; there yet remain plain vestiges of the grand causeway, which is open like a magnificent avenue, and the Indians have a bad road or pathway on it. The ground or soil of the plain is a perfectly black, rich, soapy earth, like a stiff clay or marle, wet and boggy near shore, but, further in, firm and hard enough in the summer season, but wet and in some places under water during the winter.

THIS vast plain together with the forests contiguous to it, if permitted (by the Siminoles who are sovereigns of these realms) to be in possession and under the culture of industrious planters and mechanicks, would in a little time exhibit other scenes than it does at present, delightful as it is; for by the arts of agriculture and commerce, almost every desirable thing in life might be produced and made plentiful here, and thereby establish a rich, populous and delightful region; as this soil and climate appears to be of a nature favourable for the production of almost all the fruits of the earth, as Corn*

* Zea

Rice, Indigo, Sugar–cane, Flax, Cotton, Silk, Cochineal and all the varieties of esculent vegetables; and I suppose no part of the earth affords such endless range and exuberant pasture for cattle, deer, sheep, &c. the waters every where, even in the holes in the earth abound with varieties of excellent fish; and the forests and native meadows with wild game, as bear, deer, turkeys, quail, and in the winter season geese, ducks and other fowl; and lying contiguous to one of the most beautiful navigable rivers in the world; and not more than thirty miles from St. Marks on the great bay of Mexico; is most conveniently situated for the West–India trade and the commerce of all the world.

AFTER indulging my imagination in the contemplation of these grand diversified scenes, we turned to the right hand, riding over the charming green terrace dividing the forests from the plains, and then entering the groves again, continued eight or nine miles up the river, four or five miles distance from its banks; having continually in view on one side or other, expansive green fields, groves and high forests; the meadows glittering with distant lakes and ponds, alive with cattle, deer and turkies, and frequently present to view remains of ancient Spanish plantations. At length, towards evening, we turned about and came within sight of the river, where falling on the Indian trading path, we continued along it to the landing–place opposite the town, when hallooing and discharging our pieces, an Indian with a canoe came presently over and conducted us to the town before dark.

ON our arrival at the trading house, our chief was visited by the head men of the town, when instantly the White King's arrival in town was anounced; a messenger had before been sent in to prepare a feast, the king and his retinue having killed several bears. A fire is now kindled in the area of the public square; the royal standard is displayed, and the drum beats to give notice to the town of the royal feast.

THE ribs and the choice pieces of the three great fat bears already well barbecued or broiled, are brought to the banqueting house in the square, with hot bread; and honeyed water for drink.

Travels Through North and South Carolina

WHEN the feast was over in the square, (where only the chiefs and warriors were admitted, with the white people) the chief priest, attended by slaves, came with baskets and carried off the remainder of the victuals &c. which was distributed amongst the families of the town; the king then withdrew, repairing to the council house in the square, whither the chiefs and warriors, old and young, and such of the whites as chose, repaired also; the king, war–chief and several ancient chiefs and warriors were seated on the royal cabins, the rest of the head men and warriors, old and young, sat on the cabins on the right hand of the king's, and the cabins or seats on the left, and on the same elevation are always assigned for the white people, Indians of other towns, and such of their own people as chose.

OUR chief, with the rest of the white people in town, took their seats according to order; Tobacco and pipes are brought, the calamut is lighted and smoked, circulating according to the usual forms and ceremony, and afterwards black drink concluded the feast. The king conversed, drank Cassine and associated familiarly with his people and with us.

AFTER the public entertainment was over, the young people began their music and dancing in the square, whither the young of both sexes repaired, as well as the old and middle aged: this frolick continued all night.

THE White King of Talahasochte is a middle aged man, of moderate stature, and though of a lofty and majestic countenance and deportment, yet I am convinced this dignity which really seems graceful, is not the effect of vain supercilious pride, for his smiling countenance and his cheerful familarity bespeak magnanimity and benignity.

NEXT a council and treaty was held, they requested to have a trading house again established in the town, assuring us that every possible means should constantly be pursued to prevent any disturbance in future on their part; they informed us that the murderers of M'Gee*

* M'Gee was the leader of a family of white people from Georgia, destined across the isthmus, to the Mobile river; they travelled on horse–back as far as this town, where they procured canoes of the Indians, continuing their travels, descending the river and coasting the main S. W. but at night, when on shore hunting provisions, their camp was surprised and attacked by a predatory band of Indians, who flew M'Gee and the rest of the men and carried off the plunder and a woman to their towns.

and his associates, were to be put to death, that two of them were already shot, and they were in pursuit of the other.

OUR chief trader in answer, informed them that the re—establishment of friendship and trade was the chief object of his visit, and that he was happy to find his old friends of Talahasochte in the fame good disposition, as they ever were towards him and the white people, that it was his with to trade with them, and that he was now come to collect his pack—horses to bring them goods. The king and the chiefs having been already acquainted with my business and pursuits amongst them, received me very kindly; the king in particular complimented me, saying that I was as one of his own children or people, and should be protected accordingly, while I remained with them, adding, "Our whole country is before you, where you may range about at pleasure, gather physic plants and flowers, and every other production;" thus the treaty terminated friendly and peaceably.

NEXT day early in the morning we left the town and the river, in order to fix our encampment in the forests about twelve miles from the river, our companions with the pack—horses went a head to the place of rendezvous, and our chief conducted me another way to shew me a very curious place, called the Alligator—Hole, which was lately formed by an extraordinary eruption or jet of water; it is one of those vast circular sinks, which we behold almost every where about us as we traversed these forests, after we left the Alachua savanna: this remarkable one is on the verge of a spacious meadow, the surface of the ground round about uneven by means of gentle rising knolls; some detatched groups of rocks and large spreading Live—Oaks shade it on every side; it is about sixty yards over, and the surface of the water six or seven feet below the rim of the funnel or bason; the water is transparent, cool and pleasant to drink, and well stored with fish; a very large alligator at present is lord or chief; many have been killed here, but the throne is never long vacant, the vast neighbouring ponds so abound with them.

THE account that this gentleman, who was an eye—witness of the last eruption, gave me of its first appearance; being very wonderful, I proceed to relate what he told me whilst we were in town, which was confirmed by the Indians, and one or more of our companions, who also saw its progress, as well as my own observations after I came to the ground

Travels Through North and South Carolina

THIS trader being near the place (before it had any visible existence in its present appearance) about three years ago (as he was looking for some horses which he expected to find in these parts) when, on a sudden, he was astonished by an inexpressible rushing noise, like a mighty hurricane or thunder storm, and looking around, he saw the earth overflowed by torrents of water, which came, wave after wave, rushing down a vale or plain very near him, which it filled with water, and soon began to overwhelm the higher grounds, attended with a terrific noise and tremor of the earth; recovering from his first surprise, he immediately resolved to proceed for the place from whence the noise seemed to come, and soon came in sight of the incomparable fountain, and saw, with amazement, the floods rushing upwards many feet high, and the expanding waters, which prevailed every way, spreading themselves far and near: he at length concluded (he said) that the fountains of the deep were again broken up, and that an universal deluge had commenced, and instantly turned about and fled to alarm the town, about nine miles distance, but before he could reach it he met several of the inhabitants, who, already alarmed by the unusual noise, were hurrying on towards the place, upon which he returned with the Indians, taking their stand on an eminence to watch its progress and the event: it continued to jet and flow in this manner for several days, forming a large, rapid creek or river, descending and following the various courses and windings of the valley, for the distance of seven or eight miles, emptying itself into a vast savanna where was a lake and sink which received and gave vent to its waters.

THE fountain, however, gradually ceased to overflow, and finally withdrew itself beneath the common surface of the earth, leaving this capacious bason of waters, which, though continually near full, hath never since overflowed. There yet remains, and will, I suppose, remain for ages, the dry bed or the river or canal, generally four, five and six feet below the natural surface of the land; the perpendicular, ragged banks of which, on each side, shew the different stratas of the earth, and at places, where ridges or a swelling bank crossed and opposed its course and fury, are vast heaps of fragments of rocks, white chalk, stones and pebbles, which were collected and thrown into the lateral vallies, until the main stream prevailed over and forced them aside, overflowing the levels and meadows, for some miles distance from the principal stream, on either side. We continued down the great vale, along its banks, quite to the savanna and lake where it vented itself, while its ancient subterranean channel was gradually opening, which, I imagine, from some hidden event or cause had been choked up, and which, we may suppose, was the immediate cause of the eruption.

Travels Through North and South Carolina

IN the evening having gained our encampment, on a grassy knoll or eminence, under the cover of spreading Oaks, just by the grotto or sink of the lake, which lay as a sparkling gem on the flowery bosom of the ample savanna; our roving associates soon came in from ranging the forests; we continued our encampment at this place for several days, ranging around the delightful country to a great distance, every days excursion presenting new scenes of wonder and delight.

EARLY in the morning our chief invited me with him on a visit to the town, to take a final leave of the White King. We were graciously received, and treated with the utmost civility and hospitality; there was a noble entertainment and repast provided against our arrival, consisting of bears ribs, venison, varieties of fish, roasted turkies (which they call the white man's dish) hot corn cakes, and a very agreeable, cooling sort of jelly, which they call conte; this is prepared from the root of the China brier (Smilax pseudo China; Smilax aspera, fructu nigro, radice nodosa, magna, laevi, farinacea. Sloan, tom I. p. 31. t. 143. f. I. habit. Jamaica, Virginia, Carolina and Florida;) they chop the roots in pieces, which are afterwards well pounded in a wooden mortar, then being mixed with clean water, in a tray or trough, they strain it through baskets, the sediment, which settles to the bottom of the second vessel, is afterwards dried in the open air, and is then a very fine, reddish flour or meal; a small quantity of this mixed with warm water and sweetened with honey, when cool, becomes a beautiful, delicious jelly, very nourishing and wholesome; they also mix it with fine Corn flour, which being fried in fresh bear's oil makes very good hot cakes or fritters.

ON our taking leave of the king and head men, they intreated our chief to represent to the white people, their unfeigned desire to bury in oblivion the late breach of amity and intermission of commerce, which they trusted would never be reflected on the people of Talahasochte; and lastly, that we would speedily return with merchandize as heretofore; all which was cheerfully consented to, assuring them their wishes and sentiments fully coincided with ours.

THE chief trader, intending to shew me some remarkable barren plains, on our return to our encampment; about noon we sat off; when we came within sight of them, I was struck with astonishment at their dreary appearance; the view Southerly seemed endless wastes, presenting rocky, gravelly and sandy barren plains, producing scarcely any vegetable substances, except a few shrubby, crooked Pine trees, growing out of heaps of white rocks, which represented ruins of villages, planted over the plains; with clumps of

163

mean shrubs, which served only to perpetuate the persecuting power and rage of fire, and to testify the aridity of the soil; the shrubs I observed were chiefly the following, Myrica cerifera, two or three varieties, one of which is very dwarfish; the leaves small, yet toothed or sinuated, of a yellowish green colour, owing to a farinaceous pubesence or vesicula which covers their surfaces; Prinos, varieties, Andromeda ferruginae, Andr. nitida, varieties, Rhamnus frangula, Sideroxilon fericium, Ilex aquifolium, Ilex myrtifolium, Empetrum, Kalmia ciliata, Cassine, and a great variety of shrub Oaks, evergreen and deciduous, some of them singularly beautiful; Corypha repens, with a great variety of herbage, particularly Cacalia, Prenanthus, Chrysocoma, Helianthus, Silphium, Lobelia, Globularia, Helenium, Polygala, varieties, Olinopodium, Cactus, various species, Euphorbia, various species, Asclepias carnosa, very beautiful and singular, Sophora, Dianthus, Cisus, Sisymbrium, Pedicularis, Gerardia, Lechea, Gnaphalium, Smilax sarsaparilla, Smilax pumila, Solidago, Aster, Lupinus filifolius, Galega, Hedysarum, &c. with various species of grasses; but there appeared vast spaces of gravel and plains of flat rocks, just even with the surface of the earth, which seemed entirely destitute of any vegetation, unless we may except some different kinds of mosses of the crustaceous sorts, as lichen, alga, &c. and coralloides. After passing several miles on the borders of these deserts, frequently alighting on them for observation and making collections; they at length gradually united or joined with infinite savannas and ponds, stretching beyond the fight Southerly, parallel with the rocky barrens, being seperated only by a narrow, low, rocky ridge of open groves, consisting of low, spreading Live Oaks, Zanthoxilon, Ilex, Sideroxilon, &c. and here and there, standing either in groups or alone, the pompous Palm tree, gloriously erect or gracefully bowing towards the earth; exhibiting a most pleasing contrast and wild Indian scene of primitive unmodified nature, ample and magnificent. We at length came a–breast of the expansive, glittering lake, which divided the ample meadows, one end of which stretching towards a verdant eminence, formed a little bay, which was partly encircled by groups of white, chalky rocks, shaded with Live Oaks, Bays, Zanthoxilon and Palm trees. We turned our horses to graze in the green lawns, whilst we traversed the groves and meadows. Here the palmated Convolvulus trailed over the rocks, with the Hedera carnosa (Fol. quinatis inciso–serratis, perennentibus) and the fantastic Clitoria, decorating the shrubs with garlands (Clit. caule volubili fol. ternatis pennetisque, flor. majore caeruleo, vexillo rotundiore, filiquis longissimis compressis.)

SOON after entering the forests, we were met in the path by a small company of Indians, smiling and beckoning to us long before we joined them; this was a family of

Travels Through North and South Carolina

Talahasochte who had been out on a hunt, and were returning home loaded with barbecued meat, hides and honey; their company consisted of the man, his wife and children, well mounted on fine horses, with a number of pack–horses; the man presently offered us a fawn–skin of honey, which we gladly accepted, and at parting I presented him with some fish hooks, sewing needles, &c. For in my travels amongst the Indians, I always furnished myself with such useful and acceptable little articles of light carriage, for presents; we parted and before night rejoined our companions at the Long Pond.

ON our return to camp in the evening, we were saluted by a party of young Indian warriors, who had pitched their camp on a green eminence near the lake, and at a small distance from our camp, under a little grove of Oaks and Palms. This company consisted of seven young Siminoles, under the conduct of a young prince or chief of Talahasochte, a town Southward in the isthmus, they were all dressed and painted with singular elegance, and richly ornamented with silver plates, chains, &c. after the Siminole mode, with waving plumes of feathers on their crests. On our coming up to them they arose and shook hands; we alighted and sat a while with them by their cheerful fire.

THE young prince informed our chief, that he was in pursuit of a young fellow, who had fled from the town, carrying off with him one of his favourite young wives or concubines; he said merrily he would have the ears of both of them before he returned; he was rather above the middle stature, and the most perfect human figure I ever saw; of an amiable engaging countenance, air and deportment; free and familiar in conversation, yet retaining a becoming gracefulness and dignity. We arose, took leave of them, and crossed a little vale covered with a charming green turf, already illumined by the soft light of the full moon.

SOON after joining our companions at camp, our neighbours the prince and his associates paid us a visit; we treated them with the best fare we had, having till this time preserved some of our spirituous liquors; they left us with perfect cordiality and cheerfulness, wishing us a good repose, and retired to their own camp, having a band of music with them, consisting of a drum, flutes and a rattle gourd, they entertained us during the night with their music, vocal and instrumental.

THERE is a languishing softness and melancholy air in the Indian convivial songs, especially of the amorous class, irresistibly moving, attractive, and exquisitely pleasing, especially in these solitary recesses when all nature is silent.

165

Travels Through North and South Carolina

BEHOLD how gracious and beneficent smiles the roseate morn! now the sun arises and fills the plains with light, his glories appear on the forests, encompassing the meadows, and gild the top of the terebinthine Pine and exalted Palms, now gently rustling by the pressure of the waking breezes: the music of the seraphic crane resounds in the skies, in seperate squadrons they sail, encircling their precincts, slowly descend beating the dense air, and alight on the green dewy verge of the expansive lake; its surface yet smoaking with the grey ascending mists, which, condensed aloft in clouds of vapour, are born away by the morning breezes and at last gradually vanish on the distant horizon. All nature awakes to life and activity.

THE ground during our progress this morning, every where about us presenting to view, those funnels, sinks and wells in groups of rocks, amidst the groves, as already recited.

NEAR our next encampment one more conspicuous than I had elsewhere observed presented, I took occasion from this favourable circumstance of observing them in all their variety of appearances: its outer superficial margin being fifty or sixty yards over, which equally and uniformly on every side sloped downwards towards the center; on one side of it was a considerable path–way or road leading down to the water, worn by the frequent resort of wild creatures for drink, when the waters were risen even or above the rocky bed, but at this time they were sunk many yards below the surface of the earth, we descended first to the bed of rocks, which was perforated with perpendicular tubes, exactly like a walled well, four, five or six feet in diameter, and may be compared to cells in an honeycomb, through which appeared the water at bottom, many of these were broken or worn one into another, forming one vast well with uneven walls, consisting of projecting jambs, pilasters or buttresses and excavated semicircular niches, as if a piece were taken out of an honey–comb; the bed of rocks is from fifteen to twenty feet deep or in thickness, though not of one solid mass, but of many generally horizontal laminae, or strata of various thickness, from eighteen inches to two or three feet, and admit water to weep through, trickling down; drop after drop, or chasing each other in winding little rills down to the bottom; one side of the vast cool grotto was so shattered and broken in, I thought it possible to descend down to the water at bottom, and my companion assuring me that the Indians and traders frequently go down for drink, encouraged me to make the attempt as he agreed to accompany me.

HAVING provided ourselves with a long snagged sapling, called an Indian ladder, and each of us a pole, by the assistance of these we both descended safely to the bottom, which we found nearly level and not quite covered over with water; on one side was a bed of gravel and fragments of rocks or sones, and on the other a pool of water near two feet deep, which moved with a slow current under the walls on a bed of clay and gravel.

AFTER our return to the surface of the earth, I again ranged about the groves and grottos, examining a multitude of them; being on the margin of one in the open forest, and observing some curious vegetable productions growing on the side of the sloping funnel toward its center, the surface of the ground covered with grass and herbage; unapprehensive of danger, I descended precipitately towards the group of shrubs, when I was surprised and providentially stopped in my career, at the ground sounding hollow under my feet, and observing chasms through the ground, I quickly drew back, and returning again with a pole with which I beat in the earth, when to my astonishment and dread appeared the mouth of a well through the rocks, and observed the water glimmering at the bottom. Being wearied with excursions, we returned to our pleasant situation on the verge of the lawn.

NEXT day we sat off on our return to the lower trading–house, proposing to encamp at a savanna, about twelve miles distance from this, where we were to halt again and stay a day or two, in order to collect together another party of horses, which had been stationed about that range; the young wild horses often breaking from the company, rendered our progress slow and troublesome; we however arrived at the appointed place long before night.

I HAD an opportunity this day of collecting a variety of specimens and seeds of vegetables, some of which appeared new to me, particularly Sophora, Cistus, Tradescantia, Hypoxis, Tatropa, Gerardia, Pedicularis, Mimosa sensitiva, Helonias, Melanthium, Lillium, Aletris, Agave, cactus, Zamia, Empetrum, Erythryna, Echium, &c.

NEXT day, the people being again engaged in their business of ranging the forests and plains, in search of their horses, I accompanied them, and in our rambles we again visited the great savanna and lake, called the Long Pond: the lake is nearly in the middle of the spacious lawn, of an oblong form; above two miles wide and seven in length; one end approaching the high, green banks adjoining the forests, where there is an enchanting grove and grotto of pellucid waters, inhabited with multitudes of fish, continually ascending and descending through the clean, white rocks, gradually sloping from the green verged shore, by gradual steps, from smooth, flat pavements washed by the swelling undulations of the waters.

ARRIVED in the evening at camp, where we found the rest of our companions busily employed in securing the young freakish horses. The next day was employed in like manner, breaking and tutoring the young steeds to their duty. The day following we took a final leave of this land of meadows, lakes, groves and grottos, directing our course for the trading path, having traversed a country, in appearance, little differing from the region lying upon Little St. Juan; we gained about twelve miles on our way, and in the evening encamped on a narrow ridge, dividing two savannas from each other, near the edge of a deep pond; here our people made a large pen or pound to secure their wild horses during the night. There was a little hommock or islet containing a few acres of high ground, at some distance from the shore, in the drowned savanna, almost every tree of which was loaded with nests of various tribes of water fowl, as ardea alba, ar. violacea, ar. cerulea, ar. stellaris crestate, ar. stellaris maxima, ar. virescens, colymbus, tantalus, mergus and others; these nests were all alive with young, generally almost full grown, not yet fledged, but covered with whitish or cream coloured soft down. We visited this bird isle, and some of our people taking sticks or poles with them, soon beat down, loaded themselves with these squabs and returned to camp; they were almost a lump of fat, and made us a rich supper; some we roasted and made others into a pilloe with rice: most of them, except the bitterns and tantali, were so excessively fishy in taste and smell, I could not relish them. It is incredible what prodigious numbers there were, old and young, on this little islet, and the confused noise which they kept up continually, the young crying for food incessantly, even whilst in their throats, and the old alarmed and displeased at our near residence, and the depredations we had made upon them; their various languages, cries and fluttering caused an inexpressible uproar, like a public fair or market in a populous trading city, when suddenly surprised by some unexpected, calamitous event.

ABOUT midnight, having fallen asleep, I was awakened and greatly surprised at finding most of my companions up in arms, and furiously engaged with a large alligator but a few yards from me. One of our company, it seems, awoke in the night, and perceived the monster within a few paces of the camp, who giving the alarm to the rest, they readily came to his assistance, for it was a rare piece of sport; some took fire-brands and cast them at his head, whilst others formed javelins of saplins, pointed and hardened with fire; these they thrust down his throat into his bowels, which caused the monster to roar and bellow hideously, but his strength and fury was so great that he easily wrenched or

168

twisted them out of their hands, which he wielded and brandished about and kept his enemies at distance for a time; some were for putting an end to his life and sufferings with a rifle ball, but the majority thought this would too soon deprive them of the diversion and pleasure of exercising their various inventions of torture; they at length however grew tired, and agreed in one opinion, that he had suffered sufficiently, and put an end to his existence. This crocodile was about twelve feet in length: we supposed that he had been allured by the fishy scent of our birds, and encouraged to undertake and pursue this hazardous adventure which cost him his life: this, with other instances already recited, may be sufficient to prove the intrepidity and subtilty of those voracious, formidable animals.

WE sat off early next morning, and soon after falling into the trading path, accomplished about twenty miles of our journey, and in the evening encamped as usual, near the banks of savannas and ponds, for the benefit of water and accommodations of pasture for our creatures. Next day we passed over part of the great and beautiful Alachua Savanna, whose exuberant green meadows, with the fertile hills which immediately encircle it, would if peopled and cultivated after the manner of the civilized countries of Europe, without crouding or incommoding families, at a moderate estimation, accommodate in the happiest manner, above one hundred thousand human inhabitants, besides millions of domestic animals; and I make no doubt this place will at some future day be one of the most populous and delightful seats on earth.

WE came to camp in the evening, on the banks of a creek but a few miles distance from Cuscowilla, and two days more moderate travelling brought us safe back again to the lower trading–house, on St. Juan, having been blessed with health and prosperous journey.

ON my arrival at the stores, I was happy to find all well as we had left them, and our bringing with us friendly talks from the Siminole towns, and the Nation likewise, compleated the hopes and wishes of the trading company, with respect to their commercial concerns with the Indians, which, as the chearing light of the sun–beams after a dark, tempestuous night, diffused joy and conviviality throughout the little community, where were a number of men with their families, who had been put out of employment and subsistence, anxiously waiting the happy event.

CHAP. VIII.

AS a loading could not be procured until late in the autumn, for the schooner that was to return to Georgia, this circumstance allowed me time and opportunity to continue my excursions in this land of flowers, as well as at the same time to augment my collections of seeds, growing roots, &c.

I RESOLVED upon another little voyage up the river; and after resting a few days and refitting my bark, I got on board the necessary stores, and furnishing myself with boxes to plant roots in, with my fuzee, amunition and fishing tackle, I sat sail, and in the evening arrived at Mount Royal. Next morning being moderately calm and serene, I sat sail with a gentle leading breeze, which delightfully wafted me across the lake to the west coast, landing on an airy, sandy beach, a pleasant, cool situation, where I passed the night, but not without frequent attacks from the musquitoes, and next day visited the Great Springs, where I remained until the succeeding day, encreasing my collections of specimens, seeds and roots, and then recrossed the lake to the Eastern coast. This shore is generally bolder and more rocky than the Western, it being exposed to the lash of the surf, occasioned by the W. and N. W. winds, which are brisk and constant from nine or ten o'clock in the morning till towards midnight, almost the year round; though the S. winds are considerable in the spring, and by short intervals during the summer and winter; and the N. E. though sometimes very violent in the spring and autumn, does not continue long. The day was employed in coasting slowly, and making collections. In the evening I made a harbour under cover of a long point of flat rocks, which defended the mole from the surf; having safely moored my bark, and chosen my camping ground just by, during the fine evening I reconnoitred the adjacent groves and lawns; here is a deserted plantation, the property of Dr. Stork, where he once resided. I observed many lovely shrubs and plants in the old fields and Orange groves, particularly several species of Convolvulus and Ipomea, the former having very large, white, sweet scented flowers; they are great ramblers, climbing and strolling on the shrubs and hedges. Next morning I re–embarked and continued traversing the bold coast North–Eastward, and searching the shores at all convenient landings, where I was amply rewarded for my assiduity in the society of beauties in the blooming realms of Florida. Came to again, at an old deserted plantation, the property of a British gentleman, but some years since vacated. A very spacious frame building was settling to the ground and mouldering to earth; here are very extensive old fields, where were growing the West–Indian or perennial Cotton and

Indigo, which had been cultivated here, and some scattered remains of the ancient Orange groves, which had been left standing at the clearing of the plantation.

I HAVE often been affected with extreme regret, at beholding the destruction and devastation which has been committed, or indiscreetly exercised on those extensive, fruitful Orange groves, on the banks of St. Juan, by the new planters under the British government, some hundred acres of which, at a single plantation, has been entirely destroyed to make room for the Indigo, Cotton, Corn, Batatas, &c. or as they say to extirpate the musquitoes, alledging that groves near their dwellings are haunts and shelters for those persecuting insects; some plantations have not a single tree standing, and where any have been left, it is only a small coppice or clump, nakedly exposed and destitute; perhaps fifty or an hundred trees standing near the dwelling–house, having no lofty cool grove of expensive Live Oaks, Laurel Magnolias and Palms to shade and protect them, exhibiting a mournful, sallow countenance; their native perfectly formed and glossy green foliage as if violated, defaced and torn to pieces by the bleak winds, scorched by the burning sun–beams in summer, and chilled by the winter frosts.

IN the evening I took up my quarters in the beautiful isle in sight of Mount Royal. Next day, after collecting what was new and worthy of particular notice, I sat sail again and called by the way at Mount Royal, in the evening arrived safe at the stores, bringing along with me valuable collections.

CHAP. IX.

AT the trading–house I found a very large party of the Lower Creeks encamped in a grove, just without the pallisadoes; this was a predatory band of the Siminoles, consisting of about forty warriors destined against the Chactaws of West Florida. They had just arrived here from St. Augustine, where they had been with a large troop of horses for sale and furnished themselves with a very liberal supply of spirituous liquors, about twenty kegs, each containing five gallons.

THESE sons of Mars had the continence and fortitude to withstand the temptation of even tasting a drop of it until their arrival here, where they purposed to supply themselves with necessary articles to equip them for the expedition, and proceed on directly; but here meeting with our young traders and pack–horse men, they were soon prevailed on to broach their beloved nectar; which in the end caused some disturbance, and the consumption of most of their liquor, for after they had once got a smack of it, they never were sober for ten days, and by that time there was but little left.

IN a few days this festival exhibited one of the most ludicrous bachanalian scenes that is possible to be conceived, white and red men and women without distinction, passed the day merrily with these jovial, amorous topers, and the nights in convivial songs, dances and sacrifices to Venus, as long as they could stand or move; for in these frolicks both sexes take those liberties with each other, and act, without constraint or shame, such scenes as they would abhor when sober or in their senses; and would endanger their ears and even their lives; but at last their liquor running low, and being most of them sick through intoxication, they became more sober, and now the dejected lifeless sots would pawn every thing they were in possession of, for a mouthful of spirits to settle their stomachs, as they termed it. This was the time for the wenches to make their market, as they had the fortitude and subtilty by dissimulation and artifice to save their share of the liquor during the frolick, and that by a very singular stratagem, for, at these riots, every fellow who joins in the club, has his own quart bottle of rum in his hand, holding it by the neck so sure that he never looses hold of it day or night, drunk or sober, as long as the frolick continues, and with this, his beloved friend, he roves about continually, singing, roaring and reeling to and fro, either alone or arm in arm with a brother toper, presenting his bottle to every one, offering a drink, and is sure to meet his beloved female if he can, whom he complaisantly begs to drink with him, but the modest fair, veiling her face in a mantle, refuses (at the beginning of the frolick) but he presses and at last insists; she being furnished with an empty bottle, concealed in her mantle, at last consents, and taking a good long draught, blushes, drops her pretty face on her bosom and artfully discharge the rum into her bottle, and by repeating this artifice soon fills it; this she privately conveys to her secret store, and then returns to the jovial game, and so on during the festival; and when the comic farce is over, the wench retails this precious cordial to them at her own price.

THERE were a few of the chiefs, particularly the Long Warrior their leader, who had the prudence and fortitude to resist the alluring temptation during the whole farce; but though he was a powerful chief, a king and a very cunning man, he was not able to controul these madmen, although he was acknowledged by the Indians to have communion with powerful invisible beings or spirits, and on that account esteemed worthy of homage and great respect.

Travels Through North and South Carolina

AFTER the Indians became sober they began to prepare for their departure; in the morning early the Long Warrior and chiefs sent a messenger to Mr. M'Latche, desiring to have a talk with him upon matters of moment; accordingly about noon they arrived; the conference was held in the piazza of the council house; the Long Warrior and chiefs who attended him, took their seats upon a long bench adjoining the side or front of the house, reaching the whole length of it, on one hand; and the principal white traders on the other, all on the same seat; I was admitted at this conference, Mr. M`Latche and the Long Warrior sat next to each other, my late companion, the old trader and myself sat next to him.

THE Long Warrior spake, saying, that he and his companions were going to fight their enemies the Chactaws, and that some of his associates being in want of blankets, shirts and some other articles, which they declined supplying themselves with at St. Augustine, because they had rather stick close to their old friend Mr. Spalding, and bring their buckskins, furs and other produce of their country to his trading house, (which they knew were acceptable) to purchase what they wanted; But not having the skins, &c. with them to pay for such things as they had occasion for, yet doubted not, but that on their return, they should bring with them sufficient not only to pay their debts, about to be contracted, but be able to make other considerable purchases, as the principal object of this expedition was hunting on the plentiful borders of the Chactaws. Mr. M'Latche hesitating, and expressing some dissatisfaction at his request; particularly at the length of time and great uncertainty of obtaining pay for the goods, and moreover his being only an agent for Messrs. Spalding & Co. and the magnitude and unprecedented terms of the Long Warrior's demands, required the company's assent and directions before he could comply with their request.

THIS answer displeased the Indian chief, and I observed great agitation and tumult in his passions, from his actions, hurry and rapidity of speech and expression; the old interpreter who sat by asked me if I fully understood the debate, I answered that I apprehended the Long Warrior was displeased, he told me he was so, and then recapitulated what has been said respecting his questions and Mr. M'Latche's answer; adding that upon his hesitation he immediately replied, in seeming disgust and great expressions of anger, "Do you presume to refuse me credit; certainly you know who I am and what power I have; but perhaps you do not know that if the matter required it, and I pleased, that I could command and cause the terrible thunder*

173

* It thundered, lightened and rained in a violent manner during these debates.

now rolling in the skies above, to descend upon your head, in rapid fiery shafts, and lay you prostrate at my feet, and consume your stores, turning them instantly into dust and ashes." Mr. M'Latche calmly replied, that he was fully sensible that the Long Warrior was a great man, a powerful chief of the bands of the respectable Siminoles, that his name was terrible to his enemies, but still he doubted if any man upon earth had such power, but rather believed that thunder and lightning was under the direction of the Great Spirit, but however, since we are not disposed to deny your power, supernatural influence and intercourse with the elements and spiritual agents, or withhold the respect and homage due to so great a prince of the Siminoles, friends and allies to the white people; if you think fit now in the presence of us all here, command and cause yon terrible thunder with its rapid fiery shafts, to descend upon the top of that Live Oak*

* A large ancient Live Oak stood in the yard about fifty yards distant.

in front of us, rend it in pieces, scatter his brawny limbs on the earth and consume them to ashes before our eyes, we will then own your supernatural power and dread your displeasure.

AFTER some silence the prince became more calm and easy, and returned for answer, that recollecting the former friendship and good understanding, which had ever subsisted betwixt the white people and red people of the Siminole bands, and in particular, the many acts of friendship and kindness received from Mr. M'Latche, he would look over this affront; he acknowledged his reasoning and expostulations to be just and manly, that he should suppress his resentment, and withhold his power and vengeance at present. Mr. M'Latche concluded, by saying that he was not in the least intimidated by his threats of destroying him with thunder and lightning, neither was he disposed in any manner to displease the Siminoles, and should certainly comply with his requisitions, as far as he could proceed without the advice and directions of the company, and finally agreed to supply him and his followers with such things as they stood most in need of, such as shirts, blankets and some paints, one half to be paid for directly, and the remainder to stand on credit until their return from the expedition. This determination entirely satisfied the Indians. We broke up the conference in perfect amity and good humour, and they returned to their camp and in the evening, ratified it with feasting and dancing, which continued all next day with tolerable decorum. An occurrence happened this day, by which I had an opportunity of observing their extraordinary veneration or dread of the rattle snake; I was in the forenoon busy in my apartment in the council–house, drawing some curious flowers; when, on a sudden, my attention was taken off by a tumult without, at the Indian camp; I stepped to the door opening to the piazza, where I met my friend the old interpreter, who informed me that there was a very large rattle snake in the Indian camp, which had taken possession of it, having driven the men, women and children out, and he heard them saying that they would send for Puc–Puggy (for that was the name which they had given me, signifying the Flower Hunter) to kill him or take him out of their camp; I answered that I desired to have nothing to do with him, apprehending some disagreeable consequences, and desired that the Indians might be acquainted that I was engaged in business that required application and quiet, and was determined to avoid it if possible; my old friend turned about to carry my answer to the Indians, I presently heard them approaching and calling for Puc–Puggy; starting up to escape from their sight by a back door, a party consisting of three young fellows, richly dressed and ornamented, stepped in, and with a countenance and action of noble simplicity, amity and complaisance, requested me to accompany them to their encampment; I desired them to excuse me at this time; they plead and entreated me to go with them, in order to free them from a great rattle snake which had entered their camp, that none of them had freedom or courage to expel him, and understanding that it was my pleasure to collect all their animals and other natural productions of their land, desired that I would come with them and take him away, that I was welcome to him. I at length consented and attended on them to their encampment, where I beheld the Indians greatly disturbed indeed. The men with sticks and tomahawks, and the women and children collected together at a distance in affright and trepidation, whilst the dreaded and revered serpent leisurely traversed their camp, visiting the fire places from one to another, picking up fragments of their provisions and licking their platters. The men gathered around me, exciting me to remove him: being armed with a lightwood knot, I approached the reptile, who instantly collected himself in a vast coil (their attitude of defence) I cast my missile weapon at him, which luckily taking his head, dispatched him instantly, and laid him trembling at my feet; I took out my knife, severed his head from his body, then turning about, the Indians complimented me with every demonstration of satisfaction and approbation for my heroism, and friendship for them. I carried off the head of the serpent bleeding in my hand as a trophy of victory, and taking out the mortal fangs, deposited them carefully amongst my collection. I had not been long retired to my apartment before I was again

175

roused from it by a tumult in the yard, and hearing Puc–Puggy called on, I started up, when instantly the old interpreter met me again, and told me the Indians were approaching in order to scratch me; I asked him for what; he answer for killing the rattle snake within their camp. Before I could make any reply or effect my escape, three young fellows singing, arm in arm, came up to me; I observed one of the there was a young prince who had, on my first interview with him, declared himself my friend and protector, when he told me that if ever occasion should offer in his presence, he would risk his life to defend mine or my property. This young champion stood by his two associates, one on each side of him, the two affecting a countenance and air of displeasure and importance, instantly presenting their scratching instruments, and flourishing them, spoke boldly, and said that I was too heroic and violent, that it would be good for me to loose some of my blood to make me more mild and tame, and for that purpose they were come to scratch me; they gave me no time to expostulate or reply, but attempted to lay hold on me, which I resisted, and my friend, the young prince, interposed and pushed them off, saying that I was a brave warrior and his friend, that they should not insult me, when instantly they altered their countenance and behaviour; they all whooped in chorus, took me friendly by the hand, clapped me on the shoulder and laid their hands on their breasts in token of sincere friendship, and laughing aloud, said I was a sincere friend to the Siminoles, a worthy and brave warrior, and that no one should hereafter attempt to injure me: they then all three joined arm in arm again and went off, shouting and proclaiming Puc–Puggy was their friend, &c. Thus it seemed that the whole was a ludicrous farce to satisfy their people and appease the manes*

* These people never kill the rattle snake or any other serpent, saying if they do so, the spirit of the killed snake will excite or influence his living kindred or relatives to revenge the injury or violence done to him when alive.

of the slain rattle snake.

THE next day was employed by the Indians in preparations for their departure, such as taking up their goods from the trading house, collecting together their horses, making up their packs, &c. and the evening joyfully spent in songs and dances. The succeeding morning after exhibiting the war farce they decamped, proceeding on their expedition against their enemy.

CHAP. X.

BUT let us again resume the subject of the rattle snake; a wonderful creature, when we consider his form, nature and disposition, it is certain that he is capable by a puncture or scratch of one of his fangs, not only to kill the largest animal in America, and that in a few minutes time, but to turn the whole body into corruption; but such is the nature of this dreaded reptile, that he cannot run or creep faster than a man or child can walk, and he is never known to strike until he is first assaulted or fears himself in danger, and even then always gives the earliest warning by the rattles at the extremity of his tail. I have in the course of my travels in the Southern states (where they are the largest, most numerous and supposed to be the most venemous and vindictive) stept unknowingly so close as almost to touch one of them with my feet, and when I perceived him he was already drawn up in circular coils ready for a blow. But however incredible it may appear, the generous, I may say magnanimous creature lay as still and motionless as if inanimate, his head crouched in, his eyes almost shut, I precipitately withdrew, unless when I have been so shocked with surprise and horror as to be in a manner rivetted to the spot, for a short time not having strength to go away, when he often slowly extends himself and quietly moves off in a direct line, unless pursued when he erects his tail as far as the rattles extend, and gives the warning alarm by intervals, but if you pursue and overtake him with a shew of enmity, he instantly throws himself into the spiral coil, his tail by the rapidity of its motion appears like a vapour, making a quick tremulous sound, his whole body swells through rage, continually rising and falling as a bellows; his beautiful particoloured skin becomes speckled and rough by dilatation, his head and neck are flattened, his cheeks swollen and his lips constricted, discovering his mortal fangs; his eyes red as burning coals, and his brandishing forked tongue of the colour of the hottest flame, continually menaces death and destruction, yet never strikes unless sure of his mark.

THE rattle snake is the largest serpent yet known to exist in North America, I have heard of their having been seen formerly, at the first settling of of Georgia, seven, eight and even ten feet in length, and six or eight inches diameter, but there are none of that size now to be seen, yet I have seen them above six feet in length, and about six inches in thickness, or as large as a man's leg, but their general size is four, five and six feet in length. They are supposed to have the power of fascination in an eminent degree, so as to inthral their prey. It is generally believed that they charm birds, rabbits, squirrels and

177

other animals, and by stedfastly looking at them possess them with infatuation; be the cause what it may, the miserable creatures undoubtedly strive by every possible means to escape, but alas! their endeavours are in vain, they at last loose the power of resistance, and flutter or move slowly, but reluctantly towards the yawning jaws of their devourers, and creep into their mouths or lay down and suffer themselves to be taken and swallowed.

SINCE, within the circle of my acquaintance, I am known to be an advocate or vindicator of the benevolent and peaceable disposition of animal creation in general, not only towards mankind, whom they seem to venerate, but also towards one another, except where hunger or the rational and necessary provocations of the sensual appetites interfere. I shall mention a few instances, amongst many, which I have had an opportunity of remarking during my travels, particularly with regard to the animal I have been treating of, I shall strictly confine myself to facts.

WHEN on the sea coast of Georgia, I consented, with a few friends, to make a party of amusement at fishing and fowling on Sapello, one of the sea coast islands; we accordingly descended the Alatamaha, crossed the sound and landed on the North end of the island, near the inlet, fixing our encampment at a pleasant situation, under the shade of a grove of Live Oaks and Laurels*

* Magnolia grandiflora, called by the inhabitants the Laurel.

on the high banks of a creek which we ascended, winding through a salt marsh, which had its source from a swamp and savanna in the island: our situation elevated and open, commanded a comprehensive landscape; the great ocean, the foaming surf breaking on the sandy beach, the snowy breakers on the bar, the endless chain of islands, checkered sound and high continent all appearing before us. The diverting toils of the day were not fruitless, affording us opportunities of furnishing ourselves plentifully with a variety of game, fish and oysters for our supper.

ABOUT two hundred yards from our camp was a cool spring, amidst a grove of the odoriferous Myrica; the winding path to this salubrious fountain led through a grassy savanna; I visited the spring several times in the night, but little did I know, or any of my careless drowsy companions, that every time we visited the fountain we were in

178

imminent danger, as I am going to relate; early in the morning, excited by unconquerable thirst, I arose and went to the spring, and having, thoughtless of harm or danger, nearly half past the dewy vale, along the serpentine foot path, my hasty steps were suddenly stopped by the sight of a hideous serpent, the formidable rattle snake, in a high spiral coil, forming a circular mound half the height of my knees, within six inches of the narrow path; as soon as I recovered my senses and strength from so sudden a surprise, I started back out of his reach, where I stood to view him: he lay quiet whilst I surveyed him, appearing no way surprised or disturbed, but kept his half–shut eyes fixed on me; my imagination and spirits were in a tumult, almost equally divided betwixt thanksgiving to the Supreme Creator and preserver, and the dignified nature of the generous though terrible creature, who had suffered us all to pass many times by him during the night, without injuring us in the least, although we must have touched him, or our steps guided therefrom by a supreme guardian spirit: I hastened back to acquaint my associates, but with a determination to protect the life of the generous serpent; I presently brought my companions to the place, who were, beyond expression, surprised and terrified at the sight of the animal, and in a moment acknowledged their escape from destruction to be miraculous; and I am proud to assert, that all of us, except one person, agreed to let him lay undisturbed, and that person at length was prevailed upon to suffer him to escape.

AGAIN, when in my youth, attending my father on a journey to the Catskill Mountains, in the government of New–York; having nearly ascended the peak of Giliad, being youthful and vigorous in the pursuit of botanical and novel objects, I had gained the summit of a steep rocky precipice, a–head of our guide, when, just entering a shady vale, I saw at the root of a small shrub, a singular and beautiful appearance, which I remember to have instantly apprehended to be a large kind of Fungus which we call Jews ears, and was just drawing back my foot to kick it over, when at the instant, my father being near, cried out, a rattle snake my son, and jerked me back, which probably saved my life; I had never before seen one, this was of the kind which our guide called a yellow one, it was very beautiful, speckled and clouded. My father plead for his life, but our guide was inexorable, saying he never spared the life of a rattle snake, and killed him; my father took his skin and fangs.

SOME years after this, when again in company with my father on a journey into East Florida, on the banks of St. Juan, at Fort Picolata, attending the congress at a treaty between that government and the Creek Nation, for obtaining a territory from that people to annex to the new government. After the Indians and a detachment from the garrison of

179

Travels Through North and South Carolina

St. Augustine had arrived and encamped separately, near the fort, some days elapsed before the business of the treaty came on, waiting the arrival of a vessel from St. Augustine, on board of which were the presents for the Indians. My father employed this time of leisure in little excursions round about the fort; and one morning, being the day the treaty commenced, I attended him on a botanical excursion, some time after we had been rambling in a swamp about a quarter of a mile from the camp, I being a−head a few paces my father bid me observe the rattle snake before and just at my feet, I stopped and saw the monster formed in a high spiral coil, not half his length from my feet, another step forward would have put my life in his power, as I must have touched if not stumbled over him; the fright and perturbation of my spirits at once excited resentment, at that time I was entirely insensible to gratitude or mercy; I instantly cut off a little sapling and soon dispatched him: this serpent was about six feet in length, and as thick as an ordinary mans leg. The rencounter deterred us from proceeding on our researches for that day. So I cut off a long tough withe or vine, which fastening round the neck of the slain serpent I dragged him after me, his scaly body founding over the ground, and entering the camp with him in triumph, was soon surrounded by the amazed multitude, both Indians and my countrymen. The adventure soon reached the ears of the commander, who sent an officer to request that, if the snake had not bit himself, he might have him served up for his dinner; I readily delivered up the body of the snake to the cooks, and being that day invited to dine at the governor's table, saw the snake served up in several dishes: governor Grant being fond of the flesh of the rattle snake; I tasted of it but could not swallow it. I however, was sorry after killing the serpent when cooly recollecting every circumstance, he certainly had it in his power to kill me almost instantly, and I make no doubt but that he was conscious of it. I promised myself that I would never again be accessary to the death of a rattle snake, which promise I have invaribly kept to. This dreaded animal is easily killed, a stick no thicker than a man's thumb is sufficient to kill the largest at one stroke, if well directed either on the head or across the back, nor can they make their escape by running off, nor indeed do they attempt it when attacked.

THE moccasin snake is a large and horrid serpent to all appearance, and there are very terrifying stories related of him by the inhabitants of the Southern states, where they greatly abound, particularly in East Florida: that their bite is always incurable, the flesh for a considerable space about the wound rotting to the bone, which then becomes caros, and a general mortification ensues, which infallibly destroys the patient; the members of the body rotting and dying by piecemeal, and that there is no remedy to prevent a lingering miserable death but by immediately cutting away the flesh to the bone, for some distance round about the wound. In shape and proportion of parts they much resemble the rattle snake, and are marked or clouded much after the same manner, but their colours more dull and obscure; and in their disposition seem to agree with that dreaded reptile, being slow of progression, and throw themselves in a spiral coil ready for a blow when attacked. They have one peculiar quality, which is this, when discovered, and observing their enemy to take notice of them, after throwing themselves in a coil, they gradually raise their upper mandible or jaw until it falls back nearly touching their neck, at the same time slowly vibrating their long purple forked tongue, their crooked poisonous fangs directed right at you, gives the creature a most terrifying appearance. They are from three to four and even five feet in length, and as thick as a man's leg; they are not numerous, yet too common, and a sufficient terror to the miserable naked slaves, who are compelled to labour in the swamps and low lands where they only abound.

I NEVER could find any that knew an instance of any person's loosing their life from the bite of them, only by hearsay. Yet I am convinced it is highly prudent for every person to be on their guard against them. They appear to be of the viper tribe, from their swelling of their body and flattening their neck when provoked, and from their large poisonous fangs; their head, mouth and eyes are remarkably large.

THERE is another snake in Carolina and Florida called the moccasin, very different from this, which is a very beautiful creature, and I believe not of a distructive or vindictive nature; these when grown to their greatest size are about five feet in length, and near as thick as a man's arm; their skin scaly but smooth and shining, of a pale grey and sky colour ground, uniformly marked with transverse undulatory ringlets or blotches of a deep nut brown, edged with red or bright Spanish brown; they appear innocent, very active and swift, endeavouring to escape from one; they have no poisonous fangs. These are seen in high forest lands, about rotten logs or decayed fallen limbs of trees, and they harbour about old log buildings. They seem to be a species, if not the very same snake which in Pennsylvania and Virginia, are called the wampom snake, but here in warmer Southern climes they grow to a much larger size, and from the same accident their colour may be more variable and deeper. They are by the inhabitants asserted to be dangerously venemous, their bite incurable, &c. But as I could never learn an instance of their bite being mortal or attended with any dangerous consequence, and having had frequent opportunities of observing their nature and disposition, I am inclined to pronounce them an innocent creature, with respect to mankind.

Travels Through North and South Carolina

THE bastard rattle snake, by some called ground rattle snake, is a dangerous little creature, their bite is certainly mortal if present medical relief is not administered: they seem to be much of the nature of the asp or adder of the old world.

THIS little viper is in form and colour much like the rattle snake, but not so bright and uniformly marked; their head is broader and shorter in proportion with the other parts of their body; their nose prominent and turned upwards; their tail becomes suddenly small from the vent to the extremity, which terminates with three minute articulations, resembling rattles; when irritated they turn up their tail which vibrates so quick as to appear like a mist or vapour, but causes little or no found or noise, yet it is the common report of the inhabitants, that they cause that remarkable vehement noise, so frequently observed in forests in the heat of summer and autumn, very terrifying to strangers, which is, probably, caused by a very sable, small insect of the genus cicadae, or which are called locusts in America, yet it is possible I may be mistaken in this conjecture. This dangerous viper is from eight to ten inches in length, and of proportionable thickness; they are a spiteful, snappish creature, throwing themselves into a little coil, swell and flatten themselves, continually darting out their head, and they seem capable of springing beyond their length. They seem destitute of the pacific disposition and magnanimity of the rattle snake, and are unworthy of an alliance with him; no man ever saves their lives, yet they remain too numerous, even in the oldest settled parts of the country.

THE green snake is a beautiful innocent creature; they are from two to three feet in length, but not so thick as a persons little finger, of the finest green colour. They are very abundant, commonly seen on the limbs of trees and shrubs: they prey upon insects and reptiles, particularly the little green chameleon; and the forked tailed hawk or kite feeds on both of them, snatching them off the boughs of the trees.

THE ribband snake is another very beautiful innocent serpent; they are eighteen inches in length, and about the thickness of a man's little finger; the head is very small; the ground colour of a full, clear vermilion, variegated with transverse bars or zones of a dark brown, which people fancy represents a ribband wound round the creature's body: they are altogether inoffensive to man, and are in a manner domestic, frequenting old wooden buildings, open grounds and plantations.

THE chicken snake is a large, strong and swift serpent, six or seven feet in length, but scarcely so thick as a man's wrist; they are of a cinerious, earthy colour, and striped longitudinally with broad lines or lists, of a dusky or blackish colour. They are a domestic snake, haunting about houses and plantations, and would be useful to man if tamed and properly tutored, being great devourers of rats, but they are apt to disturb hen roosts and prey upon chickens. They are as innocent as a worm with respect to venom, are easily tamed and soon become very familiar.

THE pine or bull snake is very large and inoffensive with respect to mankind, but devour squirrels, birds, rabbits and every other creature they can take as food. They are the largest snake yet known in North America, except the rattle snake, and perhaps exceed him in length; they are pied black and white; they utter a terrible loud hissing noise, sounding very hollow and like distant thunder, when irritated, or at the time of incubation, when the males contend with each other for the desired female. These serpents are also called horn snakes, from their tail terminating with a hard, horny spur, which they vibrate very quick when disturbed, but they never attempt to strike with it; they have dens in the earth, whither they retreat precipitately when apprehensive of danger.

THERE are many other species of snakes in the regions of Florida and Carolina, as the water snake, black snake, garter snake, copper belly, ring neck and two or three varieties of vipers besides those already noticed in my journal. Since I have begun to mention the animals of these regions, this may be a proper place to enumerate the other tribes which I observed during my perigrinations. I shall begin with the frogs (RANAE.)

(1) THE largest frog known in Florida and on the sea coast of Carolina, is about eight or nine inches in length from the nose to the extremity of the toes; they are of a dusky brown or black colour on the upper side, and their belly or under side white, spotted and clouded with dusky spots of various size and figure; their legs and thighs also are variegated with transverse ringlets, of dark brown or black, and are yellow and green about their mouth and lips: they live in wet swamps and marshes, on the shores of large rivers and lakes; their voice is loud and hideous, greatly resembling the grunting of a swine, but not near as loud as the voice of the bull frog of Virginia and Pennsylvania, neither do they arrive to half their size, the bull frog being frequently eighteen inches in length, and their roaring as loud as that of a bull.

(2) THE bell frog, so called because their voice is fancied to be exactly like the sound of a loud cow bell. This tribe being very numerous, and uttering their voices in companies

or by large districts, when one begins another answers, thus the sound is caught and repeated from one to another, to a great distance round about, causing a surprising noise for a few minutes, rising and sinking according as the wind sets, when it nearly dies away, or is softly kept up by distant disricts or communities, thus the noise is repeated continually, and as one becomes familiarised to it is not unmusical, though at first, to strangers, it seems clamorous and disgusting.

(3) A BEAUTIFUL green frog inhabits the grassy, marshy shores of these large rivers. They are very numerous, and their noise exactly resembles the barking of little dogs, or the yelping of puppies; these, likewise make a great clamour, but as their notes are fine, and uttered in chorus, by separate bands or communities, far and near, rising and falling with the gentle breezes, affords a pleasing kind of music.

(4) THERE is besides this a less green frog, which are very common about houses: their notes are remarkably like that of young chickens; these raise their chorus immediately preceeding a shower of rain, with which they seem delighted.

(5) A LITTLE grey speckled frog are in prodigious numbers in and about the ponds and savannas on high land, particularly in Pine forests; their language or noise is also uttered in chorus, by large communities or separate bands; each particular note resembles the noise made by striking two pebbles together under the surface of the water, which when thousands near you utter their notes at the same time, and being wasted to your ears by a sudden flow of wind, is very surprising, and does not ill resemble the rushing noise made by a vast quantity of gravel and pebbles together, at once precipitated from a great height.

(6) THERE is yet an extreme diminutive species of frogs, which inhabits the grassy verges of ponds in savannas: these are called savanna crickets, are of a dark ash or dusky colour, and have a very picked nose. At the times of very great rains in the autumn, when the savannas are in a manner inundated, they are to be seen in incredible multitudes clambering up the tall grass, weeds, &c. round the verges of the savannas, bordering on the higher ground, and by an inattentive person might be taken for spiders or other insects. Their note is very feeble, not unlike the chattering of young birds or crickets.

(7) THE shad frog, so called in Pennsylvania from their appearing and croaking in the spring season, at the time the people fish for shad: these are a beautiful spotted frog, of a slender form, five or six inches in length from the nose to the extremities; of a dark olive

green, blotched with clouds and ringlets of a dusky colour: these are remarkable jumpers, and enterprising hunters, leaving their ponds to a great distance in search of prey. They abound in rivers, swamps and marshes, in the Southern regions; in the evening and sultry summer days, particularly in times of drought, are very noisy, and at some distance one would be almost persuaded that there were assemblies of men in serious debate. These have also a sucking or clucking noise, like that which is made by sucking in the tongue under the roof of the mouth. These are the kinds of water frogs that have come under my observation, yet I am persuaded that there are yet remaining several other species.

(8) THE high land frogs, commonly called toads, are of two species, the red and black. The former, which is of a reddish brown or brick colour, is the largest, and may weigh upwards of one pound when full grown; they have a disagreeable look, and when irritated, they swell and raise themselves up on their four legs and croak, but are no ways venomous or hurtful to man. The other species are one third less, and of a black or dark dusky colour; the legs and thighs of both are marked with blotches and ringlets of a darker colour, which appear more conspicuous when provoked: the smaller black species are the most numerous. Early in the spring season, they assemble by numberless multitudes in the drains and ponds, when their universal croaking and shouts are great indeed, yet in some degree not unharmonious: after this breeding time they crawl out of the waters and spread themselves all over the country. Their spawn being hatched in the warm water, the larva is there nourished, passing through the like metamorphoses as the water frogs, and as soon as they obtain four feet, whilst yet no larger than crickets, they leave the fluid nursery–bed and hop over the dry land after their parents.

THE food of these amphibious creatures, when out of the water, is every kind of insect, reptile, &c. they can take, even ants and spiders, nature having furnished them with an extreme long tongue, which exudes a viscid or glutinous liquid, they being secreted under covert, spring suddenly upon their prey, or dart forth their tongues as quick as lightning, and instrantly drag into their devouring jaws the unwary insect. But whether they prey upon one another as the water frogs do, I know not.

THERE are several species of the lizard kind besides the alligator, which is by naturalist allowed to be a species of that genus.

THE green lizard or little green chameleon is a pretty innocent creature; the largest I have seen were not more than seven inches in length; they appear commonly of a fine green colour, having a large red gill under their throat; they have the faculty of changing colour, which, notwithstanding the specious reasoning of physiologists, is a very surprising phenomenon. The striped lizard, called scorpion, and the blue bellied squamous lizards I have already mentioned. There is a large copper coloured lizard, and a very slender one of a fine blue colour, and very swift; the tail of this last, which is very long and slender, is as subject to be broken off as that of the glass snake. These two last are become very scarce, and when seen are discovered about old log buildings.

HERE are several species of the tortoise, besides those already mentioned; as the small land tortoise, already described by every traveller. There is a good figure and description of him in G. Edwards's Gl. Nat Hist. vol. II. p. 205. There are two species of fresh–water tortoises inhabiting the tide water rivers, one of which is large, weighing ten or twelve pounds, the back shell of nearly an oval form, and raised very high, the belly shell flat and entire, but deeply scolloped opposite their legs. The other species are small comparatively, and the back shell lightly raised; both species are food for mankind and esteemed delicious.

OF beasts the otter (lutra) is common, but more so in West–Florida, towards the mountains. The several species of mustela are common, as the mink, weasel and polecat; (putorius) racoons and opossums, are in great abundance, these animals are esteemed delicious and healthy food. There are two species of wild–rats, but neither of them near as large as the European house–rat, which are common enough in the settlements of the white people: here are very few mice, yet I have seen some, particularly in Charleston; I saw two in a little wire cage, at a gentleman's house, which were as white as snow, and their eyes red. There are yet a few beavers in East–Florida and Georgia, but they abound most in the north of Georgia, and in West–Florida, near the mountains. But the muskrat (castor cauda lanciolata) are never seen in Carolina, Georgia or Florida, within one hundred miles of the sea coast and very few in the most northern parts of these regions; which must be considered as a most favourable circumstance, by the people in countries where there is so much banking and draining of the land, they being the most destructive creatures to dykes.

THE roe–buck I have already mentioned. The bears are yet too numerous: they are a strong creature, and prey on the fruits of the country, and will likewise devour young calves, swine and sheep, but I never could learn a well attested instance of their attacking mankind; they weigh from five hundred to six hundred weight when full grown and fat, their flesh is greatly esteemed as food by the natives.

THE wild–cat, felis cauda truncata, (lynx) are common enough; they are a fierce and bold little animal, preying on young pigs, fawns, turkies, &c. they are not half the size of a common cur dog, are generally of a greyish colour, and somewhat tabbied; their sides bordering on the belly is varied with yellowish brown spots, and almost black waved streaks, and brindled. I have been credibly informed that the wolves here are frequently seen pied, black and white, and of other mixed colours. They assemble in companies in the night time, howl and bark altogether, especially in cold winter nights, which is terrifying to the wandering bewildered traveller.

THE foxes of Carolina and Florida are of the smaller red species; they bark in the night round about plantations, but do not bark twice in the same place; they move precipitately and in a few minutes are heard on the opposite side of the plantation, or at a great distance: it is said that dogs are terrified at the noise, and cannot be persuaded or compelled to pursue them, they commit depredations on young pigs, lambs, poultry, &c.

THE mole is not so common here as in the northern states.

THE bats of Florida seem to be the same species of those in Pennsylvania and Virginia, and very little different from the European.

HERE are several species of squirrels, (sciurus) peculiar to the lower countries, or maritime parts of Carolina and the Floridas, and some of them are very beautiful creatures.

THE great black fox squirrel is above two feet in length from the nose to the end of the tail, which for about two inches is milk white, as are the ears and nose. The red fox squirrel is of the same size and form, of a light reddish brown upper side, and white under side, the ears and tip end of the tail white.

The grey fox squirrel is rather larger than either of the foregoing, their belly white, as are the ears, nose, and tip of the tail: these three seem to be varieties of the same species.

THE common grey squirrel is about half the size of the preceding.

187

THE black squirrel is about the same size, and all over of a shining jet black.

THE little grey squirrel is much less than either of the preceding species, they are of a brownish grey upper side, and white belly.

THE ground squirrel, or little striped squirrel of Pennsylvania and the northern regions, are never seen here, and very rarely in the mountains northwest of these territories; but the flying squirrel, (sciurus volans) are very common.

THE rabbit (lepus minor, cauda abrupta, pupillis atris) are pretty common, and no ways differing from those of Pennsylvania and the northern states.

HAVING mentioned most of the animals in these parts of America, which are most remarkable or useful, there remains however yet some observations on birds, which by some may be thought not impertinent.

THERE are but few that have fallen under my observation but have been mentioned by the zoologists, and most of them very well figured in Catesby's, or Edwards's works.

BUT these authors have done very little toward illucidating the subject on the migration of birds, or accounting for the annual appearance and disappearance, and vanishing of these beautiful and entertaining beings, who visit us at certain stated seasons; Catesby has said very little on this curious subject, but Edwards more, and perhaps all, or as much as could be said in truth, by the most able and ingenious, who had not the advantage and opportunity of occular observation, which can only be acquired by travelling, and residing a whole year at least in the various climates from north to south to the full extent of their peregrinations, or minutely examining the tracts and observations of curious and industrious travellers who have published their memoirs on this subject. There may perhaps be some persons who consider this enquiry not to be productive of any real benefit to mankind, and pronounce such attention to natural history merely speculative, and only fit to amuse and entertain the idle virtuoso; however, the ancients thought otherwise, for with them, the knowledge of the passage of birds was the study of their priests and philosophers, and was considered a matter of real and indispensable use to the state, next to astronomy, as we find their system and practice of agriculture was in a great degree regulated by the arrival and disappearance of birds of passage, and perhaps a calender under such a regulation at this time, might be useful to the husbandman and gardener.

BUT however attentive and observant the ancients were on this branch of science, they seem to have been very ignorant, or erroneous in their conjectures concerning what became of birds, after their disappearance, until their return again. In the southern and temperate climates some imagined they went to the moon: in the northern regions they supposed that they retired to caves and hollow trees, for shelter and security, where they remained in a dormant state during the cold season; and even at this day, very celebrated men have asserted that swallows (hirundo) at the approach of winter, voluntarily plunge into lakes and rivers, descend to the bottom, and there creep into the mud and slime, where they continue overwhelmed by ice in a torpid state, until the returning summer warms them again into life, when they rise, return to the surface of the water, immediately take wing, and again people the air. This notion, though the latest seem the most difficult to reconcile to reason or common sense; that a bird so swift of flight that can with ease and pleasure move through the air even swifter than the winds, and in a few hours time shift themselves twenty degrees from north to south, even from frozen regions to climes where frost is never seen, and where the air and plains are replenished with flying insects of infinite variety, their favourite and only food.

PENNSYLVANIA and Virginia appear to me to be the climates in North–America, where the greatest variety and abundance of these winged emigrants choose to celebrate their nuptials, and rear their offspring, which they annually return with, to their winter habitations in the southern regions of N. America; and most of these beautiful creatures who annually people and harmonize our forests and groves in the spring and summer season, are birds of passage from the southward. The eagle, i. e. falco leucocephalus, or bald eagle, falco maximus, or great grey eagle, falco major cauda ferruginio, falco pullarius, falco columbarius, strix pythaulis, strix acclamatus, strix assio, tetrao tympanus, or pheasant of Pennsylvania, tetrao urogallus, or mountain cock or grous of Pennsylvania, tetrao minor sive coturnix, or partridge of Pennsylvania, picus, or woodpeckers of several species, corvus carnivorus, or raven, corvus frugivora, or crow, corvus glandarius f. corvus cristatus, or blue jay, aluda maxima, regulus atrofuscus minor, or marsh wren, sitta, or nuthatch, meleagris, are perhaps nearly all the land birds which continue the year round in Pennsylvania. I might add to these the blue bird, motacilla fialis, mock bird, turdus polyglottos, and sometimes the robin readbreast, turdus migratorius, in extraordinary warm winters, and although I do not pretend to assert as a known truth, yet it may be found on future observation that most of these above mentioned are strangers, or not really bred where they wintered, but are more northern families, or sojourners, bound southerly to more temperate habitations; thus pushing each other southerly, and possessing their vacated places, and then back again at the return of spring.

VERY few tribes of birds build, or rear their young, in the south or maritime parts of Virginia and Carolina, Georgia and Florida; yet all these numerous tribes, particularly of the soft billed kinds, which breed in Pennsylvania, pass in the spring season through these regions in a few weeks time, making but very short stages by the way; and again, but few of them winter there, on their return southerly; and as I have never travelled the continent south of New Orleans, or the point of Florida, where few or none of them are to be seen in the winter, I am entirely ignorant how far southward they continue their route during their absence from Pennsylvania, but perhaps none of them pass the tropic.

WHEN in my residence in Carolina and Florida, I have seen vast residence of the house swallow (hirundo pelasgia) and bank martin (hirundo riparia) passing onward north toward Pennsylvania, where they breed in the spring, about the middle of March, and likewise in the autumn in September or October, and large slights on their return southward; and it is observable that they always avail themselves of the advantage of high and favourable winds which likewise do all birds of passage. The pewit, or black cap flycatcher, of Catesby, is the first bird of passage which appears in the spring in Pennsylvania, which is generally about the first, or middle of March, and then wherever they appear, we may plant peas and beans in the open grounds, (vitia sativa) French beans (phaccolus) sow raddishes, (raphanus) lettuce, (lactuca) onions, (cepa) pastinaca, daucus, and almost every kind of exculent garden seeds, without fear or danger from frosts; for although we have sometimes frosts after their first appearance for a night or two yet not so severe as to injure the young plants.

IN the spring of the year the small birds of passage appear very suddenly in Pennsylvania, which is not a little surprising, and no less pleasing: at once the woods, the groves, and meads, are filled with their melody, as if they dropped down from the skies. The reason or probable cause is their setting off with high and fair winds from the southward; for a strong south and south–west wind about the beginning of April never fails bringing millions of these welcome visitors.

BEING willing to contribute my mite towards illustrating the subject of the peregrination of the tribes of birds of N. America, I shall subjoin a nomenclature of the birds of passage, agreeable to my observation, when on my travels from New–England to New–Orleans, on the Missiippi, and point of Florida.

LAND birds which are seen in Pennsylvania, Maryland, Virginia, N. and S. Carolina, Georgia and Florida, from the sea coast Westward, to the Apalachian mountains, viz.

* THESE arrive in Pennsylvania in the spring season from the South, which after building nests, and rearing their young, return again Southerly in the autumn.

** THESE arrive in Pennsylvania in the autumn, from the North, where they continue during the winter, and return again the spring following, I suppose to breed and rear their young; and these kinds continue their journies as far South as Carolilina and Florida.

*** THESE arrive in the spring in Carolina and Florida from the South, breed and rear their young, and return South again at the approach of winter, but never reach Pennsylvania, or the Northern States.

****THESE are natives of Carolina and Florida, where they breed and continue the year round.

***** THESE breed and continue the year round in Pennsylvania.

STRIX. The OWL.

** Strix arcticus, capite levi corpore toto niveo, the great white owl.

***** Strix pythaules, capite aurito, corpore rufo, the great horned owl.

** Strix maximus, capite aurito, corpore niveo, the great horned white owl.

***** Strix acclamator, capite levi, corpore grisco, the whooting owl.

** Strix peregrinator, capite aurito, corpore versicolore, the sharp winged owl.

***** Strix assio, capite aurito, corpore ferruginio, the little screech owl.

VULTUR. The VULTURE.

**** Vultur aura, the turkey–buzzard.

**** Vultur sacra, the white tailed vulture.

**** Vultur atratus, black vulture, or carrion crow.

FALCO. Eagle and Hawk.

***** Falco regalis, the great grey eagle.

***** F. leucocephalus, the bald eagle.

* F. piscatorius, the fishing eagle.

***** F. Aquilinus, cauda ferrug. great eagle hawk.

***** F. gallinarius, the hen hawk.

***** F. pullarius, the chicken hawk.

* F. columbarius, the pidgeon hawk.

***** F. niger, the black hawk.

* F. ranivorus, the marsh hawk.

* F. sparverius, the least hawk or sparrow hawk.

MILVUS. Kite Hawk.

a Kite hawks These are characterised by having long sharp pointed wings, being of swift flight, sailing without flapping their wings, lean light bodies, and feeding out of their claws on the wing, as they gently sail round and round.

Pica glandaria cerulea non cristata, the little jay of East Florida.

**** Falco furcatus, the forked tail hawk, or kite.

**** F. glaucus, the sharp winged hawk, of a pale sky–blue colour, the tip of the wings black.

**** F. subcerulius, the sharp winged hawk, of a dark or dusky blue colour.

**** Psitticus Caroliniensis, the parrot of Carolina, or parrakeet.

CORVUS. The Crow kind.

* Corvus carnivorus, the raven.

**** C. maritimus, the great sea–side crow, or rook.

***** C. frugivorus, the common crow.

***** C. cristatus, f. pica glandaria, the blue jay.

***** C. Floridanus, pica glandaria minor, the little jay of Florida.

***** Gracula quiscula, the purple jackdaw of the sea coast.

* Gracula purpurea, the lesser purple jackdaw, or crow blackbird.

* Cuculus Caroliniensis, the cuckoo of Carolina.

PICUS. Woodpeckers.

***** Picus principalis, the greatest crested woodpecker, having a white back.

* P. pileatus, the great red crested black woodpecker.

* P. erythrocephalus, read headed woodpecker.

* P. auratus, the gold winged woodpecker.

**** P. Carolinus, the red bellied woodpecker.

**** P. pubescens, the least spotted woodpecker.

**** P. villosus, the hariy, speckled and crested woodpecker.

**** P. varius, yellow bellied woodpecker.

**** Sitta Europea, grey black capped nuthatch.

** S. varia, ventre rubro, the black capped, red bellied nuthatch.

** Certhia rufa, little brown variegated creeper.

* C. pinus, the pine creeper.

* C. picta, blue and white striped or pied creeper.

* Alcedo alcyon, the great crested king−fisher.

* Torchilus colubris, the humming bird.

* Lanius griscus, the little grey butcher−bird of Pennsylvania.

* L. garrulus, the little black capped butcher–bird of Florida.

* L. tyrannus, the king bird.

* Muscitapa nunciola, the pewit, or black cap flycatcher.

* M. cristata, the great crested yellow bellied flycatcher.

* M. rapax, the lesser pewit, or brown and greenish flycatcher.

* M. subviridis, the little olive cold, flycatcher.

* Muscicapa cantatrix, the little domestic flycatcher or green wren.

* M. sylvicola, the little red eye'd flycatcher.

* Columba Caroliniensis, the turtle dove.

***** C. passerina, the ground dove.

** C. migratoria, the pigeon of passage or wild pigeon.

* Alauda magna, the great meadow lark.

** A. campestris, gutture flavo, the skylark.

** A. migratoria, corpore toto ferrugineo, the little brown lark.

***** Turdus migratorius, the fieldfare, or robin redbreast.

* T. rufus, the great, or fox coloured thrush.

* T. polyglottos, the mocking bird.

* T. melodes, the wood thrush.

* T. minimus, vertice aurio, the least golden crown thrush.

* Orioulus Baltimore, Baltimore bird or hang nest.

* O. spurius, the goldfinch or icterus minor.

* Merula flammula, sand–hill redbird of Carolina.

* M. Marilandica, the summer red bird.

* Garrulus australis, the yellow breasted chat.

* Lucar lividus, apice nigra, the cat bird, or chicken bird.

***** Ampelis garrulus, crown bird or cedar bird.

GRANIVOROUS TRIBES.

***** Meleagris americanus, the wild turkey.

***** Tetrao lagopus, the mountain cock, or grous.

***** T. tympanus, the pheasant of Pennsylvania.

***** T. minor, s. coturnix, the quail or partridge.

***** Loxia cardinalis, the red bird, or Virginia nightingale.

** L. rostra forficato, the cross beak.

* L. cerulea, the blue cross beak.

* Emberiza oryzivora, (1) the rice bird.

* (1 2) Are generally supposed to be male and female of the same species (2) or the pied

196

rice bird the male, and (1) or the yellow, the female.

*** E. livida, the blue or slate coloured rice bird.

* E. varia, (2) the pied rice bird.

*** Linaria ciris, the painted finch, or nonpareil.

* L. cyanea, the blue linnet.

***** Carduelus Americanus, the goldfinch.

** C. pinus, the lesser goldfinch.

** C. pusilus, the least finch.

* Fringilla erythrophthalma, the towhe bird.

** F. purpurea, the purple finch.

** F. canabina, the hemp bird.

** F. rusa, the red, or fox–coloured ground or hedge sparrow.

** F. fusca, the large brown white throat sparrow

* Passer domesticus, the little house sparrow or chipping bird.

* P. palustris, the reed sparrow.

* P. agrestis, the little field sparrow.

** P. nivalis, the snow bird.

* Calandra pratensis, the May bird.

* Sturuus predatorius, the red winged sterling, or corn thief.

* S. stercorarius, the cowpen bird.

* Motacilla sialis, the blue bird. (Rebicula Americana, Cat.)

* M. fluviatilis, the water wagtail.

* M. domestica (regulus rufus) the house wren.

***** * M. palustris, (reg. minor) the marsh wren.

* M. Caroliniana, (reg. magnus) the great wren of Carolina, the body of a dark brown, the throat and breast of a pale clay colour.

* Regulus griceus, the little bluish grey wren.

** R. cristatus, the golden crown wren.

** R. cristatus alter vertice rubini coloris, the ruby crown wren. (G. Edwards.)

* R. peregrinus, gutture flavo, the olive coloured yellow throated wren.

* Ruticilla Americana, the redstart.

* Luscinia, s. philomela Americana, the yellow hooded titmouse.

* Parus cristatus, bluish grey crested titmouse.

***** P. Europeus, the black cap titmouse.

* P. luteus, the summer yellow bird.

* P. cedrus, uropygio slavo, the yellow rump.

* P. varius, various coloured little finch creeper.

* P. peregrinus, little chocolate breast titmouse.

* P. aureus vertice rubro, the yellow red pole.

* P. aurio vertice, the golden crown flycatcher.

* P. viridis gutture nigro, the green black throated flycatcher.

* P. alis aureis, the golden winged flycatcher.

* P. aureus alis ceruleis. the blue winged yellow bird.

* P. griccus gutture luteo, the yellow throated creeper.

* Hirundo pelasgia, cauda aculeata, the house swallow.

* H. purpurea, the great purple martin.

* H. riparia vertice purpurea, the bank martin.

* H. cerdo, the chimney swallow.

*** Caprimulgus lucifugus, the great bat, or chuck wills widow.

* C. Americanus, night hawk, or whip poor will.

AMPHIBIOUS, or AQUATIC BIRDS, Or such as obtain their food, and and reside in, and near the water. GRUS. The Crane.

**** Grus clamator, vertice papilloso, corpore niveo remigibus nigris, the great whooping crane.

*** G. Pratensis, corpore cinereo, vertice papilloso, the great savanna crane.

ARDEA. The Heron.

***** Ardea Herodias, the great bluish grey crested heron.

* A. immaculata, the great white river heron.

* A. alba minor, the little white heron.

*** A. purpurea cristata, the little crested purple or blue heron.

* A. varra cristata, the grey white crested heron.

*** A. maculata cristata, the speckled crested heron, or crabcatcher.

* A. mugitans, the marsh bitern, or Indian hen.

* A. clamator, corpore subceruleo, the quaw bird, or frogcatcher.

*** A. subfusca stillata, the little brownish spotted bitern.

*** A. violacca, the crested blue bitern, (called poor Jobe.)

* A. viriscens, the green bitern or poke.

* A. viriscens minor, the lesser green bitern.

* A. parva, the least brown and striped bitern.

* Platalea ajaja, the spoonbill, seen as far North as Alatamaha river in Georgia.

TANTALUS. The Wood Pelicane.

*** Tantalus loculator, the wood pelicane.

*** T. alber, the white Spanish curlew.

*** T. fuscus, the dusky and white Spanish curlew.

**** T. Pictus, (Epnouskyka Indian) the crying bird, beautifully speckled.

**** T. Ichthyophagus, the gannet, perhaps little different from the Ibis.

**** Numenius, alba varia, the white godwit.

***** N. pectore ruso, the great red breasted godwit

***** N. Americana, the greater godwit.

***** N. fluvialis, the red shank or pool snipe.

***** N. magnus rufus, the great sea coast curlew.

* N. minor campestris, the lesser field curlew.

***** N. cinereus, the sea side lesser curlew.

* Scolopax Americana rufa, great red woodcock.

* S. minor arvensis, the meadow snipe.

* Tringa rufa, the red cootfooted tring.

T. cinerea, gutture albo, the white throated cootfooted tringa.

* T. vertice nigro, black cap cootfooted tringa.

***** T. maculata, the sspotted tringa.

***** T. griceus, the little pond snipe.

***** T. fusca, the little brown or ash coloured pool snipe.

***** T. parva, the little trings of the sea shore, called sand birds.

* Morinella Americana, the turnstone or dotrill.

** Cygnus ferus, the wild swan.

** Anser Canadensis, the Canadian goose.

** A. aliis ceruliis, the blue winged goose.

** A. fuscus maculatus, the laughing goose.

** A. branta, corpore albo, remigibus nigris, the white brant goose.

** A. branta grisca maculata, the great particoloured brant, or grey goose.

** Anas fera torquata major, caput et collum viridi splendentis, dorsum grisco fuscum, pectore rufescente speculum violacrum, the great wild duck, called duck and mallard.

** A. nigra maxima, the great black duck.

** A. bucephala, the bull—neck and buffaloe head.

** A. subcerulea, the blue bill.

** A. leucocephala, the black white faced duck.

** A. caudacuta, the sprig tail duck.

** A. rustica, the little brown and white duck.

202

** A. principalis, maculata, the various coloured duck, his neck and breast as tho' ornamented with chains of beads.

** A. minor picta, the little black and white duck called butterback.

QUERQUIDULAE. Teal.

* Anas sponsa, the summer duck.

** A. discors, the blue winged teal.

** A. migratoria, the least green winged teal.

* A. fistulosa, whistling duck.

** Mergus major pectore rufo, great fishing duck

** M. cucullatus, the round crested duck.

* Colymous migratorius, the eel crow.

**** C. Floridanus, the great black cormorant of Florida, having a red beak.

**** C. colubrinus, cauda elongata, the snake bird of Florida.

***** C. musicus, the great black and white pied diver or loon.

** Colymbus arcticus, the great speckled diver.

***** C. auritus et cornutus, the little cared brown dobekick.

***** C. minor fuscus, little crested brown dobekick.

*** Phaeaton aethereus, the tropic bird.

***** Larus alber, the great white gull.

***** L. griceus, the great grey gull.

***** L. alba minor, the little white river gull.

**** Onocratalus Americanus, the American sea pelicane

**** Petrella pintada, the pintado bird.

***** Rynchops niger, the shearwater or razor bill.

*** Pelicanus aquilus, the frigat or man of war bird.

*** P. sula, the booby.

*** Sterna stolida, the sea swallow, or noddy.

CHARADRUS. The Plover Kind.

* Charadrus vociterus, the kildea or chattering plover.

* C. maculatus, the great field spotted plover.

* C. minor, the little sea side ring necked plover.

* Hematopus ostrealegus, the will willet or oister catcher.

**** Fulica Floridana, the great blue or slate coloured coot of Florida.

* Rallus Virginianus, the sorce bird or little brown rail, also called widgeon in Pennsyl.

*** R. aquaticus minor, the little dark blue water rail.

* R. rufus Americanus, the greater brown rail.

**** R. major subceruleus, the blue or slate coloured water rail of Florida.

* Phoenicopterus ruber, the flamingo, seen about the point of Florida, rarely as far N. as St. Augustine.

I AM convinced there are yet several kinds of land birds, and a great number of aquatic fowl that have not come under my particular notice, therefore shall leave them to the investigation of future travelling naturalists of greater ability and industry.

THERE yet remain some observations on the passage, and breeding of birds, &c. which may be proper to notice in this place.

I SHALL first mention the rice bird, (emberiza oryza vora.) It is the common received opinion that they are male and female of the same species, i. e. the black pied rice bird the male, and a yellowish clay coloured one the female: the last mentioned appearing only in the autumn, when the oryz zizania are about ripening, yet in my opinion there are some strong circumstances which seem to operate against such a conjecture, though generally believed.

IN the spring about the middle of May, the black pied rice bird (which is called the male) appear in Pennsylvania; at that time the great yellow ephemera, called May fly, and a species of locusta appear in incredible multitudes, the favourite delicious food of these birds, when they are sprightly, vociferous, and pleasingly tuneful.

WHEN I was at St. Augustine, in E. Florida, in the beginning of April, the same species of grasshoppers were in multitudes on the fields and commons about the town, when great flights of these male rice birds suddenly arrived from the South, who by feeding on these insects became extremely fat and delicious, they continued here two or three weeks, until their food became scarce, when they disappeared, I suppose pursuing their journey North after the locusta and ephemera; there were a few of the yellow kind, or true rice bird, to be seen amongst them. Now these pied rice birds seem to observe the same order and time in their migrations Northerly, with the other spring birds of passage, and are undoubtedly on their way to their breeding place; but then there are no females with them, at least not one to ten thousand of the male colour, which cannot be supposed are a sufficient number to pair and breed by. Being in Charleston in the month of June, I observed at a gentleman's door, a cage full of rice birds, that is of the yellow or female

205

colour, who were very merry and vociferous, having the same variable music with the pied or male kind, which I thought extraordinary, and observing it to the gentleman, he assured me that they were all of the male kind, taken the preceding spring, but had changed their colour, and would be next spring of the colour of the pied, thus changing colour with the seasons of the year. If this is really the case, it appears they are both of the same species intermixt, spring and fall. In the spring they are gay, vociferous and tuneful birds.

AMPELIS garrulus, crown bird or cedar bird. These birds feed on various sorts of succulent fruit and berries, associating in little flocks or flights, and are to be seen in all the regions from Canada to New Orleans on the Mississippi, and how much farther South and South–West I know not. They observe no fixed time of appearance in Pennsylvania, but are to be seen a few days every month of the year, so that it is difficult to determine at what season they breed, or where. The longest period of their appearance in Pennsylvania is in the spring and first of June, at the time the early cherries are ripe, when they are numerous; and in the autumn when the Cedar berries are ripe (Juniperus Americana;) they arrive in large flights, who, with the robins (turdus migratorius) and yellow rump (parus cedrus) soon strip those trees of their berries, after which they disappear again; but in November and December they appear in smaller flights, feeding on the fruit of the Pesimmon (Dyospyros Virginiana;) and some are seen till March, subsisting upon Smilax berries, Privet (Ligustrum ruelgare) and other permanent fruits; after which they disappear until May and June. I have been informed by some people in Pennsylvania, that they have found their nests at these seasons in Pennsylvania.

LINARIA ciris (emberiza ciris Linn.) or painted finch, or nonpareil of Catesby are not seen North of Cape Fear in North Carolina, and seldom ten miles from the sea coast, or perhaps twenty or thirty miles, near the banks of great rivers, in fragrant groves of the Orange (Citrus aurantium) Zanthoxilon, Laurus Borbonia, Cassine, Sideroxilon, &c.

LINARIA cianea (tanagra Linn.) the blue linet, is supposed by some to be the nonpareil, in an early stage of life, not being yet arrived to his brilliancy and variety of colours; but this is certainly a mistake, for the blue linet is longer and of a slenderer configuration, and their notes more variable, vehement and sonorous; and the inhabit the continent and sea coast islands from Mexico to Nova–Scotia, from the sea coast West beyond the Apalachean and Cherokee mountains. The songs of the nonpareil are remarkably low, soft and warbling, exceedingly tender and soothing.

Travels Through North and South Carolina

CATESBY in his history of Carolina, speaking of the cat–bird (muscicapa vertice nigro) says, "They have but one note, which resembles the mewing of a cat;" a mistake very injurious to the same of that bird. He, in reality, being one of our most eminent songsters, little inferior to the philomela or mock–bird; and in some remarkable instances, perhaps, exceeds them both, in particular as a buffoon or mimick; he endeavours to imitate every bird and animal, and in many attempts does not ill succeed, even in rehearsing the songs, which he attentively listens to, from the shepherdess and rural swain, and will endeavour and succeed to admiration, in repeating the melodious and variable airs from instrumental music, and this in his wild state of nature. They being a kind of domestic bird during their spring and summer residence in Pennsylvania, building their nests in gardens and sheltering themselves in groves near the houses; they cause great trouble and vexation to hens that have broods of chickens, by imitating their distressing cries, in which they seem to enjoy much delight, and cause some amusement to persons who are diverted at such incidents. They are the first bird heard singing in the morning, even before break of day.

THEY seem to be a tribe of birds seperated by nature from the motacilla, with which the zoologists have classed them, and appear allied to a tribe peculiar to America, to which Edwards has given the name of manakin: in their nature they seem to take place between the thrush (turdus) and motacilla, their beak being longer, stronger and straiter than the motacilla, and formed for eating fruit, which is their chief food, yet they will feed on reptile insects, but never attempt to take their prey on the wing.

CATESBY is chargeable with the like mistake with respect to the little thrush (t. minor) and the fox coloured thrush (t. rufes) both eminent singers, and the latter little inferior to the mock–bird. The former for his shrill, sonorous and elevated strains in the high, shady forests; and the latter for variety, softness and constant responses in the hegdes and groves near houses.

BUT yet Catesby has some right of claim to our excuse and justification, for his detraction of the fame due to these eminent musicians of the groves and forests, when we consider that he resided and made his collections and observations, in the regions which are the winter retreats and residence of these birds, where they rarely sing, as it is observable and most true, that it is only at the time of incubation, that birds sing in their wild state of nature. The cat–bird, great and less thrush and field fare seldom or never build in Carolina beneath the mountains, except the great or fox coloured thrush in a few instances, but all these breed in Pennsylvania.

Travels Through North and South Carolina

THE parakeet (psitlicus Carolinienses) never reach so far North as Pennsylvania, which to me is unaccountable, considering they are a bird of such singular rapid flight, they could easily perform the journey in ten or twelve hours from North Carolina, where they are very numerous, and we abound with all the fruits which they delight in.

I WAS assured in Carolina, that these birds, for a month or two in the coldest winter weather, house themselves in hollow Cypress trees, clinging fast to each other like bees in a hive, where they continue in a torpid state until the warmth of the returning spring reanimates them, when they issue forth from their late dark, cold winter cloisters. But I lived several years in North Carolina and never was witness to an instance of it, yet I do not at all doubt but there have been instances of belated flocks thus surprised by sudden severe cold, and forced into such shelter, and the extraordinary severity and perseverance of the season might have benumbed them into a torpid, sleepy state; but that they all willingly should yield to so disagreeable and hazardous a situation, does not seem reasonable or natural, when we consider that they are a bird of the swiftest flight and impatient of severe cold. They are easily tamed, when they become docile and familiar, but never learn to imitate the human language.

BOTH species of the Baltimore bird (oriolus, Linn. icterus, Cat.) are spring birds of passage, and breed in Pennsylvania; they have loud and musical notes.

THE yellow breasted chat (oenanthe, Cat. motacilla trochilus, Linn.) is in many instances a very singular bird; the variableness and mimickry of his notes or speech, imitating various creatures; and a surprising faculty of uttering a coarse, hollow sounding noise in their throats or crops, which at times seems to be at a great distance, though uttered by a bird very near, and vice versa. They arrive in Pennsylvania from the South late in the month of May, breed and return again early in autumn.

IT is a matter of enquiry, who should have induced the zoologists to class this bird with the motacilla, when they discover no one characteristic to induce such an alliance. This bird having a remarkable thick, strong bill, more like the frugivorous tribes; and in my opinion they are guilty of the like oversight in classing the summer red−bird with the muscicapa, this bird having a thick, strong bill, approaching nearer the sterling (sturnus.)

THESE historical observations being noted, we will will again resume the subject of our journal.

CHAP. XI.

AFTER the predatory band of Siminoles, under the conduct of the Long Warrior, had decamped, Mr. M'Latche invited me with him on a visit to an Indian town, about twelve miles distance from the trading–house, to regale ourselves at a feast of Water mellons and Oranges, the Indians having brought a canoe load of them to the trading–house the day preceding, which they disposed of to the traders. This was a circumstance pretty extraordinary to me, it being late in September, a season of the year when the Citruel are ripe and gone in Georgia and Carolina, but here the weather yet continued hot and sultry, and consequently this cool, exhilerating fruit was still in high relish and estimation.

AFTER breakfasting, having each of us a Siminole horse completely equipped, we sat off: the ride was agreeable and variously entertaining; we kept no road or pathway constantly, but as Indian hunting tracks, by chance suited our course, through high, open Pine forests, green lawns and flowery savannas in youthful verdure and gaity, having been lately burnt, but now overrun with a green enamelled carpet, checquered with hommocks of trees of dark green foliage, intersected with serpentine rivulets, their banks adorned with shrubberies of various tribes, as Andromeda fomosissima, And. nitida, And. virides, And. calyculata, And. axilaris, Halmea spuria, Annona alba, &c. About noon we arrived at the town, the same little village I passed by on my ascent of the river, on the banks of the little lake below Charlotia.

WE were received and entertained friendly by the Indians, the chief of the village conducting us to a grand, airy pavilion in the center of the village. It was four square; a range of pillars or posts on each side supporting a canopy composed of Palmetto leaves, woven or thatched together, which shaded a level platform in the center that was ascended to from each side, by two steps or flights, each about twelve inches high, and seven or eight feet in breadth, all covered with carpets or matts, curiously woven of split canes dyed of various colours; here being seated or reclining ourselves, after smoking tobacco, baskets of choicest fruits were brought and set before us.

THE fields surrounding the town and groves were plentifully stored with Corn, Citruels, Pumpkins, Squashes, Beans, Peas, Potatoes, Peaches, Figs, Oranges, &c.

TOWARDS evening we took our leave, and arrived at the stores before night, having in the course of the day collected a variety of curious specimens of vegetables, seeds and roots.

THE company being busily employed in forming their packs of leather and loading the vessel, and I being eager to augment my collections during my stay here, I crossed the river with a party of our people, who were transporting a gang of horses to range in the meadows and plains on the side opposite to the trading–house we carried them over in a large flat or scow. The river was here above a mile wide, but divided into a number of streams by numerous islands, which occasioned the voyage to be very troublesome, as most of the horses were lately taken wild out of their ranges, and many of them young and untutored; being under the necessity of passing near the points of the islands, they grew restless and impatient to land, and it was with great difficulty we kept them on board, and at last when within a quarter of a mile of the opposite shore, passing between two islands, the horses became ungovernable, and most of them plunged into the river and forced over board one of our people; I being a pretty good swimmer, in the midst of the bustle, and to avoid being beat over and perhaps wounded, I leapt out and caught hold of the dock of one of the horses; we all landed safe on one of the islands, about one hundred and fifty yards distance, and the flat followed us: after a deal of trouble and loss of time we got the horses again into the scow, where securing them by withs and vines, we again sat off, and soon landed safe on the main, at a high bluff or bank of the river, where, after turning the horses to pasture and resting ourselves, we sat off on a visit to a plantation on the river, six or eight miles distance: on the way thither we discovered a bee tree, which we cut down and regaled ourselves on the delicious honey; leaving one of our companions to protect the remainder until our return with a tub, to collect it and carry it with us, and in the evening we all returned safe with our sweet booty to the trading–house.

THE vessel being loaded and ready to depart, I got all my collections on board. My trusty and fortunate bark I presented to the old interpreter, Job Wiggens, often my travelling companion, friend and benefactor, and taking an affectionate and final leave of the worthy C. M'Latche and the whole trading company, we sat sail in a neat little schooner for Frederica in Georgia, about the last of September. We had a pleasant and prosperous voyage down the grand river St. Juans, frequently visiting the plantations on the banks of the river, especially at such times as opposed by contrary winds, and according to promise did not neglect calling on the generous and friendly Mr. Marshall, who received me so politely, and treated me with such unparalleled friendship and hospitality, when ascending the river alone, last spring.

WE never once went out to sea during the voyage, for when we had descended the river below the Cow–Ford, we entered the sound by a channel between Fort George Island and the main, through which we passed, and continued sailing between the sea coast islands and the main to Frederica on St. Simons.

ON my arrival at Frederica, I was again, as usual, friendly received and accommodated by the excellent J. Spalding, Esq. and here learning that the honourable Henry Lawrens, Esq. had a large ship loading at Sunbury for Liverpool, I determined to embrace so favourable an offer for conveying my collection to Europe, and hearing at the same time that Mr. Lawrens was daily expected in a vessel of his own, at his plantations on Broton island and New Hope, in order to take a loading of rice for the cargo of the ship at Sunbury; I transported my collections to Broton, where meeting with Mr. Lawrens, he generally permitted me to put my things on board his vessel, and gave me room with himself in the cabin, and the merchant in Liverpool, to whom the ship was consigned, being his friend and correspondent, and a friend of Dr. Fothergill's, Mr. Lawrens proposed to recommend my collections and letters to his care.

THESE favourable circumstances thus co–operating, after bidding adieu to my friends and liberal patrons in these parts, I embarked on board this vessel, and after a short and pleasant passage through the sound, arrived at Sunbury, from whence, after shipping my collections, I sat sail again for Charleston, South Carolina; where being arrived I spent the season in short excursions until next spring, and during this time of my recess I had liesure to plan my future travels, agreeable to Dr. Fothergill's instructions and the council and advice of Dr. Chalmers of Charleston, with other gentlemen of that city, eminent for the promotion of science and encouraging merit and industry.

IT was agreed that my future rout should be directed West and South–West, into the Cherokee country and the regions of the Muscogulges or Creeks.

PART III

CHAP. I.

APRIL 22d, 1776, I sat off from Charleston for the Cherokee nation, and after riding this day about twenty–five miles, arrived in the evening at Jacksonsburg, a village on Ponpon river. The next day's journey was about the same distance, to a public house or inn on the road.

THE next day, early in the morning, I sat off again, and about noon stopped at a public house to dine; after the meridan heats were abated, proceeding on till evening, obtained good quarters at a private house, having rode this day about thirty miles. At this plantation I observed a large orchard of the European Mulberry trees (Morns alba) some of which were grafted on stocks of the native Mulberry (Morus rubra;) these trees were cultivated for the purpose of feeding silk–worms (phalaena bombyca.) Having breakfasted I sat forward again.

I soon entered a high forest, continuing the space of fifteen miles to the Three Sisters, a public ferry on Savanna River: the country generally very level; the soil a dark, loose, fertile mould, on a stratum of cinerious coloured tennacious clay; the ground shaded with its native forests, consisting of the great Black Oak, Quercus tictoria, Q. rubra, Q. phellos, Q. prinos, Q. hemispherica, Juglans nigra, J. rustica, J. exaltata, Magnolia grandiflora, Fraxinus excelsior, Acer rubrum, Liriodendron tulipifera, Populus heterophylla, Morus rubra, Nyssa sylvatica, Platanus occidentales, Tilia, Ulmus campestris, U. subiser, Laurus sassafras, L. Borbonia, Ilex aquifolium, Fagus sylvatica, Cornus Florida, Halesia, Æsculus pavia, Sambucus, Callicarpa and Stewartia malachodendron, with a variety of other trees and shrubs. This ancient sublime forest is frequently intersected with extensive avenues, vistas and green lawns, opening to extensive savannas and far distant Rice plantaions, agreeably employs the imagination and captivates the senses by their magnificence and grandeur.

THE gay mock–bird, vocal and joyous, mounts aloft on silvered wings, rolls over and over, then gently descends and presides in the choir of the tuneful tribes.

HAVING dined at the ferry, I crossed the river into Georgia; on landing and ascending the bank, which has here a North prospect, I observed the Dirca palustris, growing six or seven feet high. I rode about twelve miles further through Pine forests and savannas; in the evening I took up my quarters at a delightful habitation, though not a common tavern; having ordered my horse a stable and provender, and refreshed my spirits with a draught of cooling liquor, I betook myself to contemplation in the groves and lawns; directing my steps towards the river, I observed in a high Pine forest on the border of a savanna, a great number of cattle herded together, and on my nearer approach discovered it to be a cow pen; on my coming up I was kindly saluted by my host and his wife, who I found were superintending a number of slaves, women, boys and girls, that were milking the cows. Here were about forty milch cows and as many young calves, for in these Southern countries the calves run with the cows a whole year, the people milking them at the same time. The pen including two or three acres of ground, more or less, according to the stock, adjoining a rivulet or run of water, is inclosed by a fence; in this inclosure the calves are kept while the cows are out at range; a small part of this pen is partioned off to receive the cows when they come up at evening; here are several stakes drove into the ground, and there is a gate in the partition fence for a communication between the two pens. When the milkmaid has taken her share of milk, she looses the calf, who strips the cow, which is next morning turned out again to range.

I FOUND these people, contrary to what a traveller might, perhaps, reasonably expect, from their occupation and remote situation from the capital or any commercial town, to be civil and courteous, and though educated as it were in the woods, no strangers to sensibility and those moral virtues which grace and ornament the most approved and admired characters in civil society.

AFTER the vessels were filled with milk, the daily and liberal aid of the friendly kine, and the good wife, with her maids and servants, were returning with it to the dairy: the gentleman was at leisure to attend to my enquiries and observations, which he did with complaisance, and apparent pleasure. On my observing to him that his stock of horned cattle must be very considerable to afford so many milch cows at one time, he answered, that he had about fifteen hundred head: "my stock is but young, having lately removed from some distance to this place; I found it convenient to part with most of my old stock and begin here anew; Heaven is pleased to bless my endeavours and industry with success even beyond my own expectations." Yet continuing my interrogatories on this subject: your stock I apprehend must be very profitable, being so convenient to the capital and sea port, in affording a vast quantity of bees, butter, and cheese, for the market, and must thereby contribute greatly towards your emolument: "yes, I find my stock of cattle very profitable, and I constantly contribute towards supplying the markets with bees, but as to the articles of butter and cheese, I make no more than what is expended in my own houshold, and I have a considerable family of black people who though they are slaves must be fed, and cared for; those I have were either chosen for their good qualities, or born in the family, and finding from long experience and observation, that the better they are fed, clothed and treated, the more service and profit we may expect to derive from their labour: in short, I find my stock produces no more milk, or any article of food or nourishment, than what is expended to the best advantage amongst my family and slaves."

HE added, come along with me towards the river bank, where I have some men at work squaring Pine and Cypress timber for the West–India market; I will shew you their days work, when you will readily grant that I have reason to acknowledge myself sufficiently gratified for the little attention bestowed towards them. At yonder little new habitation near the bluff, on the banks of the river I have settled my eldest son; it is but a few days since he was married to a deserving young woman.

HAVING at length arrived near the high banks of the majestic Savanna, we stood at the timber landing: almost every object in our progress having contributed to demonstrate this good man's system of economy to be not only practicable but eligible, and the slaves appeared on all sides as a crowd of witnesses to justify his industry, humanity and liberal spirit.

THE slaves comparatively of a gigantic stature, fat and muscular, mounted on the massive timber logs, the regular heavy strokes of their gleaming axes re–echo in the deep forests, at the same time contented and joyful the sooty sons of Afric forgeting their bondage, in chorus sing the virtues and beneficence of their master in songs of their own composition.

THE log or timber landing is a capacious open area, the lofty pines*

* Pinus palutstris, Linn. the long leaved Pitch pine, or yellow Pine.

having been felled and cleared away for a considerable distance round about, near an almost perpendicular bluff or steep bank of the river, rising up immediately from the water to the height of sixty or seventy feet. The logs being dragged by timber wheels to this yard, and landed as near the brink of this high bank as possible with safety, and laid by the side of each other, are rolled off and precipitated down the bank into the river, where being formed into rafts, they are conducted by slaves down to Savanna, about fifty miles below this place.

HAVING contemplated these scenes of art and industry, my venerable host in company with his son, conducted me to the neat habitation which is situated in a spacious airy forest, a little distance from the river bank, commanding a comprehensive and varied prospect; an extensive reach of the river in front, on the right hand a spacious lawn or savanna, on the left the timber yard, the vast fertile low lands and forest on the river upwards, and the plantations adjoining; a cool evening arrived after a sultry day, as we approach the door conducted by the young man, his lovely bride arrayed in native innocence and becoming modesty, with an air and smile of grace and benignity, meets and salutes us: (what a Venus! what an Adonis! said I in silent transport; every action and feature seemed to reveal the celestial endowments of the mind: though a native sprightliness and sensibility appeared, yet virtue and discretion direct and rule. The dress of this beauteous sylvan queen was plain but clean, neat and elegant, all of cotton and of her own spinning and weaving.)

NEXT morning early I sat forward prosecuting my tour. I pursued the high road leading from Savanna to Augusta for the distance of one hundred miles or more, and then recrossed the river at Silver Bluff, a pleasant villa, the property and seat of G. Golphin, Esquire, a gentleman of very distinguished talents and great liberality, who possessed the most extensive trade, connections and influence, amongst the South and South-West Indian tribes, particularly with the Creeks and Chactaws, of whom I fortunately obtained letters of recommendation and credit to the principal traders residing in the Indian towns.

SILVER-BLUFF is a very celebrated place; it is a considerable height upon the Carolina shore of the Savanna river, perhaps thirty feet higher than the low lands on the opposite shore, which are subject to be overflowed in the spring and fall: this steep bank rises perpendicular out of the river, discovering various strata of earth; the surface for a considerable depth is a loose sandy loam, with a mixture of sea shells, especially ostreae; the next stratum is clay, then sand, next marl, then clays again of various colours and qualities, which last insensibly mixes or unites with a deep stratum of blackish or dark slate coloured saline and sulphureous earth, which seems to be of an aluminous or vitriolic quality, and lies in nearly horizontal lamina or strata of various thickness, we discovered bellemnites, pyrites, markasites and sulphureous nodules, shining like brass, some single of various forms, and others conglomerated, lying in this black slaty–like mucaeus earth; as also sticks, limbs and trunks of trees, leaves, acorns and their cups, all transmuted or changed black, hard and shining as charcoal; we also see animal substances, as if petrified, or what are called sharks teeth, (dentes charchariae) but these heterogeneous substances or petrifactions are the most abundant and conspicuous where there is a looser kind of earth, either immediately upon this vast stratum of black earth, or in the divisions of the lamina. The surface of the ground upon this bluff, which extends a mile and an half or two miles on the river, and is from an half mile to a mile in breadth, nearly level, and a good fertile soil, as is evident from the vast Oaks, Hickory, Mulberry, Black walnut and other trees and shrubs, which are left standing in the old fields which are spread abroad to a great distance, and discover various monuments and vestiges of the residence of the ancients, as Indian conical mounts, terraces, areas, &c. as well as remains or traces of fortresses of regular formation, as if constructed after the modes of European military architects, and are supposed to be ancient camps of the Spaniards who formerly fixed themselves at this place in hopes of finding silver.

BUT perhaps Mr. Golphin's buildings and improvements will prove to be the foundation of monuments of infinitely greater celebrity and permanency than either of the preceding establishment.

THE place which at this day is called fort Moore, is a stupendous bluff, or high perpendicular bank of earth, rising out of the river on the Carolina shore, perhaps ninety or one hundred feet above the common surface of the water, and exhibits a singular and pleasing spectacle to a stranger, especially from the opposite shore, or as we pass up or down the river, presenting a view of prodigious walls of party–coloured earths, chiefly clays and marl of various colours, as brown, red, yellows, blue, purple, white, &c. in horizontal strata, one over the other.

WAITING for the ferry boat to carry me over, I walked almost round the under side of the bluff, betwixt its steep wall and the water of the river, which glided rapidly under my feet; I came to the carcase of a calf, which the people told me had fallen down from the edge of the precipice above, being invited too far by grass and sweet herbs, which they say frequently happens at this place. In early times, the Carolinians had a fort, and kept a good garrison here as a frontier and Indian trading post, but Augusta superceding it, this place was dismantled, and since that time, which probably cannot exceed thirty years, the river hath so much encroached upon the Carolina shore, that its bed now lies where the site of the fort then was; indeed some told me that the opposite Georgia shore, where there is now a fine house and corn field, occupies the place.

THE site of Augusta is perhaps the most delightful and eligible of any in Georgia for a city, an extensive level plain on the banks of a fine navigable river, which has its numerous sources in the Cherokee mountains, a fruitful and temperate region; whence after roving and winding about those fertile heights, they meander through a fertile hilly country, and one after another combine in forming the Tugilo and Broad rivers, and then the famous Savanna river, thence continues near an hundred miles more, following its meanders and falls over the cataracts at Augusta, which crosses the river at the upper end of the town: these falls are four or five feet perpendicular height in the summer season when the river is low: from these cataracts upwards, this river with all its tributaries, as Broad river, Little river, Tugilo, &c. are one continued rapid, with some short intervals of still water, navigable for canoes. But from Augusta downwards to the ocean, a distance of near three hundred miles by water. The Savanna uninterruptedly flows with a gentle meandring course, and is navigable for vessels of twenty or thirty tons burthen to Savanna, where ships of three hundred tons lie in a capacious and secure harbour.

AUGUSTA thus seated at the head of navigation, and just below the conflux of several of its most considerable branches, without a competitor, commands the trade and commerce of vast fruitful regions above it, and from every side to a great distance; and I do not hesitate to pronounce as my opinion, will very soon become the metropolis of Georgia.

* A few years after the above remark, the seat of government was removed from Savanna to Augusta.

I CHOSE to take this route up Savanna river, in preference to the strait and shorter road from Charleston to the Cherokee country by fort Ninety Six, because by keeping near this great river, I had frequent opportunities of visiting its steep banks, vast swamps and low grounds, and had the advantage without great delay, or deviating from the main high road, of observing the various soils and situations of the countries through which this famous river pursues its course, and of examining the various productions, mineral, vegetable and animal; whereas had I pursued the great trading path by Ninety–Six, should have been led over a high, dry, sandy and gravelly ridge, and a great part of the distance an old settled or resorted part of the country, and consequently void of the varieties of original or novel productions of nature.

BEFORE I leave Augusta, I shall recite a curious phenomenon, which may furnish ample matter for philosophical discussion to the curious naturalists. On the Georgia side of the river, about fifteen miles below Silver Bluff, the high road crosses a ridge of high swelling hills of uncommon elevation, and perhaps seventy feet higher than the surface of the river; these hills are from three feet below the common vegetative surface, to the depth of twenty or thirty feet, composed entirely of fossil oyster shells, internally of the colour and consistency of clear white marble; they are of an incredible magnitude, generally fifteen or twenty inches in length, from six to eight wide and two to four in thickness, and their hollows sufficient to receive an ordinary man's foot; they appear all to have been opened before the period of petrefaction, a transmutation they seem evidently to have suffered; they are undoubtedly very ancient or perhaps antideluvian. The adjacent inhabitants burn them to lime for building, for which purpose they serve very well; and would undoubtedly afford an excellent manure when their lands require it, these hills being now remarkably fertile. The heaps of shells lie upon a stratum of yellowish sandy mould, of several feet in depth, upon a foundation of soft white rocks that has the outward appearance of free–stone, but on strict examination is really a testaceous concrete or composition of sand and pulverised sea shell; in short, this testaceous rock approaches near in quality and appearance to the Bahama or Bermudian white rock.

THESE hills are shaded with glorious Magnolia grandiflora, Morus rubra, Tilia, Quercus, Ulmus, Juglans, &c. with aromatic groves of fragrant Callicanthus Floridus, Rhododendron ferruginium Laurus Indica, &c. Æsculus pavia, Cornus Florida, Azalea coccinea, Philadelphus inodorous and others; but who would have expected to see the Dirca palustris and Dodecathean meadea grow in abundance in this hot climate! it is true they are seen in the rich and deep shaded vales, between the hills and North exposure; but they attain to a degree of magnitude and splendor never seen in Pennsylvania.

CHAP. II.

AFTER conferring with gentlemen in Augusta, conversant in Indian affairs, concerning my future travels in those distant, unexplored regions, and obtaining letters to their agents in the Indian territories, I sat off, proceeding for Fort James Dartmouth, at the confluence of Broad River with Savanna, the road leading me near the banks of the river for the distance of near thirty miles, crossing two or three of its considerable branches, besides rivulets and smaller brooks. The surface of the land uneven, by means of ridges or chains of swelling hills and corresponding vales, with level downs; the soil a loose, greyish brown loamy mould on the hills, but darker and more cohesive and humid in the vales and downs; this superficial, vegetative earth, covers a deep stratum of very tenaceous yellowish clay: the downs afford grass and various herbage; the vales and hills forest trees and shrubs of various tribes, i. e. Quercus tinctoria, Q. alba, Q. rubra, Q. lobata, Acer rubrum, A. Saccharinum, A. glaucum, Morus rubra, Gleditsia triacanthus, Juglans hickory, various species, Quercus phillos, Quer. dentata, s. hemispherica, Quercus aquatica, or Maryland Water Oak, Ulmus sylvatica, Liriodendron, Liquid–amber, Diospyros, Cornus Florida, Prunus Indica, Prunus padus and Æsculus pavia: and near water courses in the vales, Stewartia malachodendron, Halesia, Æsculus sylvatica, Styrax, Carpinus, Magnolia acuminata, Mag. tripetala, Mag. auriculata, Azalea, &c. The rich humid lands in the vales bordering on creeks and bases of the hills, lifewife produce various trees, shrubs and plants, as Cercis, Corylus, Ptelea, Evonimus, Philadelphus inodorous, Staphylea trifoliata, Chionanthus, Hamamelis, Callicarpa, Sambucus, Cornus alba, Viburnum dentatum, Spirea opulifolia, Cornus sanguinea, Cephalanthus, &c. and of herbaccae a vast variety and abundance, as Verbisina, Rudbeckea, Phaciolus, Tripsacum, Aconitum napellus, Delphinium, Angelica luceda, Tradescantia, Trillium fessile, Trillium canuum, Actaea, Chelone, Glycine apios, Convalaria racemosa, Mediola, Carduus, Bidens frondosa, Arum triphyllum, Corepsis alternifolia. Circea, Commelina, Aster, Solidago, Eupatorium, Helianthus and Silphium, together with a variety of other tribes and species now to me. In the evening I arrived at Little river, and took up my quarters at a public house on its banks, near its banks with the Savanna. This is a beautiful rapid water, about fifty yards over; on a branch of this river is situated the town of Wrightsborough.

NEAR the ford, on the banks of this river, I first observed a very curious shrub, a beautiful evergreen, which appears to be allied to the Rhododendron, though the seed vessels seem to bear more the characteristics of the Kalmia. This shrub grows in copses or little groves, in open, high situations, where trees of large growth are but scatteringly planted; many simple stems arise together from a root or source erect, four, five and six feet high; their limbs or branches, which are produced towards the top of the stems, also

219

stand nearly erect, lightly diverging from the main stems, which are furnished with moderately large ovate pointed intire leaves, of a pale or yellowish green colour; these leaves are of a firm, compact texture, both surfaces smooth and shining, and stand nearly erect upon short petioles; the branches terminate with long, loose panicles or spikes of white flowers, whose sedgments are five, long and narrow.

I AROSE early next morning and continued my journey for Fort James. This day's progress was agreeably entertaining, from the novelty and variety of objects and views; the wild country now almost depopulated, vast forests, expansive plains and detached groves; then chains of hills whose gravelly, dry, barren summits present detached piles of rocks, which delude and flatter the hopes and expectations of the solitary traveller, full sure of hospitable habitations; heaps of white, gnawed bones of the ancient buffaloe, elk and deer, indiscrimintaely mixed with those of men, half grown over with moss, altogether, exhibit scenes of uncultivated nature, on reflection, perhaps, rather disagreeable to a mind of delicate feelings and sensibility, since some of these objects recognize past transactions and events, perhaps not altogether reconcilable to justice and humanity.

HOW harmonious and sweetly murmur the purling rills and fleeting brooks, roving along the shadowy vales, passing through dark, subterranean caverns, or dashing over steep rocky precipices, their cold, humid banks condensing the volatile vapours, which fall and coalesce in chrystaline drops, on the leaves and elastic twigs of the aromatic shrubs and incarnate flowers. In these cool, sequestered, rocky vales, we behold the following celebrated beauties of the hills, i. e. fragrant Calycanthus, blushing Rhododendron ferruginium, delicate Philadelphus inodorus, which displays the white wavy mantle, with the sky robed Delphinium, perfumed Convalaria and fiery Azalea, flaming on the ascending hills or wavy surface of the gliding brooks. The epithet fiery, I annex to this most celebrated species of Azalea, as being expressive of the appearance of it in flower, which are in general of the colour of the finest red lead, orange and bright gold, as well as yellow and cream colour; these various splendid colours are not only in separate plants, but frequently all the varieties and shades are seen in separate branches on the same plant, and the clusters of the blossoms cover the shrubs in such incredible profusion on the hill sides, that suddenly opening to view from dark shades, we are alarmed with the apprehension of the hills being set on fire. This is certainly the most gay and brilliant flowering shrub yet known: they grow in little copses or clumps, in open forests as well as dark groves, with other shrubs, and about the bases of hills, especially where brooks and rivulets wind about them; the bushes seldom rise above six or seven feet in height, and generally but three, four and five, but branch and spread their tops greatly; the young leaves are but very small whilst the shrubs are in bloom, from which circumstance the plant exhibits a greater shew of splendour.

TOWARDS evening I crossed Broad river at a good ford, just above its confluence with the Savanna, and arrived at Fort James, which is a four square stockade, with saliant bastions at each angle, mounted with a block–house, where are some swivel guns, one story higher than the curtains, which are pierced with loop–holes, breast high, and defended by small arms; the fortification encloses about an acre of ground, where is the governor's or commandant's house, a good building, which is flanked on each side by buildings for the officers and barracks for the garrison, consisting of fifty ranges, including officers, each having a good horse well equipt, a rifle, two dragoon pistols and a hanger, besides a powder horn, shot pouch and tomahawk. The fort stands on an eminence in the forks between the Savanna and Broad rivers, about one mile above Fort Charlotta, which is situated near the banks of the Savanna, on the Carolina side; Fort James is situated nearly at an equal distance from the banks of the two rivers, and from the extreme point of the land that separates them. The point or peninsula between the two rivers, for the distance of two miles back from the fort, is laid out for a town, by the name of Dartmouth, in honour to the earl of Dartmouth, who, by his interest and influence in the British councils, obtained from the king a grant and powers in favour of the Indian trading company of Georgia, to treat with the Creeks for the cession of a quantity of land sufficient to discharge their debts to the traders, for the security and defence of which territory this fortress was established.

THIS territory, called the New Purchase, contains about two millions of acres, lying upon the head of Great Ogechee, between the banks of the Savanna and Alatamaha, touching on the Ocone and taking within its precincts all the waters of Broad and Little rivers, comprehends a body of excellent fertile land, well watered by innumerable rivers, creeks and brooks.

I MADE a little excursion up the Savanna river, four or five miles above the fort, with the surgeon of the garrison, who was so polite as to attend me to shew me some remarkable Indian monuments, which are worthy of every travellers notice. These wonderful labours of the ancients stand in a level plain, very near the bank of the river, now twenty or thirty yards from it; they consist of conical mounts of earth and four square terraces, &c. The great mount is in the form of a cone, about forty or fifty feet high, and the circumference of its base two or three hundred yards, entirely composed of the loamy rich earth of the low grounds; the top or apix is flat; a spiral path or track leading from the ground up to the top is still visible, where now grows a large, beautiful spreading Red Cedar (Juniperus Americana;) there appears four niches, excavated out of the sides of this hill, at different heights from the safe, fronting the four cardinal points; these niches or sentry boxes are entered into from the winding path, and seem to have been ment for resting places or look–outs. The circumjacent level grounds are cleared and planted with Indian Corn at present, and I think the proprietor of these lands, who accompanied us to this place, said that the mount itself yielded above one hundred bushels in one season: the land hereabouts is indeed exceeding fertile and productive.

IT is altogether unknown to us, what could have induced the Indians to raise such a heap of earth in this place, the ground for a great space around being subject to inundations, at least once a year, from which circumstance we may conclude they had no town or settled habitations here: some imagine these tumuli were constructed for look–out towers. It is reasonable to suppose, however, that they were to serve some important purpose in those days, as they were public works, and would have required the united labour and attention of a whole nation, circumstanced as they were, to have constructed one of them almost in an age. There are several less ones round about the great one, with some very large tetragon terraces on each side, near one hundred yards in length, and their surface four, six, eight and ten feet above the ground on which they stand.

WE may however hazard a conjecture, that a there is generally a narrow space or ridge in these low lands, immediately bordering on the rivers bank, which is eight or ten feet higher than the adjoining low grounds, that lie betwixt the stream and the heights of the adjacent main land, which, when the river overflows its banks, are many feet under water, when, at the same time, this ridge on the river bank is above water and dry, and at such inundations appears as an islands in the river. Now these people might have had a town on this ridge, and this mount raised for a retreat and refuge in case of an inundation, which are unforeseen and surprise them very suddenly, spring and autumn.

HAVING finished my collections and observations, which were extended to a considerable distance in the environs of Dartmouth; May 10th sat off again, proceeding for Keowe, rode six or eight miles up the river above the fort, crossed over into Carolina and soon got into the high road, but had not proceeded far when I was surprised by a

222

sudden very heavy shower of rain, attended with terrific thunder, but luckily found present shelter at a farm house, where I continued above and hour before its fury abated, when I proceeded again, and notwithstanding this detention and obstacles in consequence of the heavy rains in raising the creeks, travelled thirty–five miles, and arrived in the evening at Mr. Cameron's, deputy commissary for Indian affairs for the Cherokee nation, to whom I was recommended by letters from the honourable John Stewart, superintendant, residing in Charleston, mentioning my business in the Cherokee country.

THE road this day had led me over an uneven country, its surface undulated by ridges or chains of hills, sometimes rough with rocks and stones, yet generally productive of forests, with a variety of vegetables of inferior growth, i. e. Quercus, various species, Juglans hickory, varieties, Liriodendron, Fraxinus, Fagus sylvatica, Fagus castania, Fagus pumila, s. Chinkapin, Nyssa sylvatica, Acer rubrum, Æsculus sylvatica, Magnolia acuminata, Magnolia tripetala, Andromeda arborea, Hopea tinctoria, Æsculus pavia, Vibernum, Azalea flammea and other species; Hydrangea, Calycanthus, &c.

THE season being uncommonly wet, almost daily showers of rain and frequently attended with tremenduous thunder, rendered travelling disagreeable, toilsome and hazardous, through an uninhabited wilderness, abounding with rivers and brooks; I was prevailed upon by Mr. Cameron to stay at his house a few days, until the rains ceased and the rivers could be more easily forded.

THE Angelica lucido or Nondo grows here in abundance; its aromatic carminative root is in taste much like that of the Ginseng (Panax) though more of the taste and scent of Anise seed; it is in high estimation with the Indians as well as white inhabitants, and sells at a great price to the Southern Indians of Florida, who dwell near the sea coast where this never grows spontaneously. I observed a charming species of Malva, having panicles of large splended purple or deep blue flowers, and another species of Malva, very singular indeed, for it is a climber; the leaves are broad, which, with the whole plant, are hoary; the flowers are very small, of a greenish white: and here grows in abundance a beautiful species of Delphinium; the flowers differ in no respect from those of the common branching Larkspur of the gardens; they are of a fine deep blue colour, and disposed in long sparsed spikes; the leaves are compound, almost linear, but the segments not so fine cut as those of the garden Larkspur.

Travels Through North and South Carolina

THE weather now settled and fair, I prepared to proceed for Fort Prince George Keowe, having obtained of the agreeable and liberal Mr. Cameron, ample testimonials and letters of recommendation to the traders in the nation; this gentleman also very obligingly sent a young Negro slave along, to assist and pilot me as far as Senica.

MAY 15th I left Lough–abber, the seat of Mr. Cameron. In the course of this day's journey I crossed several rivers and brooks, all branches of Savanna, now called Keowe, above its confluence with the Tugilo, the West main branch. The face of the country uneven, by means of ridges of hills and water courses; the hills somewhat rocky near their summits and at the banks of rivers and creeks, but very fertile, as there is a good depth of a loose dark and moist vegetative mould, on a stratum of reddish brown tenaceous clay, and sometimes a deep stratum of dusky brown marl. The vegetable productions observed during this day's progress, were generally the same as already recited since leaving Dartmouth. The flaming Azalea abound and illuminate the hill sides, and a new and singularly beautiful species of Æsculus pavia, situated above them, towards the summits of these low hills; this conspicuously beautiful flowering shrub, grows to the height of five or six feet, many divergent crooked stems arise together from a root or source, which dividing their branches, wreath about every way, after a very irregular and free order; the exterior subdivisions of these limbs terminate with a heavy cluster or thyrsis of rose or pink coloured flowers, speckled or variegated with crimson, larger, more expansive and regular in their formation than those of the Pavia; and these heavy spikes of flowers, charged with the morning dews, bend the slender flexile stems to the ground: the compound leaves are of the configuration of those of the Pavia, but broader and their veins more prominent. The shrubs growing about the tops of the more barren grassy hills, where large trees are few and scattered shew themselves to great advantage, and make a fine appearance.

THERE are abundance of Grape vines (Vitis vinifera) which ramble and spread themselves over the shrubs and low trees in these situations, and I was assured produce fruit affording an excellent juice; the grapes are of various colours when ripe, of the figure and about the size of the European wine grapes. Arrived at Sinica in the evening, after travelling forty five miles through an uninhabited wilderness.

THE Cherokee town of Sinica is a very respectable settlement, situated on the East bank of the Keowe river, though the greatest number of Indian habitations are on the opposite shore, where likewise stands the council–house in a level plain betwixt the river and a range of beautiful lofty hills, which rise magnificently, and seem to bend over the green plains and the river; but the chief's house, with those of the traders, and some Indian dwellings are seated on the ascent of the heights on the opposite shore; this situation in point of prospect far excels the other, as it overlooks the whole settlement, the extensive fruitful plains on the river above and below, and the plantations of the inhabitants, commanding a most comprehensive diversified view of the opposite elevations.

SINICA is a new town rebuilt since the late Indian war, when the Cherokees were vanquished and compelled to sue for peace, by general Middleton, commander of the Carolinian auxiliaries acting against them, when the lower and middle settlements were broken up: the number of inhabitants are now estimated at about five hundred, and they are able to muster about one hundred warriors.

NEXT day I left Sinica alone, and after riding about sixteen miles, chiefly through high forests of excellent land at a little distance from the river, arrived in the evening at fort Prince George Keowe.

KEOWE is a most charming situation, and the adjacent heights are naturally so formed and disposed, as with little expensive of military architecture to be rendered almost impregnable; in a fertile vale, at this season, enamelled with the incarnate fragrant strawberries and blooming plants, through which the beautiful river meanders, sometimes gently flowing, but more frequently agitated, gliding swiftly between the fruitful strawberry banks, environed at various distances, by high hills and mountains, some rising boldly almost upright upon the verge of the expansive lawn, so as to overlook and shadow it, whilst others more lofty, superb, misty and blue, majestically mount far above.

THE evening still and calm, all silent and peaceable, a vivifying gentle breeze continually wafted from the fragrant strawberry fields, and aromatic Calycanthean groves on the surrounding heights, the wary moor fowl thundering in the distant echoing hills, how the groves and hills ring with the shrill perpetual voice of the whip–poor–will!

ABANDONED as my situation now was, yet thank heaven many objects met together at this time, and conspired to conciliate, and in some degree compose my mind, heretofore somewhat dejected and unharmonized: all alone in a wild Indian country, a thousand miles from my native land, and a vast distance from any settlements of white people. It is true, here were some of my own colour, yet they were strangers, and though friendly and hospitable, their manners and customs of living so different from what I had been accustomed to, administered but little to my consolation: some hundred miles yet to travel, the savage vindictive inhabitants lately ill–treated by the frontier Virginians, blood being spilt between them and the injury not yet wiped away by formal treaty; the Cherokees extremely jealous of white people travelling about their mountains, especially if they should be seen peeping in amongst the rocks or digging up their earth.

THE vale of Keowe is seven or eight miles in extent, that is from the little town of Kulsage*

* Sugar Town.

about a mile above, thence down the river six or seven miles, where a high ridge of hills on each side of the river almost terminates the vale, but opens again below the narrow ridge, and continues ten or twelve miles down to Sinica, and in width one and two miles: this fertile vale within the remembrance of some old traders with whom I conversed, was one continued settlement, the swelling sides of the adjoining hills were then covered with habitations, and the rich level grounds beneath lying on the river, was cultivated and planted, which now exhibit a very different spectacle, humiliating indeed to the present generation, the posterity and feeble remains of the once potent and renowned Cherokees: the vestiges of the ancient Indian dwellings are yet visible on the feet of the hills bordering and fronting on the vale, such as posts or pillars of their habitations, &c.

THERE are several Indian mounts or tumuli, and terraces, monuments of the ancients, at the old site of Keowe, near the sort Prince George, but no Indian habitations at present; and here are several dwellings inhabited by white people concerned in the Indian trade; Mr. D. Homes is the principal trader here.

THE old sort Prince George now bears no marks of a fortress, but serves for a trading house.

CHAP. III.

I WAITED two or three days at this post expecting the return of an Indian, who was out hunting; this man was recommended to me as a suitable person for a protector and guide to the Indian settlements over the hills, but upon information that he would not be in shortly, and there being no other person suitable for the purpose, rather than be detained, and perhaps thereby frustrated in my purposes, determined to set off alone and run all risks.

I crossed the river at a good ford just below the old fort. The river here is near one hundred yards over: after an agreeable progress for about two miles over delightful strawberry plains, and gently swelling green hills, began to ascend more steep and rocky ridges. Having gained a very considerable elevation, and looking around, I enjoyed a very comprehensive and delightful view: Keowe which I had but just lost sight of, appears again, and the serpentine river speeding through the lucid green plain apparently just under my feet. After observing this delightful landscape I continued on again three or four miles, keeping the trading path which led me over uneven rocky land, and crossing rivulets and brooks, rapidly descending over rocky precipices, when I came into a charming vale, embellished with a delightful glittering river, which meandered through it, and crossed my road: on my left hand upon the grassy bases of the rising hills, appears the remains of a town of the ancients, as the tumuli, terraces, posts or pillars, old Peach and Plumb orchards, &c. sufficiently testify. These vales and swelling base of the surrounding hills, afford vast crops of excellent grass and herbage fit for pasturage and hay; of the latter Plantago Virginica, Sanguis orba, Geum, Fragaria, &c. The Panax quinquifolium, or Ginseng, now appears plentifully on the North exposure of the hill, growing out of the rich mellow humid earth amongst the stones or fragments of rocks.

HAVING crossed the vales, began to ascend again the more lofty ridges of hills, then continued about eight miles over more gentle pyramidal hills, narrow vales and lawns, the soil exceedingly fertile, producing lofty forests and odoriferous groves of Calycanthus, near the banks of rivers, with Halesia, Philadelphus inodorus, Rhododendron ferruginium, Aazalea, Stewartia montana*

* This is a new species of Stewartia, unknown to the European botanist, and not mentioned in any catalogues.

fol. ovatis acuminatis serratis, flor. nivea, staminum corona fulgida, pericarp. pomum exsuccum, apice acuminato dehiscens, Cornus Florida, Styrax, all in full bloom, and

227

decorated with the following sweet roving climbers, i. e. Bignonia sempervirens, Big. crucigera, Lonicera sempervirens, Rosa paniculata, &c.

NOW at once the mount divides, and discloses to view the ample Occonne vale, encircled by a wreath of uniform hills; their swelling bases clad in cheerful verdure, over which issuing from between the mountains, plays along a glittering river, meandering through the meadows, which crossing at the upper end of the vale, I began to ascend the Occonne mountain. On the foot of the hills are the ruins of the antient Occonne town: the first step after leaving the verdant beds of the hills was a very high rocky chain of pointed hills, extremely well ambered with the following trees: Quercus tinctoria, Querc. alba, Querc rubra, Fraxinus excelsior, Juglans hickory, various species, Ulmus, Tilia, Acer saccharinum, Morus, Juglans nigra, Juglans alba, Annona glabra, Robinia pseudacacia, Magnolia acuminata, Æsculus sylvatica, with many more, particularly a species of Robinia new to me, though perhaps the same as figured and described by Catesby in his Nat. Hist. Carol. This beautiful flowering tree grows twenty and thirty feet high, with a crooked leaning trunk, the branches spread greatly, and wreath about, some almost touching the ground; however there appears a singular pleasing wildness and freedom in its manner of growth, the slender subdivisions of the branches terminate with heavy compound panicles of rose or pink coloured flowers, amidst a wreath of beautiful pinnated leaves.

MY next flight was up a very high peak, to the top of the Occonne mountain, where I rested; and turning about found that I was now in a very elevated situation, from whence I enjoyed a view inexpressibly magnificent and comprehensive. The mountainous wilderness through which I had lately traversed down to the region of Augusta, appearing regularly undulated as the great ocean after a tempest; the undulations gradually depressing, yet perfectly regular, as the squammae of fish or imbrications of tile on a roof: the nearest ground to me of a perfect full green, next more glaucous, and lastly almost blue as the ether with which the the most distant curve of the horizon seems to be blended.

MY imagination thus wholly engaged in the contemplation of this magnificent landscape, infinitely varied, and without bound, I was almost insensible or regardless of the charming objects more within my reach: a new species of Rhododendron foremost in the assembly of mountain beauties, next the flaming Azalea, Kalmia latifolia, incarnate Robinia, snowy mantled Philadelphus inodorus, perfumed Calycanthus, &c.

Travels Through North and South Carolina

THIS species of Rhododendron grows six or seven feet high, many nearly erect stems arise together from the root forming a group or coppice. The leaves are three or four inches in length, of an oblong figure, broadest toward the extremity, and terminating with an obtuse point; their upper surface of a deep green and polished, but the nether surface of a rusty iron colour, which seems to be effected by innumerable minute reddish vesicles, beneath a fine short downy pubescence; the numerous flexile branches terminate with a loose spiked raceme, or cluster of large deep rose coloured flowers, each flower being affixed in the diffused cluster by a long peduncle, which with the whole plant possess an agreeable perfume.

AFTER being recovered of the fatigue and labour in ascending the mountain, I began again to prosecute my task, proceeding through a shady forest, and soon after gained the most elevated crest of the Occonne mountain, and then began to descend the other side; the winding rough road carrying me over rocky hills and levels, shaded by incomparable forests, the soil exceedingly rich, and of an excellent quality for the production of every vegetable suited to the climate, and seems peculiarly adapted for the cultivation of Vines (Vitis vinifera) Olives, (Olea Europea) the Almond tree (Amygdalus communis) Fig (Ficus carica) and perhaps the Pomgranate (Punica granatum) as well as Peaches, (Amyg. Persica) Prunus, Pyrus, of every variety: arising again steep rocky ascents, and then rich levels, where grew many trees and plants common in Pennsylvania, New–York and even Canada, as Pinus strobus, Pin. sylvestris, Pin. abies, Acer saccharinum, Acer striatum, s. Pennysylvanicnm, Populus trimula, Betula nigra, Juglans alba, &c. but what seems remarkable, the yellow Jessamine, (Bignonia sempervirens) which is killed by a very slight frost in the open air in Pennsylvania, here on the summits of the Cherokee mountains associates with the Canadian vegetables, and appears roving with them in perfect bloom and gaiety; as likewise Halesia diptera, and Hal. tetraptera, mountain Stewartia, Styrax, Ptelea, and Æsculus pavia, but all these bear our hardest frosts in Pennsylvania. Now I enter a charming narrow vale, through which flows a rapid large creek, on whose banks are happily associated the shrubs already recited, together with the following; Staphylaea, Euonismus Americana, Hamamelis, Azalea, various species, Aristalochia frutescens, s.. odoratissima, which rambles over the trees and shrubs on the prolisic banks of these mountain brooks. Passed through magnificent high forests, and then came upon the borders of an ample meadow on the left, embroidered by the shade of a high circular amphitheatre of hills, the circular ridges rising magnificently one over the other: on the green turfy bases of these ascents appear the ruins of a town of the ancients; the upper end of this spacious green plain is divided by a promontory or spur of the

229

ridges before me, which projects into it; my road led me up into an opening of the ascents through which the glittering brook which watered the meadows ran rapidly down, dashing and roaring over high rocky steps. Continued yet ascending until I gained the top of an elevated rocky ridge, when appeared before me a gap or opening between other yet more lofty ascents, thro' which continuing as the rough rocky road led me, close by the winding banks of a large rapid brook, which at length turning to the left, pouring down rocky precipices, glided off through dark groves and high forests, conveying streams of fertility and pleasure to the fields below.

THE surface of the land now for three or four miles is level, yet uneven, occasioned by natural mounds or rocky knobs, but covered with a good staple of rich earth, which affords forests of timber trees and shrubs. After this, gently descending again, I travelled some miles over a varied situation of ground, exhibiting views of grand forests, dark detached groves, vales and meadows, as heretofore, and producing the like vegetable and other works of nature; the meadows affording exuberant pasturage for cattle, and the bases of the encircling hills, flowering plants, and fruitful strawberry beds: observed frequently ruins of the habitations or villages of the ancients. Crossed a delightful river, the main branch of Tugilo, when I began to ascend again, first over swelling turfy ridges, varied with groves of stately forest trees, then ascending again more steep, grassy hill sides, rested on the top of mount Magnolia, which appeared to me to be the highest ridge of the Cherokee mountains, which separates the waters of Savanna river from those of the Tanale or great main branch of the Cherokee river, which running rapidly a North–West course thro' the mountains, is joined from the North–East by the Holstein, thence taking a West course yet amongst the mountains receiving into it from either hand many large rivers, leaves the mountains immediately after being joined by a large river from the East, becomes a mighty river by the name of Hogehege, thence meanders many hundred miles through a vast country consisting of forests, meadows, groves, expansive savannas, fields and swelling hills, most fertile and delightful, flows into the beautiful Ohio, and in conjunction with its transparent waters, becomes tributary to the sovereign Missisippi.

THIS exalted peak I named mount Magnolia

* Magnolia auriculata.

from a new and beautiful species of that celebrated family of flowering trees, which here, at the cascades of Falling Creek, grows in a high degree of perfection, for although I had noticed this curious tree several times before, particularly on the high ridges betwixt Sinica and Keowe, and on ascending the first mountain after leaving Keowe, when I observed it in flower, but here it flourishes and commands our attention.

THIS tree, or perhaps rather a shrub, rises eighteen to thirty feet in height, there are usually many stems from a root or source, which lean a little, or slightly diverge from each other, in this respect imitating the Magnolia tripetala; the crooked wreathing branches arising and subdividing from the main stem without order or uniformity, their extremities turn upwards, producing a very large rosaceous, perfectly white, double or polypetalous flower, which is of a most fragrant scent; this fine flower fits in the center of a radices of very large leaves, which are of a singular figure, somewhat lanciolate, but broad towards their extremities, terminating with an acuminated point, and backwards they attenuate and become very narrow towards their bases, terminating that way with two long, narrow ears or lappets, one on each side of the insertion of the petiole; the leaves have only short footstalks, sitting very near each other, at the extremities of the floriferous branches, from whence they spread themselves after a regular order, like the spokes of a wheel, their margins touching or lightly laping upon each other, form an expansive umbrella superbly crowned or crested with the fragrant flower, representing a white plume; the blossom is succeeded by a very large crimson cone or strobile, containing a great number of scarlet berries, which, when ripe, spring from their cells and are for a time suspended by a white silky web or thread. The leaves of these trees which grow in a rich, light, humid soil, when fully expanded and at maturity, are frequently above two feet in length and six or eight inches where broadest. I discovered in the maritime parts of Georgia, particularly on the banks of the Alatamaha, another new species of Magnolia, whose leaves were nearly of the figure of those of this tree, but they were much less in size, not more than six or seven inches in length, and the strobile very small, oblong, sharp pointed and of a sine deep crimson colour, but I never saw the flower. These trees grow strait and erect, thirty feet or more in height, and of a sharp conical form, much resembling the Cucumber tree (Mag. acuminata) in figure.

THIS day being remarkably warm and sultry, which, together with the labour and fatigue of ascending the mountains, made me very thirsty and in some degree sunk my spirits. Now past mid–day. I sought a cool shaded retreat, where was water for refreshment and grazing for my horse, my faithful slave and only companion. After proceeding a little farther, descending the other side of the mountain, I perceived at some distance before me, on my right hand, a level plain supporting a grand high forest and groves; the nearer I approach my steps are the more accelerated from the flattering prospect opening to view; I now enter upon the verge of the dark forest, charming solitude! as I advanced through the animating shades, observed on the farther grassy verge a shady grove, thither I directed my steps; on approaching these shades, between the stately columns of the superb forest trees, presented to view, rushing from rocky precipices under the shade of the pensile hills, the unparalleled cascade of Falling Creek, rolling and leaping off the rocks, which uniting below, spread a broad, glittering sheet of chrystal waters, over a vast convex elivation of plain, smooth rocks, and are immediately received by a spacious bason, where, trembling in the centre through hurry and agitation, they gently subside, encircling the painted still verge, from whence gliding swiftly, they soon form a delightful little river, which continuing to flow more moderately, is restrained for a moment, gently undulating in a little lake, they then pass on rapidly to a high perpendicular steep of rocks, from whence these delightful waters are hurried down with irresistible rapidity. I here seated myself on the moss clad rocks, under the shade of spreading trees and floriferous fragrant shrubs, in full view of the cascades.

AT this rural retirement were assembled a charming circle of mountain vegetable beauties, Magnolia auriculata, Rhododendron ferruginium, Kalmia latifolia, Robinia montana, Azalea flammula, Rosa paniculata, Calycanthus Floridus, Philadelphus inodorus, perfumed Convalaria majalis, Anemone thalictroides, Auemone hepatica, Erythronium maculatum, Leontice thalictroides, Trillium fessile, Trillium cesnum, Cypripedium, Arethuza, Ophrys, Sanguinaria, Viola uvuleria, Epigea, Mitchella repens, Stewartia, Halesia, Sryrax, Lonicera, &c. some of these roving beauties are strolling over the mossy, shelving, humid rocks, or from off the expansive wavy boughs of trees, bending over the floods, salute their delusive shades, playing on the surface, some plunge their perfumed heads and bathe their flexile limbs in the silver stream, whilst others by the mountain breezes are tossed about, their blooming tufts bespangled with pearly and chrystaline dewdrops collected from the falling mists, glisten in the rain bow arch. Having collected some valuable specimens at this friendly retreat, I continued my lonesome pilgrimage. My road for a considerable time led me winding and turning about the steep rocky hills; the descent of some of which were very rough and troublesome, by means of fragments of rocks, slippery clay and talc; but after this I entered a spacious forest, the land having gradually acquired a more level surface; a prettey grassy vale appears on my right, through which my wandering path led me, close by the banks of a delightful creek, which sometimes falling over steps of rocks, glides gently with serpentine meanders through the meadows.

AFTER crossing this delightful brook and mead, the land rises again with sublime magnificence, and I am led over hills and vales, groves and high forests, vocal with the melody of the feathered longsters, the snow—white cascades glittering on the sides of the distant hills.

IT was now after noon; I approached a charming vale, amidst sublimely high forests, awful shades! darkness gathers around, far distant thunder rolls over the trembling hills; the black clouds with august majesty and power, moves slowly forwards, shading regions of towering hills, and threatning all the destructions of a thunder storm; all around is now still as death, not a whisper is heard, but a total inactivity and silence seems to pervade the earth; the birds afraid to utter a chirrup, and in low tremulous voices take leave of each other, seeking covert and safety; every insect is silenced, and nothing heard but the roaring of the approaching hurricane; the mighty cloud now expands its sable wings, extending from North to South, and is driven irresistibly on by the tumultuous winds, spreading his livid wings around the gloomy concave, armed with terrors of thunder and fiery shafts of lightning; now the lofty forests bend low beneath its fury, their limbs and wavy boughs are tossed about and catch hold of each other; the mountains tremble and seem to real about, and the ancient hills to be shaken to their foundations: the furious storm sweeps along, smoking through the vale and over the resounding hills; the face of the earth is obscured by the deluge descending from the firmament, and I am deafened by the din of thunder; the tempestuous scene damps my spirits, and my horse sinks under me at the tremendous peals, as I hasten on for the plain.

THE storm abating, I saw an Indian hunting cabin on the side of a hill, a very agreeable prospect, especially in my present condition; I made up to it and took quiet possession, there being no one to dispute it with me except a few bats and whip poorwills, who had repaired thither for shelter from the violence of the hurricane.

HAVING turned out my horse in the sweet meadows adjoining, and finding some dry wood under shelter of the old cabin, I struck up a fire, dried my clothes and comforted myself with a frugal repast of biscuit and dried beef, which was all the food my viaticum afforded me by this time, excepting a small piece of cheese which I had furnished myself with at Charleston and kept till this time.

Travels Through North and South Carolina

THE night was clear, calm and cool, and I rested quietly. Next morning at day break I was awakened and summoned to resume my daily task, by the shrill cries of the social night hawk and active merry mock–bird. By the time the rising sun had gilded the tops of the towering hills, the mountains and vales rang with the harmonious shouts of the pious and cheerful tenants of the groves and meads.

I OBSERVED growing in great abundance in these mountain meadows, Sanguiforba Canadensis and Heracleum maximum, the latter exhibiting a fine shew, being rendered conspicuous even at a great distance, by its great height and spread, vast pennatified leaves and expansive umbels of snow–white flowers; the swelling bases of the surrounding hills fronting the meadows, present, for my acceptance, the fragrant red strawberry, in painted beds of many acres surface, indeed I may safely say many hundreds.

AFTER passing through this meadow, the road led me over the bases of a ridge of hills, which as a bold promontory dividing the fields I had just passed, form expansive green lawns. On these towering hills appeared the ruins of the ancient famous town of Sticoe. Here was a vast Indian mount or tumulus and great terrace, on which stood the council–house, with banks encompassing their circus; here were also old Peach and Plumb orchards, some of the trees appeared yet thriving and fruitful; presently after leaving these ruins, the vale and fields are divided by means of a spur of the mountains pushing forward; here likewise the road forked, the left hand path continued up the mountains to the Overhill towns; I followed the vale to the right hand, and soon began again to ascend the hills, riding several miles over very rough, stony land, yielding the like vegetable productions as heretofore; and descending again gradually, by a dubious winding path, leading into a narrow vale and lawn, through which rolled on before me a delightful brook, water of the Tanase; I crossed it and continued a mile or two down the meadows, when the high mountains on each side suddenly receding, discover the opening of the extensive and fruitful vale of Cowe, through which meanders the head branch of the Tanase, almost from its source, sixty miles, following its course down to Cowe.

I LEFT the stream for a little while, passing swiftly and foaming over its rocky bed, lashing the steep craggy banks, and then suddenly sunk from my sight, murmuring hollow and deep under the rocky surface of the ground: on my right hand the vale expands, receiving a pretty silvery brook of water, which came hastily down from the adjacent hills, and entered the river a little distance before me; I now turn from the heights on my left, the road leading into the level lawns, to avoid the hollow rocky grounds, full of holes and cavities, arching over the river, through which the waters are seen gliding along, but the river is soon liberated from these solitary and gloomy recesses, and appears waving through the green plain before me. I continued several miles, pursuing my serpentine path, through and over the meadows and green fields, and crossing the river, which is here incredibly increased in size, by the continual accession of brooks flowing in from the hills on each side, dividing their green turfy beds, forming them into parterres, vistas and verdant swelling knolls, profusely productive of flowers and fragrant strawberries, their rich juice dying my horses feet and ancles.

THESE swelling hills, the prolific beds on which the towering mountains repose, seem to have been the common situations of the towns of the acients, as appear from the remaining ruins of them yet to be seen; and the level rich vale and meadows in front, their planting grounds.

CONTINUING yet ten or twelve miles down the vale, my road leading at times closes to the banks of the river, the Azalea, Kalmia, Rhododendron, Philadelphus, &c. beautifying his now elevated shores, and painting the coves with a rich and cheerful scenery, continually unfolding new prospects as I traverse the shores; the towering mountains seem continually in motion as I pass along pompously rising their superb crests towards the lofty skies, traversing the far distant horizon.

THE Tanase is now greatly increased from the conflux of the multitude of rivulets and brooks, descending from the hills on either side, generously contributing to establish his future fame, already a spacious river.

THE mountains recede, the vale expands, two beautiful rivulets stream down through lateral vales, gliding in serpentine mazes over the green turfy knolls, and enter the Tanase nearly opposite to each other. Strait forward the expansive green vale seems yet infinite: now on the right hand a lofty pyramidal hill terminates a spur of the adjacent mountain, and advances almost into the river; but immediately after doubling this promontory, an expanded wing of the vale spreads on my right, down which came precipitately, a very beautiful creek, which flowed into the river just before me: but now behold, high upon the side of a distant mountain overlooking the vale, the fountain of this brisk flowing creek; the uparalleled water fall appears as a vast edifice with chrystal front, or a field of ice lying on the bosom of the hill.

Travels Through North and South Carolina

I NOW approach the river at the fording place, which was greatly swolen by the floods of rain that fell the day before, and ran with foaming rapidity, but observing that it had fell several feet perpendicular, and perceiving the bottom or bed of the river to be level, and covered evenly with pebbles, I ventured to cross over, however I was obliged to swim two or three yards at the deepest chanel of it, and landed safely on the banks of a fine meadow, which lay on the opposite shore, where I immediately alighted and spread abroad on the turf my linen, books and specimens of plants, &c. to dry, turned out my steed to graze and then avanced into to the strawberry plains to regale on the fragrant, delicious fruit, welcomed by communities of the splendid meleagris, the capricious roe–buck and all the free and happy tribes which possess and inhabit those prolific fields, who appeared to invite and joined with me in the participation of the bountiful repast presented to us from the lap of nature.

I MOUNTED again and followed the trading path about a quarter of a mile through the fields, then gently ascended the green beds of the hills, and entered the forests, being a point of a chain of hills projecting into the green vale or low lands of the river; this forest continued about a mile, the surface of the land level but rough, being covered with stones or fragments of rocks, and very large, smooth pebbles of various shapes and sizes, some of ten or fifteen pounds weight: I observed on each side of the road many vast heaps of these stones, Indian graves undoubtedly

* At this place was fought a bloody and decisive battle between the Indians and the Carolinians, under the conduct of general Middleton, when a great number of Cherokee warriors were slain, which shook their power, terrified and humbled them, insomuch that they deserted most of their settlements in the low countries, and betook themselves to the mountains as less accessible to the regular forces of the white people.

AFTER I left the graves, the ample vale soon offered on my right hand, through the tall forest trees, charming views, and which exhibited a pleasing contrast, immediately out of the gloomy shades and scenes of death, into expansive, lucid, green, flowery fields, expanding between retiring hills and turfy eminences, the rapid Tanase gliding through as a vast serpent rushing after his prey.

Travels Through North and South Carolina

MY winding path now leads me again over the green fields into the meadows, sometimes visiting the decorated banks of the river, as it meanders through the meadows, or boldy sweeps along the bases of the mountains, its surface receiving the images reflected from the flowery banks above.

THUS was my agreeable progress for about fifteen miles, since I came upon the sources of the Tanase, at the head of this charming vale: in the evening espying a human habitation at the foot of the sloping green hills, beneath lofty forests of the mountains on the left hand, and at the same time observed a man crossing the river from the opposite shore in a canoe and coming towards me, I waited his approach, who hailing me, I answered I was for Cowe; he intreated me very civilly to call at his house, adding that he would presently come to me.

I WAS received and entertained here until next day with the most perfect civility. After I had dined, towards evening, a company of Indian girls, inhabitants of a village in the hills at a small distance, called, having baskets of strawberries; and this man, who kept here a trading–house, and being married to a Cherokee woman of family, was indulged to keep a stock of cattle, and his help–mate being an excellent house–wife and a very agreeable good woman, treated us with cream and strawberries.

NEXT morning after breakfasting on excellent coffee, relished with bucanned venison, hot corn cakes, excellent butter and cheese, sat forwards again for Cowe, which was about fifteen miles distance, keeping the trading path which coursed through the low lands between the hills and the river, now spacious and well beaten by travellers, but somewhat intricate to a stranger, from the frequent colateral roads falling into it from villages or towns over the hills: after riding about four miles, mostly through fields and plantations, the soil incredibly fertile, arrived at the town of Echoe, consisting of many good houses, well inhabited; I passed through and continued three miles farther to Nucasse, and three miles more brought me to Whatoga: riding through this large town, the road carried me winding about through their little plantations of Corn, Beans, &c. up to the council–house, which was a very large dome or rotunda, situated on the top of an ancient artificial mount, and here my road terminated; all before me and on every side appeared little plantations of young Corn, Beans, &c. divided from each other by narrow strips or borders of grass, which marked the bounds of each one's property, their habitation standing in the midst: finding no common high road to lead me through the town, I was now at a stand how to proceed farther, when observing an Indian man at the door of his habitation, three or four hundred yards distance from me, beckoning to come to him, I ventured to ride through their lots, being careful to do no injury to the young plants, the rising hopes of their labour and industry, crossed a little grassy vale watered by a silver stream, which gently undulated through, then ascended a green hill to the house, (where I was cheerfully welcomed at the door and led in by the chief, giving the care of my horse to two handsome youths, his sons. During my continuance here, about half an hour, I experienced the most perfect and agreeable hospitality conferred on me by these happy people; I mean happy in their dispositions, in their apprehensions of rectitude with regard to our social or moral conduct: O divine simplicity and truth, friendship without fallacy or guile, hospitality disinterested, native, undefiled, unmodifyed by artificial refinements.

MY venerable host gracefully and with an air of respect, led me into an airy, cool apartment, where being seated on cabins, his women brought in a refreshing repast, consisting of sodden venison, hot corn cakes, &c. with a pleasant cooling liquor made of hommony well boiled, mixed afterwards with milk; this is served up either before or after eating in a large bowl, with a very large spoon or ladle to sup it with.

AFTER partaking of this simple but healthy and liberal collation and the dishes cleared off, Tobacco and pipes were brought, and the chief filling one of them, whose stem, about four feet long, was sheathed in a beautiful speckled snake skin, and adorned with feathers and strings of wampum, lights it and smoaks a few whiffs, puffing the smoak first towards the sun, then to the four cardinal points and lastly over my breast, hands it towards me, which I cheerfully received from him and smoaked, when we fell into conversation; he first enquired if I came from Charleston? if I Knew John Stewart, Esq,? how long since I left Charleston? &c. Having satisfied him in my answers in the best manner I could, he was greatly pleased, which I was convinced of by his attention to me, his cheerful manners and his ordering my horse a plentiful bait of corn, which last instance of respect is conferred on those only to whom they manifest the highest esteem, saying that corn was given by the Great Spirit only for food to man.

I ACQUAINTED this ancient prince and patriarch of the nature and design of my peregrinations, and that I was now for Cowe, but having lost my road in the town, requested that I might be informed. He cheerfully replied, that he was pleased I was come in their country, where I should meet with friendship and protection, and that he would himself lead me into the right path.

Travels Through North and South Carolina

AFTER ordering my horse to the door we went forth together, he on foot and I leading my horse by the bridle, thus walking together near two miles, we shook hands and parted, he returning home and I continuing my journey for Cowe.

THIS prince is the chief of Whatoga, a man universally beloved, and particularly esteemed by the whites for his pacific and equitable disposition, and revered by all for his exemplary virtues, just, moderate, magnanimous and intrepid.

HE was tall and perfectly formed; his countenance cheerful and lofty and at the same time truly characteristic of the red men, that is, the brow ferocious and the eye active, piercing or fiery, as an eagle. He appeared to be about sixty years of age, yet upright and muscular, and his limbs active as youth.

AFTER leaving my princely friend, I travelled about five miles through old plantations, now under grass, but appeared to have been planted the last season; the soil exceeding fertile, loose, black, deep and fat. I arrived at Cowe about noon; this settlement is esteemed the capital town; it is situated on the bases of the hills on both sides of the river, near to its bank, and here terminates the great vale of Cowe, exhibiting one of the most charming natural mountainous landscapes perhaps any where to be seen; ridges of hills rising grand and sublimely one above and beyond another, some boldly and majestically advancing into the verdant plain, their feet bathed with the silver flood of the Tanase, whilst others far distant, veiled in blue mists, sublimely mount aloft, with yet greater majesty lift up their pompous crests and overlook vast regions.

THE vale is closed at Cowe by a ridge of mighty hills, called the Jore mountain, said to be the highest land in the Cherokee country, which crosses the Tanase here.

ON my arrival at this town I waited on the gentlemen to whom I was recommended by letter, and was received with respect and every demonstration of hospitality and friendship.

I TOOK my residence with Mr. Galahan the chief trader here, an ancient respectable man who had been many years a trader in this country, and is esteemed and beloved by the Indians for his humanity, probity and equitable dealings with them, which to be just and candid I am obliged to observe (and blush for my countrymen at the recital) is somewhat of a prodigy, as it is a fact, I am afraid too true, that the white traders in their commerce

239

with the Indians, give great and frequent occasions of complaint of their dishonesty and violence; but yet there are a few exceptions, as in the conduct of this gentleman, who furnishes a living instance of the truth of the old proverb, that "Honesty is the best policy," for this old honest Hibernian has often been protected by the Indians, when all others round about him have been ruined, their property seized and themselves driven out of the country or slain by the injured, provoked natives.

NEXT day after my arrival I crossed the river in a canoe, on a visit to a trader who resided amongst the habitations on the other shore.

AFTER dinner, on his mentioning some curious scenes amongst the hills, some miles distance from the river, we agreed to spend the afternoon in observations on the mountains.

AFTER riding near two miles through Indian plantations of Corn, which was well cultivated, kept clean of weeds and was well advanced, being near eighteen inches in height, and the Beans planted at the Corn hills were above ground; we leave the fields on our right, turning towards the mountains and ascending through a delightful green vale or lawn, which conducted us in amongst the pyramidal hills and crossing a brisk flowing creek, meandering through the meads which continued near two miles, dividing and branching in amongst the hills; we then mounted their steep ascents, rising gradually by ridges or steps one above another, frequently crossing narrow, fertile dales as we ascended; the air feels cool and animating, being charged with the fragrant breath of the mountain beauties, the blooming mountain cluster Rose, blushing Rhododendron and fair Lilly of the valley: having now attained the summit of this very elevated ridge, we enjoyed a fine prospect indeed; the enchanting Vale of Keowe, perhaps as celebrated for fertility, fruitfulness and beautiful prospects as the Fields of Pharsalia or the Vale of Tempe: the town, the elevated peeks of the Jore mountains, a very distant prospect of the Jore village in a beautiful lawn, lifted up many thousand feet higher than our present situation, besides a view of many other villages and settlements on the sides of the mountains, at various distances and elevations; the silver rivulets gliding by them and snow white cataracts glimmering on the sides of the lofty hills; the bold promontories of the Jore mountain stepping into the Tanase river, whilst his foaming waters rushed between them.

Travels Through North and South Carolina

AFTER viewing this very entertaining scene we began to descend the mountain on the other side, which exhibited the same order of gradations of ridges and vales as on our ascent, and at length rested on a very expansive, fertile plain, amidst the towering hills, over which we rode a long time, through magnificent high forests, extensive green fields, meadows and lawns. Here had formerly been a very flourishing settlement, but the Indians deserted it in search of fresh planting land, which they soon found in a rich vale but a few miles distance over a ridge of hills. Soon after entering on these charming, sequestered, prolific fields, we came to a fine little river, which crossing, and riding over fruitful strawberry beds and green lawns, on the sides of a circular ridge of hills in front of us, and going round the bases of this promontory, came to a fine meadow on an arm of the vale, through which meandered a brook, its humid vapours bedewing the fragrant strawberries which hung in heavy red clusters over the grassy verge; we crossed the rivulet, then rising a sloping, green, turfy ascent, alighted on the borders of a grand forest of stately trees, which we penetrated on foot a little distance to a horse–stamp, where was a large squadron of those useful creatures, belonging to my friend and companion, the trader, on the sight of whom they assembled together from all quarters; some at a distance saluted him with shrill neighings of gratitude, or came prancing up to lick the salt out of his hand; whilst the younger and more timorous came galloping onward, but coyly wheeled off, and fetching a circuit stood aloof, but as soon as their lord and master strewed the chrystaline salty bait on the hard beaten ground, they all, old and young, docile and timorous, soon formed themselves in ranks and fell to licking up the delicious morsel.

IT was a fine sight; more beautiful creatures I never saw; there were of them of all colours, sizes and dispositions. Every year as they become of age he sends off a troop of them down to Charleston, where they are sold to the highest bidder.

HAVING paid our attention to this useful part of the creation, who, if they are under our dominion, have consequently a right to our protection and favour. We returned to our trusty servants that were regaling themselves in the exuberant sweet pastures and strawberry fields in sight, and mounted again; proceeding on our return to town, continued through part of this high forest skirting on the meadows; began to ascend the hills of a ridge which we were under the necessity of crossing, and having gained its summit, enjoyed a most enchanting view, a vast expanse of green meadows and strawberry fields; a meandering river gliding through, saluting in its various turnings the swelling, green, turfy knolls, embellished with parterres of flowers and fruitful strawberry

241

beds; flocks of turkies strolling about them; herds of deer prancing in the meads or bounding over the hills; companies of young, innocent Cherokee virgins, some busily gathering the rich fragrant fruit, others having already filled their baskets, lay reclined under the shade of floriferous and fragrant native bowers of Magnolia, Azalea, Philadelphus, perfumed Calycanthus, sweet Yellow Jessamine and cerulian Glycine frutescens, disclosing their beauties to the fluttering breeze, and bathing their limbs in the cool fleeting streams; whilst other parties, more gay and libertine, were yet Collecting strawberries or wantonly chasing their companions, tantalising them, staining their lips and cheeks with the rich fruit.

THIS sylvan scene of primitive innocence was enchanting, and perhaps too enticing for hearty young men long to continue idle spectators.

IN fine, nature prevailing over reason, we wished at least to have a more active part in their delicious sports. Thus precipitately resolving, we cautiously made our approaches, yet undiscovered, almost to the joyous scene of action. Now, although we meant no other than an innocent frolic with this gay assembly of hamadryades, we shall leave it to the person of feeling and sensibility to form an idea to what lengths our passions might have hurried us, thus warmed and excited, had it not been for the vigilance and care of some envious matrons who lay in ambush, and espying us gave the alarm, time enough for the nymphs to rally and assemble together; we however pursued and gained ground on a group of them, who had incautiously strolled to a greater distance from their guardians, and finding their retreat now like to be cut off, took shelter under cover of a little grove, but on perceiving themselves to be discovered by us, kept their station, peeping through the bushes; when observing our approaches, they confidently discovered themselves and decently advanced to meet us, half unveiling their blooming faces, incarnated with the modest maiden blush, and with native innocence and cheerfulness presented their little baskets, merrily telling us their fruit was ripe and sound.

WE accepted a basket, sat down and regaled ourselves on the delicious fruit, encircled by the whole assembly of the innocently jocose sylvan nymphs; by this time the several parties under the conduct of the elder matrons, had disposed themselves in companies on the green, turfy banks.

MY young companion, the trader, by concessions and suitable apologies for the bold intrusion, having compromised the matter with them, engaged them to bring their

242

collections to his house at a stipulated price, we parted friendly.

AND now taking leave of these Elysian fields, we again mounted the hills, which we crossed, and traversing obliquely their flowery beds, arrived in town in the cool of the evening.

CHAP. IV.

AFTER waiting two days at Cowe expecting a guide and protector to the Overhill towns, and at last being disappointed, I resolved to pursue the journey alone, though against the advice of the traders; the Overhill Indians being in an ill humour with the whites, in consequence of some late skirmishes between them and the frontier Virginians, most of the Overhill traders having left the nation.

EARLY in the morning I sat off attended by my worthy old friend Mr. Gallahan, who obligingly accompanied me near fifteen miles, we passed through the Jore village, which is pleasingly situated in a little vale on the side of the mountain, a pretty rivulet or creek winds about through the vale, just under the village; here I observed a little grove of the Casine yapon, which was the only place I had seen it grow in the Cherokee country, the Indians call it the beloved tree, and are very careful to keep them pruned and cultivated, they drink a very strong infusion of the leaves, buds and tender branches of this plant, which is so celebrated, indeed venerated by the Creeks, and all the Southern maritime nations of Indians; then continued travelling down the vale about two miles, the road deviating, turning and winding about the hills, and through groves and lawns, watered by brooks and rivulets, rapidly rushing from the towering hill on every side, and flowing into the Jore, which is a considerable branch of the Tanase.

BEGAN now to ascend the mountain, following a small arm or branch of the vale, which led to a gap or narrow defile, compressed by the high pending hills on each side, down which came rapidly a considerable branch of the Jore, dashing and roaring over rocky precipices.

NOW leaving Roaring creek on our right and accomplishing two or three ascents or ridges, another branch of the trading path from the Overhills to Cowe came in on our right, and here my transitory companion Mr. Gallahan parted from me, taking this road back to Cowe, when I was left again wandering alone in the dreary mountains, not indeed totally pathless, nor in my present situation entirely agreeable, although such scenes of primitive unmodified nature always pleased me.

MAY we suppose that mankind feel in their hearts, a predilection for the society of each other; or are we delighted with scenes of human arts and cultivation, where the passions are flattered and entertained with variety of objects for gratification?

I FOUND myself unable notwithstanding the attentive admonitions and pursuasive arguments of reason, entirely to erase from my mind, those impressions which I had received from the society of the amiable and polite inhabitants of Charleston; and I could not help comparing my present situation in some degree to Nebuchadnezzar's, when expelled from the society of men, and constrained to roam in the mountains and wilderness, there to herd and feed with the wild beasts of the forest.

AFTER parting with my late companion, I went forward with all the alacrity that prudence would admit of, that I might as soon as possible see the end of my toil and hazard, being determined at all events to cross the Jore mountain, said to be the highest land in the Cherokee country.

AFTER a gentle descent I entered on an extreme stony narrow vale, through which coasted swiftly a large creek, twelve or fifteen yards wide, roaring over a rocky bed, which I crossed with difficulty and danger; the ford being incommoded by shelving rocks, full of holes and cliffs; after leaving this rocky creek my path led me upon another narrow vale or glade, down which came in great haste another noisy brook, which I repeatedly crossed and recrossed, sometimes riding on narrow level grassy verges close to its banks, still ascending, the vale gradually terminated, being shut up by stupendous rocky hills on each side, leaving a very narrow gap or defile, towards which my road led me, ascending the steep sides of the mountains, when, after rising several wearisome ascents, and finding myself over heated and tired, I halted at a little grassy lawn through which meandered a sweet rivulet; here I turned my horse to graze, and sat down to rest on a green bank just beneath a high frowning promontory, or obtuse point of a ridge of the mountain yet above me, the friendly rivulet making a circuit by my feet, and now a little rested, I took out of my wallet some biscuit and cheese, and a piece of neat's tongue, composing myself to ease and refreshment; when suddenly appeared within a few yards, advancing towards me from behind the point, a stout likely young Indian fellow, armed

244

with a rifle gun, and two dogs attending, upon sight of me he stood, and seemed a little surprised, as I was very much; but instantly recollecting himself and assuming a countenance of benignity and cheerfulness, came briskly to me and shook hands heartily; and smilingly enquired from whence I came, and whither going, but speaking only in the Cherokee tongue, our conversation was not continued to a great length. I presented him with some choice Tobacco, which was accepted with courtesy and evident pleasure, and to my enquiries concerning the roads and distance to the Overhill towns, he answered me with perfect cheerfulness and good temper; we then again shook hands and parted in friendship, he descended the hills, singing as he went.

OF vegetable productions observed in this region, were the following viz. Acer striatum, Ac. rubrum, Juglans nigra, Jug. alba, Jug. Hickory, Magnolia acuminata, Quercus alba, Q. tinctoria, Q. rubra, Q. prinus, with the other varieties common in Virginia: Panax ginseng, Angelica lucida, Convalaria majalis, Halesia, Stewartia, Styrax, Staphylea, Evonimus, Viburnum, Cornus Florida, Betula nigra, Morus, Telea, Ulmus, Fraxinus, Hopea tinctorea, Annona, Bignonia sempervirens, Aristalocha frutescens, Bignonia radicans, &c. Being now refreshed by a simple but healthy meal, I began again to ascend the Jore mountains, which I at length accomplished, and rested on the most elevated peak; from whence I beheld with rapture and astonishment, a sublimely awful scene of power and magnificence, a world of mountains piled upon mountains. Having contemplated this amazing prospect of grandeur, I descended the pinnacles, and again falling into the trading path, continued gently descending through a grassy plain, scatteringly planted with large trees, and at a distance surrounded with high forests, I was on this elevated region sensible of an alteration in the air, from warm to cold, and found that vegetation was here greatly behind, in plants of the same kind of the country below; for instance, when I left Charleston, the yellow Jasmine was rather past the blooming days, and here the buds were just beginning to swell, though some were in bloom: continued more than a mile through this elevated plain to the pitch of the mountain, from whence presented to view an expansive prospect, exhibiting scenes of mountainous landscape, Westward vast and varied, perhaps not to be exceeded any where.

My first descent and progress down the West side of the mountain was remarkably gradual, easy and pleasant, through grassy open forests for the distance of two or three miles; when my changeable path suddenly turned round an obtuse point of a ridge, and descended precipitately down a steep rocky hill for a mile or more, which was very toublesome, being incommoded with shattered fragments of the mountains, and in other places with boggy sinks, occasioned by oozy springs and rills stagnate sinking in miceous earth; some of these steep soft rocky banks or precipices seem to be continually crumbling to earth; and in these mouldering cliffs I discovered veins or stratas of most pure and clear white earth*

* Mica nitida, specimens of this earth have been exported to England, for the purpose of making Porcelain or China ware.

having a faint bluish or pearl colour gleam, somewhat exhibiting the appearance of the little cliffs or wavy crests of new fallen snowdrifts; we likewise observe in these dissolving rocky cliffs, veins of isinglass, (Mica. S. vitrum Muscoviticum) some of the flakes or laminae incredibly large, entire and transparent, and would serve the purpose of lights for windows very well, or for lanthorns; and here appeared stratas of black lead (stibium.)

AT length, after much toil and exercise, I was a little releived by a narrow grassy vale or lawn at the foot of this steep descent, through which coursed along a considerable rapid brook, on whose banks grew in great perfection the glorious Magnolia auriculata, together with the other conspicuous flowering and aromatic shrubs already mentioned; and I observed here in the rich bottoms near the creek, a new species of Hydrastis, having very large sinuated leaves and white flowers: after this I continued several miles over ridges and grassy vales, watered with delightful rivulets.

NEXT day proceeding on eight or ten miles, generally through spacious high forests and flowery lawns; the soil prolific, being of an excellent quality for agriculture; came near the banks of a large creek or river, where this high forest ended on my left hand, the trees became more scattered and insensibly united with a grassy glade or lawn bordering on the river; on the opposite bank of which appeared a very extensive forest, consisting entirely of the Hemlock spruce (P. abies) almost encircled by distant ridges of lofty hills.

SOON after crossing this large branch of the Tanase, I observed descending the heights at some distance, a company of Indians, all well mounted on horse back; they came rapidly forward; on their nearer approach I observed a chief at the head of the carravan, and apprehending him to be the Little Carpenter, emperor or grand chief of the Cherokees; as they came up I turned off from the path to make way, in token of respect, which

246

compliment was accepted and gratefully and magnanimously returned, for his highness with a gracious and cheerful smile came up to me, and clapping his hand on his breast, offered it to me, saying, I am Ata–cul–culla, and heartily shook hands with me, and asked me if I knew it; I answered that the Good Spirit who goes before me spoke to me, and said, that is the great Ata–cul–culla, and added that I was of the tribe of white men, of Pennsylvania, who esteem themselves brothers and friends to the red men, but particularly so to the Cherokees, and that notwithstanding we dwelt at so great a distance we were united in love and friendship, and that the name of Ata–cul–culla was dear to his white brothers of Pennsylvania.

AFTER this compliment, which seemed to be acceptable, he enquired if I came lately from Charleston, and if John Stewart was well, saying that the was going to see him; I replied that I came lately from Charleston on a friendly visit to the Cherokees; that I had the honour of a personal acquaintance with the superintendant, the beloved man, who I saw well but the day before I sat off, and who, by letters to the principal white men in the nation, recommended me to the friendship and protection of the Cherokees: to which the great chief was pleased to answer very respectfully, that I was welcome in their country as a friend and brother; and then shaking hands heartily bid me farewell, and his retinue confirmed it by an united voice of assent. After giving my name to the chief, requesting my compliments to the superintendant, the emperor moved, continuing his journey for Charleston, and I yet persisting in my intentions of visiting the Overhill towns continued on; leaving the great forest I mounted the high hills, descending them again on the other side and so on repeatedly for several miles, without observing any variation in the natural productions since passing the Jore; and observing the slow progress of vegetation in this mountainous, high country; and, upon serious consideration, it appeared very plainly that I could not, with entire safety, range the Overhill settlements until the treaty was over, which would not come on till late in June, I suddenly came to a resolution to defer these researches at this time, and leave them for the employment of another season and a more favourable opportunity, and return to Dartmouth in Georgia, to be ready to join a company of adventurers who were to set off in July for Mobile in West Florida. The leader of this company had been recommended to me as a fit person to assist me on so long and hazardous a journey, through the vast territories of the Creeks.

THEREFORE next day I turned about on my return, proceeding moderately, being engaged in noting such objects as appeared to be of any moment, and collecting specimens, and in the evening of next day arrived again at Cowe.

Travels Through North and South Carolina

NEXT morning Mr. Galahan conducted me to the chief of Cowe, who during my absence had returned from the chace. The remainder of this day I spent in observations in and about the town, reviewing my specimens, &c.

THE town of Cowe consists of about one hundred dwellings, near the banks of the Tanase, on both sides of the river.

THE Cherokees construct their habitations on a different plan from the Creeks, that is but one oblong four square building, of one story high; the materials consisting of logs or trunks of trees, stripped of their bark, notched at their ends, fixed one upon another, and afterwards plaistered well, both inside and out, with clay well tempered with dry grass, and the whole covered or roofed with the bark of the Chesnut tree or long broad shingles. This building is however partitioned transversely, forming three apartments, which communicate with each other by inside doors; each house or habitation has besides a little conical house, covered with dirt, which is called the winter or hot–house; this stands a few yards distance from the mansion–house, opposite the front door.

THE council or town–house is a large rotunda, capable of accomodating several hundred people; it stands on the top of an ancient artificial mount of earth, of about twenty feet perpendicular, and the rotunda on the top of it being above thirty feet more, gives the whole fabric an elevation of about sixty feet from the common surface of the ground. But it may be proper to observe, that this mount on which the rotunda stands, is of a much ancienter date than the building, and perhaps was raised for another purpose. The Cherokees themselves are as ignorant as we are, by what people or for what purpose these artificial hills were raised; they have various stories concerning them, the best of which amounts to no more than mere conjecture, and leave us entirely in the dark; but they have a tradition common with the other nations of Indians, that they found them in much the same condition as they now appear, when their forefathers arrived from the West and possessed themselves of the country, after vanquishing the nations of red men who then inhabited it, who themselves found these mounts when they took possession of the country, the former possessors delivering the same story concerning them: perhaps they were designed and apropriated by the people who constructed them, to some religious purpose, as great altars and temples similar to the high places and sacred groves anciently amongst the Canaanites and other nations of Palestine and Judea.

Travels Through North and South Carolina

THE rotunda is constructed after the following manner, they first fix in the ground a circular range of posts or trunks of trees, about six feet high, at equal distances, which are notched at top, to receive into them, from one to another, a range of beams or wall plates; within this is another circular order of very large and strong pillars, above twelve feet high, notched in like manner at top, to receive another range of wall plates, and within this is yet another or third range of stronger and higher pillars, but fewer in number, and standing at a greater distance from each other; and lastly, in the centre stands a very strong pillar, which forms the pinnacle of the building, and to which the rafters centre at top; these rafters are strengthened and bound together by cross beams and laths, which sustain the roof or covering, which is a layer of bark neatly placed, and tight enough to exclude the rain, and sometimes they cast a thin superficies of earth over all. There is but one large door, which serves at the same time to admit light from without and the smoak to escape when a fire is kindled; but as there is but a small fire kept, sufficient to give light at night, and that fed with dry small sound wood divested of its bark, there is but little smoak; all around the inside of the building, betwixt the second range of pillars and the wall, is a range of cabins or sophas, consisting of two or three steps, one above or behind the other, in theatrical order, where the assembly sit or lean down; these sophas are covered with matts or carpets, very curiously made of thin splints of Ash or Oak, woven or platted together; near the great pillar in the centre the fire is kindled for light, near which the musicians seat themselves, and round about this the performers exhibit their dances and other shews at public festivals, which happen almost every night throughout the year.

ABOUT the close of the evening I accompanied Mr. Galahan and other white traders to the rotunda, where was a grand festival, music and dancing. This assembly was held principally to rehearse the ball–play dance, this town being challenged to play against another the next day.

THE people being assembled and seated in order, and the musicians having taken their station, the ball opens, first with a long harangue or oration, spoken by an aged chief, in commendation of the manly exercise of the ball–play, recounting the many and brilliant victories which the town of Cowe had gained over the other towns in the nation, not forgetting or neglecting to recite his own exploits, together with those of other aged men now present, coadjutors in the performance of these athletic games in their youthful days.

Travels Through North and South Carolina

THIS oration was delivered with great spirit and eloquence, and was meant to influence the passions of the young men present, excite them to emulation and inspire them with ambition.

THIS prologue being at an end, the musicians began, both vocal and instrumental, when presently a company of girls, hand in hand, dressed in clean white robes and ornamented with beads, bracelets and a profusion of gay ribbands, entering the door, immediately began to sing their responses in a gentle, low and sweet voice, and formed themselves in a semicircular file or line, in two ranks, back to back, facing the spectators and musicians, moving slowly round and round; this continued about a quarter of an hour, when we were surprised by a sudden very loud and shrill whoop, uttered at once by a company of young fellows, who came in briskly after one another, with rackets or hurls in one hand. These champions likewise were well dressed, painted and ornamented with silver bracelets, gorgets and wampum, neatly ornamented with moccasins and high waving plumes in their diadems, who immediately formed themselves in a semicircular rank also, in front of the girls, when these changed their order, and formed a single rank parallel to the men, raising their voices in responses to the tunes of the young champions, the semicircles continually moving round. There was something singular and diverting in their step and motions, and I imagine not to be learned to exactness but with great attention and perseverance; the step, if it can be so termed, was performed after the following manner, i. e. first, the motion began at one end of the semicircle, gently rising up and down upon their toes and heels alternately, when the first was up on tip–toe, the next began to raise the heel, and by the time the first rested again on the heel, the second was on tip toe, thus from one end of the rank to the other, so that some were always up and some down, alternately and regularly, without the least baulk or confusion; and they at the same time, and in the same motion, moved on obliquely or sideways, so that the circle performed a double or complex motion in its progression, and at stated times exhibited a grand or universal movement, instantly and unexpectedly to the spectators, by each rank turning to right and left, taking each others places; the movements were managed with inconceivable alertness and address, and accompanied with an instantaneous and universal elevation of the voice and shrill short whoop.

THE Cherokees besides the ball play dance, have a variety of others equally entertaining; the men especially exercise themselves with a variety of gesticulations and capers, some of which are ludicrous and diverting enough; and they have others which are of the martial order, and others of the chace; these seem to be somewhat of a tragical nature,

250

wherein they exhibit astonishing feats of military prowess, masculine strength and activity. Indeed all their dances and musical entertainments seem to be theatrical exhibitions or plays, varied with comic and sometimes lascivious interludes; the women however conduct themselves with a very becoming grace and decency, insomuch that in amorous interludes, when their responses and gestures seem consenting to natural liberties, they veil themselves, just discovering a glance of their sparkling eyes and blushing faces, expressive of sensibility.

NEXT morning early I sat off on my return, and meeting with no material occurrences on the road, in two days arrived safe at Keowe, where I tarried two or three days, employed in augmenting my collections of specimens, and waiting for Mr. Galahan who was to call on me here, to accompany him to Sinica, where he and other traders where to meet Mr. Cameron, the deputy commissary, who were to hold a congress at that town, with the chiefs of the Lower Cherokees, to consult preliminaries introductory to a general congress and treaty with these Indians, which was to be convened next June, and held in the Overhill towns.

I OBSERVED in the environs of Keowe, on the bases of the rocky hills, immediately ascending from the low grounds near the river bank, a great number of very singular antiquities, the work of the ancients; they seem to me to have been altars for sacrifice or sepulchres; they were constructed of four flat stones, two set on an edge for the sides, one closed one end, and a very large flat one lay horizontally at top, so that the other end was open; this fabric was four or five feet in length, two feet high and three in width. I enquired of the trader what they were, who could not tell me certainly, but supposed them to be ancient Indian ovens; the Indians can give no account of them: they are on the surface of the ground and are of different dimensions.

I ACCOMPANIED the traders to Sinica, where we found the commissary and the Indian chiefs convened in counsel; continued at Sinica sometime, employing myself in observations and making collections of every thing worthy of notice; and finding the Indians to be yet unsettled in their determination and not in a good humour, I abandoned the project of visiting the regions beyond the Cherokee mountains for this season; sat off for my return to fort James Dartmouth, lodged this night in the forests near the banks of a delightful large creek, a branch of Keowe river, and next day arrived safe at Dartmouth.

List of the towns and villages in the Cherokee nation inhabited at this day, viz.

On the Tanase East of the Jore mountains.
4 towns.

- No. 1 Echoe
- 2 Nucasse
- 3 Whatoga
- 4 Cowe

Inland on the branches of the Tanase.
4 towns.

- 5 Ticoloosa
- 6 Jore
- 7 Conisca
- 8 Nowe

On the Tanase over the Jore mountains.
8 towns.

- 9 Tomothle
- 10 Noewe
- 11 Tellico
- 12 Clennuse
- 13 Ocunnolufte
- 14 Chewe
- 15 Quanuse
- 16 Tellowe

Inland towns on the branches of the Tanase and other waters over the Jore mountains.
5 towns.

- 17 Tellico
- 18 Chatuga
- 19 Hiwasse
- 20 Chewase
- 21 Nuanha

Overhill towns on the Tanase or Cherokee river.
6 towns.

- 22 Tallase
- 23 Chelowe
- 24 Sette
- 25 Chote great
- 26 Joco
- 27 Tahasse

Overhill towns on the Tanase or Cherokee river.
5 towns.

- 28 Tamahle
- 29 Tuskege
- 30———. Big Island
- 31 Nilaque
- 32 Niowe

Lower towns East of the mountains, viz.

On the Savanna or Keowe river.

- No. 1 Sinica
- 2 Keowe
- 3 Kulsage

On Tugilo river.

- 4 Tugilo
- 5 Estotowe

On Flint river.

- 6 Qualatche
- 7 Chote

Towns on the waters of other rivers.

Estotowe great. Allagae. Jore. Nae oche

In all forty–three towns.

CHAP. V.

BEING returned from the Cherokee country to Dartmouth, I understood that the company of adventurers for West Florida were very forward in their preparations, and would be ready to set off in a few weeks, so that I had but a little time allowed me to make provision and equip myself for the prosecution of so long and hazardous a journey.

OUR place of rendezvous was at fort Charlotte, on the opposite side of the river Savanna, and about a mile from fort James. Having a desire to make little botanical excursions towards the head of Broad river, in order to collect some curiosities which I had observed thereabouts, which being accomplished,

Travels Through North and South Carolina

JUNE 22d set out from fort Charlotte in company with Mr. Whitfield, who was chief of our caravan. We travelled about twenty miles and lodged at the farm of Mons. St. Pierre, a French gentleman, who received and entertained us with great politeness and hospitality. The mansion–house is situated on the top of a very high hill near the banks of the river Savanna, which overlooks his very extensive and well cultivated plantations of Indian Corn (Zea) Rice, Wheat, Oats, Indigo, Convolvulus Batata, &c. these are rich low lands, lying very level betwixt these natural heights and the river; his gardens occupy the gentle descent on one side of the mount, and a very thriving vineyard consisting of about five acres on the other side.

NEXT morning after breakfast we sat off again, continuing nine or ten miles farther down the river, when we stopped at a plantation, the property of one of our companions, where we were joined by the rest of the company. After dining here we prepared to depart, and the gentleman of the house taking an affectionate leave of his wife and children, we sat off again, and proceeding six miles farther down the river, we crossed over into Georgia, taking a road which led us into the great trading path from Augusta to the Creek nation. As the soil, situation and productions of these parts, for several days journey, differ very little from the Northern districts of Georgia, already recited, when on the survey of the New Purchase, I apprehend it needless to enter again into a detail of particulars, since it would produce but little more than a recapitulation of that journey.

EARLY in the evening of the 27th we arrived at the Flat–rock, where we lodged. This is a common rendezvous or camping place for traders and Indians. It is an expansive clean flat or horizontal rock, but a little above the surface of the ground, and near the banks of a delightful rivulet of excellent water which is one of the head branches of Great Ogeche: in the loose, rich soil verging round this rock, grew several very curious herbaceous plants, particularly one of singular elegance and beauty, which I take to be a species of Ipomea (Ipomea, caule erecto, ramoso, tripedali, sol. radicalibus, pinnatifidis, liniaribus, humi–straits, florib. incarnatis intus maculis coccinaeis adsperso.) It grows erect, three feet high, with a strong stem, which is decorated with plumed or pinnatifid liniar leaves, somewhat resembling those of the Delphinium or Ipomea quamoclet; from about one half its length upwards, it sends out on all sides, ascendent branches which divide again and again; these terminate with large tubular or funnel formed flowers; their limbs equally divided into five segments; these beautiful flowers are of a perfect rose colour, elegantly besprinkled on the inside of their petals with crimson specks; the flowers are in great abundance and together with the branches and delicately fine cut leaves, compose a conical spike or compound pannicle. I saw a species of this plant, if not the very same, growing on the sea coast islands near St. Augustine. The blue flowered Malva and Delphinium were its associates about the Flat–rock.

THERE are extensive Cane brakes or Cane meadows spread abroad round about, which afford the most acceptable and nourishing food for cattle.

THIS evening two companies of Indian traders from Augusta arrived and encamped near us; and as they were bound to the Nation, we concluded to unite in company with them, they generously offering us their assistance, having many spare horses and others lightly loaded, several of ours by this time being jaded, this was a favorable opportunity of relief in case of necessity.

NEXT morning, as soon as the horses were packed and in readiness, we decamped and set forward together.

I THOUGHT it worthy of taking notice of a singular method the traders make use of to reduce the wild young horses to their hard duty. When any one persists in refusing to receive his load, if threats, the discipline of the whip and other common abuse prove insufficient, after being haltered, a pack–horseman catches the tip end of one of his ears betwixt his teeth and pinches it, when instantly the furious strong creature, trembling, stands perfectly still until he is loaded.

OUR caravan consisting of about twenty men and sixty horses, we made a formidable appearance, having now little to apprehend from predatory bands or out–laws.

THIS day's journey was for the most part over high gravelly ridges, and on the most elevated hills appeared emerging out of the earth, rocky cliffs of a dark reddish brown colour; their composition seemed to be a coarse, sandy, ferruginous concrete, but so firmly cemented as to constitute a perfect hard stone or rock, and appeared to be excavated or worn into cavities and furrows by the violence of the dashing billows and rapid currents of the ocean, which heretofore probably washed them; there were however strata or veins in these rocks, of a finer composition and compact consistence, and seemed ponderous, rich iron ore. A little depth below the sandy, gravelly surface lies a stratum of very compact reddish yellow clay and fragments of ochre. The trees and shrubs common on these gravelly ridges are as follows, Diospyros, Quercus rubra, Q.

nigra, Q. tinctoria or great Black Oak, Q. alba, Q. lobata, post White Oak, Q. incana, foliis ovalibus integerrimis subtus incanis, Pinus lutea, Pinus taeda, foliis geminatis et trinis, strobilo ovato brevi, cortice rimoso, Pinus palustris, foliis trinis Iongissimis, strobilo elongato, Cornus Florida, Andromeda arborea, Nyssa sylvatica, Juglans hickory, Prunus padus, &c. Of herbacia, Solidago, Eupatorium Sylphium, Rudbeckia, Gerardia, Asclepias, Agave Virginica, Eryngium, Thapsia, Euphorbia, Polymnia, &c.

IN the course of this day's journey we crossed two considerable rivulets, running swiftly over rocky beds. There is some very good land on the gradual descents of the ridges and their bottoms bordering on creeks, and very extensive grassy savannas and Cane meadows always in view on one hand or the other. At evening we came to camp on the banks of a beautiful creek, a branch of Great Ogeche, called Rocky Comfort, where we found excellent accommodations, here being pleasant grassy open plains to spread our beds upon, environed with extensive Cane meadows, affording the best of food for our quadrupeds.

THE next day's journey led us over a level district; the land generally very fertile and of a good quality for agriculture, the vegetable surface being of a dark, loose, rich mould, on a stratum of stiff reddish brown clay. crossing several considerable creeks, branches of the Ocone, North branch of the Alatamaha, at evening, July 1st, encamped on the banks of the Ocone, in a delightful grove of forest trees, consisting of Oak, Ash, Mulberry, Hickory, Black Walnut, Elm, Sassafras, Gleditsia, &c. This flourishing grove was an appendage of the high forests we had passed through, and projected into an extensive, green, open, level plain, consisting of old Indian fields and plantations, being the rich low lands of the river, and stretching along its banks upwards to a very great distance, charmingly diversified and decorated with detached groves and clumps of various trees and shrubs, and indented on its verge by advancing and retreating promontories of the high land.

OUR encampment was fixed on the site of the old Ocone town, which, about sixty years ago, was evacuated by the Indians, who finding their situation disagreeable from its vicinity to the white people, left it, moving upwards into the Nation or Upper Creeks, and there built a town, but that situation not suiting their roving disposition, they grew sickly and tired of it, and resolved to seek a habitation more agreeable to their minds; they all arose, directing their migration South–Eastward towards the sea coast, and in the course of their journey, observing the delightful appearance of the extensive plains of Alachua and the fertile hills environing it, they sat down and built a town on the banks of a spacious and beautiful lake, at a small distance from the plains, naming this new town Cuscowilla: this situation pleased them, the vast desarts, forests, lake and savannas around, affording unbounded range of the best hunting ground for bear and deer, their favourite game. But although this situation was healthy and delightful to the utmost degree, affording them variety and plenty of every desirable thing in their estimation, yet troubles and afflictions found them out. This territory, to the promontory of Florida, was then claimed by the Tomocos, Utinas, Calloosas, Yamases and other remnant tribes of the ancient Floridans and the more Northern refugees, driven away by the Carolinians, now in alliance and under the protection of the Spaniards, who assisting them, attacked the new settlement and for many years were very troublesome, but the Alachuas or Ocones being strengthened by other emigrants and fugitive bands from the Upper Creeks, with whom they were confederated, and who gradually established other towns in this low country, stretching a line of settlements across the isthmus, extending from the Alatamaha to the bay of Apalache: these uniting were at length able to face their enemies and even attack them in their own settlements, and in the end, with the assistance of the Upper Creeks, their uncles, vanquished their enemies and destroyed them, and then fell upon the Spanish settlements, which they also entirely broke up. But having treated of these matters in the journal of my travels into East Florida, I end this digression and proceed again on my journey.

AFTER crossing the Ocone by fording it, which is about two hundred and fifty yards over, we travelled about twenty miles and came to camp in the evening; passed over a pleasant territory, presenting varying scenes of gentle swelling hills and levels, affording sublime forests, contrasted by expansive illumined green fields, native meadows and Cane brakes; the vegetables, trees, shrubs and plants the same as already noticed without any material variation. The next day's journey was about twenty miles, having crossed the Oakmulge by fording it three or four hundred yards over. This river is the main branch of the beautiful Alatamaha; on the East bank of the river lies the famous Oakmulge fields, where are yet conspicuous very wonderful remains of the power and grandeur of the ancients of this part of America, in the ruins of a capital town and settlement, as vast artificial hills, terraces, &c. already particularly mentioned in my tour through the lower districts of Georgia. The Oakmulge here is about forty miles distance from the Ocone, the other arm of the Alatamaha. In the evening we came to camp near the banks of Stony Creek, a large rapid water about six miles beyond the river.

Travels Through North and South Carolina

NEXT day we travelled about twenty miles farther, crossing two considerable creeks named Great and Little Tobosochte, and at evening encamped close by a beautiful large brook called Sweet Water, the glittering wavy flood passing along actively over a bed of pebbles and gravel. The territory through which we passed from the banks of the Oakmulge to this place, exhibited a delightful diversified rural scene, and promises a happy, fruitful and salubrious region, when cultivated by industrious inhabitants, generally ridges of low swelling hills and plains supporting grand forests, vast Cane meadows, savannas and verdant lawns.

I OBSERVED here a very singular and beautiful shrub, which I suppose is a species of Hydrangia (H. quercifolia.) It grows in coppices or clumps near or on the banks of rivers and creeks; many stems usually arise from a root, spreading itself greatly on all sides by suckers or offsets; the stems grow five or six feet high, declining or diverging from each other, and are covered with several barks or rinds, the last of which being of a cinerious dirt colour and very thin, at a certain age of the stems or shoots, cracks through to the next bark, and is peeled off by the winds, discovering the under, smooth, dark reddish brown bark, which also cracks and peels off the next year, in like manner as the former; thus every year forming a new bark; the stems divide regularly or oppositely, though the branches are crooked or wreathe about horizontally, and these again divide, forming others which terminate with large heavy pannicles or thyrsi of flowers, but these flowers are of two kinds; the numerous partial spikes which compose the pannicles and consist of a multitude of very small fruitful flowers, terminate with one or more very large expansive neutral or mock flowers, standing on a long, slender, stiff peduncle; these flowers are composed of four broad oval petals or segments, of a dark rose or crimson colour at first, but as they become older acquire a deeper red or purplish hue, and lastly are of a brown or ferruginous colour; these have no perfect parts of generation of either sex, but discover in their centre two, three or four papiliae or rudiments; these neutral flowers, with the whole pannicle, are truly permanent, remaining on the plant for years, until they dry and decay; the leaves which clothe the plants are very large, pinnatifid or palmated and serrated, or toothed, very much resembling the leaves of some of our Oaks; they sit opposite, supported by slender petioles and are of a fine, full green colour.

NEXT day after noon we crossed Flint river by fording it, about two hundred and fifty yards over, and at evening came to camp near the banks of a large and deep creek, a branch of the Flint. The high land excellent, affording grand forests, and the low ground vast timber and Canes of great height and thickness, Arundo gigantea. I observed growing on the steep dry banks of this creek, a species of shrub Hypericum, of extraordinary shew and beauty (Hypericum aureum.) It grows erect, three or four feet high, forming a globular top, representing a perfect little tree; the leaves are large, oblong, firm of texture, smooth and shining; the flowers are very large, their petals broad and conspicuous, which, with their tufts of golden filaments, give the little bushes a very splendid appearance.

THE adjacent low grounds and Cane swamp afforded excellent food and range for our horses, who, by this time, through fatigue of constant travelling, heat of the climate and season, were tired and dispirited, we came to camp sooner than usual and started later next day, that they might have time to rest and recruit themselves. The territory lying upon this creek and the space between it and the river, presents every appearance of a delightful and fruitful region in some future day, it being a rich soil and exceedingly well situated for every branch of agriculture and grazing, diversified with hills and dales, savannas and vast Cane meadows, and watered by innumerable rivulets and brooks, all contiguous to the Flint river: an arm of the great Chata Uche or Apalachucla offers an uninterrupted navigation to the bay of Mexico and Atlantic ocean, and thence to the West India islands and over the whole world.

OUR horses being hunted up and packed, sat forward again, proceeding moderately, ascending a higher country and more uneven by means of ridges of gentle hills; the country however very pleasing, being diversified with expansive groves, savannas and Cane meadows, abounding with creeks and brooks gliding through the plains or roving about the hills, their banks bordered with forests and groves, consisting of varieties of trees, shrubs and plants; the summits of the hills frequently presenting to view piles and cliffs of the ferruginous rocks, the same species as observed on the ridges between the Flat–rock and Rocky Comfort.

NEXT day we travelled but a few miles; the heat and the burning flies tormenting our horses to such a degree, as to excite compassion even in the hearts of pack–horsemen. These biting flies are of several species, and their numbers incredible; we travelled almost from sun–rise to his setting, amidst a flying host of these persecuting spirits, who formed a vast cloud around our caravan so thick as to obscure every distant object; but our van always bore the brunt of the conflict; the head, neck and shoulders of the leading horses were continually in a gore of blood: some of these flies were near as large as humble bees; this is the hippobosca. They are armed with a strong sharp beak or

260

probosces, shaped like a lancet, and sheathed in flexible thin valves; with this beak they instantly pierce the veins of the creatures, making a large orifice from whence the blood springs in large drops, rolling down as tears, causing a fierce pain or aching for a considerable time after the wound is made; there are three or four species of this genus of less size but equally vexatious, as they are vastly more numerous, active and sanguineous; particularly, one about half the size of the first mentioned, the next less of a dusky colour with a green head; another yet somewhat less, of a splendid green and the head of a gold colour; the sting of this last is intolerable, no less acute than a prick from a redhot needle, or a spark of fire on the skin; these are called the burning flies. Besides the preceding tormentors, there are three or four species of the afilus or smaller biting flies; one of a greyish dusky colour, another much of the same colour, having spotted wings and a green head, and another very small and perfectly black: this last species lie in ambush in shrubby thickets and Cane brakes near water; whenever we approach the cool shades near creeks, impatient for repose and relief, almost sinking under the persecutions from the evil spirits, who continually surround and follow us over the burning desart ridges and plains, and here in some hopes of momentary peace and quietness, under cover of the cool humid groves, we are surprised and quickly invested with dark clouds of these persecuting demons, besides musquitoes and gnats (culex et cynips.)

THE next day being in like manner oppressed and harassed by the stinging flies and heats; we halted at noon, being unable longer to support ourselves under such grievances, even in our present situation charming to the senses; on the acclivity of a high swelling ridge planted with open airy groves of the superb terebenthine Pines, glittering rills playing beneath, and pellucid brooks meandering through an expansive green savanna, their banks ornamented with coppices of blooming aromatic shrubs and plants perfuming the air. The meridian heats just allayed, the sun is veiled in a dark cloud, rising North–Westward; the air still, gloomy and sultry; the animal spirits sink under the conflict, and we fall into a kind of mortal torpor rather than refreshing repose; and startled or terrified at each others plaintive murmurs and groans: now the earth trembles under the peals of incessant distant thunder, the hurricane comes on roaring, and I am shocked again to life: I raise my head and rub open my eyes, pained with gleams and flashes of lightning; when just attempting to wake up my afflicted brethren and companions, almost overwhelmed with floods of rain, the dark cloud opens over my head, diveloping a vast river of the etherial fire, I am instantly struck dumb, inactive and benumbed; at length the pulse of life begins to vibrate, the animal spirits begin to exert their powers, and I am by degrees revived.

Travels Through North and South Carolina

IN the evening this surprising heavy tempest passed off, we had a serene sky and a pleasant cool night; having had time enough to collect a great quantity of wood and Pine knots to feed our fires and keep up a light in our camp, which was a lucky precaution, as we found it absolutely necessary to dry our clothes and warm ourselves, for all our skins and bedding were cast over the packs of merchandize to prevent them and our provision from being injured by the deluge of rain; next day was cool and pleasant, the air having recovered its elasticity and vivific spirit; I found myself cheerful and invigorated; indeed all around us appeared reanimated, and nature presents her cheerful countenance; the vegetables smile in their blooming decorations and sparkling crystaline dew–drop.

THE birds sing merrily in the groves, and the alert roe–buck whistles and bounds over the ample meads and green turfy hills. After leaving our encampment we travelled over a delightful territory, presenting to view variable sylvan scenes, consisting of chains of low hills affording high forests, with expansive savannas, Cane meadows and lawns between, watered with rivulets and glittering brooks; towards evening we came to camp on the banks of Pintchlucco, a large branch of the Chata Uche river.

THE next day's journey was over an uneven hilly country, but the soil generally fertile and of a quality and situation favourable to agriculture and grazing, the summits of the ridges rough with ferruginous rocks, in high cliffs and fragments, scattered over the surface of the ground; observed also high cliffs of stiff reddish brown clay, with veins or strata of ferruginous stones, either in detached masses or conglomerated nodules or hematites with veins or masses of ochre.

NEXT day after traversing a very delightful territory, exhibiting a charming rural scenery of primitive nature, gently descending and passing alternately easy declivities or magnificent terraces supporting sublime forests, almost endless grassy fields, detatched groves and green lawns for the distance of nine or ten miles, we arrived at the banks of the Chata Uche river opposite the Uche town, where after unloading our horses, the Indians came over to us in large canoes, by means of which, with the cheerful and liberal assistance of the Indians, ferried over their merchandize, and afterwards driving our horses altogether into the river swam them over: the river here is about three or four hundred yards wide, carries fifteen or twenty feet water and flows down with an active current; the water is clear, cool and salubrious.

Travels Through North and South Carolina

THE Uche town is situated in a vast plain, on the gradual ascent as we rise from a narrow strip of low ground immediately bordering on the river: it is the largest, most compact and best situated Indian town I ever saw; the habitations are large and neatly built; the walls of the houses are constructed of a wooden frame, then lathed and plaistered inside and out with a reddish well tempered clay or morter, which gives them the appearance of red brick walls, and these houses are neatly covered or roofed with Cypress bark or shingles of that tree. The town appeared to be populous and thriving, full of youth and young children: I suppose the number of inhabitants, men, women and children, might amount to one thousand or fifteen hundred, as it is said they are able to muster five hundred gun–men or warriors. Their own national language is altogether or radically different from the Creek or Muscogulge tongue, and is called the Savanna or Savanuca tongue; I was told by the traders it was the same or a dialect of the Shawanese. They are in confederacy with the Creeks, but do not mix with them, and on account of their numbers and strength, are of importance enough to excite and draw upon them the jealousy of the whole Muscogulge confederacy, and are usually at variance, yet are wise enough to unite against a common enemy, to support the interest and glory of the general Creek confederacy.

AFTER a little refreshment at this beautiful town, we repacked and sat off again for the Apalachucla town, where we arrived after riding over a level plain, consisting of ancient Indian plantations, a beautiful landscape diversified with groves and lawns.

THIS is esteemed the mother town or capital of the Creek or Muscogulge confederacy: sacred to peace; no captives are put to death or human blood split here. And when a general peace is proposed, deputies from all the towns in the confederacy assemble at this capital, in order to deliberate upon a subject of so high importance for the prosperity of the commonwealth.

AND on the contrary the great Coweta town, about twelve miles higher up this river, is called the bloody town, where the Micos chiefs and warriors assemble when a general war is proposed, and here captives and state malefactors are put to death.

THE time of my continuance here, which was about a week, was employed in excursions round about this settlement. One day the chief trader of Apalachucla obliged me with his company on a walk of about a mile and an half down the river, to view the ruins and site of the ancient Apalachucla: it had been situated on a peninsula formed by a doubling of

263

the river, and indeed appears to have been a very famous capital by the artificial mounds or terraces, and a very populous settlement, from its extent and expansive old fields, stretching beyond the scope of the sight along the low grounds of the river. We viewed the mounds or terraces, on which formerly stood their town house or rotunda and square or areopagus, and a little back of this, on a level height or natural step, above the low grounds is a vast artificial terrace or four square mound, now seven or eight feet higher than the common surface of the ground; in front of one square or side of this mound adjoins a very extensive oblong square yard or artificial level plain, sunk a little below the common surface, and surrounded with a bank or narrow terrace, formed with the earth thrown out of this yard at the time of its formation : the Creeks or present inhabitants have a tradition that this was the work of the ancients, many ages prior to their arrival and possessing this country.

THIS old town was avacuated about twenty years ago by the general consent of the inhabitants, on account of its unhealthy situation, owing to the frequent inundations of the river over the low grounds; and moreover they grew timorous and dejected, apprehending themselves to be haunted and possessed with vengeful spirits, on account of human blood that had been undeservedly*

* About fifty or sixty years ago almost all the white traders then in the Nation were massacred in his town, whither they had repaired from the different towns, in hope of an assylum or refuge, in consequence of the alarm, having been timely apprised of the hostile intentions of the Indians by their temporary wives, they all met together in one house, under the avowed protection of the chiefs of the town, waiting the event; but whilst the chiefs were assembled in council, deliberating on ways and means to protect them, the Indians in multitudes surrounded the house and sat fire to it; they all, to the number of eighteen or twenty, perished with the house in the flames. The trader shewed me the ruins of the house where they were burnt.

spilt in this old town, having been repeatedly warned by apparitions and dreams to leave it.

AT the time of their leaving this old town, like the ruin or dispersion of the ancient Babel, the inhabitants separated from each other, forming several bands under the conduct or auspices of the chief of each family or tribe. The greatest number, however, chose to sit down and build the present new Apalachucla town, upon a high bank of the river above the inundations. The other bands pursued different routs, as their inclinations led them, settling villages lower down the river; some continued their migration towards the sea coast, seeking their kindred and countrymen amongst the Lower Creeks in East Florida, where they settled themselves. My intelligent friend, the trader of Apalachucla, having from a long residence amongst these Indians acquired an extensive knowledge of their customs and affairs, I enquired of him what were his sentiments with respect to their wandering, unsettled disposition; their so frequently breaking up their old towns and settling new ones, &c. His answers and opinions were, the necessity they were under of having fresh or new strong land for their plantations; and new, convenient and extensive range or hunting ground, which unavoidably forces them into contentions and wars with their confederates and neighbouring tribes; to avoid which they had rather move and seek a plentiful and peaceable retreat, even at a distance, than to contend with friends and relatives or embroil themselves in destructive wars with their neighbours, when either can be avoided with so little inconvenience. With regard to the Muscogulges, the first object in order to obtain these conveniencies was the destruction of the Yamases, who held the possession of Florida and were in close alliance with the Spaniards, their declared and most inveterate enemy, which they at length fully accomplished; and by this conquest they gained a vast and invaluable territory, comprehending a delightful region and a most plentiful country for their favourite game, bear and deer. But not yet satisfied, having already so far conquered the powerful Cherokees, as, in a manner, to force them in alliance, and compelled the warlike Chicasaws to sue for peace and alliance with them; they then grew arrogant and insatiable, and turned their covetous looks towards the potent and intrepid Chactaws, the only Indian enemy they had to fear, meaning to break them up and possess themselves of that extensive, fruitful and delightful country, and make it a part of their vast empire; but the Chactaws, a powerful, hardy, subtile and intrepid race, estimated at twenty thousand warriors, are likely to afford sufficient exercise for the proud and restless spirits of the Muscogulges, at least for some years to come, and they appear to be so equally matched with the Chactaws, it seems doubtful which of these powerful nations will rise victorious. The Creeks have sworn, it seems, that they never will make peace with this enemy as long as the rivers flow or the sun pursues his course through the skies.

THUS we see that war or the exercise of arms originates from the same motives, and operates in the spirits of the wild red men of America, as it formerly did with the renowned Greeks and Romans or modern civilized nations, and not from a ferocious, capricious desire of sheding human blood as carnivorous savages; neither does the eager avarice of plunder stimulate them to acts of madness and cruelty, that being a trifling object in their estimation, a duffield blanket, a polished rifle gun, or embroidered mantle; no, their martial prowess and objects of desire and ambition proceed from greater principles and more magnanimous intentions, even that of reuniting all nations and languages under one universal confederacy or commonwealth.

THE vegetable productions in the rich low ground, near the banks of this great river, of trees and shrubs, are as follow, Platanus occidentalis, Liriodendron tulipifera, Populus heterophylla, Laurus sassafras, Laurus Borbonia, Laurus benzoin, Betula lenta, Salix fluvialis, Magnolia grandiflora, Annona glabra, Ulmus campestris, Ulmus suberifera, Carpinus, Quercus, various species, Juglans, various species, Æsculus pavia, Æsculus sylvatica, s. Virginiana, Morus, Hopea tinctoria, Fagus sylvatica, of surprising magnitude and comeliness, &c. The land rises from the river with sublime magnificence, gradually retreating by flights or steps one behind and above the other, in beautiful theatrical order, each step or terrace holding up a level plain; and as we travel back from the river the steps are higher, and the corresponding levels are more and more expansive; the ascents produce grand high forests, and the plains present to view a delightful varied landscape, consisting of extensive grassy fields, detached groves of high forest trees, and clumps of lower trees, evergreen shrubs and herbage; green knolls, with serpentine, wavy, glittering brooks coursing through the green plains, and dark promontories, or obtuse projections of the side–long acclivities, alternately advancing or receding on the verge of the illumined native fields, to the utmost extent of sight; the summits of the acclivities afford, besides the forest trees already recited, Halesia, Ptelea, Circis, Cornus Florida and Amorpha. The upper mound or terrace holds up a dilated level plain of excellent land, for the distance of five or six miles in width, which is a high forest of the majestic trees already mentioned, as Quercus tinctoria, Juglans nigra, Morus, Ulmus, Telea, Gleditsia, Juglans hickory, &c. The land after this distance, though almost flat and level, becomes leaner; the vegetative mould or surface is shallower, on a stratum of tenacious humid clay, for the distance of fifteen or twenty miles, more or less, according to the distance of the next great river; presenting to our view a fine expanse of level grassy plains, detached forests and groves of Quercus alba, Q. lobata, Q. phillos, Q. heimspherica, Q. aquatica, with entire groves of the splendid Nyssa sylvatica and perfumed Liquid–amber styraciflua, vast Cane meadows, and lastly a chain of grassy savannas: immediately from this we began to ascend gradually, the most elevated, gravelly and stony ridge, consisting of parallel chains of broken swelling hills, the very highest chain, frequently presenting to view cliffs of the ferrugineous rocks and red clay already noticed. This last mentioned high ridge divides the waters of the great rivers from each other, whence arise the sources of their numerous lateral branches, gradually increasing as they wind about the hills, fertilizing the vales, and level plains, by their inundations, as they pour forth from the vast humid forests and shaded prolific hills and lastly, flow down, with an easy, meandering, steady course, into the rivers to which they are tributary.

OUR horses by this time having recruited themselves, by ranging at liberty and feeding in the rich young cane swamps, in the vicinity of Apalachucla, we resumed our journey for Mobile, having here repaired our equipage and replenished ourselves with fresh supplies of provisions. Our caravan was now reduced to its original number; the companies of traders who joined us at the Flat−rock, on our arrival at this town separated from us, betaking themselves to the several towns in the Nation, where they were respectively bound. I shall just mention a very curious non−descript shrub, which I observed growing in the shady forests, beneath the ascents, next bordering on the rich low lands of the river.

THIS stoloniferous shrub grows five or six feet in height; many stems usually ascend from a root or the same source; these several stems diverge from each other, or incline a little towards the earth, covered with a smooth whitish bark, divided oppositely, and the branches wreath and twist about, being ornamented with compound leaves; there being five lanciolate serrated leaves, associated upon one general long slender petiole, which stand oppositely, on the branches, which terminate with a spike, or pannicle of white flowers, which have an agreeable scent; from the characters of the flowers, this shrub appears to be a species of Æsculus or Pavia, but as I could find none of the fruit and but a few flowers, quite out of season and imperfect, I am not certain.

CHAP. VI.

JULY 13th we left the Apalachucla town, and three days journey brought us to Talasse, a town on the Tallapoose river, North−East great branch of the Alabama or Mobile river, having passed over a vast level plain country of expansive savannas, groves, Cane swamps and open Pine forests, watered by innumerable rivulets and books, tributary to Apalachucla and Mobile; we now alter our course, turning to the left hand, Southerly, and descending near the river banks, continually in sight of the Indian plantations and commons adjacent to their towns. Passed by Otasse, an ancient famous Muscogulge town. The next settlement we came to was Coolome, where we stayed two days, and having letters for Mr. Germany, the principal trader of Coolome, I meant to consult with him in matters relative to my affairs and future proceedings.

HERE are very extensive old fields, the abandoned plantations and commons of the old town, on the East side of the river, but the settlement is removed, and the new town now stands on the opposite shore, in a charming fruitful plain, under an elevated ridge of hills, the swelling beds or bases of which are covered with a pleasing verdure of grass, but the last ascent is steeper, and towards the summit discovers shelving rocky cliffs, which appear to be continually splitting and bursting to pieces, scattering their thin exfoliations over the tops of the grassy knolls beneath. The plain is narrow where the town is built: their houses are neat, commodious buildings, a wooden frame with plaistered walls, and roofed with Cypress bark or shingles; every habitation consists of four oblong square houses, of one story, of the same form and dimensions, and so situated as to form an exact square, encompassing an area or court yard of about a quarter of an acre of ground, leaving an entrance into it at each corner. Here is a beautiful new square or areopagus, in the centre of the new town; but the stores of the principal trader and two or three Indian habitations, stand near the banks of the opposite shore on the site of the old Coolome town. The Tallapoose river is here three hundred yards over, and about fifteen or twenty feet water, which is very clear, agreeable to the taste, esteemed salubrious, and runs with a steady, active current.

BEING now recruited and refited, having obtained a guide to set us in the great trading path for West Florida, early in the morning we sat off for Mobile: our progress for about eighteen miles was through a magnificent forest, just without or skirting on the Indian plantations, frequently having a view of their distant towns, over plains or old fields, and at evening came to camp under shelter of a grove of venerable spreading Oaks, on the verge of the great plains; their enormous limbs loaded with Tillandsia ulneadscites, waving in the winds; these Oaks were some shelter to us from the violence of an extraordinary shower of rain, which suddenly came down in such floods as to inundate the earth, and kept us standing on our feet the whole night, for the surface of the ground was under water almost till morning. Early next morning, our guide having performed his duty, took leave, returning home, and we continued on our journey, entering on the great plains; we had not proceeded far before our people roused a litter of young wolves, to which giving chase we soon caught one of them, it being entangled in high grass, one of our people caught it by the hind legs and another beat out its brains with the but of his gun,—— barbarous sport!—— This creature was about half the size of a small cur–dog, and quite black.

WE continued over these expansive illumined grassy plains, or native fields, above twenty miles in length, and in width eight or nine, lying parallel to the river, which was about ten miles distance; they are invested by high forests, extensive points or promontories, which project into the plains on each side, dividing them into many vast fields opening on either hand as we passed along, which presents a magnificent and pleasing sylvan landscape of primitive, uncultivated nature. Crossed several very considerable creeks, their serpentine courses being directed across the plain by gently swelling knolls, perceptible at a distance, but seem to vanish or disappear as we come upon them; the creeks were waters of the Alabama, the name of the East arm of the Mobile below the confluence of the Tallapoose. These rivulets were ornamented by groves of various trees and shrubs, which do not spread far from their banks; I observed amongst them the wild Crab (Pyrus coronaria) and Prunus Indica or wild Plumb, Cornus Florida, and on the grassy turf adjoining grew abundance of Strawberry vines; the surface of the plains or fields is clad with tall grass, intermixed with a variety of herbage; the most conspicuous, both for beauty and novelty, is a tall species of Silphium; the radical leaves are large, long and lightly sinuated, but those which garnish the stem are few and less sinuated; these leaves with the whole plant, except the flowers, appear of a whitish green colour, which is owing to a fine soft silky down or pubescence; the flower stem, which is eight or ten feet in length when standing erect, terminates upwards with a long heavy spike of large golden yellow radiated flowers; the stem is usually seen bowing on one side or other, occasioned by the weight of the flowers, and many of them are broke, just under the pannicle or spike, by their own weight, after storms and heavy rains, which often cracks or splits the stem, from whence exudes a gummy or resinous substance, which the sun and air harden into semi–pellucid drops or tears of a pale amber colour; this resin possesses a very agreeable fragrance and bitterish taste, somewhat like frankincense or turpentine, which is chewed by the Indians and traders, to cleanse their teeth and mouth, and sweeten their breath.

THE upper stratum or vegetative mould of these plains is perfectly black, soapy and rich, especially after rains, and renders the road very slippery; it lies on a deep bed of white, testaceous, limestone rock, which in some places resembles chalk, and in other places are strata or subterrene banks of various kinds of sea shells, as ostrea, &c. these dissolving near the surface of the earth, and mixing with the superficial mould, render it extremely

269

productive.

IMMEDIATELY after leaving the plains we enter the grand high forests. There were stately trees of the Robinea pseudacacia, Telea, Morus, Ulmus, Juglans exaltata, Juglans nigra, Pyrus coronaria, Cornus Florida, Cercis, &c. Our road now for several miles led us near the Alabama, within two or three miles of its bank; the surface of the land is considerably broken into hills and vales, some of them of considerable elevation, but covered with forests of stately trees, such as already mentioned, but they are of a much larger growth than those of the same kind which grow in the Southern or inhabited parts of Georgia and Carolia. We now leave the river at a good distance, the Alabama bearing away Southerly, and enter a vast open forest which continued above seventy miles, East and West, without any considerable variation, generally a level plain, except near the banks of creeks that course through; the soil on the surface is a dusky brownish mould or sandy loam, on a foundation of stiff clay, and the surface pebbles or gravel mixed with clay on the summits of the ridges; the forests consist chiefly of Oak, Hickory, Ash, Sour Gum (Nyssa sylvatica) Sweet Gum (Liquid–amber styraciflua) Beech, Mulberry, Scarlet maple, Black walnut, Dog–wood, Cornus Florida, Æsculus pavia, Prunus Indica, Ptelea and an abundance of Chesnut (Fag. castania) on the hills, with Pinus taeda and Pinus lutea. During our progress over this vast high forest, we crossed extensive open plains, the soil gravelly, producing a few trees and shrubs or undergrowth, which were entangled with Grape vines (Vitis campestris) of a peculiar species; the bunches (racemes) of fruit were very large, as were the grapes that composed them, though yet green and not fully grown, but when ripe are of various colours, and their juice sweet and rich. The Indians gather great quantities of them, which they prepare for keeping, by first sweating them on hurdles over a gentle fire, and afterwards dry them on their bunches in the sun and air, and store them up for provisions: these Grape vines do not climb into high trees, but creep along from one low shrub to another, extending their branches to a great distance horizontally round about, and it is very pleasing to behold the clusters pendant from the vines, almost touching the earth, indeed some of them lie upon the ground.

WE now enter a very remarkable grove of Dog wood trees (Cornus Florida) which continued nine or ten miles unalterable, except here and there a towering Magnolia grandiflora; the land on which they stand is an exact level; the surface a shallow, loose, black mould, on a stratum of stiff, yellowish clay; these trees were about twelve feet high, spreading horizontally; their limbs meeting and interlocking with each other, formed one vast, shady, cool grove, so dense and humid as to exclude the sun–beams and prevent the

270

intrusion of almost every other vegetable, affording us a most desirable shelter from the fervid fun–beams at noon–day. This admirable grove by way of eminence has acquired the name of the Dog woods.

DURING a progress of near seventy miles, through this high forest, there constantly presented to view on one hand or the other, spacious groves of this fine flowering tree, which must, in the spring season, when covered with blosoms present a most pleasing scene; when at the same time a variety of other sweet shrubs display their beauty, adorned in their gay apparel, as the Halesia, Stewartia, Æsculus pavia, Æsc. alba, Æsc. Florid. ramis divaricatis, thyrsis grandis, flosculis expansis incarnatis, Azalea, &c. intangled with garlands of Bignonea crucigera, Big. radicans, Big. sempervirens, Glycine frutescens, Lonicera sempervirens, &c. and at the same time the superb Magnolia grandiflora, standing in front of the dark groves, towering far above the common level.

THE evening cool, we encamped on the banks of a glittering rivulet amidst a spicy grove of the Illisium Floridanum.

EARLY next morning we arose, hunted up our horses and proceeded on, continuing about twenty miles, over a district which presented to view another landscape, expansive plains of Cane meadows, and detached groves, contrasted by swelling ridges, and vales supporting grand forests of the trees already noted, embellished with delightful creeks and brooks, their low grounds producing very tall canes, and their higher banks groves of the Illisium, Callicanthus, Stewartia, Halesia, Styrax and others, particulary Magnolia auriculata. In the evening we forded the river Schambe about fifty yards over, the stream active but shallow, which carries its waters into the bay of Pensacola. Came to camp, on the banks of a beautiful creek, by a charming grove of the Illisium Floridanum; from this we travelled over a level country above fifty miles, very gently but perceptably descending South–Eastward before us; this district exhibited a landscape very different from what had presented to view since we left the nation, and not much unlike the low countries of Carolina; it is in fact one vast flat grassy savanna and Cane meadows, intersected or variously scrolled over with narrow forests and groves, on the banks of creeks and rivulets, or hommocks and swamps at their sources; with long leaved Pines, scatteringly planted, amongst the grass, and on the high sandy knolls and swelling ridges, Quercus nigra, Quercus flammula, Quercus incana, with various other trees and shrubs as already noted, inhabiting such situations; the rivulets however exhibited a different appearance, they are shallower, course more swift over gravelly beds, and their banks adorned with Illisium groves, Magnolias, Azaleas, Halesia, Andromedas, &c. The highest hills near large creeks afford high forests with abundance of Chesnut trees.

WE now approach the bay of Mobile, gently ascending a hilly district, being the highest forest adjoining the extensive rich low lands of the river; these heights are somewhat encumbered with pebbles, fragments and cliffs of rusty ferrugineous rocks, the stones were ponderous and indicated very rich iron ore; here was a small district of good land, on the acclivities and bases of these ridges, and a level forest below, watered by a fine creek, running into the Mobile. From hence we proceeded, again descending, and travelled about nine miles generally over a level country consisting of savannas, Cane swamps, and gentle rising knolls, producing Pinus taeda, Nyssa sylvatica, Quercus rubra, Fagus castania, Fraxinus, with other trees. Arrived at Taensa, a pretty high bluff, on the Eastern channel of the great Mobile river, about thirty miles above fort Conde, or city of Mobile, at the head of the bay.

NEXT day early in the morning I embarked in a boat, proceeded for Mobile; along the banks of islands (near twenty miles) which lay in the middle of the river, between the Eastern and Western shores of the main: the banks of these low flat rich islands are well cultivated, having on them extensive farms and some good habitations, chiefly the property of French gentlemen, who reside in the city, as being more pleasant and healthy. Leaving these islands, we continued ten or twelve miles between the Eastern main and a chain of low grassy islands, too low and wet for cultivation; then crossed over the head of the bay and arrived in town in the evening.

THE city of Mobile is situated on the easy ascent of a rising bank, extending near half a mile back on the level plain above; it has been near a mile in length, though now chiefly in ruins, many houses vacant and mouldering to earth; yet there are a few good buildings inhabited by French gentlemen, English, Scotch and Irish, and emigrants from the Northern British colonies. Messrs. Swanson and M'Gillivary who have the management of the Indian trade, carried on to the Chicasaws, Chactaws, Upper and Lower Creeks, &c. have made here very extraordinary improvements in buildings.

THE fort Conde, which stands very near the bay, towards the lower end of the town is a large regular fortress of brick.

Travels Through North and South Carolina

THE principal French buildings are constructed of brick, and are of one story, but on an extensive scale, four square, encompassing on three sides a large area or court yard, the principal apartment is on the side fronting the street; they seem in some degree to have copied after the Creek habitation in the general plan; those of the poorer class are constructed of a strong frame of Cypress, filled in with brick, plaistered and white–washed inside and out.

JULY 31st, 1778, the air being very hot and sultry, thermometer up at 87. excessive thunder, and repeated heavy showers of rain, from morning until evening.

NOT having an immediate opportunity from hence to Manchac, a British settlement on the Mississipi, I endeavoured to procure a light canoe, with which I designed to pursue my travels along shore to the settlements about Pearl river.

AUGUST 5th, sat off from Mobile up the river in a trading boat, and was landed at Taensa bluff, the seat of Major Farmer, to make good my engagements, in consequence of an invitation from that worthy gentleman, to spend some days in his family; here I obtained the use of a light canoe, to continue my voyage up the river. The settlement of Taensa is on the site of an ancient town of a tribe of Indians of that name, which is apparent from many artificial mounds of earth and other ruins. Besides Mr. Farmer's dwellings, there are many others inhabited by French families; who are chiefly his tenants. It is a most delightful situation, commanding a spacious prospect up and down the river, and the low lands of his extensive plantations on the opposite shore. In my excursions about this place, I observed many curious vegetable productions, particularly a species of Myrica (Myrica inodora) this very beautiful evergreen shrub, which the French inhabitants call the Wax tree, grows in wet sandy ground about the edges of swamps, it rises erect nine or ten feet, dividing itself into a multitude of nearly erect branches, which are garnished with many shining deep green entire leaves of a lanciolate figure; the branches produce abundance of large round berries, nearly the size of bird cherries, which are covered with a scale or coat of white wax; no part of this plant possesses any degree of fragrance. It is in high estimation with the inhabitants for the production of wax for candles, for which purpose it answers equally well with bees–wax, or preferable, as it is harder and more lasting in burning.

EARLY on a fine morning I sat sail up the river, took the East channel, and passed along by well cultivated plantations, on the fertile islands, in the river on my left hand; these

273

islands exhibit every shew of fertility, the native productions exceed any thing I had ever seen, particularly the Reeds or Canes (Arundo gigantea) grow to a great height and thickness.

EARLY one morning, passing along by some old uncultivated fields, a few miles above Taensa, I was struck with surprise at the appearance of a blooming plant, gilded with the richest golden yellow, stepping on shore, I discovered it to be a new species of the Oenothera (Oenothera grandiflora) Caule erecto, ramoso, piloso, 7, 8 pedali, foliis semi–amplexi–caulibus, lanceolatis, serrato–dentatis, floribus magnis, fulgidis, sessilibus, capsulis cylindricis, 4 angulis, perhaps the most pompous and brilliant herbaceous plant yet known to exist. It is an annual or biennial, rising erect seven or eight feet, branching on all sides from near the earth upwards, the lower branches extensive, and the succeeding gradually shorter to the top of the plant, forming a pyramid in figure; the leaves are of a broad lanceolate shape, dentated or deeply serrated, terminating with a slender point, and of a deep full green colour; the large expanded flowers, that so ornament this plant, are of a splendid perfect yellow colour; but when they contract again, before they drop off, the underside of the petals next the calyx becomes of a reddish flesh colour, inclining to vermilion, the flowers begin to open in the evening, are fully expanded during the night, and are in their beauty next morning, but close and wither before noon. There is a daily profuse succession for many weeks, and one single plant at the same instant presents to view many hundred flowers. I have measured these flowers above five inches in diameter, they have an agreeable scent.

AFTER leaving these splendid fields of the golden Oenothera, I passed by old deserted plantations and high forests, and now having advanced above ten miles, landed at a bluff, where mooring my bark in a safe harbour, I ascended the bank of the river, and penetrating the groves, came presently to old fields, where I observed ruins of ancient habitations, there being abundance of Peach and Fig trees, loaded with fruit, which affording a very acceptable desert after the heats and toil of the day, and evening drawing on apace, I concluded to take up my quarters here for the night. The Fig trees were large as well as their fruit, which was when ripe, of the shape of pears and as large, and of a dark bluish purple colour.

NEXT morning I arose early, continuing my voyage, passed by, on each hand, high forests and rich swamps, and frequently ruins of ancient French plantations; the Canes, and Cypress trees of an astonishing magnitude, as were the trees of other tribes, indicating an excellent soil. Came too at noon, and advancing forward from the river, and penetrating the awful shades, passed between the stately columns of the Magnolia grandiflora, and came to the ascents supporting the high forests and expansive plains above—What a sylvan scene is here! the pompous Magnolia, reigns sovereign of the forests; how sweet the aromatic Illisium groves? how gaily flutters the radiated wings of the Magnolia auriculata? each branch supporting an expanded umbrella, superbly crested with a silver plume, fragrant blossom, or crimson studded strobile and fruits! I recline on the verdant bank, and view the beauties of the groves. Æsculus pavia, Prunus nemoralis, floribus racemosis, foliis sempervirentibus, nitidis. Æsculus alba, Hydrangia quercifolia, Cassine, Magnolia pyramidata, foliis ovatis, oblongis, acuminatis, basi auriculatis, strobilo oblongo ovato, Myrica, Rhamnus frangula, Halefea, Bignonia, Azalea, Lonicera, Sideroxilon, with many more.

RETURNED to the river, re–imbarked, and at evening came too, in sight of the confluence or junction of the two large arms of the great Mobile river i. e. the Tombigbe or Chicasaw with the Alabama or Coosau. About one hundred and fifty miles above this conflux at Ft. Thoulouse, the Alabama receives into it from the East the great Talapoose river, when the former takes the name of Coosau, which it bears to its source, which is in the So. West promontories of the Cherokee or Apalachean Mountains in the Chickasaw territories.

OBSERVED very large alligators, basking on the shores, as well as swimming in the river and lagoons.

NEXT morning entered the Tombigbe, and ascended that fine river; just within its capes, on the left hand is a large lagoon, or capacious bay of still water, containing many acres in surface, which at a distant view presents a very singular and diverting scene, a delusive green wavy plain of the Nymphaea Nilumbo, the surface of the water is overspread with its round floating leaves, whilst these are shadowed by a forest of umbragious leaves with gay flowers, waving to and fro on flexible stems, three or four feet high: these fine flowers are double as a rose, and when expanded are seven or eight inches in diameter, of a lively lemon yellow colour. The seed vessel when ripe, is a large truncated, dry, porous capsule, its plane or disk regularly perforated, each cell containing an oval osseous gland or nut, of the size of a filbert; when these are fully grown, before they become quite hard, they are sweet and pleasant eating, and taste like chesnuts: I fed freely on them without any injury, but found them laxative. I have observed this aquatic plant, in my travels

275

along the Eastern shores of this continent, in the large rivers and lakes, from New–Jersey to this place, particularly in a large pond or lake near Cape Fear river in North Carolina; this pond is about two miles over and twelve feet water, notwithstanding which its surface is almost covered with the leaves of this plant; they also abound in Wakamaw lake near the same river, and in Savanna river at Augusta, and all over East Florida.

PROCEEDING up the river, came to at a very high steep bluff of red and particoloured tenacious clay, under a deep stratum of loose sandy mould; after ascending this steep bank of the river, I found myself in an old field, and penetrating the forests surrounding, observed them to be young growth, covering very extensive old plantations, which was evident from the ridges and hillocks which once raised their Corn (Zea) Batatas, &c. I suppose this to be the site of an ancient fortified post of the French, as there appears vestiges of a rampart and other traces of a fortress; perhaps fort Louis de la Mobile, but in all probability it will not remain long visible, the stream of the river making daily encroachments on it, by carrying away the land on which it stood.

OBSERVED here amongst other vegetable productions, a new species, or at least a variety of Halesia diptera; these trees are of the size and figure of ordinary Mulberry trees, their stems short and tops regular and spreading, and the leaves large and broad, in size and figure resembling those of our common wild Mulberry.

OPPOSITE this bluff, on the other side of the river, is a district of swamp or low land, the richest I ever saw, or perhaps any where to be seen; as for the trees I shall forbear to describe them, because it would appear incredible, let it suffice to mention, that the Cypress, Ash, Platanus, Populus, Liquid–amber, and others, are by far the tallest, straitest and every way the most enormous that I have seen or heard of. And as a proof of the extraordinary fertility of the soil, the reeds or canes (Arundo gigantea) grow here thirty or forty feet high, and as thick as a man's arm, or three or four inches in diameter; I suppose one joint of some of them would contain above a quart of water, and these reeds serve very well for setting poles, or masts for barks and canoes. Continued yet ascending this fine river, passing by the most delightful and fertile situations, observed frequently, on bluffs of high land, deserted plantations (the houses always burnt down to the ground) and ancient Indian villages. But observing little variation in the natural vegetable productions, the current of the river pressing down with increased force and velocity, I turned about descending the river, and next evening came to at a large well cultivated plantation, where lodged all night, and the evening following returned to Taensa.

Travels Through North and South Carolina

NEXT day I felt symptoms of a fever, which in a few days laid me up and became dangerous. But a dose of Tart. Emet. broke its violence, and care and good attendance after a few days, in some degree restored my health, at least, so far as to enable me to rove about the neighbouring forests; and here being informed of a certain plant of extraordinary medical virtues, and in high estimation with the inhabitants, which grew in the hilly land about thirty miles higher up the river, I resolved to set out in search of it, the Major being so polite and obliging as to furnish me with horses to ride, and a Negro to pilot and take care of me.

SAT off in the morning, and in the course of the days journey crossed several creeks and brooks, one of which swam our horses. On passing by a swamp at the head of a bay or lagoon of the river, I observed a species of Cypress; it differs a little from the white Cedar of New–Jersey and Pennsylvania (Cupressus thyoides) the trunk is short and the limbs spreading horizontally, the branches fuller of leaves and the cones larger and of a crimson or reddish purple colour when ripe.

AFTER leaving the low grounds and ascending the hills, discovered the plant I went in search of, which I had before frequently observed in my descent from the Creek nation down towards Taensa. This plant appears to be a species of Collinsonia; it is diuretic and carminative, and esteemed a powerful febrifuge, an infusion of its tops is ordinarily drank at breakfast, and is of an exceeding pleasant taste and flavor; when in flower; which is the time the inhabitants gather it for preservation and use; it possesses a lively aromatic scent, partaking of lemon and aniseed. Lodged this night at a plantation near the river, and met with civility and good entertainment. The man and his three sons are famous hunters. I was assured from good authority that the old gentleman, for his own part, kills three hundred deer annually, besides bears, tygers and wolves.

NEXT morning early, sat off again, on my return, and taking a different path back, for the sake of variety, though somewhat farther about and at a greater distance from the banks of the river, observed abundance of the tall blue Sage; it grows six or seven feet high; many stems arise from one root or source; these stems are thick, woody and quadrangular, the angles obtuse; the narrow lanciolate and serrated leaves are placed opposite, and are sessile, lightly embracing the branches, which terminate with spikes of large flowers of a celestial blue colour.

Travels Through North and South Carolina

THESE stony, gravelly heights produce a variety of herbacious plants, but one in particular I shall mention on account of its singular beauty; I believe it is a species Gerardea (Gerardea sammea) it grows erect, a single stem from a root, three or four feet in height, branching very regularly from about one half its length upwards, forming a cone or pyramid, profusely garnished with large tubular labiated scarlet or flame coloured flowers, which give the plant a very splendid appearance, even at a great distance. Returned home in the evening fully satisfied with the day's excursion, from the discovery of many curious and beautiful vegetables.

HAVING advice from Mobile of an opportunity to Manchac, although my health was not established, feverish symptoms continuing to lurk about me, I resolved, notwithstanding, immediately to embrace this offer, and embarked again, descending the river to the city in company with Dr. Grant, a physician of the garrison, and late in the evening arrived in town, having suffered a smart fit of the fever by the way.

IN the course of conversation with the doctor, I remarked that during my travels since leaving the Creek nation, and when there, I had not seen any honey bees; he replied that there were few or none West of the isthmus of Florida, and but one hive in Mobile, which was lately brought there from Europe; the English supposing that there were none in the country, not finding any when they took possession of it after the Spanish and French: I had been assured by the traders that there were none in West Florida, which to me seemed extraordinary and almost incredible, since they are so numerous all along the Eastern continent from Nova–Scotia to East Florida, even in the wild forests, as to be thought, by the generality of the inhabitants, aborigines of this continent.

THE boat in which I had taken a passage to Pearl river, not being in readiness to depart for several days to come, I sought opportunities to fill up this time to the best advantage possible, and hearing of a boat going to the river Perdedo, for the purpose of securing the remains of a wreck, I apprehended this a favourable time to go and search that coast, the captain civilly offering me a passage and birth with him in a handsome light sailing–boat. Sat sail early on a fine morning and having a brisk leading breeze, came to in the evening just within Mobile point, collected a quantity of drift wood to keep up a light and smoke away the musquetoes, and rested well on the clean sandy beach until the cool morning awoke us. We hoisted sail again and soon doubled the point or East promontory of the cape of the bay, stretching out many miles and pointing towards Dauphin island, between which and this cape is the ship channel.

Travels Through North and South Carolina

COASTING along the sea–shore Eastward, we soon came up to the wreck, which being already stripped of her sails, &c. our captain kept on for Pensacola, where we arrived late in the evening.

MY arrival at this capital, at present the seat of government, was merely accidental and undesigned; and having left at Mobile all my papers and testimonials, I designed to conceal my avocations, but my name being made known to Dr. Lorimer, one of the honourable council, he sent me a very polite invitation, and requested that he might acquaint governor Chester of my arrival, who he knew would expect that I should wait on him, and would be pleased to see me; I begged to be excused, at this time, as the boat would sail back for Mobile in a few hours, in which I was under the necessity of returning or loose my passage to the Missisipi; but during this expostulation I received a letter from Mr. Livingston the secretary, whom I waited upon, and was received very respectfully and treated with the utmost politeness and affability; soon after the governor's chariot passed by, his excellency returning from a morning visit to his farm a few miles from Pensacola. Mr. Livingston went with me and introduced me to the governor, who commended my pursuits, and invited me to continue in West Florida in researches after subjects of natural history, &c. nobly offering to bear my expences, and a residence in his own family as long as I chose to continue in the colony; very judiciously observing that a complete investigation of its natural history could not be accomplished in a short space of time, since it would require the revolution of the seasons to discover and view vegetable nature in all her various perfections.

THE captain of our fortunate bark by this time being ready to sail, I took leave of his excellency the governor, and bid adieu to my friends Dr. Lorimer, Mr. Livingston and others: sat sail about noon on our return, and came to again within the capes of Mobile river.

SINCE I have hitherto given a superficial account of the towns, ports, improvements and other remarkable productions of nature, and human arts and industry, during the course of my perigrination, I shall not pass by Pensacola and its environs. This city is delightfully situated (and commands some natural advantages, superior to any other port in this province, in point of naval commerce, and such as human art and strength can never supply) upon gentle rising ascents environing a spacious harbour, safe and capacious enough to shelter all the navies of Europe, and excellent ground for anchorage; the West end of St. Rose island stretches across the great bay St. Maria Galves, and its

South–West projecting point forms the harbour of Pensacola, which with the road or entrance is defended by a block–house built on the extremity of that point, which at the same time serves the purpose of a fortress and look–out tower. There are several rivers which run into this great bay from the continent, but none of them navigable, for large craft, to any considerable distance into the country, the Shambe is the largest, which admits shallops some miles up, and Perreaugues upwards of fifty miles. There are some spots of good high land, and rich swamps, favourable for the production of rice on the banks of this river, which have given rise to some plantations producing Indigo, Rice, Corn, Batatas, &c. these rivers dividing and spreading abroad their numerous branches, over the expansive flat low country (between the two great rivers Apalachucla and Mobile) which consists of savannas and Cane meadows, fills them with brooks and water courses, and render them exuberant pasture for cattle.

THERE are several hundred habitations in Pensacola: the governor's palace is a large stone building ornamented with a tower, built by the Spaniards. The town is defended by a large stockado fortress, the plan a tetragon with salient angles at each corner, where is a block–house or round tower, one story higher than the curtains, where are light cannon mounted, it is constructed of wood. Within this fortress is the council chamber, here the records are kept, houses for the officers and barracks for the accommodation of the garrison, arsenal, magazine, &c. The secretary resides in a spacious, neat building: there are several merchants and gentlemen of other professions, who have respectable and convenient buildings in the town.

THERE were growing on the sand hills, environing Pensacola, several curious non–described plants; particularly one of the verticilate order, about eighteen inches in height, the flowers which formed loose spikes, were large and of a fine scarlet colour, but not having time, to examine the fructification, or collect good specimens, am ignorant of what order, or genus, it belongs to. And in the level wet savannas grew plentifully a new and very elegant species of Saracinia (Saracinia lacunosa) the leaves of this plant, which are twelve or fourteen inches in length, stand nearly erect, are round, tubular and ventricose; but not ridged with longitudinal angles or prominent nerves, as the leaves of the Saracinia flava are; the aperture at top may be shut up by a cap or lid, of a helmet form, which is an appendage of the leaf, turning over the orifice in that singular manner, the ventricose, or inflated part of the leaf, which is of a pale, but vivid green colour, is beautifully ornamented with rose coloured studs or blisters, and the inner surface curiously inscribed, or variegated with crimson veins or fibres. It was past the time for flowering, but the plant in any situation is a very great curiosity.

NEXT morning early we arose from our hard sandy sea–beaten couch, being disturbed the whole night by the troublesome musquitoes; sat sail, and before night returned safe to the city of Mobile.

CHAP. VII.

THE next day after my return to Mobile, I found myself very ill, and not a little alarmed by an excessive pain in my head, attended with a high fever, this disorder soon settled in my eyes, nature pursuing that way to expel the malady, causing a most painful defluxion of pellucid, corrosive water; notwithstanding I next day sat off on board a large trading boat, the property of a French gentleman, and commanded by him (he being general interpreter for the Chactaw nation) on his return to his plantations, on the banks of Pearl river; our bark was large, well equiped for sailing, and manned with three stout Negroes, to row in case of necessity. We embarked in the evening, and came to about six miles below the town, at a pleasant farm, the master of which (who was a Frenchman) entertained us in a very polite and friendly manner. The wind favourable, next morning early we sat sail again, and having made extraordinary way, about noon came up abreast of a high steep bluff, or perpendicular cliffs of high land, touching on the bay of the West coast, where we went on shore, to give liberty to the slaves to rest and refresh themselves. In the mean time I accompanied the captain on an excursion into the spacious level forests, which spread abroad from the shore to a great distance back, observed vestiges of an ancient fortress and settlement, and there yet remain a few pieces of iron cannon; but what principally attracted my notice, was three vast iron pots or kettles, each of many hundred gallons contents, upon enquiry, my associate informed me they were for the purpose of boiling tar to pitch, there being vast forests of Pine trees in the vicinity of this place. In Carolina the inhabitants pursue a different method; when they design to make pitch, they dig large holes in the ground, near the tar kiln, which they line with a thick coat of good clay, into which they conduct a sufficient quantity of tar, and set it on fire, suffering it to flame and evaporate a length of time sufficient to convert it into pitch, and when cool, lade it into barrels, and so on until they have consumed all the tar, or made a sufficient quantity of pitch for their purpose.

AFTER re–imbarking, and leaving this bluff a few miles, we put into shore again, and came to a farm house, a little distance from the water, where we supplied ourselves with Corn meal, Batatas, bacon, &c. The French gentleman active and cheerful, her eyes seemed as brisk and sparkling as youth, but of a diminutive size, not half the stature and weight of her son; it was now above fifty years since she came into America from old France.

I EMBARKED again, proceeding down the bay, and in the evening doubled the west point or cape of the bay, being a promontory of the main, between which and Dauphin island, we entered the channel Oleron; from this time, until we arrived at this gentleman's habitation on Pearl river, I was incapable of making any observations, for my eyes could not bear the light, as the least ray admitted seemed as the piercing of a sword, and by the time I had arrived at Pearl river, the excruciating pain had rendered me almost frantic and stupified for want of sleep, of which I was totally deprived, and the corroding water, every few minutes, streaming from my eyes, had stripped the skin off my face, in the same manner as scalding water would have done. I continued three days with this friendly Frenchman, who tried every remedy, that he or his family could recollect, to administer relief, but to no purpose, my situation was now become dangerous, and I expected to sink under the malady, as I believe my friends here did. At last the man informed me, on Pearl island, about twelve miles distance, resided an English gentleman, who had a variety of medicines, and if I chose to go to him he would take me there; I accordingly bid adieu to this hospitable family, and sat off with him in a convenient boat, before night arrived at Mr. Rumsey's, who received me kindly, and treated me with the utmost humanity, during a stay of four or five weeks: the night however after my arrival here I sincerely thought would be my last, and my torments were so extreme as to desire it; having survived this tedious night, I in some degree recovered my senses and asked Mr. Rumsey if he had any Cantharides, who soon prepared a blister plaister for me, which I directed to be placed betwixt my shoulders, this produced the desired relief and more than answered my expectation, for it had not been there a quarter of an hour before I fell asleep, and remained so a whole day, when I awoke intirely relieved from pain, my senses in perfect harmony and mind composed; I do not know how to express myself on this occasion; all was peace and tranquility; although I had my sight perfectly, yet my body seemed but as a light shadow, and my existence as a pleasing delirium, for I sometimes doubted of its reality. I however from that moment began to mend, until my health was perfectly restored, but it was several weeks before I could expose my eyes to open day light, and at last I found my left eye considerably injured, which suffered the greatest pain and weight of the disease.

Travels Through North and South Carolina

As soon as I acquired strength to walk about, and bear the least impression of open day light on my eyes, I made frequent, indeed I may say daily excursions in and about this island, strolling through its awful shades, venerable groves and sublime forests, consisting of the Live Oaks and Magnolia grandiflora, Laurus Borbonia, Olea Americana, Fagus sylvatica, Laur. Sassafras, Quercus hemispherica, Telea, Liquid–amber styraciflua, Morus, Gleditsia, Callicarpa, Halesia, &c.

THE island is six or seven miles in length, and four or five in width, including the salt marshes and plains, which invest it on every side, I believe we may only except a narrow strand at the South end of it, washed by Lake Borgone at the Regullets, which is a promontory composed of banks, of seashells and sand, cast up by the force of winds, and the surf of the lake; these shells are chiefly a small species of white clam shells, called les coquelles. Here are a few shrubs growing on these shelly heights, viz. Rhamnus frangula, Sideroxilon, Myrica, Zanthoxilon clava Herculis, Juniperus Americana, Lysium salsum; together with several new genera and species of the herbacious and suffruticose tribes, Croton, Stillingia, &c. but particularly a species of Mimosa (Mimosa virgatia) which in respect of the elegancy of its pinnated leaves, cannot be exceeded by any of that celebrated family. It is a perennial plant, sending up many nearly erect stems, from the root or source, these divide themselves into many ascendant slender rods like branches, which are ornamented with double pinnated leaves, of a most delicate formation. The compound flowers, are of a pale, greenish yellow, collected together in a small oblong head, upon a long slender peduncle, the legumes are large, lunated and slat, placed in a spiral or contorted manner, each containing several hard compressed seed, or little beans.

THE interior and by far the greater part of the island consists of high land; the soil to appearance a heap of sea sand in some places, with an admixture of sea shells, this soil, notwithstanding its sandy and steril appearance, when divested of its natural vegetative attire, has, from what cause I know not, a continual resource of fertility within itself, the surface of the earth, after being cleared of its original vegetable productions, exposed a few seasons to the sun, winds and triturations of agriculture, appears scarcely any thing but heaps of white sand, yet it produces Corn (Zea) Indigo, Batatas, Beans Peas, Cotton, Tobacco, and almost every sort of esculent vegetable, in a degree of luxuriancy very surprising and unexpected, year after year, incessantly, without any addition of artificial manure or compost; there is indeed a foundation of strong adhesive clay, consisting of stratas of various colours, which I discovered by examining a well, lately dug in Mr. Rumsey's yard; but its lying at a great depth under the surface, the roots of small shrubs

283

and herbage, cannot reach near to it, or receive any benefit, unless we may suppose, that ascending fumes or exhalations, from this bed of clay, may have a vivific nutritive quality, and be received by the fibres of the roots, or being condensed in the atmosphere by nocturnal chills, fall with dews upon the leaves and twigs of these plants, and there absorbed, become nutritive or exhilerating to them.

BESIDES the native forest trees and shrubs already noted, manured fruit trees arrive in this island to the utmost degree of perfection, as Pears, Peaches, Figs, Grape Vines, Plumbs &c. of the last mentioned genus, there is a native species grows in this island, which produce their large oblong crimson fruit in prodigious abundance; the fruit though of a most inticing appearance, are rather too tart, yet are agreeable eating, at sultry noon, in this burning climate, they afford a most delicious and reviving marmalade, when preserved in sugar, and make excellent tarts: the tree grows about twelve feet high, the top spreading, the branches spiny and the leaves broad, nervous, serrated, and terminate with a subulated point.

My eyes having acquired sufficient strength to endure the open day–light, I sat off from Pearl island, for Manchac on the Mississipi, in a handsome large boat with three Negroes to navigate her; leaving the friendly Mr. Rumsey's seat on Pearl Island, we descend a creek from the landing near his house; this creek led us about a mile, winding through salt sedgy marshes, into Lake Pontchartrain, along whose North shores, we coasted about twenty miles, having low, reedy marshes, on our starboard: these marshes were very extensive between us and the far distant high forests on the main, when at evening the shore becomes bolder, with sandy elevations, affording a few dwarf Oaks, Zanthoxilon, Myrica and Rham. frangula. We came to in a little bay, kindled a fire, and after supper betook ourselves to repose; our situation open, airy and cool, on clean sand banks; we rested quietly, though sometimes roused by alarms from the crocodile, which are here in great numbers, and of an enormous bulk and strength.

NEXT day early we got under way, pursuing our former course, nearly West ward, keeping the North shore several leagues; immediately back of this high sandy strand; (which is cast up by the beating surf and winds, setting from sea ward, across the widest part of the lake) the ground suddenly falls, and becomes extensive flat Cypress swamps, the sources of creeks and rivers, which run into the lake, or Pearl River, or at other places, the high forests of the main now gradually approaching the lake, advance up to the very shore, where we find houses, plantations and new settlements: we came to at one of them charmingly situated, sat sail again, and came up to the mouth of the beautiful Taensapaoa, which takes that name from a nation of Indians, who formerly possessed the territories lying on its banks, which are fertile and delightful regions. This river is narrow at its entrance, but deep, and said to be navigable for large barks and perreauguas, upwards of fifty miles, just within its capes, on the leeward shore, are heights, or a group of low hills (composed of the small clam shells, called les coquelles) which gradually depress as we retreat back from the river, and the surface of the land is more level; these shells dissolving and mixing with the surface, render the vegetative mould black, rich, and productive. Here are a few habitations, and some fields cleared and cultivated; but the inhabitants neglect agriculture; and generally employ themselves in hunting, and fishing: we however furnished ourselves here with a sufficiency of excellent Batatas. I observed no new vegetable productions, except a species of Cleome, (Cleome lupinifolia) this plant possesses a very strong scent, somewhat like Gum Assasetida, notwithstanding which the inhabitants give it a place in soups and and sauces.

FROM Taensapaoa, we still coasted Westward, three or four miles, to the straits that communicate to the lake Mauripas; entering which and continuing six or eight miles, having low swampy land on each side, the channel divides, forming an island in the middle of the pass, we took the right hand channel, which continuing three or four miles, when the channels reunite in full view of the charming lake. We came to at an elevated point, or promontory on the starboard main shore, it being the North cape, from whence I enjoyed a very pleasing and complete view of the beautiful lake Mauripas, entering which next morning with a steady favourable gale, soon wasted us nine or ten miles over to the mouth of the river Amete; ascended between its low banks; the land on each side a level swamp, about two feet above the surface of the water, supporting a thick forest of trees, consisting chiefly of Fraxinus, Nyssa aquatica, Nyssa multiflora, Cupressus disticha, Quercus phillos, Acer rubrum, Ac. negundo, Acer glaucum, Sambuces, Laurus Borbonia, Carpinus, Ulmus and others. The soil or earth humid, black and rich. There is scarcely a perceptible current; the water dark, deep, turgid and stagnate, being from shore to shore covered with a scum or pelliele of a green and purpleish cast, and is perpetually throwing up from the muddy bottom to its surface minute air bladders or bubbles; in short, these dark loathsome waters, from every appearance seem to be a strong extract, or tincture of the leaves of the trees, herbs and reeds, arising from the shores, and which almost overspread them, and float on the surface, insomuch that a great part of these stagnate rivers, during the summer and autumnal seasons, are constrained to pass under a load of grass and weeds; which are continually vegetating and spreading over the surface from the banks, until the rising floods of winter and spring, rushing down from the main, sweep them way, and purify the waters. Late in the evening we discovered a narrow ridge of land close to the river bank, high and dry enough to suffer us to kindle up a fire, and space sufficient to spread our bedding on. But here, fire and smoke were insufficient to expel the hosts of musquitoes that invested our camp, and kept us awake during the long and tedious night, so that the alligators had no chance of taking us napping. We were glad to rise early in the morning, proceeding up the Amete. The land now gradually rises, the banks become higher, the soil drier and firmer four or five feet above the surface of the river; the trees are of an incredible magnitude, particulary Platanus occidentalis, Fraxinus, Ulmus, Quercus hemispherica, &c. The Cana Indica grows here in surprising luxuriance, presenting a glorious shew; the stem rises six, seven and nine feet high, terminating upwards with spikes of scarlet flowers.

Now having advanced near thirty miles up the Amete, we arrived at a very large plantation, the property of a Scotch gentleman, who received me with civility, intreating me to reside with him, but being impatient to get to the river, and pleading the necessity of prosecuting my travels with alacrity, on account of the season being so far advanced, I was permited to proceed, and sat off next morning; still ascending the Amete about twenty miles farther, and arrived at the forks; where the Iberville comes in on the left hand, ascending which a little way, we soon came to the landing, where are ware–houses for disposing merchandize; this being the extremity of navigation up this canal, and here small vessels load and unload. From this place to Manchac, on the banks of the Mississipi, just above the mouth of the canal, is nine miles by land; the road strait, spacious, and perfectly level, under the shadow of a grand forest; the trees of the first order in magnitude and beauty, as Magnolia grandiflora, Liriodendron tulipifera, Platanus, Juglans nigra, Fraxinus excelsior, Morus rubra, Laurus sasafras, Laurus Borbonia, Telea, Liquid–amber styraciflua, &c.

AT evening arrived at Manchac, when I directed my steps to the banks of the Mississipi, where I stood for a time as it were fascinated by the magnificence of the great sire*

* Which is the meaning of the word Mississipi.

of rivers.

Travels Through North and South Carolina

THE depth of the river here, even in this season, at its lowest ebb is astonishing, not less than forty fathoms, and the width about a mile or some what less; but it is not expansion of surface alone that strike us with ideas of magnificence, the altitude, and theatrical ascents of its pensile banks, the steady course of the mighty flood, the trees, high forests, even every particular object, as well as societies, bear the stamp of superiority and excellence; all unite or combine in exhibiting a prospect of the grand sublime. The banks of the river at Manchac, though frequently overflowed by the vernal inundations, are fifty feet perpendicular height above the surface of the water (by which the channel at those times must be about two hundred and ninety feet deep) and these precipices being an accumulation of the sediment of muddy waters, annually brought down with the floods, of a light loamy consistance, are continually cracking and parting, present to view deep yawning chasms, in time split off, as the active perpetual current undermines, and the mighty masses of earth tumbe headlong into the river, whose impetuous current sweeps away and lodges them elsewhere. There is yet visible some remains of a high artificial bank, in front of the buildings of the town, formerly cast up by the French, to resist the inundations, but found to be ineffectual, and now in part tumbled down the precipice, as the river daily incroaches on the bluff; some of the habitations are in danger, and most be very soon removed or swallowed up in the deep gulph of waters. A few of the buildings that have been established by the English, since taking possession of the colony, are large and commodious, particularly the warehouses of Messrs. Swanson & Co. Indian traders and merchants.

THE Spaniards have a small fortress and garrison on the point of land below the Iberville, close by the banks of the river, which has a communication with Manchac, by a slender narrow wooden bridge across the channel of Iberville, supported on wooden pillars, and not a bow shot from the habitations of Manchac. The Iberville in the summer season is dry, and its bed twelve or fifteen feet above the surface of the Mississipi; but in the winter and spring has a great depth of water, and a very rapid stream which flows into the Amete, thence down through the lakes into the bay of Pearls to the ocean.

HAVING recommendations to the inhabitants of Batonrouge, now called New Richmond, more than forty miles higher up the river; and one of these gentlemen being present at Manchac, gave me a friendly and polite invitation to accompany him on his return home. A pleasant morning, we sat off after breakfast, well accommodated in a handsome convenient boat, rowed by three blacks. Two miles above Manchac we put into shore at Alabama, this Indian village is delightfully situated on several swelling

287

green hills, gradually ascending from the verge of the river: they are a remnant of the ancient Alabama nation, who inhabited the East arm of the great Mobile river, which bears their name to this day, now possessed by the Creeks or Muscogulges, who conquered the former.

MY friend having purchased some baskets and earthen–ware, the manufactures of these people, we left the village, and proceeded twelve miles higher up the river, landed again at a very large and well cultivated plantation, where we lodged all night. Observed growing in a spacious garden adjacent to the house, many useful as well as curious exoticks, particularly the delicate and sweet Tube–rose (Polyanthus tuberosa) it grows here in the open garden, the flowers were very large and abundant on the stems, which were five, six or seven feet high, but I saw none here having double flowers. In one corner of the garden was a pond or marsh, round about which grew luxuriantly the Scotch grass (Panicum sirtellum, gramen panicum maximum, spica devisa, ariftis armatum, Sloan, Jam. Cat. p. 20.) the people introduced this valuable grass from the West–India islands: they mow or reap it at any time, and feed it green to cows or horses; it is nourishing food for all cattle. The Humble plant (Mimosa pudica) grows here five or six feet high, rambling like Brier vines over the fences and shrubs all about the garden. The people here say it is an indigenous plant, but this I doubt, as it is not seen growing wild in the forests and fields, and it differs in no respect from that which we protect in green houses and stoves, except in the extent and luxuriancy of its branches, which may be owing to the productive virgin mould and temperature of the climate; the people however pay no attention to its culture, but rather condemn it as a noxious, troublesome weed, for wherever it gets footing, it spreads itself by its seed in so great abundance as to oppress and even extirpate more useful vegetables.

NEXT day we likewise visited several delightful and spacious plantations on the banks of the river, during our progress upwards; in the evening arrived at my friend's habitation, a very delightful villa, with extensive plantations of Corn (Zea) Indigo, Cotton and some Rice.

A DAY or two after our arrival we agreed upon a visit to Point Coupe, a flourishing French settlement on the Spanish shore of the Mississipi.

EARLY next morning we sat off in a neat Cypress boat with three oars, proceeding up the river, and by night got to a large plantation near the White cliffs, now called Brown's cliffs, in honour of the late governor of West Florida, now of the Bahama Islands, who is proprietor of a large district of country, lying on and adjacent to the Cliffs. At the time of my residence with Mr. Rumsey at Pearl island, governor Brown, then on his passage to his government of the Bahamas, paid Mr. Rumsey a visit, who politely introduced me to his excellency, acquainting him with my character and pursuits; he desired me to explore his territory, and give him my opinion of the quality of the White plains.

AUGUST 27th, 1787, having in readiness horses well equipt, early in the morning we sat off for the plains. About a mile from the river we crossed a deep gully and small rivulet, then immediately entered the Cane forests, following a strait avenue cut through them, off from the river, which continued about eight miles, the ground gradually but imperceptibly rising before us; when at once opens to view expansive plains, which are a range of native grassy fields of many miles extent, lying parallel with the river, surrounded and intersected with Cane brakes and high forests of stately trees; the soil black, extremely rich and productive, but the virgin mould becomes thiner and less fertile as it verges on to the plains, which are so barren as scarcely to produce a bush or even grass, in the middle or highest parts; the upper stratum or surface of the earth is a whitish clay or chalk, with veins of sea shells, chiefly of those little clams called les coqueles, or interspersed with the white earth or clay, so tenacious and hard as to render it quite sterile, scarcely any vegetable growth to be seen, except short grass, crustaceous mosses, and some places quite bare, where it is on the surface, but where it lies from eighteen inches to two or three feet below, it has the virtue of fertilizing the virgin mould above, rendering it black, humid, soapy, and incredibly productive.

I OBSERVED two or three scrubby Pine trees or rather dwarf bushes, upon the highest ridge of these plains, which are viewed here as a curiosity, there being no Pine forests within several leagues distance from the banks of this great river, but, on the contrary, seemingly an endless wilderness of Canes and the most magnificent forests of the trees already noted, but particularly Platanus occidentalis, Liriodendron, Magnolia grandiflora, Liquid–amber styraciflua, Juglans nigra, Juglans exaltata, Telea, Morus rubra, Gleditsia triacanthus, Laurus Borbonia and Laurus sassafras; this last grows here to a vast tree, forty or fifty feet strait trunk; its timber is found to be very useful, sawn into boards and scantling, or hewn into posts for building and fencing.

ON the more fertile borders of the plains, adjoining the surrounding forests, are Sideroxilon, Pyrus coronaria and Strawberry vines (Fragaria) but no fruit on them; the

289

inhabitants assured me they were fruitful in their season, very large, of a fine red colour, delicious and fragrant.

HAVING made our tour and observations on the White plains, we returned to the river at the close of the day, and next morning sat off for Point Coupe; passed under the high painted cliffs, and then set our course across the Mississipi, which is here near two miles over: touched at a large island near the middle of the river, being led there, a little out of our way, in pursuit of a bear crossing from the main, but he out−swam us, reached the island and made a safe retreat in the forests entangled with vines; we however pursued him on shore, but to no purpose. After resting a while we re−embarked and continued our voyage, coasting the East shore of the island to the upper end, here we landed again, on an extended projecting point of clean sand and pebbles, where were to be seen pieces of coal sticking in the gravel and sand, together with other fragments of the fossil kingdom, brought down by inundations and lodged there. We observed a large kind of muscle in the sand; the shell of an oval form, having horns or protuberances near half an inch in length and as thick as a crow−quill, which I suppose serve the purpose of grapnels to hold their ground against the violence of the current. Here were great numbers of wild fowl, wading in the shoal water that covers the sandy points, to a vast distance from the shores: they were geese, brant, gannet, and the great and beautiful whooping crane (grus alber.) Embarked again, doubled the point of the island and arrived at Point Coupe in the evening.

WE made our visit to a French gentleman, an ancient man and wealthy planter, who, according to the history he favoured us with of his own life and adventures, must have been very aged; his hair was of a silky white, yet his complexion was florid and constitution athletic. He said that soon after he came to America, with many families of his countrymen, they ascended the river to the Cliffs of the Natches, where they sat down, being entertained by the natives; and under cover of a strong fortress and garrison, established a settlement, and by cultivating the land and forming plantations, in league and friendship with the Indians, in a few years they became a populous, rich and growing colony; when, through the imprudent and tyrannical conduct of the commandant towards the Natches, the ancients of the country, a very powerful and civilized nation of red men, who were sovereigns of the soil, and possessed the country round about them, they became tired of these comers, and exasperated at their cruelty and licentiousness, at length determined to revenge themselves of such inhumanity and ingratitude, secretly conspired their destruction, and their measures were so well concerted with other Indian tribes, that if it had not been for the treachery of one of their princesses, with whom the commander was in favour (for by her influence her nation attempted the destruction of the settlement, before their auxilaries joined them, which afforded an opportunity for some few of the settlers to escape) they would have fully accomplished their purpose, however the settlement was entirely broken up, most of the inhabitants being slaughtered in one night, and the few who escaped betook themselves to their canoes, descending the river until they arrived at this place, where they established themselves again; and this gentleman had only time and opportunity to take into his boat one heifer calf, which he assured us was the mother of the numerous herds he now possesses, consisting of many hundred head. Here is now a very respectable village, defended by a strong fortress and garrison of Spaniards, the commander being governor of the district.

THE French here are able, ingenious and industrious planters: they live easy and plentifully, and are far more regular and commendable in the enjoyment of their earnings than their neighbours the English; their dress of their own manufactures, well wrought and neatly made up, yet not extravagant or foppish; manners and conversation easy, moral and entertaining.

NEXT morning we sat off again on our return home, and called by the way of the Cliffs, which is a perpendicular bank or bluff, rising up out of the river near one hundred feet above the present surface of the water, whose active current sweeps along by it. From eight or nine feet below the loamy vegetative mould at top, to within four or five feet of the water, these cliffs present to view stratas of clay, marle and chalk, of all colours, as brown, red, yellow, white, blue and purple; there are separate strata of these various colours, as well as mixed or particoloured: the lowest stratum next the water is exactly of the same black mud or rich soil of the adjacent low Cypress swamps, above and below the bluff; and here in the cliffs we see vast stumps of Cypress and other trees, which at this day grow in these low, wet swamps, and which range on a level with them. These stumps are sound, stand upright, and seem to be rotted off about two or three feet above the spread of their roots; their trunks, limbs, &c. lie in all directions about them. But when these swampy forests were growing, and by what cause they were cut off and overwhelmed by the various strata of earth, which now rise near one hundred feet above, at the brink of the cliffs, and two or three times that height but a few hundred yards back, is a phenomenon perhaps not easily developed; the swelling heights rising gradually over and beyond this precipice are now adorned with high forests of stately Magnolia, Liquid–amber, Fagus, Quercus, Laurus, Morus, Juglans, Telea, Halesia, Æsculus,

Callicarpa, Liriodendron, &c. Arrived in the evening at the plantation below the Cliffs, and next day got safe back to my friend's habitation.

OBSERVED few vegetable productions different from what grow in Carolina and Georgia; perhaps in the spring and early summer season, here may be some new plants, particularly in the high forests and ridges, at some distance from the river: there is however growing in the rich high lands, near on the banks of the river, which I observed in the settlement of Baton Rouge, an arborescent aromatic vine, which mounts to the tops of the highest trees, by twisting or writhing spirally round them; some of these vines are as thick as a man's leg, of a soft spungy texture, and flexible, covered with a Cinnamon coloured bark, which is highly aromatic or spicy. The large oblong leaves sit opposite on the branches, and are of a full deep green colour, but its season of flowering being past, and the seed was scattered, I am entirely ignorant to what genus it belongs; perhaps it is a non–descript or new genus: here is likewise a new and beautiful species of Verbena, with decumbent branches and lacerated deep green leaves; the branches terminate with corymbi of Violet blue flowers, this pretty plant grows in old fields where there is a good soil.

THE severe disorder in my eyes subverted the plan of my peregrinations, and contracted the span of my pilgrimage South–Westward. This disappointment affected me very sensibly, but resignation and reason resuming their empire over my mind, I submitted and determined to return to Carolina.

RECEIVING information that the company's schooner was ready to sail for Mobile, I embarked on board a trading boat for Manchac, where arriving in the evening, I took leave next morning of Messrs. Swanson & Co. and sat off for the forks of the Amite, and next day sat sail, descending the tardy current of the Amite. Observing two bears crossing the river a–head, though our pieces were ready charged, and the yawl along side to receive us, we pursued them in vain, they swam swiftly across and escaped in the forests on the island of Orleans. The breeze dying away at evening, we came to anchor, and had variety of amusements at fishing and fowling.

NEXT day, November 13th 1777, with a steady leading breeze, entered and sailed over the lake Maurepas, and through the streights into the Pontchartrain, and continued under sail, but at midnight by keeping too near the West shore we ran aground on a sand–bar, where we lay beating the hard sandy bottom until morning, and our yawl parting from us in the night, which we never recovered, we were left to the mercy of the winds and floods, but before noon the wind coming briskly from North–East, drove the sea into the lake, we got off, made sail again, and before night passed through the Regullets, entering the ocean through the bay of Pearls, sailing through the sound betwixt Cat island and the strand of the continent; passing by the beautiful bay St. Louis, into which descend many delightful rivers, which flow from the lower or maritime settlements of the Chactaws or Flat–heads. Continuing through the sound between the oyster banks and shoals of Ship and Horn islands, and the high and bold coast of Biloxi on the main, got through the narrow pass Aux Christian and soon came up abreast of Isle Dauphin, betwixt whose shoals and the West Cape of Mobile Bay we got a–ground on some sunken oyster banks, but next day a brisk Southerly wind raised the sea on the coast, which lifted us off again, and setting sail, shot through the Pass au Oleron, and entering the bay, by night came to anchor safe again at the city of Mobile.

AFTER having made up my collections of growing roots, seeds and curious specimens, left them to the care of Messrs. Swanson and M'Gillavry, to be forwarded to Dr. Fothergill of London. I prepared to set off again to Augusta in Georgia, through the Creek Nation, the only practicable way of returning by land, being frustrated of pursuing my intended rout which I had meditated, through the territories of the Siminoles or Lower Creeks, they being a treacherous people, lying so far from the eye and controul of the nation with whom they are confederate: there having lately been depredations and murders committed by them at the bay of Apalache, on some families of white people who were migrating from Georgia, with an intention of setling on the Mobile. Having to pass the distance of near two hundred miles to the first town of the nation, through a solitary, uninhabited wilderness, the bloody field of Schambe, where those contending bands of American bravos, Creeks and Chactaws, often meet in dire conflict: for the better convenience and security, I joined company with a caravan of traders, now about setting off for the nation.

OBSERVED growing in a garden in Mobile, two large trees of the Juglans pecan, and the Discorea bulbifera, this last curious plant bears a large kidney shaped root, one, two or three at the bosom of the leaves, several feet from the ground, as they climb up poles or supports set by their roots; these roots when boilen or roasted, are esteemed a pleasant wholesome food, and taste like the ordinary Yam.

CHAP. VIII.

NOVEMBER 27th 1777, sat off from Mobile, in a large boat with the principal trader of the company, and at evening arrived at Taensa, where were the pack–horsemen with the merchandize, and next morning as soon as we had our horses in readiness, I took my last leave of Major Farmer, and left Taensa. Our caravan consisting of between twenty and thirty horses, sixteen of which were loaded, two pack–horsemen, and myself, under the direction of Mr. Tap——y the chief trader. One of our young men was a Mustee Creek, his mother being a Chactaw slave, and his father a half breed, betwixt a Creek and a white man. I loaded one horse with my effects, some presents to the Indians, to enable me to purchase a fresh horse, in case of necessity, for my old trusty slave which had served me faithfully almost three years, having carried me on his back at least six thousand miles, was by this time almost worn out, and I expected every hour he would give up, especially after I found the manner of these traders' travelling; who seldom decamp until the sun is high and hot; each one having a whip made of the toughest cowskin, they start all at once, the horses having ranged themselves in regular Indian file, the veteran in the van, and the younger in the rear; then the chief drives with the crack of his whip, and a whoop or shriek, which rings through the forests and plains, speaks in Indian, commanding them to proceed, which is repeated by all the company, when we start at once, keeping up a brisk and constant trot, which is incessantly urged and continued as long as the miserable creatures are able to move forward, and then come to camp, though frequently in the middle of the afternoon, which is the pleasantest time of the day for travelling: and every horse has a bell on, which being stopped when we start in the morning with a twist of grass or leaves, soon shakes out, and they are never stopped again during the day; the constant ringing and clattering of the bells, smacking of the whips, whooping and too frequent cursing these miserable quadrupeds, cause an incessant uproar and confusion, inexpressibly disagreeable.

AFTER three days travelling in this mad manner, my old servant was on the point of giving out, and several of the company's horses were tired, but were relieved of their burthens by the led horses which attended for that purpose. I was now driven to disagreeable extremities, and had no other alternative, but either to leave my horse in the woods, pay a very extravagant hire for a doubtful passage to the Nation, or separate myself from my companions, and wait the recovery of my horse alone: the traders gave me no other comfortable advice in this dilemma, than that, there was a company of traders on the road a–head of us from the nation, to Mobile, who had a large gang of led horses with them for sale, when they should arrive; and expected from the advice which he had received at Mobile before we set off from thence, that this company must be very near to us, and probably would be up tomorrow, or at least in two or three days: and this man condescended so far as to moderate a little his mode of travelling, that I might have a chance of keeping up with them until the evening of next day; besides I had the comfort of observing that the traders and pack–horsemen carried themselves towards me, with evident signs of humanity and friendship, often expressing sentiments of sympathy, and saying I must not be left alone to perish in the wilderness.

ALTHOUGH my apprehensions on this occasion, were somewhat tumultuous, since there was little hope, on the principle of reason, should I be left alone, of escaping cruel captivity, and perhaps being murdered by the Chactaws; for the company of traders was my only security, as the Indians never attack the traders on the road, though they be trading with nations at enmity with them. Yet I had secret hopes of relief and deliverance, that cheered me, and inspired confidence and peace of mind.

Now I am come within the atmosphere of the Illisium groves, how reanimating is the fragrance! every part of this plant above ground possesses an aromatic scent, but the large stillated pericarpes is the most fragrant part of it, which continually perspires an oleagenous sweat, as warm and vivific as Cloves or Mace, I never saw it grow naturally further North than Lat. 33°, on the Mobile river and its branches, and but one place in East Florida near Lake George, Lat. 28°.

ABOUT the middle of the afternoon, we were joyfully surprised at the distant prospect of the trading company coming up, and we soon met, saluting each other several times with a general Indian whoop, or shouts of friendship; then each company came to camp within a few paces of each other; and before night I struck up a bargain with them for a handsome strong young horse, which cost me about ten pounds sterling. I was now constrained to leave my old slave behind, to feed in rich Cane pastures, where he was to remain and recruit until the return of his new master from Mobile; from whom I extorted a promise to use him gently, and if possibly, not to make a pack–horse of him.

NEXT morning we decamped, proceeding again on my travels, now alert and cheerful. crossed a brisk rivulet ripling over a gravelly bed, and winding through aromatic groves of the Illisium Floridanum, then gently descended to the high forests, leaving Deadman's creek, for at this creek a white man was found dead, supposed to have been murdered, from which circumstance it has its name.

A FEW days before we arrived at the Nation we met a company of emigrants from Georgia; a man, his wife, a young woman, several young children and three stout young men, with about a dozen horses loaded with their property. They informed us their design was to settle on the Alabama, a few miles above the confluence of the Tombigbe.

BEING now near the Nation, the chief trader with another of our company sat off a–head for his town, to give notice to the Nation, as he said, of his approach with the merchandize, each of them taking the best horse they could pick out of the gang, leaving the goods to the conduct and care of the young Mustee and myself. Early in the evening we came to the banks of a large deep creek, a considerable branch of the Alabama: the waters ran furiously, being overcharged with the floods of rain which had fallen the day before. We discoverd immediately that there was no possibility of crossing it by fording; its depth and rapidity would have swept our horses, loads and all, instantly from our sight; my companion, after consideration, said we must make a raft to ferry over our goods, which we immediately set about, after unloading our horses and turning them out to range. I undertook to collect dry Canes, and my companion dry timber or logs and vines to bind them together: having gathered the necessary materials, and laid them in order on the brink of the river, ready to work upon, we betook ourselves to repose, and early next morning sat about building our raft. This was a novel scene to me, and I could not, until finished and put to practice, well comprehend how it could possibly answer the effect desired. In the first place we laid, parallel to each other, dry, sound trunks of trees, about nine feet in length, and eight or nine inches diameter, which binding fast together with Grape vines and withs, until we had formed this first floor, about twelve or fourteen feet in length, then binding the dry Canes in bundles, each near as thick as a man's body, with which we formed the upper stratum, laying them close by the side of each other and binding them fast; after this manner our raft was constructed: then having two strong Grape vines, each long enough to cross the river, we fastened one to each end of the raft, which now being completed, and loading on as much as it would safely carry, the Indian took the end of one of the vines in his mouth, plunged into the river and swam over with it, and the vine fixed to the other end was committed to my charge, to steady the raft and haul it back again after being unloaded; as soon as he had safe landed and hauled taught his vine, I pushed off the raft, which he drew over as quick as possible, I steadying it with my vine: in this manner, though with inexpressible danger of loosing our effects, we ferried all safe over: the last load, with other articles, contained my property, with all my clothes, which I stripped off, except my breeches, for they contained matters of more value and consequence than all the rest of my property put together; besides I did not choose to expose myself entirely naked to the alligators and serpents in crossing the flood. Now seeing all the goods safe over, and the horses at a landing place on the banks of the river about fifty yards above, I drove them all in together, when, seeing them safe landed, I plunged in after them, and being a tollerable swimmer, soon reached the opposite shore; but my difficulties at this place were not yet at an end, for our horses all landing just below the mouth of a considerable branch of this river, of fifteen or twenty feet width, and its perpendicular banks almost as many feet in height above its swift waters, over which we were obliged to carry every article of our effects, and this by no other bridge than a sapling felled across it, which is called a raccoon bridge, and over this my Indian friend would trip as quick and light as that quadruped, with one hundred weight of leather on his back, when I was scarcely able to shuffle myself along over it astride. At last having re–packed and sat off again, without any material occurrence intervening; in the evening we arrived at the banks of the great Tallapoose river, and came to camp under shelter of some Indian cabins, in expansive fields, close to the river bank, opposite the town of Savannuca. Late in the evening a young white man, in great haste and seeming confusion, joined our camp, who immediately related, that being on his journey from Pensacola, it happened that the very night after we had passed the company of emigrants, he met them and joined their camp in the evening, when, just at dark, the Chactaws surrounded them, plundered their camp and carried all the people off captive, except himself, he having the good fortune to escape with his horse, though closely pursued.

NEXT morning very early, though very cold and the surface of the earth as hoary as if covered with a fall of snow; the trader standing on the opposite shore entirely naked except a breech–clout, and encircled by a company of red men in the like habit, hailed us, and presently, with canoes, brought us all over with the merchandize, and conducted us safe to the town of Mucclasse, a mile or two distant.

THE next day was a day of rest and audience: the following was devoted to feasting, and the evening concluded in celebrating the nuptials of the young Mustee with a Creek girl of Mucclasse, daughter of the chief and sister to our trader's wife. The trader's house and stores formed a compleat square, after the mode of the habitations of the Muscogulges, that is, four oblong buildings of equal dimensions, two opposite to each other,

297

encompassing an area of about a quarter of an acre; on one side of this a fence enclosed a yard of near an acre of ground, and at one of the farther corners of which a booth or pavilion was formed of green boughs, having two Laurel trees planted in front (Magnolia grandiflora.) This was the secret nuptial chamber. Dancing, music and feasting continued the forepart of the night, and towards morning the happy couple privately withdrew, and continued alone all the next day, no one presuming to approach the sacred, mysterious thalame.

THE trader obliged me with his company on a visit to the Alabama, an Indian town at the confluence of the two fine rivers, the Tallapoose and Coosau, which here resign their names to the great Alabama, where are to be seen traces of the ancient French fortress, Thoulouse; here are yet lying, half buried in the earth, a few pieces of ordnance, four and six pounders. I observed, in a very thriving condition, two or three very large Apple trees, planted here by the French. This is, perhaps, one of the most elegible situations for a city in the world, a level plain between the conflux of two majestic rivers, which are exactly of equal magnitude in appearance, each navigable for vessels and perreauguas at least five hundred miles above it, and spreading their numerous branches over the most fertile and delightful regions, many hundred miles before we reach their sources in the Apalachean mountains.

STAYED all night at Alabama, where we had a grand entertainment at the public square, with music and dancing, and returned next day to Mucclasse, where being informed of a company of traders about setting off from Tuckabatche for Augusta, I made a visit to that town to know the truth of it, but on my arrival there they were gone, but being informed of another caravan who were to start from the Ottasse town in two or three weeks time, I returned to Mucclasse in order to prepare for my departure.

ON my arrival, I was not a little surprised at a tragical revolution in the family of my friend the trader, his stores shut up, and guarded by a party of Indians: in a few minutes however, the whole affair was related to me. It appeared that this son of Adonis, had been detected in an amorous intrigue, with the wife of a young chief, the day after his arrival: the chief being out on a hunt, but arrived next day, who upon information of the affair, and the fact being confirmed, he with his friends and kindred resolved to exact legal satisfaction, which in this case is cutting off both ears of the delinquent, close to the head, which is called cropping. This being determined upon, he took the most secret and effectual methods to effect his purpose. About a dozen young Indian fellows, conducted

298

by their chief (the injured husband) having provided and armed themselves with knotty cudgels of green Hickory, which they concealed under their mantles, in the dusk of the evening paid a pretended friendly visit to the trader at his own house; when the chief feigning a private matter of business, took him aside in the yard; then whistling through his singers (the signal preconcerted) he was instantly surrounded, knocked down, and then stripped to his skin, and beaten with their knotty bludgeons; however he had the subtilty to feign himself speechless before they really killed him, which he supposed was their intention; when he had now lain for dead, the executioner drew out his knife with an intention of taking off his ears; this small respite gave him time to reflect a little; when he instantly sprang up, ran off, leaped the fence and had the good fortune to get into a dark swamp, overgrown with vines and thickets, where he miraculously eluded the earnest researches of his enemies, and finally made a safe retreat to the house of his father–in–law, the chief of the town; throwing himself under his protection, who gave his word that he would do him all the favour that lay in his power. This account I had from his own month, who hearing of my return, the next morning after my arrival, sent a trusty messenger, by whom I found means of access to him. He farther informed me that there had been a council of the chiefs of the town convened, to deliberate on the affair, and their final determination was that he must loose his ears, or forfeit all his goods, which amounted to upwards of one thousand pounds sterling, and even that forfeiture would not save his ears, unless Mr. Golphin interposed in his behalf; and after all the injured Indian declares that he will have his life. He entreated me with tears to make what speed I could to Silver Bluff, represent his dangerous situation to Mr. Golphin, and solicit that gentleman's most speedy and effectual interference; which I assured him I would undertake.

Now having all things prepared for my departure, early in the morning, after taking leave of my distressed friend the trader of Mucclasse, I sat off; passed through continued plantations and Indian towns on my way up the Tallapoose river, being every where treated by the inhabitants with marks of friendship, even as though I had been their countryman and relation. Called by the way at the beautiful town of Coolome, where I tarried some time with Mr. Germany the chief trader of the town, an elderly gentleman, but active, cheerful and very agreeable; who received and treated me with the utmost civility and friendship: his wife is a Creek woman, of a very amiable and worthy character and disposition, industrious, prudent and affectionate; and by whom he had several children, whom he is desirous to send to Savanna or Charleston, for their education, but cannot prevail on his wife to consent to it: this affair affects him very

299

sensibly, for he has accumulated a pretty fortune by his industry and commendable conduct.

LEAVING Coolome, I re-crossed the river at Tuccabache, an ancient and large town, thence continuing up the river, and at evening arrived at Attasse, where I continued near a week, waiting the preparations of the traders, with whom I was to join in company to Augusta.

THE next day after my arrival, I was introduced to the ancient chiefs, at the public square or areopagus, and in the evening in company with the traders, who are numerous in this town, repaired to the great rotunda, where were assembled the greatest number of ancient venerable chiefs and warriors that I had ever beheld; we spent the evening and greater part of the night together, in drinking Cassine and smoking Tobacco. The great counsel-house or rotunda is appropriated to much the same purpose as the public square, but more private, and seems particularly dedicated to political affairs; women and youth are never admitted; and I suppose it is death for a female to presume to enter the door, or approach within its pale. It is a vast conical building or circular dome, capable of accomodating many hundred people; constructed and furnished within, exactly in the same manner as those of the Cherokees already described, but much larger than any I had seen there; there are people appointed to take care of it, to have it daily swept clean, to provide canes for fuel or to give light.

As their vigils and manner of conducting their vespers and mystical fire in this rotunda, is extremely singular, and altogether different from the customs and usages of any other people, I shall proceed to describe it. In the first place, the governor or officer who has the management of this business, with his servants attending, orders the black drink to be brewed, which is a decoction or infusion of the leaves and tender shoots of the Cassine: this is done under an open shed or pavilion, at twenty or thirty yards distance, directly opposite the door of the council-house. Next he orders bundles of dry Canes to be brought in; these are previously split and broke in pieces to about the length of two feet, and then placed obliquely crossways upon one another on the floor, forming a spiral circle round about the great centre pillar, rising to a foot or eighteen inches in height from the ground; and this circle spreading as it proceeds round and round, often repeated from right to left, every revolution encreases its diameter, and at length extends to the distance of ten or twelve feet from the centre, more or less, according to the length of time the assembly or meeting is to continue. By the time these preparations are accomplished it is night, and the assembly taken their seats in order. The exterior extremity or outer end of the spiral circle takes fire and immediately rises into a bright flame (but how this is effected I did not plainly apprehend; I saw no person set fire to it; there might have been fire left on the hearth, however I neither saw nor smelt fire or smoke until the blaze instantly ascended upwards) which gradually and slowly creeps round the centre pillar, with the course of the sun, feeding on the dry Canes, and affords a cheerful, gentle and sufficient light until the circle is consumed, when the council breaks up. Soon after this illumination takes place, the aged chiefs and warriors being seated on their cabbins or sophas, on the side of the house opposite the door, in three classes or ranks, rising a little, one above or behind the other; and the white people and red people of confederate towns in the like order on the left hand: a transverse range of pillars, supporting a thin clay wall about breast high, separates them: the king's cabbin or seat is in front, the next back of it the head warriors, and the third or last accommodates the young warriors, &c. the great war chief's seat or place is on the same cabbin with, and immediately to the left hand of the king and next to the white people, and to the right hand of the mico or king the most venerable head men and warriors are seated. The assembly being now seated in order, and the house illuminated, two middle aged men, who perform the office of slaves or servants, pro tempore, come in together at the door, each having very large conch shells full of black drink, advancing with slow, uniform and steady steps, their eyes or countenances lifted up, singing very low but sweetly, advance within six on eight paces of the king's and white people's cabbins, when they stop together, and each rests his shell on a tripos or little table, but presently takes it up again, and, bowing very low, advances obsequiously, crossing or intersecting each other about midway: he who rested his shell before the white people now stands before the king, and the other who stopped before the king stands before the white people, when each presents his shell, one to the king and the other to the chief of the white people, and as soon as he raises it to his mouth the slave utters or sings two notes, each of which continues as long as he has breath, and as long as these notes continue, so long must the person drink, or at least keep the shell to his mouth. These two long notes are very solemn, and at once strike the imagination with a religious awe or homage to the Supreme, founding some what like a–hoo—ojah and a–lu—yah. After this manner the whole assembly are treated, as long as the drink and light continues to hold out, and as soon as the drinking begins, Tobacco and pipes are brought. The skin of a wild cat or young tyger stuffed with Tobacco is brought, and laid at the king's feet, with the great or royal pipe beautifully adorned; the skin is usually of the animals of the king's family or tribe, as the wild–cat, otter, bear, rattle–snake, &c. A skin of Tobacco is like–wise brought and cast at the feet of the white chief of the town, and from him it passes on from one to another to fill their pipes from, though each person has besides his own peculiar skin of Tobacco. The king or chief smokes first in the great pipe a few whiffs, blowing it off ceremoniously, first towards the sun, or as it is generally supposed to the Great Spirit, for it is puffed upwards, next towards the four cardinal points, then towards the white people in the house, then the great pipe is taken from the hand of the mico by a save, and presented to the chief white man, and then to the great war chief, whence it circulates through the rank of head men and warriors, then returns to the king. After this each one fills his pipe from his own or his neighbours skin.

THE great or public square generally stands alone, in the centre and highest part of the town, it consists of foursquare or cubical buildings, or houses of one story, uniform, and of the same dimensions, so situated as to form an exact tetragon, encompassing an area of half an acre of ground, more or less, according to the strength or largeness of the town, or will of the inhabitants; there is a passage or avenue at each corner of equal width; each building is constructed of a wooden frame fixed strong in the earth, the walls filled in, and neatly plaistered with clay mortar; close on three sides, that is the back and two ends, except within about two feet of the wall plate or eves, which is left open for the purpose of a window and to admit a free passage of the air; the front or side next to the area is quite open like a piazza. One of these buildings which is properly the counsel–house, where the mico chiefs and wariors, with the citizens who have business, or choose to repair thither, assemble every day in counsel; to hear, decide and rectify all grievances, complaints and contentions, arising betwixt the citizens; give audience–to ambassadors, and strangers, hear news and talks from confederate towns, allies or distant nations; to consult about the particular affairs of the town, as erecting habitations for new citizens, or establishing young families, concerning agriculture &c. &c. and this building is somewhat different from the other three; it is closely shut up on three sides, that is, the back and two ends, and besides a partition wall longitudinally from end to end divides it into two apartments, the back part totally dark, only three small arched apertures or holes opening into it from the front apartment or piazza, and are little larger than just to admit a man to crawl in upon his hands and knees. This secluded place appears to me to be designed as a sanctuary*

*Sanctorum or sacred temple, and it is said to be death for any person but the mico, war–chief and high priest to enter in, and none are admitted but by permission of the priests, who guard it day and night.

dedicated to religion or rather priest craft; for here are deposited all the sacred things, as the physic pot, rattles, chaplets of deer's hoofs and other apparatus of conjuration; and likewise the calumet or great pipe of peace, the imperial standard, or eagle's tail, which is made of the feathers of the white eagles tail

*** Vultura sacra.

curiously formed and displayed like an open fan on a sceptre or staff, as white and clean as possible when displayed for peace; but when for war, the feathers are painted or tinged with vermilion. The piazza or front of this building, is equally divided into three apartments, by two transverse walls or partitions, about breast high, each having three orders or ranges of seats or cabins stepping one above and behind the other, which accommodate the senate and audience, in the like order as observed in the rotunda. The other three buildings which compose the square, are alike furnished with three ranges of cabins or sophas, and serve for a banqueting–house, to shelter and accommodate the audience and spectators at all times, particularly at feasts or public entertainments, where all classes of citizens resort day and night in the summer or moderate season; the children and females however are seldom or never seen in the public square.

THE pillars and walls of the houses of the square were decorated with various paintings and sculptures; which I suppose to be hieroglyphic, and as an historic legendary of political and sacerdotal affairs: but they are extremely picturesque or caricature, as men in variety of attitudes, some ludicrous enough, others having the head of some kind of animal as those of a duck, turkey, bear, fox, wolf, buck, &c. and again those kind of creatures are represented having the human head. These designs were not ill executed, the outlines bold, free and well proportioned. The pillars supporting the front or piazza of the council house of the square, were ingeniously formed in the likeness of vast speckled serpents, ascending upward; the Otasses being of the snake family or tribe. At this time the town was fasting, taking medicine, and I think I may say praying, to avert a grevious calamity of sickness, which had lately afflicted them, and laid in the grave abundance of their citizens; they fast seven or eight days, during which time they eat or drink nothing but a meagre gruel, made of a little corn–flour and water; taking at the same time by way of medicine or physic, a strong decoction of the roots of the Iris versicolor, which is a powerful cathartic; they hold this root in high estimation, every town cultivates a little

303

plantation of it having a large artificial pond, just without the town, planted and almost overgrown with it, where they usually dig clay for pottery, and mortar and plaster for their buildings, and I observed where they had lately been digging up this root.

IN the midst of a large oblong square adjoining this town (which was surrounded with a low bank or terrace) is standing a high pillar, round like a pin or needle, it is about forty feet in height, and between two and three feet in diameter at the earth, gradually tapering upwards to a point; it is one piece of Pine wood, and arises from the centre of a low circular, artificial hill, but it leans a little to one side. I enquired of the Indians and traders what it was designed for, who answered they knew not: the Indians said that their ancestors found it in the same situation, when they first arrived and possessed the country, adding, that the red men or Indians, then the possessors, whom they vanquished, were as ignorant as themselves concerning it, saying that their ancestors likewise sound it standing so. This monument, simple as it is, may be worthy the observations of a traveller, since it naturally excites at least the following queries: for what purpose was it designed? its great antiquity and incorruptibility—— what method or machines they employed to bring it to the spot, and how they raised it erect? There is no tree or species of the Pine, whose wood, i. e. so large a portion of the trunk, is supposed to be incorruptible, exposed in the open air to all weathers, but the long–leaved Pine (Pin. palustris) and there is none growing within twelve or fifteen miles of this place, that tree being naturally produced only on the high, dry, barren ridges, where there is a sandy soil and grassy wet savannas. A great number of men uniting their strength, probably carried it to the place on handspikes, or some such contrivance.

ON the Sabbath day before I sat off from this place, I could not help observing the solemnity of the town, the silence and the retiredness of the red inhabitants, but a very few of them were to be seen, the doors of their dwellings shut, and if a child chanced to stray out, it was quickly drawn in doors again: I asked the meaning of this, and was immediately answered, that it being the white people's beloved day or Sabbath, the Indians kept it religiously sacred to the Great Spirit.

LAST night was clear and cold, wind North West, and this morning January 2d, 1778, the face of the earth was perfectly white with a beautiful sparkling frost. Sat off for Augusta with a company of traders, four men with about thirty horses, twenty of which were loaded with leather and furs, each pack or load supposed to weigh one hundred and fifty pounds upon an average; in three days we arrived at the Apalachucla or Chata Uche river, crossed at the point towns Chehaw and Usseta; these towns almost join each other, yet speak two languages, as radically different perhaps as the Muscogulge's and Chinese. After leaving the river we met with nothing material, or worth particular observation, until our arrival at Oakmulge, towards evening, where we encamped in expansive ancient Indian fields, in view of the foaming flood of the river, now raging over its banks. Here were two companies of traders from Augusta, bound to the Nation, consisting of fifteen or twenty men, with seventy or eighty horses, most of which had their loads of merchandize; they crossed the river this morning and lost six horses in the attempt; they were drowned, being entangled in the vines under water at landing. But the river now falling again, we were in hopes that by next morning the waters would be again confined within the banks. We immediately sat about rigging our portable leather boat, about eight feet long, which was of thick soal leather, folded up and carried on the top of a pack of deer skins; the people soon got her rigged, which was effected after the following manner. We in the first place cut down a White–Oak sapling, and by notching this at each end, bent it up, which formed the keel, stem and stern post of one piece, this being placed in the bottom of the boat, and pretty strong hoop–poles being fixed in the bottom across the keel, and, turning up their ends, expanded the hull of the boat, which being fastened by thongs to two other poles bent round, the outside of the rim forms the gunwales, thus in an hour's time our bark was rigged, to which afterwards we added two little oars or sculls. Our boat being now in readiness, and our horses turned out to pasture, each one retired to repose, or to such exercise as most effectually contributed to divert the mind. I was at this time rather dejected, and sought comfort in retirement. Turning my course to the expansive fields, fragrant groves and sublime forests. Returned to camp by dusk, where I found my companions cheerful and thoughtless rather to an extreme. It was a calm still evening and warm, the wood–cock (scolopax) chirruping high up in the air, gently descends by spiral circular tract, and alights on the humid plain: this bird appears in Pennsylvania early in the spring, when the Elm and Maple begin to flower, and here the scarlet Maple, Elm and Alder began to shew their flowers, the yellow Jasmin just ready to open its fragrant golden blossoms, and the gay Azalea also preparing to expand its beauties.

THE morning cool and pleasant, after reconnoitering the shores of the rivers, and consulting with our brethren in distress, who had not yet decamped, resolving to stay and lend their assistance in passing over this rapid gulph, we were encouraged to proceed, and launching our barke into the raging flood, after many successful trips ferried over all the goods, then drove in our horses altogether, and had the pleasure of seeing them all safely landed on the opposite shore; and lastly I embarked with three of our people, and several packs of leather, we then put off from shore, bidding adieu to our generous friends left behind, who re–echoed our shouts upon our safe landing. We proceeded again, crossed the Oconne in the same manner, and with the like success, and came to camp in the fertile fields, on the banks of that beautiful river, and proceeding thence next day, in the evening came to camp on the waters of great Ogeche, and the following day, after crossing several of its considerable branches, came to camp, and next day crossed the main branch of that famous river, which being wide and very rapid proved difficult and dangerous fording, yet we crossed without any loss, but some of our pack–horses were badly bruised, being swept off their feet and dashed against the rocks, my horse too being carried away with the current, and plunging off sunken shelving rocks into deep holes, I got very wet, but I kept my seat and landed safe: however I suffered much, it being a cold freezing day. We came to camp early, and raising great fires with Pine knots and other wood, we dried ourselves and kept warm during the long night, and after two days more hard travelling we arrived at Augusta.

BEING under a necessity of making two or three days stay here, in order to refit myself, for by this time my stock of cloths were entirely worn out. I took this opportunity of visiting my friend doctor Wells at his plantations near the city. And now being again new clothed and furnished with a tolerable Indian poney, I took leave of my host and prepared to depart for Savanna.

SOON after I left Augusta, proceeding for Savanna, the capital, a gentleman overtook me on the road, who was a native of Ireland, and had lately arrived in this part of America with a view of settling a plantation in Georgia, particularly for the culture of those very useful fruits and vegetables that are cultivated up the Mediterranean, and which so largely contribute towards supporting that lucrative branch of commerce, i. e. the Levant trade, viz. Vitis vinifera, for wine, Vitis Corinthiaca, for Currants, Vitis Allobrogica, for Raisins, Olives, Figs, Morus, for feeding silk–worms, Amygdalus communis, Pistachia, Capparis, Citrus aurantium, Cilectures limon, Citrus verrucosa, the great sweet scented Citron, &c. He was very ingenious, desirous of information and as liberal and free of communicating his own acquisitions and discoveries in useful science, and consequently a very agreeable companion. On our journey down we stopped a while to rest and refresh ourselves at the Great Springs, near the road, on our left hand, about midway between Augusta and Savanna. This amazing fountain of transparent, cool water, breaks suddenly out of the earth, at the basis of a moderately elevated hill or bank, forming at once a bason near twenty yards over, ascending through a horizontal bed of soft socks, of a heterogenious composition, chiefly a testacious concretion of broken, entire and pulverised sea shells, sand, &c. constituting a coarse kind of lime–stone. The ebullition is copious, active and continual, over the ragged apertures in the rocks, which lie seven or eight feet below, swelling the surface considerably immediately above it; the waters descend swiftly from the fountain, forming at once a large brook, six or eight yards over, and five or six feet deep. There are multitudes of fish in the fountain of various tribes, chiefly the several species of bream, trout, cat–fish and garr: it was amusing to behold the fish continually ascending and descending through the rocky apertures, Observed that we crossed no stream or brook of water within twelve or fifteen miles of this fountain, but had in view vast savannas, swamps and Cane meadows, at no great distance from our road, on our right hand, which we may presume were the resources or reservoirs which contributed to the supplies of this delightful grotto. Here were growing on the ascents from the fountain, Magnolia grandiflora, Laurus Borbonia, Quercus sempervirens, Callicarpa; at a little distance a grove of the Cassine, and in an old field, just by, are to be seen some small Indian mounts. We travelled several miles over ridges of low swelling hills, whose surfaces were covered with particoloured pebbles, streaked and clouded with red, white, brown and yellow: they were mostly broken or shivered to pieces, I believe by the ancients in forming arrow–heads, darts, knives &c. for I observed frequently some of these misshapen implements amongst them, some broken and others spoiled in the making. These stones seemed to be a species of jasper or agate.

ON my way down I also called at Silver Bluff, and waited on the honourable G. Golphin, Esq. to acknowledge my obligations to him, and likewise to fulfil my engagements on the part of Mr. T——y, trader of Mucclasse. Mr. Golphin assured me that he was in a disagreeable predicament, and that he feared the worst, but said he would do all in his power to save him.

AFTER five days pleasant travelling we arrived at Savanna in good health.

LIST of the towns and tribes in league, and which constitute the powerful confederacy or empire of the Creeks or Muscogulges, viz.

Towns on the Tallapoose or Oakfuske river, viz.

• ### These speak the Muscogulge or Creek tongue, called the Mother tongue.

♦ Oakfuske, upper.
♦ Oakfuske, lower.
♦ Ufale, upper.
♦ Ufale, lower.
♦ Sokaspoge.
♦ Tallase, great.
♦ Coolome.
♦ Ghuaclahatche.
♦ Otasse.
♦ Cluale.
♦ Fusahatche.
♦ Tuccabatche.
♦ Cunhutke.

• ### Speak the Stincard tongue.

♦ Mucclasse.
♦ Alabama.

• ### Speak the Uche tongue.

♦ Savannuca.

• ### Speak the Stincard tongue.

♦ Whittumke.
♦ Coosauda.

Towns on the Coosau river, viz.

- ### Speak a dialect of Chicasaw.

  ♦ Abacooche.
- ### Speak the Muscogulge tongue

  ♦ Pocontallahasse.
  ♦ Hickory ground, traders name.
- ### Speak Muscog. and Chicasaw.

  ♦ Natche.

Towns on the branches of the Coosau river, viz.

- ### Speak the Muscogulge tongue.

  ♦ Wiccakaw.
  Fish pond, traders name.
  ♦ Hillaba.
  ♦ Kiolege

Towns on the Apalachucla or Chata Uche river, viz.

- ### Speak the Muscogulge tongue

  ♦ Apalachucla.
  ♦ Tucpauska.
  ♦ Chockeclucca.
  ♦ Chata Uche.
  ♦ Checlucca–ninne.
  ♦ Hothletega.
  ♦ Coweta.
  ♦ Usseta.

Towns on the Apalachucla or Chata Uche river, continued, viz.

- ### Speak the Savannuca tongue.

  ♦ Uche.

- ### Speak the Muscog. tongue.

  ♦ Hooseche.

- ### Speak the Stincard.

  ♦ Chehaw.
  ♦ Echeta.
  ♦ Occone.
  ♦ Swaglaw, great.
  ♦ Swaglaw, little.

Towns on Flint river, comprehending the Siminoles or Lower Creeks.

- Suola–nocha.
- Cuscowilla or Allachua.
- Talahasochte.
- Caloosahatche.
- ——Great island. Traders name.
- ——Great hammock. Traders name.
- ——Capon. Traders name.
- ——St. Mark's. Traders name.
- ——Forks. Traders name.

WITH many others of less note.

THE Siminoles speak both the Muscogulge and Stincard tongue.

Travels Through North and South Carolina

IN all fifty–five towns, besides many villages not enumerated, and reckoning two hundred inhabitants to each town on an average, which is a moderate computation, would give eleven thousand inhabitants.

IT appears to me pretty clearly, from divers circumstances, that this powerful empire or confederacy of the Creeks or Muscogulges, arose from, and established itself upon the ruins of that of the Natches, agreeably to Monsieur Duprat. According to the Muscogulges account of themselves, they arrived from the South–West, beyond the Mississipi, some time before the English settled the colony of Carolina and built Charleston; and their story concerning their country and people, from whence they sprang, the cause of leaving their native land, the progress of their migration, &c. is very similar to that celebrated historian's account of the Natches, they might have been included as allies and confederates in that vast and powerful empire of red men. The Muscogulges gradually pushing and extending their settlements on their North–East border, until the dissolution of the Natches empire; being then the most numerous, warlike and powerful tribe, they began to subjugate the various tribes or bands (which formerly constituted the Natches) and uniting them with themselves, formed a new confederacy under the name of the Muscogulges.

THE Muscogulge tongue being now the national or sovereign language, the Chicasaws, Chactaws, and even the remains of the Natches, if we are to credit the Creeks and traders, being dialects of the Muscogulge; and probably, when the Natches were sovereigns, they called their own the national tongue, and the Creeks, Chicasaws, &c. only dialects of theirs. It is uncertain which is really the mother tongue.

As for those numerous remnant bands or tribes, included at this day within the Muscogulge confederacy, who generally speak the Stincard language, (which is radically different from the Muscogulge) they are, beyond a doubt, the shattered remains of the various nations who inhabited the lower or maritime parts of Carolina and Florida, from Cape Fear, West to the Mississipi. The Uches and Savannucas is a third language, radically different from the Muscogulge and Lingo, and seems to be a more Northern tongue; I suppose a language that prevailed amongst the numerous tribes who formerly possessed and inhabited the maritime parts of Maryland and Virginia. I was told by an old trader that the Savannuca and Shawanese speak the same language, or very near alike.

CHAP. IX.

AFTER my return from the Creek nation, I employed myself during the spring and fore part of summer, in revisiting the several districts in Georgia and the East borders of Florida, where I had noted the most curious subjects; collecting them together, and shipping them off to England. In the course of these excursions and researches, I had the opportunity of observing the new flowering shrub, resembling the Gordonia*

* On first observing the fructification and habit of this tree, I was inclined to believe it a species of Gordonia, but afterwards, upon stricter examination, and comparing its flowers and fruit with those of the Gordonia lasianthus, I presently found striking characteristics abundantly sufficient to seperate it from that genus, and to establish it the head of a new tribe, which we have honoured with the name of the illustrious Dr. Benjamin Franklin, Franklinia Alatamaha.

in perfect bloom, as well as bearing ripe fruit. It is a flowering tree, of the first order for beauty and fragrance of blossoms: the tree grows fifteen or twenty feet high, branching alternately; the leaves are oblong, broadest towards their extremities, and terminate with an acute point, which is generally a little reflexed; they are lightly serrated, attenuate downwards and sessile, or have very short petioles; they are placed in alternate order, and towards the extremities of the twigs are crouded together, but stand more sparsedly below; the flowers are very large, expand themselves perfectly, are of a snow–white colour, and ornamented with a crown or tassel of gold coloured refulgent staminae in their centre; the inferior petal or segment of the corolla is hollow, formed like a cap or helmet, and entirely includes the other four, until the moment of expansion; its exterior surface is covered with a short silky hair; the borders of the petals are crisped or plicated: these large, white flowers stand single and sessile in the bosom of the leaves, which being near together towards the extremities of the twigs, and usually many expanded at the same time, make a gay appearance; the fruit is a large, round, dry, woody apple or pericarpe, opening at each end oppositely by five alternate fissures, containing ten cells, each replete with dry woody cuniform seed. This very curious tree was first taken notice of, about ten or twelve years ago, at this place, when I attended my father (John Bartram) on a botanical excursion; but, it being then late in the autumn, we could form no opinion to what class or tribe it belonged.

WE never saw it grow in any other place, nor have I ever since seen it growing wild, in all my travels, from Pennsylvania to Point Coupe, on the banks of the Mississipi, which must be allowed a very singular and unaccountable circumstance; at this place there are two or three acres of ground where it grows plentifully.

THE other new, singular and beautiful shrub

* I gave it the name of Bignonia bractonia extempore.

now here in full bloom, I never saw grow but at two other places in all my travels, and there very sparingly, except in East Florida, in the neighbourhood of the sea–coast.

CHAP. X.

HAVING now completed my collections in Georgia, I took leave of these Southern regions, proceeding on my return to Charleston. Left Savanna in the evening, in consequence of a pressing invitation from the honourable Jonathan Bryan, Esq. who was returning from the capital, to his villa, about eight miles up Savanna river; a very delightful situation, where are spacious gardens, furnished with variety of fruit trees and flowering shrubs; observed in a low wet place at the corner of the garden, the Ado (Arum esculentum) this plant is much cultivated in the maritime parts of Georgia, and Florida, for the sake of its large Turnip–like root, which when boiled or roasted, is excellent food, and tastes like the Yam; the leaves of this magnificent plant are very large, and of a beautiful green colour, the spatha large and circulated, the spadix terminates with a very long subulated tongue, naked and perfectly white: perhaps this may be the Arum Colocasia. They have likewise, another species of the esculent Arum, called Tannier, which are large and beautiful plants, and much cultivated and esteemed for food, particularly by the Negroes.

AT night, soon after our arrival, several of his servants came home with horse loads of wild pigeons (Columba migratoria) which it seems they had collected in a short space of time at a neighbouring Bay swamp: they take them by torch light; they have particular roosting places, where they associate in incredible multitudes at evening, on low trees and bushes, in hommocks or higher knolls in the interior parts of vast swamps. Many people go out together on this kind of sport, when dark; some take with them little fascines of fat Pine splinters for torches; others sacks or bags; and others furnish themselves with poles or staves; thus accoutered and prepared, they approach their roosts, the sudden blaze of light confounds, blinds and affrights the birds, whereby multitudes drop off the limbs to the ground, and others are beaten off with their staves, which by the sudden consternation, are entirely helpless, and easily taken and put into the sacks. It is chiefly the sweet small acorns of the Quercus phillos, Quercus aquatica, Quercus sempervirens, Quercus flammula, and others, which induce these birds to migrate in the autumn to those Southern regions; where they spend their days agreeably, and feast luxuriously, during the rigour of the colds in the North, whither they return at the approach of summer to breed.

SAT off next day, and crossed the river at Zubley's ferry, about fifty miles above Savanna, and in three days after arrived at Charleston.

OBSERVED, by the way near Jacksonsburg Ponpon, growing plentifully in good moist ground, usually by the banks of canals, After fructicosus. It is a most charming autumnal flowering shrub, it will rise to the height of eight or ten feet, when supported by neighbouring trees.

AFTER a few days residence in Charleston, I sat off on my return to my native land, crossed Cowper river, about nine miles above the city, where the water was a mile wide, and the ferry–house being on the opposite shore, I hoisted my travelling blanket on a pole for a signal, which being white, the people soon came to me and carried me safe over. In three days more easy travelling, I crossed Winyaw bay, just below Georgetown, and in two days more, got to the West end of Long bay, where I lodged at a large Indigo plantation. Sat off early next morning, and after crossing over the sand ridges, which afford little else but Quercus pumila, Myrica cerifera, Cassine, Sideroxilon and Andromeda entangled with various species of Smilax, got on the bay, which is a hard sand beach, exposed for the distance of fifteen miles to the continual lash of the Atlantic ocean; at about low water mark, are cliffs of rocks of the helmintholithus, being a very firm concrete or petrifaction, consisting of various kinds of seashells, fine sand and pulverized shells; there is a reef of these rocks, thirty or forty yards farther out than low water mark, which lift their rugged backs above water, and brave the continual strokes of the waves, which, however, assisted by the constant friction of the sands, make continual inroads upon them, bore them into holes and cavities, when tempestuous seas rend them

314

to pieces, scattering the fragments over the sandy shore. It is pleasant riding on this clean hard sand, paved with shells of various colours.

OBSERVED a number of persons coming up a head which I soon perceived to be a party of Negroes: I had every reason to dread the consequence; for this being a desolate place, and I was by this time several miles from any house or plantation, and had reason to apprehend this to be a predatory band of Negroes: people being frequently attacked, robbed, and sometimes murdered by them at this place; I was unarmed, alone, and my horse tired; thus situated every way in their power, I had no alternative but to be resigned and prepare to meet them, as soon as I saw them distinctly a mile or two off, I immediately alighted to rest, and give breath to my horse, intending to attempt my safety by slight, if upon near approach they should betray hostile designs, thus prepared, when we drew near to each other, I mounted and rode briskly up, and though armed with clubs, axes and hoes, they opened to right and left, and let me pass peaceably, their chief informed me whom they belonged to, and said they were going to man a new quarter at the West end of the bay, I however kept a sharp eye about me, apprehending that this might possibly have been an advanced division, and their intentions were to ambuscade and surround me, but they kept on quietly and I was no more alarmed by them. After noon, I crossed the swash at the east end of the bay, and in the evening got to good quarters. Next morning early I sat off again, and soon crossed Little River at the boundary; which is on the line that separates North and South Carolina; in an old field, on the banks of this river, a little distance from the public house, stands a single tree of the Magnolia grandiflora, which is said to be the most northern settlement of that tree. Passed this day over expansive savannas, charmingly decorated with late autumnal flowers, as Helianthus, Rudbeckia, Silphium, Solidago, Helenium, Serratula, Cacalia, Aster, Lillium Martagon, Gentiana caerulia, Chironia, Gentiana saponaria, Asclepias coccinea, Hypericum, Rhexea pulcherima, &c. &c.

OBSERVED likewise in these Savannas abundance of the ludicrous Dionea muscipula (Dioneae, Ellis ad Linnaeum, miraculum naturae, folia biloba, radicalia, ciliata, conduplicanda, sensibilia, isecta incarcerantia. Syst. vegetab. p. 335.

THIS wonderful plant seems to be distinguished in the creation, by the Author of nature, with faculties eminently superior to every other vegetable production*

* See some account of it in the introduction.

315

specimens of it were first communicated to the curious of the old world by John Bartram, the American botanist and traveller, who contributed as much if not more than any other man towards enriching the North American botanical nomenclature, as well as its natural history.

AFTER traversing these ample savannas I gradually ascended sand hills to open Pine forests; at evening got to Old town near Brunswick, where I lodged. Brunswick is a sea–port town on the Clarendon, or Cape Fear river, about thirty miles above the capes; it is about thirty years since this was the seat of government, when Arthur Dobbs, Esq. was governor and commander in chief of the province of North Carolina. Continued up the West side of North West of Cape Fear river, and rested two or three days at the seat of F. Lucas, Esq. a few miles above Livingston's creek, a considerable branch of the North West. This creek heads in vast swamps, in the vicinity of the beautiful lake Wakamaw, which in the source of a fine river of that name, and runs a South course seventy or eighty miles, delivering its waters into Winyaw bay at George–town. The Wakamaw lake is twenty six miles in circuit, the lands on its Eastern shores are fertile and the situation delightful, gradually ascending from pleasing eminences; bounded on the North–West coast by vast rich swamps, fit for the production of Rice: the lake is twelve miles West from Esq. Moores, whose villa is on the banks of the North West.

PROCEEDING again up the North West, crossed Carver's creek, and stopped at Ashwood, the ancient seat of Colonel William Bartram; the house stands on the high banks of the river, near seventy feet in height, above the surface of the water; this high bluff continues two or three miles on the river, and commands a magnificent prospect of the low lands opposite, when in their native state, presenting to the view grand forests and expansive Cane meadows; the trees which compose these forests are generally of the following tribes, Quercus tinctoria, Querc. alba, Querc. phillos, Querc. aquatica, Querc. hemispherica, Fraxinus excelsior, Platanus occidentalis, Liriodendron tulipifera, Liquid–amber styraciflua, Ulmus, Telea, Juglans hickory, Juglans cinerea, Juglans nigra, Morus rubra, Gleditsia triacanthus, Hopea tinctoria, Nyssa aquatica, Nyssa sylvatica, Carpinus and many more; the Cupressus disticha as stately and beautiful as I have seen any where. When these lands are cleared of their timber and cultivated, they produce abundantly, particularly, Wheat, Zea, Cotton, Hemp, Flax, with variety of excellent vegetables. This perpendicular bank of the river, by which the waters swiftly glide along, discovers at once the various strata of the earth of this low maritime country. For the most part the upper stratum consists of a light, sandy, pale, yellowish mold or loam, for ten or twelve feet in depth (except the flat level land back from the rivers, where the clays or marle approach very near the surface, and the ridges of sand hills, where the clays lie much deeper) this sandy mold or loam lays upon a deep bed of black, or dark slate coloured saline and sulphureous earth, which is composed of horizontal thin flakes or laminae, separable by means of very thin, almost imperceptible veins or strata of fine miceous particles, which drain or percolate a clear water, continually exuding, or trickling down, and forming little rills and diminutive cataracts, being conducted by perpendicular chinks or fissures; in some places, a portion of this clear water or transparent vapour, seems to coagulate on the edges of the veins and fissures, leaving a reddish curd or jelly–like substance sticking to them, which I should suppose indicates it to spring from a ferruginous source, especially since it discovers a chalybeate scent and taste: in other places these fissures shew evidently a chrystallization of exceeding fine white salts, which have an alluminous or vitriolic scent: there are pyrites, marcasites, or sulphureous nodules, shining like brass, of various sizes and forms, some single and others conglomerated: other places present to view, strata of heterogenous matter, lying between the upper loamy stratum and the bed of black saline earth, consisting of various kinds of sea shells, some whole, others broken to pieces, and even pulverized, which fill up the cavities of the entire shells, and the interstices betwixt them: at other places we observe, two or three feet below the surface or virgin mold, a stratum of four, five or six feet in depth, of brownish marle, on a bed of testaceous rocks; a petrefaction composed apparently of various kinds of sea shells, belemnites, sand, &c. combined or united with a calcarious cement: these masses of rocks are in some places detached by veins and strata of a heterogenous earth, consisting of sea shells and other marine productions, as well as terrestrial, which seem to be fossile or in some degree of petrifaction, or otherwise transmuted, particularly those curious productions called birds bills or sharks teeth (dentes carchariae) belemnites, &c. loosely mixed with a desicated earth composed of sand, clay, particles of marle, vegetable rubbish, &c. And again we observe shells, marcasites, belemnites, dentes carchariae, with pieces of wood transmuted, black and hard as sea coal, singly interspersed in the black vitriolic strata of earth; when this black earth is exposed to the sun and dry air, the little thin laminae separate, and soon discover a fine, white chrystallization, or alluminous powder, but this very soon disappears, being again incorporated with the general mass, which gradually dissolves or falls like quick–lime, and appears then a greyish, extremely fine, dry miceous powder, which smells like gun–powder.

Travels Through North and South Carolina

THE North West of Cape Fear, here at Ashwood, is near three hundred yards over (when the stream is low and within its banks) and is eighty or ninety miles above the capes. Observed growing hereabouts a great variety of very curious and beautiful flowering and sweet scented shrubs, particularly Callicarpa, Æsculus pavia, floribus coccineis, caule suffructicoso, Æsculus sylvatica, floribus ex albo et carneo eleganter variegatis, caule arboreo, Ptelea trifoliata, Styrax, Stewartia, Fothergilla, Amorpha, Myrica, Stillingia fructicosa, foliis lanciolatis, utrinque glabris, fructu tricocco. Olea Americana, foliis lanciolato ellipticis, baceis atro–purpureis (Purple berried bay.) Catesby. Ilex dahoon, Cassine Yapon, Azalea, varieties, Kalmea, Cyrilla, Liquid amber peregrinum, Sideroxilon, Andromeda lucida, &c.

LEAVING Ashwood, and continuing up the West side of the river, about forty miles, in the banks of a creek, five or six feet below the sandy surface, are to be seen projecting out many feet in length, trunks of trees petrified to very hard stone; they lie between the upper sandy stratum and the common bed of blackish vitriolic earth; and these stone trees are to be seen in the same situation, sticking out of the perpendicular banks or bluffs of the river in this region: there are several trunks of large trees with their bark, stumps of their limbs and roots, lying petrified on the sand hills and Pine forests, near the road about this creek, not far from the saw–mills.

crossed Rock–fish, a large branch of the North West, near its mouth or confluence, and at evening arrived at Cross–Creeks, another very considerable branch of the river, flowing in through its West banks: this creek gave name to a fine inland trading town, on some heights or swelling hills, from whence the creek descends precipitately, then gently meanders near a mile, through lower level lands, to its confluence with the river, affording most convenient mill–seats; these prospects induced active, enterprising men to avail themselves of such advantages pointed out to them by nature, they built mills, which drew people to the place, and these observing elegible situations for other profitable improvements, bought lots and erected tenements, where they exercised mechanic arts, as smiths, wheelwrights, carpenters, coopers, tanners, &c. And at length merchants were encouraged to adventure and settle; in short, within eight or ten years from a grist–mill, saw–mill, smith–shop and a tavern, arose a flourishing commercial town, the seat of government of the county of Cumberland: the leading men of the county, seeing plainly the superior advantages of this situation, on the banks of a famous navigable river, petitioned the Assembly for a charter to empower them to purchase a district, sufficient for founding a large town, which being granted, they immeiately proceeded to mark out its precincts, and named the new city Cambelton, a compliment to—— Cambel, Esq. a gentleman of merit, and a citizen of the county. When I was here about twenty years ago, this town was marking out its bounds, and there were then about twenty habitations, and now there are above a thousand houses, many wealthy merchants, and respectable public buildings, a vast resort of inhabitants and travellers, and continual brisk commerce by waggons, from the back settlements, with large trading boats, to and from Wilmington, the seaport and flourishing trading town on the Clarendon, about forty miles above the capes, which is about one hundred miles below this town. The Clarendon or Cape Fear river has its source in the Cherokee mountains, where its numerous confederate streams unite, after leaving the first ridges of the mountains, it assumes the name of Haw river, and coursing the hilly fertile country, above one hundred and fifty miles, receives through its West banks the West branch, called Deep river, and after this union, takes the name of the North–West of Cape Fear, from whence down to Cambelton, about eighty miles, it is navigable for perriauguas of considerable burthen.

OBSERVED near Cambelton a very curious scandent Fern (Pteris scandens) rambling over low bushes, in humid situations, the lower larger fronds were digitated, or rather radiated, but towards the tops or extremities of the branches they became trifid, hastated, and lastly lanciolate; it is a delicate plant, of a yellowish lively green, and would be an ornament in a garden.

SAT off again to Cambelton, continuing yet up the North West about sixty miles, crossed over this branch, and soon after crossed the Roanoke, and then rested a few days at Mr. Lucas', a worthy old gentleman, a planter on Meherren river. Observed strolling over his fences and stables, a very singular and useful species of the Gourd (Cucurbita laginaria) their necks or handles are above two feet in length, and not above an inch in diameter; their bellies round, which would contain about a pint; they make excellent ladles, funnels, &c. At a little distance from Mr. Lucas', at the head of a swamp near the high road, I observed a very curious species of Prinos, which grows seven or eight feet high, the leaves broad, lanciolate, sharply serrated, nervous, and of a deep green colour; but its striking beauty consists in profuse clusters of fruit, collected about the cases or origin of the last spring's shoots; these berries are nearly round, about the size of middling grapes, of a fine clear scarlet colour, covered or invested with an incarnate mist or nebulae.

BEING now arrived on the South border of Virginia, and the hoary frigid season far advanced, I shall pass as speedily as possible from hence to Pennsylvania, my native

319

country; since those cultivated regions of Virginia and Maryland, through which I design to travel, have been over and over explored, and described by very able men in every branch of natural history.

AFTER leaving Meherren, I soon arrived at Alexandria in Virginia, a fine city on the West banks of the Patowmac, about the 26th of December, having had excellent roads, and pleasant, moderate weather, neither snow nor ice to be seen, except a slight fall of snow from a flying cloud, the day before I reached this place, but this evening it clouding up from the West, the wind North–East and cold. Next morning the snow was eight or ten inches deep on the ground, and the wind shifting to North–West, cleared up intensely cold; I however sat off and crossed the river just below the falls, and landed at George–town in Maryland. The snow is now deep every where around, the air cold to an extreme, and the roads deep under snow or slippery with ice, rendered the travelling uncomfortable.

BEING now arrived at Wright's ferry on the Susquehanna, I began anxiously to look towards home, but here I found almost insuperable embarrassments; the river being but half frozen over, there was no possibility of crossing here, but hearing that people crossed at Anderson's, about five miles above, early next morning I sat off again up the river, in company with several travellers, some for Philadelphia; arriving at the ferry, we were joined by a number of traders, with their pack–horses loaded with leather and furrs, where we all agreed to venture over together, and keeping at a moderate distance from each other, examining well our icy bridge, and being careful of our steps, we landed safe on the opposite shore, got to Lancaster in the evening, and next morning sat forward again towards Philadelphia, and in two days more arrived at my father's house on the banks of the river Schuylkill, within four miles of the city, January 1778.

AN
ACCOUNT
OF THE
PERSONS, MANNERS, CUSTOMS
AND
GOVERNMENT
OF THE

MUSCOGULGES OR CREEKS, CHEROKEES, CHACTAWS, &c. *ABORIGINES OF THE CONTINENT OF NORTH AMERICA.*

BY

WILLIAM BARTRAM.

PHILADELPHIA: PRINTED BY *JAMES & JOHNSON* M,DCC,XCI.

PART IV.

CHAP. I.

DESCRIPTION OF THE CHARACTER, CUSTOMS AND PERSONS OF THE AMERICAN ABORIGINES, FROM MY OWN OBSERVATIONS, AS WELL AS FROM THE GENERAL AND IMPARTIAL REPORT OF ANCIENT, RESPECTABLE MEN, EITHER OF THEIR OWN PEOPLE, OR WHITE TRADERS, WHO HAVE SPENT MANY DAYS OF THEIR LIVES AMONGST THEM.

PERSONS AND QUALIFICATIONS.

THE males of the Cherokees, Muscogulges, Siminoles, Chicasaws, Chactaws and confederate tribes of the Creeks, are tall, erect, and moderately robust, their limbs well shaped, so as generally to form a perfect human figure; their features regular, and countenance open, dignified and placid; yet the forehead and brow so formed, as to strike you instantly with heroism and bravery; the eye though rather small, yet active and full of fire; the pupil always black, and the nose commonly inclining to the aquiline.

THEIR countenance and actions exhibit an air of magnanimity, superiority and independence.

THEIR complexion of a reddish brown or copper colour; their hair long, lank, coarse and black as a raven, and reflecting the like lustre at different exposures to the light.

THE women of the Cherokees are tall, slender, erect and of a delicate frame, their features formed with perfect symetry, their countenance cheerful and friendly, and they move with a becoming grace and dignity.

THE Muscogulge women, though remarkably short of stature, are well formed; their visage round, features regular and beautiful; the brow high and arched; the eye large, black and languishing, expressive of modesty, difidence, and bashfulness; these charms are their defensive and offensive weapons, and they know very well how to play them off. And under cover of these alluring graces, are concealed the most subtile artifice; they are however loving and affectionate: they are I believe the smallest race of women yet known, seldom above five feet high, and I believe the greater number never arrive to that stature: their hands and feet not larger than those of Europeans of nine or ten years of age; yet the men are of gigantic stature, a full size larger than Europeans; many of them above six feet, and few under that, or five feet eight or ten inches. Their complexion much darker than any of the tribes to the North of them, that I have seen. This description will I believe comprehend the Muscogulges, their confederates, the Chactaws, and I believe the Chicasaws (though I have never seen their women) excepting however some bands of the Siminoles, Uches and Savannucas, who are rather taller and slenderer, and their complexion brighter

THE Cherokees are yet taller and more robust than the Muscogulges, and by far the largest race of men I have seen

* There are however, some exceptions to this general observation, as I have myself witnessed. Their pre cut grand chief or emperor (the Little Carpenter, Atta–kul–kulla) is a man of remarkable small stature, slender, and delicate frame, the only instance I saw in the nation: but he is a man of superior abilities.

their complexions brighter and somewhat of the olive cast, especially the adults; and some of their young women are nearly as fair and blooming as European women.

Travels Through North and South Carolina

THE Cherokees in their dispositions and manners are grave and steady; dignified and circumspect in their deportment; rather slow and reserved in conversation; yet frank, cheerful and humane; tenacious of the liberties and natural nights of men; secret, deliberate and determined in their councils; honest, just and liberal, and are ready always to sacrifice every pleasure and gratification, even their blood, and life itself, to defend their territory and maintain their rights. They do homage to the Muscogulges with reluctance, and are impatient under that galling yoke. I was witness to a most humiliating lash, which they passively received from their red masters, at the great congress and treaty of Augusta, when these people acceded with the Creeks, to the cession of the New Purchase; where were about three hundred of the Creeks, a great part of whom were warriors, and about one hundred Cherokees.

THE first day of convention opened with settling the preliminaries, one article of which was a demand on the part of the Georgians, to a territory lying on the Tugilo, and claimed by them both, which it seems the Cherokees had, previous to the opening of congress, privately conveyed to the Georgian, unknown to the Creeks, which the Georgians mentioning as a matter settled, the Creeks demanded in council, on what foundation they built that claim, saying they had never ceded these lands. The Georgians answered, that they bought them of their friends and brothers the Cherokees. The Creeks nettled and incensed at this, a chief and warrior started up, and with an agitated and terrific countenance, frowning menaces and disdain, fixed his eyes on the Cherokee chiefs, asked them what right they had to give away their lands, calling them old women, and saying that they had long ago obliged them to wear the petticoat; a most humiliating and degrading stroke, in the presence of the chiefs of the whole Muscogulge confederacy, of the Chicasaws, principle men and citizens of Georgia, Carolina, Virginia, Maryland and Pennsylvania, in the face of their own chiefs and citizens, and amidst the laugh and jeers of the assembly, especially the young men of Virginia, their old enemy and dreaded neighbour: but humiliating as it really was, they were obliged to bear the stigma passively, and even without a reply.

AND moreover, these arrogant bravos and usurpers, carried their pride and importance to such lengths, as even to threaten to dissolve the congress and retun home, unless the Georgians consented to annul the secret treaty with the Cherokees, and receive that territory immediately from them; as acknowledging their exclusive right of alienation, which was complied with, though violently extorted from the Cherokees, contrary to right and sanction of treaties; since the Savanna river and its waters were acknowledged

323

to be the natural and just bounds of territory betwixt the Cherokees and Muscogulges.

THE national character of the Muscogulges, when considered in a political view, exhibits a portraiture of a great or illustrious heroe. A proud, haughty and arrogant race of men; they are however, brave and valiant in war, ambitious of conquest, restless and perpetually exercising their arms, yet magnanimous and merciful to a vanquished enemy, when he submits and seeks their friendship and protection: always uniting the vanquished tribes in confederacy with them; when they immediately enjoy, unexceptionably, every right of free citizens, and are from that moment united in one common band of brotherhood: they were never known to exterminate a tribe, except the Yamasees, who would never submit on any terms, but fought it out to the last, only about forty or fifty of them escaping at the last decisive battle, who threw themselves under the protection of the Spaniards at St. Augustine.

ACCORDING to their own account, which I believe to be true, after their arrival in this country, they joined in alliance and perpetual amity, with the British colonists of South Carolina and Georgia, which they never openly violated; but on the contrary, pursued every step to strengthen the alliance; and their aged chiefs to this day, speak of it with tears of joy, and exult in that memorable transaction, as one of the most glorious events in the annals of their nation.

As an instance of their ideas of political impartial justice, and homage to the Supreme Being, as the high arbiter of human transactions, who alone claims the right of taking away the life of man: I beg leave to offer to the reader's consideration, the following event, as I had it from the mouth of a Spaniard, a respectable inhabitant of East Florida.

THE son of the Spanish governor of St. Augustine, together with two young gentlemen, his friends and associates, conceived a design of amusing themselves in a party of sport, at hunting and fishing. Having provided themselves with a convenient bark, ammunition, fishing tackle, &c. they sat sail, directing their course South, along the coast towards the point of Florida, putting into bays and rivers, as conveniency and the prospect of game invited them; the pleasing rural, and diversified scenes of the Florida coast, imperceptibly allured them far to the south, beyond the Spanish fortified post. Unfortunate youth! regardless of the advice and injunctions of their parents and friends, still pursuing the delusive objects, they enter a harbour at evening, with a view of chasing the roe–buck, and hunting up the sturdy bear, solacing themselves with delicious fruits, and reposing under aromatic shades, when alas! cruel unexpected event, in the beatific moments of their slumbers, they are surrounded, arrested and carried off by a predatory band of Creek Indians, proud of the capture, so rich a prize; they hurry away into cruel bondage the hapless youth, conducting them, by devious paths through dreary swamps and boundless savannas, to the Nation.

AT that time the Indians were at furious war with the Spaniards, scarcely any bounds set to their cruelties on either side: in short, the miserable youth were condemned to be burnt.

BUT, there being English traders in these towns, who learning the character of the captives, and expecting great rewards from the Spanish governor, if they could deliver them; they petitioned the Indians on their behalf, expressing their wishes to obtain their rescue, offering a great ransom, acquainting them at the same time, that they were young men of high rank, and one of them the governor's son.

UPON this, the head men, or chiefs of the whole nation, were convened, and after solemn and mature deliberation, they returned the traders their final answer and determination, which was as follows.

"BROTHERS and friends. We have been considering upon this business concerning the captives.—And that, under the eye and fear of the Great Spirit. You know that these people are our cruel enemies, they save no lives of us red men, who fall in their power. You say that the youth is the son of the Spanish governor, we believe it, we are sorry he has fallen into our hands, but he is our enemy; the two young men (his friends) are equally our enemies, we are sorry to see them here: but we know no difference in their flesh and blood; they are equally our enemies, if we save one we must save all three; but we cannot do it, the red men require their blood to appease the spirits of their slain relatives; they have entrusted us with the guardianship of our laws and rights, we cannot betray them.

HOWEVER we have a sacred prescription relative to this affair; which allows us to extend mercy to a certain degree: a third is saved by lot; the Great Spirit allows us to put it to that decision; he is no respecter of persons." The lots are cast. The governor's son was taken and burnt.

Travels Through North and South Carolina

IF we consider them with respect to their private character or in a moral view, they must, I think, claim our approbation, if we divest ourselves of prejudice and think freely. As moral men they certainly stand in no need of European civilization.

THEY are just, honest, liberal and hospitable to strangers; considerate, loving and affectionate to their wives and relations; fond of their children; industrious, frugal, temperate and persevering; charitable and forbearing. I have been weeks and months amongst them and in their towns, and never observed the least sign of contention or wrangling: never saw an instance of an Indian beating his wife, or even reproving her in anger. In this case they stand as examples of reproof to the most civilized nations, as not being defective in justice, gratitude and a good understanding; for indeed their wives merit their esteem and the most gentle treatment, they being industrious, frugal, careful, loving and affectionate.

THE Muscogulges are more volatile, sprightly and talkative than their Northern neighbours, the Cherokees; and, though far more distant from the white settlements than any nation East of the Mississipi or Ohio, appear evidently to have made greater advances towards the refinements of true civilization, which cannot, in the least degree, be attributed to the good examples of the white people.

THEIR internal police and family economy is what at once engages the notice of European travellers, and incontrovertibly places these people in an illustrious point of view; their liberality, intimacy and friendly intercourse one with another, without any restraint of ceremonious formality, as if they were even insensible of the use or necessity of associating the passions or affections of avarice, ambition or covetousness.

A MAN goes forth on his business or avocations, he calls in at another town, if he wants victuals, rest or—social conversation, he confidently approaches the door of the first house he chooses, saying "I am come;" the good man or woman replies, "You are; its well." Immediately victuals and drink are ready; he eats and drinks a little, then smokes Tobacco, and converses either of private matters, public talks or the news of the town. He rises and says, "I go;" the other answers, "You do!" He then proceeds again, and steps in at the next habitation he likes, or repairs to the public square, where are people always conversing by day, or dancing all night, or to some more private assembly, as he likes; he needs no one to introduce him, any more than the black–bird or thrush, when he repairs to the fruitful groves, to regale on their luxuries, and entertain the fond female with evening songs.

IT is astonishing, though a fact, as well as a sharp reproof to the white people, if they will allow themselves liberty to reflect and form a just estimate, and I must own elevates these people to the first rank amongst mankind, that they have been able to resist the continual efforts of the complicated host of vices, that have for ages overrun the nations of the old world, and so contaminated their morals; yet more so, since such vast armies of these evil spirits have invaded this continent, and closely invested them on all sides. Astonishing indeed! when we behold the ill, immoral conduct of too many white people, who reside amongst them: notwithstanding it seems natural, eligible and even easy for these simple, illiterate people, to put in practice those beautiful lectures delivered to us by the ancient sages and philosophers, and recorded for our instruction.

I SAW a young Indian in the Nation, who when present, and beholding the scenes of mad intemperance and folly acted by the white men in the town, clap his hand to his breast, and with a smile, looking aloft as if struck with astonishment, and wrapt in love and adoration to the Deity, as who should say, O thou Great and Good Spirit, we are indeed sensible of thy benignity and favour to us red men, in denying us the understanding of white men. We did not know before they came amongst us that makind could become so base, and fall so below the dignity of their nature. Defend us from their manners, laws and power.

THE Muscogulges, with their confederates, the Chactaws, Chicasaws, and perhaps the Cherokees, eminently deserve the encomium of all nations, for their wisdom and virtue in resisting and even repeling the greatest, and even the common enemy of mankind, at least of most of the European nations, I mean spirituous liquors.

THE first and most cogent article in all their treaties with the white people, is, that there shall not be any kind of spirituous liquors sold or brought into their towns; and the traders are allowed but two kegs (five gallons each) which is supposed to be sufficient for a company, to serve them on the road, and if any of this remains on their approaching the towns, they must spill it on the ground or secrete it on the road, for it must not come into the town.

ON my journey from Mobile to the Nation, just after we had passed the junction of the Pensacola road with our path, two young traders overtook us on their way to the Nation.

327

We enquired what news? They informed us that they were running about forty kegs of Jamaica spirits (which by dashing would have made at least eighty kegs) to the Nation; and after having left the town three or four days, they were surprised on the road in the evening, just after they had come to camp, by a party of Creeks, who discovering their species of merchandize, they forthwith struck their tomahawks into every keg, giving the liquor to the thirsty sand, not tasting a drop of it themselves, and they had enough to do to keep the tomahawks from their own skulls.

HOW are we to account for their excellent policy in civil government: it cannot derive its influence from coercive laws, for they have no such artificial system. Divine wisdom dictates and they obey.

WE see and know full well the direful effect of this torrent of evil, which has its source in hell, and we know surely, as well as these savages, how to divert its course and suppress its inundations. Do we want wisdom and virtue? let our youth then repair to the venerable councils of the Muscogulges.

CHAP. II. OF THEIR GOVERNMENT AND CIVIL SOCIETY.

THE constitution or system of their police is simply natural, and as little complicated as that which is supposed to direct or rule the approved economy of the ant and the bee, and seems to be nothing more than the simple dictates of natural reason, plain to every one, yet recommended to them by their wife and virtuous elders as divine, because necessary for securing mutual happiness: equally binding and effectual, as being proposed and assented to in the general combination: every one's conscience being a sufficient conviction (the golden rule, do as you would be done by) instantly presents to view, and produces a society of peace and love, which in effect better maintains human happiness, than the most complicated system of modern politics, or sumptuary laws, enforced by coercive means: for here the people are all on an equality, as to the possession and enjoyments of the common necessaries and conveniencies of life, for luxuries and superfluities they have none.

THIS natural constitution is simply subordinate, and the supreme, sovereign or executive power resides in a council of elderly chiefs, warriors and others, respectable for wisdom, valour and virtue.

Travels Through North and South Carolina

AT the head of this venerable senate, presides their mico or king, which signifies a magistrate or chief ruler: the governors of Carolina, Georgia, &c. are called mico; and the king of England is called Ant–apala–mico–clucco

* Clucco signifies great or excellent

that is the great king, over or beyond the great water.

THE king although he is acknowledged to be the first and greatest man in the town or tribe, and honoured with every due and rational mark of love and esteem, and when presiding in council, with a humility and homage as reverent as that paid to the most despotic monarch in Europe or the East, and when absent, his seat is not filled by any other person, yet he is not dreaded, and when out of the council, he associates with the people as a common man, converses with them, and they with him in perfect ease and familiarity.

THE mico or king, though elective, yet his advancement to that supreme dignity must be understood in a very different light from the elective monarchs of the old world, where the progress to magistracy is generally affected by schism and the influence of friends gained by craft, bribery and often by more violent efforts; and after the throne is obtained, by measures little better than usurpation, he must be protected and supported there, by the same base means that carried him thither.

BUT here behold the majesty of the Muscogulge mico, he does not either publicly or privately beg of the people to place him in a situation to command and rule them. No, his appearance is altogether mysterious, as a benificent deity he rises king over them, as the sun rises to bless the earth!

No one will tell you how or when he became their king; but he is universally acknowledged to be the greatest person among them, and he is loved, esteemed and reverenced, although he associates, eats, drinks and dances with them in common as another man, his dress is the same, and a stranger could not distinguish the king's habitation, from that of any other citizen by any sort of splendor or magnificence: yet he percieves they act as though their mico beheld them though invisible. In a word, their mico seems to them, the representative of Providence or the Great Spirit, whom they

329

acknowledge to preside over and influence their councils and public proceedings. He personally presides daily in their councils, either at the rotunda or public square: and even here his voice in regard to business in hand, is regarded no more, than any other chief or senator's, any other than in his advice as being the best and wisest man of the tribe, and not by virtue of regal prerogative. But whether their ultimate decisions require unanimity, or only a majority of voices, I am uncertain, but probably where there is a majority, the minority voluntarily accede.

THE most active part the mico acts, is in the civil government of the town or tribe, here he has the power and prerogative of calling a council, to deliberate on peace and war, or all public concerns, as enquiring into, and deciding upon complaints and differences, but he has not the least shadow of exclusive executive power. He is complimented with the first visits of strangers, giving audience to ambassadors, with presents, and he has also the disposal of the public granary.

THE next man in order of dignity and power, is the great war chief, he represents and exercises the dignity of the mico, in his absence in council; his voice is of the greatest weight, in military affairs: his power and authority are entirely independent of the mico, though when a mico goes on an expedition, he heads the army, and is there the war chief: there are many of these war chiefs in a town or tribe, who are captains or leaders of military parties; they are elderly men, who in their youthful days, have distinguished themselves in war by valour, subtilty and intrepidity: and these veteran chiefs, in a great degree, constitute their truly dignified and venerable senates.

THERE is in every town or tribe a high priest, usually called by the white people jugglers, or conjurers, besides several juniors or graduates. But the ancient high priest or seer, presides in spiritual affairs, and is a person of consequence; he maintains and exercises great influence in the state; particularly in military affairs, the senate never determine on an expedition against their enemy without his counsel and assistance. These people generally believe that their seer has communion with powerful invisible spirits, who they suppose have a share in the rule and government of human affairs, as well as the elements; that he can predict the result of an expedition, and his influence is so great, that they have been known frequently to stop, and turn back an army, when within a days journey of their enemy, after a march of several hundred miles, and indeed their predictions have surprized many people. They foretel rain or drougth, and pretend to bring rain at pleasure, cure diseases, and exercise witchcraft, invoke or expel evil spirits,

Travels Through North and South Carolina

and even assume the power of directing thunder and lightning.

THESE Indians are by no means idolaters, unless their puffing the Tobacco smoke towards the sun, and rejoicing at the appearance of the new moon,

* I have observed the young fellows very merry and jocose, at the appearance of the new moon, saying, how ashamed she looks under the veil, since, sleeping with the sun these two or three nights, she is ashamed to shew her face, &c

may be termed so, so far from idolatry are they, that they have no images amongst them, nor any religious rite or ceremony that I could perceive; but adore the Great Spirit, the giver and taker away of the breath of life, with the most profound and respectful homage. They believe in a future state, where the spirit exists, which they call the world of spirits, where they enjoy different degrees of tranquility or comforts, agreeable to their life spent here: a person who in this life has been an industrious hunter, provided well for his family, an intrepid and active warrior, just, upright, and done all the good he could, will, they say, in the world of spirits, live in a warm, pleasant country, where are expansive, green, flowery savannas and high forests, watered with rivers of pure waters, replenished with deer, and every species of game; a serene, unclouded and peaceful sky; in short, where there is fulness of pleasure, uninterrupted.

THEY have many accounts of trances and visions of their people, who have been supposed to be dead, but afterwards reviving have related their visions, which tend to enforce the practice of virtue and the moral duties.

BEFORE I went amongst the Indians I had often heard it reported that these people, when their parents, through extreme old age, become decrepid and helpless, in compassion for their miseries, send them to the other world, by a stroke of the tomahawk or bullet. Such a degree of depravity and species of impiety always appeared to me so incredibly inhuman and horrid, it was with the utmost difficulty that I assumed resolution sufficient to enquire into it.

THE traders assured me they knew no instance of such barbarism, but that there had been instances of the communities performing such a deed at the earnest request of the victim.

331

Travels Through North and South Carolina

WHEN I was at Mucclasse town, early one morning, at the invitation of the chief trader, we repaired to the public square, taking with us some presents for the Indian chiefs. On our arrival we took our seats in a circle of venerable men, round a fire in the centre of the area; other citizens were continually coming in, and amongst them I was struck with awe and veneration at the appearance of a very aged man; his hair, what little he had, was as white as snow, he was conducted by three young men, one having hold of each arm, and the third behind to steady him. On his approach the whole circle saluted him, "welcome," and made way for him: he looked as smiling and cheerful as youth, yet stone–blind by extreme old age; he was the most ancient chief of the town, and they all seemed to reverence him. Soon after the old man had seated himself I distributed my presents, giving him a very fine handkerchief and a twist of choice Tobacco; which passed through the hands of an elderly chief who sat next to him, telling him it was a present from one of their white brothers, lately arrived in the nation from Charleston: he received the present with a smile, and thanked me, returning the favour immediately with his own stone pipe and cat skin of Tobacco, and then complimented me with a long oration, the purport of which was the value he set on the friendship of the Carolinians: he said, that when he was a young man they had no iron hatchets, pots, hoes, knives, razors nor guns, but that they then made use of their own stone axes, clay pots, flint knives, bows and arrows; and that he was the first man who brought the white peoples goods into his town, which he did on his back from Charleston, five hundred miles on foot, for they had no horses then amongst them.

THE trader then related to me an anecdote concerning this ancient patriarch, which occurred not long since.

ONE morning after his attendants had led him to the council fire, before seating himself he addressed himself to the people after this manner—

"YOU yet love me; what can I do now to merit your regard? nothing; I am good for nothing; I cannot see to shoot the buck or hunt up the sturdy bear; I know I am but a burthen to you; I have lived long enough; now let my spirit go; I want to see the warriors of my youth in the country of spirits; (bareing his breast) here is the hatchet, take it and strike." They answered with one united voice, "We will not; we cannot; we want you here."

CHAP. III.
OF THEIR DRESS, FEASTS AND DIVERTISEMENTS.

THE youth of both sexes are fond of decorating themselves with external ornaments. The men shave their head, leaving only a narrow crest or comb, beginning at the crown of the head, where it is about two inches broad and about the same height, and stands frized upright; but this crest tending backwards, gradually widens, covering the hinder part of the head and back of the neck; this lank hair behind is ornamented with pendant silver quills, and then jointed or articulated silver plates, and usually the middle fascicle of hair, which being by far the longest, is wrapped in a large quill of silver, or the joint of a small reed, curiously sculptured and painted, the hair continuing through it terminates in a tail or tossil.

THEIR ears are lacerated, separating the border or cartilagenous limb, which at first is bound round very close and tight with leather strings or thongs, and anointed with fresh bear's oil, until healed; the weight of the lead, extends this cartilage an incredible length, which afterwards being craped, or bound round in brass or silver wire, extends it semicircularly like a bow or crescent; and it is then very elastic, even so as to spring and bound about with the least motion or flexure of the body; this is decorated with soft white plumes of heron feathers.

A VERY curious diadem or band, about four inches broad, and ingeniously wrought or woven, and curiously decorated with stones, beads, wampum, porcupine quills, &c. encircles their temples, the front peak of which is embellished with a high waving plume, of crane or heron feathers.

THE cloathing of their body is very simple and frugal. Sometimes a ruffled shirt of fine linen, next the skin, and a flap, which covers their lower parts, this garment somewhat resembles the ancient Roman breeches, or the kelt of the Highlanders; it usually consists of a piece of blue cloth, about eighteen inches wide, this they pass between their thighs, and both ends being taken up and drawn through a belt round their waist, the ends fall down, one before, and the other behind, not quite to the knee; this flap is usually plaited and indented at the ends, and ornamented with beads, tinsel lace, &c.

THE leg is furnished with cloth boots; they reach from the ancle to the calf, and are ornamented with lace, beads, silver bells, &c.

AND the stillepica or moccasin defends and adorns the feet; they seem to be an imitation of the ancient buskin or sandal; these are very ingeniously made of deer skins, dressed very soft, and curiously ornamented according to fancy.

BESIDE this attire, they have a large mantle of the finest cloth they are able to purchase, always either of scarlet or blue colour; this mantle is fancifully decorated, with rich lace or fringe round the border, and often with little round silver, or brass bells. Some have a short cloak, just large enough to cover the shoulders and breast; this is most ingeniously constructed, of feathers woven or placed in a natural imbricated manner, usually of the scarlet feathers of the flaningo, or others of the gayest colour.

THEY have large silver crescents, or gorgets, which being suspended by a ribband round the neck, lie upon the breast: and the arms are ornamented with silver bands, or bracelets, and silver and gold chains, &c. a collar invests the neck.

THE head, neck and breast, are painted with vermilion, and some of the warriors have the skin of the breast, and muscular parts of the body, very curiously inscribed, or adorned with hieroglyphick scroles, flowers, figures of animals, stars, crescents, and the sun in the centre of the breast. This painting of the flesh, I understand, is performed in their youth, by picking the skin with a needle, until the blood starts, and rubbing in a blueish tinct, which is as permanent as their life. The shirt hangs loose about the waist, like a frock, or split down before, resembling a gown, which is sometimes wrapped close, and the waist encircled by a curious belt or sash.

THE dress of the females is somewhat different from that of the men; their flap or petticoat, is made after a different manner, is larger and longer, reaching almost to the middle of the leg, and is put on differently; they have no shirt or shift but a little short waistcoat, usually made of callico, printed linen, or fine cloth, decorated with lace, beads, &c. They never wear boots or stockings, but their buskins reach to the middle of the leg. They never cut their hair, but plait it in wreathes, which is turned up, and fastened on the crown, with a silver broach, forming a wreathed top–knot, decorated with an incredibly quantity of silk ribbands, of various colours, which stream down on every side, almost to the ground. They never paint, except those of a particular class, when disposed to grant certain favours to the other sex.

BUT these decorations are only to be considered as indulgencies on particular occasions, and the privilege of youth; as at weddings, festivals, dances, &c. or when the men assemble to act the war farce, on the evening immediately preceding their march on a hostile expedition; for usually they are almost naked, contenting themselves with the flap and sometimes a shirt, boots and moccasins; the mantle is seldom worn by the men, except at night, in the winter season, when extremely cold, and by the women at dances, which serves the purpose of a veil, and the females always wear the jacket, flap, and buskin, even children as soon or before they can walk, whereas the male youth go perfectly naked until they are twelve or fifteen years of age.

THE junior priests or students, constantly wear the mantle or robe, which is white, and they have a great owl skin cased and stuffed very ingeniously, so well executed, as almost to represent the living bird, having large sparkling glass beads, or buttons fixed in the head for eyes: this insignia of wisdom and divination, they wear sometimes as a crest on the top of the head, at other times the image sits on the arm, or is borne on the hand. These bachelors are also distinguishable from the other people, by their taciturnity, grave and solemn countenance, dignified step, and singing to themselves songs or hymns, in a low sweet voice, as they stroll about the towns.

THESE people like all other nations, are fond of music and dancing: their music is both vocal and instrumental; but of the latter they have scarcely any thing worth the name, the tambour, rattlegourd, and a kind of flute, made of a joint of reed or the tibia of the deers leg: on this instrument they perform badly, and at best it is rather a hideous melancholy discord, than harmony; it is only young fellows who amuse themselves on this howling instrument, but the tambour and rattle, accompanied with their sweet low voices, produces a pathetic harmony, keeping exact time together, and the countenance of the musician, at proper times, seems to express the solemn elevated state of the mind; at that time there seems not only a harmony between him and his instrument, but instantly touches the feelings of the attentive audience, as the influence of an active and powerful spirit; there is then an united universal sensation of delight and peaceful union of souls throughout the assembly.

THEIR music, vocal and instrumental, united, keeps exact time with the performers or dancers.

Travels Through North and South Carolina

THEY have an endless variety of steps, but the most common, and that which I term the most civil, and indeed the most admired and practiced amongst themselves, is a slow shuffling alternate step; both feet move forward one after the other, first the right foot foremost, and next the left, moving one after the other, in two opposite circles, i. e. first a circle of young men, and within a circle of young women moving together opposite ways, the men with the course of the sun, and the females contrary to it, the men strike their arm with the open hand, and the girls clap hands, and raise their shrill sweet voices, answering an elevated shout of the men at stated times of termination of the stanzas; and the girls perform an interlude or chorus separately.

THEY have songs to accompany their dances, of different classes, as martial, bacchanalian and amorous, which last I must confess, are extravagantly libidinous, and they have moral songs, which seem to be the most esteemed and practised, and answer the purpose of religious lectures.

SOME of their most favorite songs and dances, they have from their enemy, the Chactaw; for it seems this people are very eminent, for poetry and music; every town amongst them strives to excel each other in composing new songs for dances; and by a custom amongst them, they must have at least one new song, for exhibition, at every annual busque.

THE young mustee, who came with me to the Mucclasses from Mobile, having Chactaw blood in his veins from his mother, was a sensible young fellow, and by his father had been instructed in reading, writing and arithmetic, and could speak English very well. He took it into his head, to travel into the Chactaw country: his views were magnanimous, and his designs in the highest degree commendable, nothing less than to inform himself of every species of arts and sciences, that might be of use and advantage, when introduced into his own country, but more particularly music and poetry: with these views he privately left the Nation, went to Mobile, and there entered into the service of the trading company to the Chactaws, as a white man; his easy, communicative, active and familiar disposition and manners, being agreeable to that people, procured him access every where, and favored his subtilty and artifice: at length, however, the Chactaws hearing of his lineage and consanguinity with the Creeks, by the father's side, pronounced him a Creek, and consequently an enemy and a spy amongst them, and secretly resolved to dispatch him. The young philosopher got notice of their suspicions, and hostile intentions, in time to make his escape, though closely pursued, he however kept a head of his sanguinary pursuers, arrived at Mobile, and threw himself under the protection of the

336

English, entered the service of the trader of Mucclasse, who was then setting off for the Nation, and notwithstanding the speed with which we travelled, narrowly escaped the ardor and vigilance of his pursuing enemies, who surprised a company of emigrants, in the desarts of Schambe, the very night after we met them, expecting to intercept him thereabout.

THE young traveller, having learned all their most celebrated new songs and poetry, at a great dance and festival in the Mucclasse, a day or two after our arrival; the youth pressed him, to give out some of his new songs, he complied with their entreaties, and the songs and dance went round with harmony and eclat; their being a young Chactaw slave girl in the circle, who soon after, discovered very affecting sensations of affliction and distress of mind, and before the conclusion of the dance, many of her companions complimented her with sympathetic sighs and tears, from their own sparkling eyes. As soon as I had an opportunity, I enquired of the young Orpheus, the cause of that song being so distressing to the young slave. He replied, that when she was lately taken captive, her father and brothers were slain in the contest, and she understanding the sense of the song, called to remembrance the tragical sate of her family, and could not forbear weeping at the recital.

The meaning of the chorus was,

> All men must surely die,
> Tho' no one knows how soon,
> Yet when the time shall come,
> The event may be joyful.

THESE doleful moral songs or elegies, have a quick and sensible effect on their passions, and discover a lively affection and sensibility; their countenance now dejected, or again, by an easy transition, becomes gently elevated, as if in solemn address or supplication, accompanied with a tremulous, sweet, lamentable voice; a stranger is for a moment lost to himself as it were, or his mind, associated with the person immediately affected, is in danger of revealing his own distress unawares.

THEY have a variety of games for exercise and pastime; some particular to the men, some to the female sex, and others wherein both sexes are engaged.

THE ball play is esteemed the most noble and manly exercise; this game is exhibited in an extensive level plain, usually contiguous to the town: the inhabitants of one town play against another, in consequence of a challenge, when the youth of both sexes are often engaged, and sometimes stake their whole substance. Here they perform amazing feats of strength and agility; the game principally consists in taking and carrying off the ball from the opposite party, after being hurled into the air, midway between two high pillars, which are the goals, and the party who bears off the ball to their pillar wins the game; each person having a racquet or hurl, which is an implement of a very curious construction, somewhat resembling a ladle or little hoop–net, with a handle near three feet in length, the hoop and handle of wood, and the neting of thongs of raw hide, or tendons of an animal.

THE foot–ball is likewise a favorite, manly diversion with them. Feasting and dancing in the square, at evening ends all their games.

THEY have besides, feasts or festivals almost for every month in the year, which are chiefly dedicated to hunting and agriculture.

THE busk or feast of first fruits is their principal festival; this seems to end the last, and begin the new year.

IT commences in August, when their new crops of Corn are arrived to perfect maturity: and every town celebrates the busk seperately, when their own harvest is ready.

IF they have any religious rite or ceremony, this festival is its most solemn celebration.

WHEN a town celebrates the busk, having previously provided themselves with new clothes, new pots, pans and other household utensils and furniture, they collect all their worn out clothes and other despicable things, sweep and cleanse their houses, squares, and the whole town, of their filth, which with all the remaining grain and other old provisions, they cast together in one common heap, and consume it with fire; after having taken medicine, and fasted for three days, all the fire in the town is extinguished; during this fast they abstain from the gratification of every appetite and passion whatever. A general amnesty is proclaimed, all malefactors may return to their town, and they are absolved from their crimes, which are now forgotten, and they restored to favor.

ON the fourth morning, the high priest, by rubbing dry wood together, produces new fire in the public square, from whence every habitation in the town is supplied with the new and pure flame.

THEN the women go forth to the harvest field, and bring from thence new Corn and fruits, which being prepared in the best manner, in various dishes, and drink withal, is brought with solemnity to the square, where the people are assembled, apparelled in their new clothes and decorations. The men having regaled themselves, the remainder is carried off and distributed amongst the families of the town. The women and children solace themselves in their separate families, and in the evening repair to the public square, where they dance, sing and rejoice during the whole night, observing a proper and exemplary decorum; this continues three days, and the four following days they receive visits, and rejoice with their friends from neighbouring towns, who have purified and prepared themselves.

CHAP. IV. CONCERNING PROPERTY, AGRICULTURE, ARTS AND MANUFACTURES.

IT has been said by historians, who have written concerning the customs and usages of the aborigines of America, that they have every thing in common, and no private property; which are terms in my opinion too vague and general, when applied to these people. From my own frequent opportunities of observation, and the information of respectable characters, who have spent many years amongst them, I venture to set this matter in a just view before my readers.

I SHALL begin with the produce of their agricultural labours.

AN Indian town is generally so situated, as to be convenient for procuring game, secure from sudden invasion, a large district of excellent arable land adjoining, or in its vicinity, if possible on an isthmus betwixt two waters, or where the doubling of a river forms a peninsula such a situation generally comprises a sufficient body of excellent land for planting Corn, Potatoes, Beans, Squash, Pumpkins, Citruls, Melons, &c. and is taken in with a small expence and trouble of fencing, to secure their crops from the invasion of predatory animals. At other times however they choose such a convenient fertile spot at some distance from their town, when circumstances will not admit of having both

339

together.

THIS is their common plantation, and the whole town plant in one vast field together, but yet the part or share of every individual family or habitation, is separated from the next adjoining, by a narrow strip, or verge of grass, or any other natural or artificial boundary.

IN the spring, the ground being already prepared, on one and the same day, early in the morning, the whole town is summoned, by the sound of a conch shell, from the mouth of the overseer, to meet at the public square, whither the people repair with their hoes and axes, and from thence proceed to their plantation, where they begin to plant, not every one in his own little district, assigned and laid out, but the whole community united, begins on one certain part of the field, where they plant on until finished, and when their rising crops are ready for dressing, and cleansing, they proceed after the same order, and so on day after day, until the crop is laid by for ripening. After the feast of the busk is over, and all the grain is ripe, the whole town again assemble, and every man carries of the fruits of his labour, from the part first allotted to him, which he deposits in his own granary; which is individually his own. But previous to their carrying off their crops from the field, there is a large crib or granary, erected in the plantation, which is called the king's crib; and to this each family carries and deposits a certain quantity, according to his ability or inclination, or none at all if he so chooses, this in appearance seems a tribute or revenue to the mico, but in fact is designed for another purpose, i.e. that of a public treasury, supplied by a few and voluntary contributions, and to which every citizen has the right of free and equal access, when his own private stores are consumed, to serve as a surplus to fly to for succour, to assist neighbouring towns, whose crops may have failed, accommodate strangers, or travellers, afford provisions or supplies, when they go forth on hostile expeditions, and for all other exigencies of the state; and this treasure is at the disposal of the king or mico; which is surely a royal attribute to have an exclusive right and ability in a community to distribute comfort and blessings to the necessitous.

As to mechanic arts or manufactures, at present they have scarcely any thing worth observation, since they are supplied with necessaries, conveniencies and even superfluities by the white traders. The men perform nothing except erecting their mean habitations, forming their canoes, stone pipes, tambour, eagles tail or standard, and some other trifling matters, for war and hunting are their principal employments. The women are more vigilant, and turn their attention to various manual employments; they make all their pottery or earthen–ware, moccasins; spin and weave the curious belts and diadems

340

for the men; fabricate lace, fringe, embroider and decorate their apparel, &c. &c.

CHAP. V. OF THEIR MARRIAGE AND FUNERAL CEREMONIES.

AS to their marriage ceremonies they are very simple, yet differ greatly in the various nations and tribes. Amongst some of the bands in the Muscogulge confederacy, I was informed the mystery is performed after the following manner. When a young man has fixed his affections, and is determined to marry, he takes a Cane or Reed, such as they stick down at the hills of their Bean vines for their support: with this (after having obtained her parents or nearest relations consent) he repairs to the habitation of his beloved, attended by his friends and associates, and in the presence of the wedding guests, he sticks his Reed down, upright in the ground, when soon after his sweet-heart comes forth with another Reed, which she sticks down by the side of his, when they are married; then they exchange Reeds, which are laid by as evidences or certificates of the marriage, which is celebrated with feasting, music and dancing: each one of their relations and friends, at the wedding, contribute something towards establishing the new family. As soon as the wedding is over, the town is convened, and the council orders or recommends a new habitation to be constructed for the accommodation of the new family; every man in the town joins in the work, which is begun and finished in a day's time.

THE greatest accomplishments to recommend a young man to his favourite maid, is to prove himself a brave warrior, and a cunning, industrious hunter.

THEY marry only for a year's time, and, according to ancient custom, at the expiration of the year they renew the marriage; but there is seldom an instance of their separating after they have children. If it should happen, the mother takes the children under her own protection, though the father is obliged to contribute towards their maintainance during their minority and the mother's widowhood.

THE Muscogulges allow of polygamy in the utmost latitude; every man takes as many wives as he chooses, but the first is queen, and the others her handmaids and associates.

Travels Through North and South Carolina

IT is common for a great man amongst them, who has already half a dozen wives, if he sees a a child of eight or nine years of age, who pleases him, and he can agree with her parents or guardians, to marry her and take her into his house at that age.

ADULTERY is always punished with cropping, which is the only corporal punishment amongst them, and death or out–lawry for murder, and infamy for less crimes, as fornication, theft, &c. which produces such repeated marks and reflections of ridicule and contempt, that generally ends in voluntary banishment; and these renegadoes and vagabonds are generally the ruffians who commit depredations and murders on the frontiers.

THE Muscogulges bury their deceased in the earth; they dig a four square deep pit under the cabin or couch which the deceased laid on, in his house, lining the grave with Cypress bark, where they place the corps in a sitting posture, as if it were alive; depositing with him his gun, tomahawk, pipe and such other matters as he had the greatest value for in his life time. His eldest wife, or the queen dowager, has the second choice of his possessions, and the remaining effects are divided amongst his other wives and children.

THE Chactaws pay their last duties and respect to the deceased in a very different manner. As soon as a person is dead, they erect a scaffold eighteen or twenty feet high, in a grove adjacent to the town, where they lay the corps, lightly covered with a mantle; here it is suffered to remain, visited and protected by the friends and relations, until the flesh becomes putrid, so as easily to part from the bones, then undertakers, who make it their business, carefully strip the flesh from the bones, wash and cleanse them, and when dry and purified by the air, having provided a curiously wrought chest or coffin, fabricated of bones and splints, they place all the bones therein; which is deposited in the bone–house, a building erected for that purpose in every town. And when this house is full a general solemn funeral takes place. When the nearest kindred or friends of the deceased, on a day appointed, repair to the bone–house, take up the respective coffins, and following one another in order of seniority, the nearest relations and connections attending their respective corps, and the multitude following after them, all as one family, with united voice of alternate Allelujah and lamentation, slowly proceeding on to the place of general interment, where they place the coffins in order, forming a pyramid*

* Some ingenious men, whom I have conversed with, have given it as their opinion, that all those pyramidal artificial hills, usually called Indian mounts were raised on this

342

occasion, and are generally sepulchres. However I am of a different opinion.

and lastly, cover all over with earth, which raises a conical hill or mount. When they return to town in order of solemn procession, concluding the day with a festival, which is called the feast of the dead.

THE Chactaws are called by the traders flats, or flat–heads, all the males having the fore and hind part of their skulls, artificially flattened, or compressed, which is effected after the following manner. As soon as the child is born, the nurse provides a cradle or wooden case, hollowed and fashioned, to receive the infant, lying prostrate on its back, and that part of the case where the head reposes, being fashioned like a brick mould. In this portable machine the little boy is fixed, a bag of sand being laid on his forehead, which by continual gentle compressure, gives the head somewhat the form of a brick from the temples upwards, and by these means they have high and lofty foreheads, sloping off backwards. These men are not so neat in the trim of their heads, as the Muscogulges are, and they are remarkably slovenly and negligent in every part of their dress; but otherwise they are said to be ingenious, sensible and virtuous men; bold and intrepid, yet quiet and peaceable, and are acknowledged by the Creeks to be brave.

THEY are supposed to be most ingenious and industrious husbandmen, having large plantations, or country farms, where they employ much of their time in agricultural improvements, after the manner of the white people; by which means their territories are more generally cultivated, and better inhabited than any other Indian republic that we know of; the number of their inhabitants is said to greatly exceed the whole Muscogulge confederacy, although their territories are not a fourth part as extensive. It appeared to me from observation, and what information I could get, that the Indians entertain rational notions of the soul's immortality, and of a future state of social existence; and accordingly, in order to inculcate morality, and promote human happiness, they applaud praiseworthy actions, as commendable and necessary for the support of civil society, and maintaining the dignity and strength of their nation or tribe, as well as securing an excellent and tranquil state and degree in the world of spirits, after their decease. And they say the Great Spirit favours all good and brave men.

CHAP. VI LANGUAGE AND MANNERS.

THE Muscogulge language is spoken throughout the confederacy, (although consisting of many nations, who have a speech peculiar to themselves) as also by their friends and allies, the Natches. The Chicasaw and Chactaw the Muscogulges say is a dialect of theirs.

THIS language is very agreeable to the ear, courteous, gentle and musical: the letter R is not sounded in one word of their language: the women in particular speak so fine and musical, as to represent the singing of birds; and when heard and not seen, one might imagine it to be the prattling of young children: the men's speech is indeed more strong and sonorous, but not harsh, and in no instance guttural, and I believe the letter R is not used to express any word, in any language of the confederacy.

THE Cherokee tongue on the contrary, is very loud, somewhat rough and very sonorous, sounding the letter R frequently, yet very agreeable and pleasant to the ear. All the Indian languages, are truly rhetorical, or figurative, assisting their speech by tropes, their hands, flexure of the head, the brow, in short, every member, naturally associate, and give their assistance to render their harrangues eloquent, persuasive and effectual.

THE pyramidal hills or artificial mounts and highways, or avenues, leading from them to artificial lakes or ponds, vast tetragon terraces, chunk yards

* Chunk yard, a term given by the white traders, to the oblong four square yards, adjoining the high mounts and rotunda of the modern Indians.—In the center of these stands the obelisk, and at each corner of the farther end stands a slave post or strong stake, where the captives that are burnt alive are bound.

and obelisks or pillars of wood, are the only monuments of labour, ingenuity and magnificence, that I have seen worthy of notice, or remark. The region lying between Savanna river and Oakmulge, East and West, and from the sea coast to the Cherokee or Apalachean mountains, North and South, is the most remarkable for their high conical hills, tetragon terraces and chunk yards; this region was last possessed by the Cherokees, since the arrival of the Europeans, but they were afterwards dispossessed by the Muscogulges, and all that country was probably many ages preceding the Cherokee

344

invasion, inhabited by one nation or confederacy, who were ruled by the same system of laws, customs and language; but so ancient, that the Cherokees, Creeks, or the nation they conquered, could render no account for what purpose these monuments were raised. The mounts and cubical yards adjoining them, seemed to have been raised in part for ornament and recreation, and likewise to serve some other public purpose, since they are always so situated as to command the most extensive prospect over the town and country adjacent. The tetragon terraces, seem to be the foundation of a fortress, and perhaps the great pyramidal mounts, served the purpose of look out towers, and high places for sacrifice. The sunken area, called by white traders the chunk yard, very likely served the same conveniency, that it has been appropriated to by the more modern and even present nations of Indians, that is, the place where they burnt and otherwise tortured the unhappy captives, that were condemned to die, as the area is surrounded by a bank, and sometimes two of them, one behind and above the other, as seats, to accommodate the spectators, at such tragical scenes, as well as the exhibition of games, shews and dances. From the river St. Juans, Southerly to the point of the peninsula of Florida, are to be seen high pyramidal mounts, with spacious and extensive avenues, leading from them out of the town, to an artificial lake or pond of water, these were evidently dignified in part, for ornament or monuments of magnificence, to perpetuate the power and grandeur of the nation, and no considerable one neither, for they exhibit scenes of power and grandeur, and must have been public edifices.

THE great mounts, highways and artificial lakes up St. Juans on the East shore just at the enterance of the great Lake George, one on the opposite shore, on the bank of the Little Lake, another on Dunn's Island, a little below Charlotteville, and one on the large beautiful island just without the Capes of Lake George, in sight of Mount Royal, and a spacious one on the West banks of the Musquitoe river near New Smyrna, are the most remarkable of this sort that occurred to me; but undoubtedly many more are yet to be discovered farther South in the peninsula, however I observed none Westward, after I left St. Juans on my journey to little St. Juan, near the bay of Apalache.

BUT in all the region of the Muscogulge country, South–West from the Oakmulge River quite to the Tallapoose, down to the city of Mobile, and thence along the sea coast, to the Mississipi, I saw no signs of mountains or highways, except at Taensa, where were several inconsiderable conical mountains, and but one instance of the tetragon terraces which was at the Apalachucla old town, on the West banks of that river; here were yet remaining conspicuous monuments, as vast four square terraces, chunk yards, &c. almost equalling those eminent ones at the Oakmulge fields; but no high conical mounts. Those Indians have a tradition that these remains are the ruins of an ancient Indian town and fortress. I was not in the interior parts of the Chactaw territories, and therefore am ignorant whether there are any mounts or monuments there.

To conclude this subject concerning the monuments of the Americans, I deem it necessary to observe as my opinion, that none of them that I have seen discover the least signs of the arts, sciences, or architecture of the Europeans or other inhabitants of the old world: yet evidently betray every sign or mark of the most distant antiquity.

FINIS.

CPSIA information can be obtained at www.ICGtesting.com
Printed in the USA
LVOW02*0834190913

353167LV00006B/241/P

9 781169 327061